What to
Say When

Other Books by Lilly Walters

Secrets of Successful Speakers: How You Can Motivate,
Captivate, and Persuade

Speak and Grow Rich

What to Say When

A Complete Resource for
Speakers, Trainers, and Executives

Lilly Walters

McGraw-Hill, Inc.
New York   San Francisco   Washington, D.C.   Auckland   Bogotá
Caracas   Lisbon   London   Madrid   Mexico City   Milan
Montreal   New Delhi   San Juan   Singapore
Sydney   Tokyo   Toronto

Library of Congress Cataloging-in-Publication Data

Walters, Lillet.
    What to say when : a complete resource for speakers, trainers,
and executives / Lilly Walters.
        p.   cm.
    Includes index.
    ISBN 0-07-068038-8
    1. Business presentations. 2. Public speaking. I. Title.
HF5718.22.W35   1995
658.4'52—dc20   94-34198
                                                       CIP

2 3 4 5 6 7 8 9 0   DOC/DOC   9 0 0 9 8 7 6 5

ISBN 0-07-068038-8

*The sponsoring editor for this book was Betsy Brown, the editing supervisor was
Jane Palmieri, and the production supervisor was Suzanne W.B. Rapcavage. It
was set in Palatino by Priscilla Beer of McGraw-Hill's Professional Book Group
composition unit.*

Printed and bound by R. R. Donnelley & Sons Company.

You have filled my life with love and laughter; your thoughts, actions, and words give meaning to otherwise heartless words like honor, courage, and compassion. Forever my model of the perfect man.

Daddy, *semper fi.*

Table of Symptoms

3. Room and Equipment Afflictions   161

4. Miscellaneous Maladies   232

5. Group Therapy: Simple Audience Participation
Exercises   279

Who's Who of the Celebrity Speakers

If you would like information about any of the speakers and seminar leaders listed below, please contact Walters International Speakers Bureau, P.O. Box 1120, Glendora, CA 91740, Phone: 818-335-8069, Fax: 818-335-6127.

Peter Adendorff, a management development consultant whose skills have been honed in helping middle and senior management in South Africa deal with the unique challenges.

Steve Allen is a comedian on radio and television and has been an actor both in Hollywood and on Broadway for over four decades. Among his numerous accomplishments are creating NBC's *Tonight Show* and the award-winning PBS series *Meeting of Minds*.

Jack Anderson was a Pulitzer-winning investigative columnist, a radio talk show host, a television personality, Washington editor of *Parade* magazine, and editor of *The National Forum, American Satire*, and *The National Gallery of Cartoons*.

Tom Antion is an entertainer/professional speaker and the author of five books, as well as the best-selling videocassette training program entitled *Make 'em Laugh* on the use of humor in business presentations.

Gary Apple has been a staff writer for several TV sitcoms and has written episodes for Fox TV's *The Simpsons*. The material in this book was taken from one of the publications he writes for: *Speaker's Idea File*.

Ralph Archbold, CPAE*, has addressed over 7000 groups through his readings of Benjamin Franklin. He is considered the leading Franklin portrayer in America.

Janet Attard is the author of *The Home Office and Small Business Answer Book*. An information highway pioneer, she manages several electronic business forums on two major on-line services (America Online and GEnie). She has been an information provider and manager for on-line services since 1988.

Michael Aun is president of an insurance and real estate company. He writes the popular column "Behind the Mike" and has coauthored three books. He is a life member of the Million-Dollar Roundtable and a world champion speaker for Toastmasters International.

Letitia Baldrige is a corporate director and the author of 13 books. She was Tiffany & Company's first woman executive and first director of public relations. During the John F. Kennedy administration, she was chief of staff for Jacqueline Kennedy and social secretary to the White House. She has served as adviser to four subsequent first ladies.

Deanna Berg, Ph.D., is an international speaker, trainer, facilitator, consultant, and coach in the areas of business change, leadership, creativity, team building, and learning organizations.

Dr. Albert Bernstein is a psychologist, consultant, and author of the best-seller *Dinosaur Brains—Neanderthals at Work*, which was translated into 16 languages worldwide.

---

*Council Peers Award of Excellence, presented by the National Speakers Association (NSA). Each year five speakers are selected. A small committee within NSA is picked to decide who the new CPAEs will be. This award is exclusive to the membership of NSA.

Perry Biddle, Ph.D., has spoken on five continents and is the author of 13 books and over 90 articles. Perry has earned four academic degrees. In August 1989, Perry was in a near-fatal car wreck and spent 14 weeks in the hospital. He has made a miraculous recovery and shares his intentional and successful use of humor in a program entitled "Laugh Yourself Well!"

Lenora Billings-Harris is a speaker and trainer in international diversity, specializing in the USA and the new South Africa.

Dr. Ken Blanchard is the best-selling author of *The One-Minute Manager* and *The Power of Ethical Management.*

Michele Blood is a motivational New Age singer and entertainer from Australia.

Dianna Booher, CSP*, has published 27 books, 15 on business and personal communication. Her latest two titles are *Communicate with Confidence* and *Clean Up Your Act.*

Nate Booth is head corporate trainer for the Anthony Robbins Companies and the author of *Willpower.* Since 1987 he has worked closely with Tony Robbins.

Bob Bostrom, Ph.D., is president of Bostrom & Associates, a management and consulting company, and professor at the University of Georgia's Department of Management. He has published leading research on sociotechnical systems, facilitation, and the uses and implications of group technology.

Terry Braverman, M.D. (mirth doctor), is a speaker, trainer, and comic impressionist. He has opened for Ben Vereen, appeared on national television, and performed at the famous Improv comedy club.

Terry Brewer is a speaker and humorist with an undergraduate degree in public speaking and a master's degree in psychology.

Deanna Jean Brown has wide experience as an executive, entrepreneur, and principal of an all-male high school. She is currently head of The 25-Hour Day, a sales training firm.

Vincent Bugliosi is a lawyer and author of the number-one selling crime book of all time: *Helter Skelter.* He has also written *Till Death Us Do Part, And the Sea Will Tell, Drugs in America,* and a new book on JFK. In his career as an attorney, his most famous case was the prose-

*Certified Speaking Professional, a designation from the National Speakers Association, USA.

cution of Charles Manson. Bugliosi's life was the basis for the TV series *The DA*.

Bob Burg is a speaker and author on business networking. His *Endless Referrals: Networking Your Everyday Contacts into Sales* is in bookstores nationwide.

Roger Burgraff, Ph.D., is an international speaker and seminar leader with over 20 years' experience in health care as well as the author of five audio album packages on management topics.

Jimmy Calano is CEO and cofounder of CareerTrack, leading a team of over 700 people. He steered CareerTrack to the top of the highly competitive training industry and developed it into a $79 million operation that trains over 750,000 people per year.

Jack Canfield is president of Self-Esteem Seminars and the author of seven books, including the 1993 release *Chicken Soup for the Soul*. He has also prepared eight audio training programs on self-esteem and peak performance.

Dave Carey is a retired U.S. Navy captain and a professional speaker, consultant, and trainer. He has more than 20 years of executive-level leadership in management and sales positions and spent over 5 years as a POW in Vietnam.

Nick Carter is vice president of Communication Research of Nightingale-Conant Corporation—the world leader in audiocassette and videocassette training systems.

Chérie Carter-Scott is the best-selling author of *Negaholics: How to Overcome Negativity and Turn Your Life Around* and *Corporate Negaholics: Deal Successfully with Negative Colleagues, Managers, and Corporations*. Her latest books include *Partnering* and *Developing Deep Feelings with Your Clients*.

Phil Cass is a well-known comedy magician in Australia and winner of two consecutive Entertainment "Mo" Awards for Best Specialty Act.

Vikki Clawson, Ph.D., is president of V. Associates and managing director of Bostrom & Associates, a management and consulting company. She holds a bachelor's in psychology, and a master's in counseling and education, and a Ph.D. in management and administration.

Philip Crosby is the author of nine books on quality management and leadership. His first book, *Quality Is Free*, is credited with beginning the quality management revolution. His works have been translated into a dozen languages and are sold all over the world.

Ron Dentinger, a banquet comedian, has been clocked at getting six laughs a minute over his 30-minute routine.

Don Dewar introduced the concept of quality circles to the United States in the 1970s. He is founder of the Association for Quality and Participation and publisher of *The Quality Digest*, one of the largest publications of its type in the world.

Jeff Dewar is an international author, speaker, and trainer famous for the compilation of statistics known as "What Does 99.9 Percent Quality Mean to You?" He is the author of many books and products on quality.

Paul C. Dinsmore is an international speaker and seminar leader on project and change management. He is the author of six books, including the American Management Association's *Handbook of Project Management* and *Human Factors in Project Management*.

John Patrick Dolan is a hard-charging trial lawyer and entrepreneur with a dynamite sense of humor. He is the author of *Negotiate Like the Pros*.

Barry Eigen, a professional keynoter and dinner speaker, is the founder and former president and CEO of HealthCal Corporation, a nationwide franchisor of medical equipment stores in 385 cities in 45 states. He is also author of the award-winning business book *How to Think Like a Boss and Get Ahead at Work*.

Dick Flavin, winner of seven Emmy awards for TV commentary, has taught courses in humor and satire at Harvard's Kennedy Institute of Politics and at Brandeis University. He has made a serious study of humor as a strategy in business and in life.

Patricia Fripp, CPAE, was the first woman president of the National Speakers Association. Author of *Get What You Want*, she speaks on change, teamwork, customer service, and positioning yourself ahead of the crowd.

Art Gliner is head joker at Humor Communication Company. He holds the "laughable" distinction of being one of the first to conduct workshops for people wanting to enjoy the practical values of humor as a tool to communicate, cope, and become more creative.

George Goldtrap is the owner of Happy Talk Speakers Services. He is also an actor, speaker, and writer.

Steve Gottlieb is recognized nationally as a witty consultant, speaker, and trainer. He has authored *Measuring and Evaluating Crime Analysis and Prevention Programs* and coauthored *Crime Analysis: From Concept to Reality* and *Crime Analysis: From First Report to Arrest*.

Ian Hamilton entered the speaking profession in 1987, after working as a stand-up comedian of international acclaim for over 30 years. His speaking topics are "How to Be More Creative," "Communication Strategies," and "Successful Team Building."

Mark Victor Hansen speaks worldwide to sales managers of State Farm, Century 21, General Dynamics, Equitable, Harley Davidson, and more. He is a very moving and motivational speaker who touches the heartstrings.

Christopher Hegarty is an author, trainer, consultant, adviser, and international award-winning speaker to more than 400 of the Fortune 500.

Hermine Hilton has been called "America's memory motivator." Her prolific output includes the books *The Executive Memory Guide* and *60 Minutes to a Better Memory*, the award-winning audiocassette, *A Head Start to Better Memory*, and the concept of "NAMEMONIKS."

Max Hitchins, an Australian speaker, was a complete failure at school. He failed Math 1 (and now owns ten hotels), failed Math 2 (now is a pilot), failed English (has written two books), failed Music (is an accomplished pianist), failed Athletics (runs marathons), failed Tennis (is an A grade player), and failed Debating (is an international speaker).

Michael Iapoce, humorist and consultant, is the author of *A Funny Thing Happened on the Way to the Boardroom* and has written humorous speech material for executives all over the country.

Danielle Kennedy, M.A., CPAE, is a celebrated author, lecturer, and inspirational speaker. She holds an honorary doctorate degree in the humanities from Clarke College. She is a member of the NSA Board of Directors and is in *Who's Who of America's Women.*

John Kinde is a humor specialist and comedy magician. He presents keynote speeches on the role of humor in life and offers workshops on humor and communications skills.

Tony King, a successful professional inventor, is CEO and founder of KOMAX. His products are licensed around the world. At California State University, he teaches a course entitled "How to Invent and Make Money at It."

Allen Klein is a jollytologist, the recipient of a Toastmasters award, and the author of two books: *Quotations to Cheer You Up When the World Is Getting You Down* and *The Healing Power of Humor*. His mother is very proud of him.

Kristin Koeppl is the owner of BREAKTHROUGH, a training and development company that focuses on human skills.

Malcolm Kushner is an attorney turned into "America's favorite humor consultant." He has been profiled in *Time* magazine and *The*

New York Times, has appeared on many radio and TV shows, and is the author of *The Light Touch: How to Use Humor for Business Success*.

Dana LaMon was the 1992 world champion of public speaking for Toastmasters International. A Yale graduate, this blind African-American went on to become an attorney, a judge, and a motivational speaker.

Al Lampkin has shared the stage with many superstars. He has performed in 25 countries on 5 continents. He has appeared in over 100 movies and television shows.

Roger Langley, the "Dean of Comedy College," is on the faculty of four colleges and has been a guest on *Today*, *The Mike Douglas Show*, and many other TV programs. He is a keynote and workshop leader on the healthy benefits of humor and living your life as a fun person.

Janet Lapp, Ph.D., is a psychologist, author, trainer, speaker, and former college professor. She is the author of *Dancing with Tigers: How to Take Risks, Not Chances; Keep Your Feet Firmly Planted in Mid-Air: A Managers Guide to Corporate Change*; and the trend-tracking newsletter *The Change Letter*.

Ron Lee, the corporate ninja, is a managing director of business theatrics in Australia, an international motivational humorist, and an executive trainer in presentation and communication using actor's techniques, humor, and martial arts.

Stew Leonard, Jr., is the president of the original Stew Leonard's in Norwalk, Connecticut. This store serves 100,000 customers a week with sales in excess of $100 million a year—the most successful retail store in the world. Leonard is featured in Tom Peters and Nancy Austin's *A Passion for Excellence*, where he is referred to as "the Disney of retail." He is currently one of the most sought-after speakers in the United States.

Art Linkletter, a brilliant motivational speaker and television and radio star for 45 years, has performed on two of the longest broadcasting shows in history, *House Party* and *People Are Funny*. He is the author of 16 books, including *Kids Say the Darndest Things*!

Florence Littauer, CPAE, is the author of 18 books that focus on personal and spiritual growth. Her best-selling titles include *Personality Plus, Your Personality Tree, Personalities in Power, Silver Boxes,* and the recent *Dare to Dream*.

Dr. Layne Longfellow is a philosopher, a psychologist, a perceptive social commentator, and a musician with a quick wit. He speaks on ethics, the environment, generational values, and the cycle of life.

Carole Lynne has been a coach for performers since 1962 and a coach for public speakers since 1975.

Doug Malouf is considered by his peers to be a master in international speaking. He has authored five books and four audiocassette programs, and travels the globe teaching people how to create and deliver a dynamic presentation.

Eileen Mason is a certified professional consultant and the author of the *Witty Words* (Sterling Publishing). Her mission is bringing humor to life!

Pat McCormick is the only American woman to win four Olympic gold medals in diving. Her daughter, Kelly McCormick, competed in the 1984–1988 Olympics—thus making Pat and Kelly the only mother and daughter entrants in U.S. Olympic history.

Jim McJunkin was a top sales trainer and manager in the office products and computer industry for many years. Today, he is a top sales consultant and trainer to many companies and is noted for his outrageous "over-the-edge" style of humor.

Ed McManus, known as "The Jokesmith," publishes a quarterly newsletter by that name for business and professional speakers. He is the author of *We're Roasting Harry Tuesday Night*.

Peter Meyer has been speaking on business strategy and management issues for a decade internationally. The Meyer Group runs public and private seminars for businesses and consultants.

Gerald C. Meyers, former chairman of the board and CEO of American Motors, is the Ford Distinguished Professor of Business at the Graduate School of Industrial Administration, Carnegie Mellon University, and Professor of Organization Behavior at the School of Business Administration, University of Michigan. He is a speaker, management consultant, and author of *When It Hits the Fan: Managing the Nine Crises of Business*.

Hope Mihalap, CPAE, is a humorous speaker, satirist, and writer. In addition to her recognition by the National Speakers Association, she holds the rarely conferred international Mark Twain Award for Humor.

Anita Cheek Milner, M.A., J.D., is known as the "change-of-life attorney"—she passed the California bar exam at the age of 50. She is a humorist and presents all over the United States.

Lee Milteer is a motivational business and leadership speaker on success principles and personal achievement.

W Mitchell has been called and is the author of *The Man Who Won't Be Defeated*. From his wheelchair, he delivers a message about mastering adversity and focuses on how people can deal with setbacks and put themselves back in charge.

Gene Mitchener, known as "The Wheelchair Comic," has headlined in comedy clubs all over the USA. He also lectures across the country on humor therapy and living life with laughter. He is the author of *When Things Get Heavy—Lighten Up!*

Judi Moreo served for 21 years as CEO of Universal Convention and Trade Associates. A motivational business speaker, she is currently a senior executive and resident of South Africa.

John Nisbet is a humorist, an actor and acting coach, and a traffic school trainer. He serves as a consultant on humor skills to speakers and presenters.

Tom Ogden has over 20 years of experience as a magician and comedian. Among his video seminars are *The Magic of Creativity* and *Teaching and Training with Magic.* His books include *200 Years of the American Circus* and *A Volunteer from the Audience.*

Alan Parisse is something of a legend in one of the fastest-changing industries today: investments. He advises a wide variety of organizations, including most major securities houses, banks, insurance companies, and real estate firms.

Scott Paton is editor-in-chief of *Quality Digest,* a monthly magazine covering all aspects of total quality management.

Lorin Paulsen, singer and performer, has served as a writer for the *Smothers Brothers Comedy Hour* and for a variety of comedians and political satirists, including his brother, Pat Paulsen (the perpetual presidential candidate). He often performs as Abe Lincoln.

Dr. Terry Paulson, CPAE, is a psychologist and author of the popular books *They Shoot Managers, Don't They? Secrets of Life Every Teen Needs to Know,* and *Making Humor Work. Business Digest* has called him the "Will Rogers of business consultants."

Alan Pease of Australia teaches sales and negotiation techniques. His products have been translated into 29 languages and are used in over 100 countries. His best-selling books include *Body Language, Talk Language, and Write Language* (with Paul Dunn).

Rosita Perez, CPAE, has served as a social worker and mental health administrator. Today, as a motivational speaker, she uses music and a guitar to share substantive messages in an atmosphere of fun and camaraderie.

Gene Perret received an Emmy award for his comedy material, has written for Phyllis Diller, Bill Cosby, and Tim Conway, and is currently head writer for Bob Hope. Perret has written 14 books on humor.

Brad Plumb is the owner of the prestigious North American Speakers Bureau. His brother, Charlie Plumb—a former POW in Vietnam—is one of the great motivational speakers.

Michael Podolinsky is the owner of TEAM Seminars. Voted "motivational speaker of the year" by his peers, he speaks on 5 continents in 11 countries on TEAM building. He has served IBM, 3M, Prudential, Mobil Oil, US West, the FBI, and over 400 other clients.

Lorna Riley, president of the American Training Association, is an award-winning sales executive, a former marketing director and teacher, and an international author and speaker.

Anthony Robbins conducts more than 100 days of seminars each year. He has distributed more than 10 million educational audiocassettes, and his *Personal Power* television show has reached 100 million people nationwide. His is the author of *Awaken the Giant Within* and the national best-seller *Unlimited Power*.

Cavett Robert is founder and president emeritus of the National Speakers Association in the United States.

Leonard Ryzman is the author of several books, including *Make Your Own Rainbow*. He makes TV and radio appearances and has international experience in speaking, management, and professional comedy.

Jeff Saltzman, cofounder of CareerTrack, also serves as the company's chief curriculum designer and copywriter. He is one of America's top trainers and has conducted seminars in sold-out auditoriums throughout the world.

Mark Sanborn is a professional speaker and the author of 4 audio training programs, 16 videos, and the book *Teambuilt: Making Teamwork Work*.

Jeff Slutsky is the author of *Streetfighting, Street Smart Marketing, Street Smart Tele-Selling*, and *How to Get Clients*. He has been featured in *The Wall Street Journal, Inc.* magazine, *USA Today*, and *Success*.

Beverly Smallwood, Ph.D., is a psychologist, speaker, trainer, consultant, university professor, mediator, and entrepreneur.

Larry Tracy heads Tracy Presentation Skills. An expert on hostile audiences, he is well known for debating foreign policy issues for the U.S. government.

Bob Treadway is a sales and business speaker whose audiences have named him the "King of Comebacks" for his ability to help them come up with the perfect responses to customers in sales conversations.

David R. Villanueva is an author, actor, and instructor as well as a scientist. Founder of DRV Shaolin Kempo Karate, he is recognized internationally for his work in helping people achieve personal excellence.

Bob Walters—the greatest philosopher and love of my life, my Dad!

Dottie Walters is my mother. Her speaking career began over 30 years ago when she wrote the first book ever for saleswomen *by* a woman: *Never Underestimate the Selling Power of a Woman*. A premier female sales motivator on the platform, she has spoken around the world. She is currently publisher of *Sharing Ideas*, the largest magazine in the world for professional speakers.

Mike Walters is my nephew—named for his uncle (see below). Mike works as the advertising manager of our magazine for professional speakers. (Yeah, yeah, nepotism, I know. But he came up with some great one-liners for this book!)

R. Michael Walters, attorney, author, and speaker, is one of the leading experts on legal issues for mobile home park owners. My big brother!

Matt Weinstein is head Emperor of Playfair, a seminar and consulting company that takes a fun-filled look at the therapeutic and financial benefits of bringing laughter and play into people's lives. He is the author of *Playfair: Everybody's Guide to Noncompetitive Play*.

Marilyn Wheeler is the author of *Problem People at Work—and How to Deal with Them* (Random House, 1994). She is a former vice president for Diane Freis, a clothing manufacturer in Hong Kong, and former marketing director for the California Mart.

Somers White, CPAE, CSP, CMC*, is a Harvard MBA who started on Wall Street and was at one time the youngest bank president in America. A former Arizona state senator, he is the author of over 400 professional articles, an 8-hour cassette album on negotiating, and 20 other cassettes.

Larry Wilde is a motivational humorist and best-selling author. His collection of 50 *Official Joke Books*—with sales of over 12 million copies—is the most successful series of its kind in publishing history.

---

*Certified Management Consultant, a designation from the Institute of Management Consultants, the highest accreditation in the management consulting profession.

Mikki Williams is an inspirational humorist and business motivator. ABC produced a TV documentary about her life called *A Better Way.* She lectures from a wealth of experience on business dynamics, personal growth, and wellness.

Steve Wilson, known as "The Joyologist," is a psychologist, writer, humor educator, and speaker who specializes in enjoying life and creating positive working environments. He is the author of the quote book *Eat Dessert First.*

Bill Wolff, a senior executive at CBS Broadcasting, is a very funny man with a serious and informative message. He is a writer and producer of documentaries on self-esteem and stress.

Marian K. Woodall is a personal speech coach, a professional speaker, and the author of four books on communication, including *14 Reasons Corporate Speeches Don't Get the Job Done* and *Speaking to a Group.*

"Look Peter! Here's another one!"

Introduction: Before You Worry About What to Say When

Nothing is more terrifying than standing up in front of a group...
  No, strike that...
  Nothing is more terrifying than standing up in front of a group and finding that something is going VERY WRONG!

Like, "I'm dying up here!"

The Bible says, "There is a time for every purpose under heaven...a time to be born, a time to die...a time to keep silent and a time to speak...."* How many times have you lamented that you had *not* opted for that "time to speak" option? Wished you'd "remained silent and been thought a fool," instead of opening your mouth and proving them right?

You can't communicate with anybody (for very long) without making a *lethal* mistake. This book gives you tips, quips, and witty ad-libs to use when you find yourself deep in deadly situations on the dais.

Wait a minute. How can you have a book with "ad-libs?" An ad-lib is something you come up with on the spur of the moment.

Yes, you're right. But it's time to let you in on a secret of professional speakers, trainers, teachers, and entertainers. All those witty ad-libs they come up with "off the cuff"† are usually lines they have rehearsed for *years*. At some time in their career, they stood in front of a group and had their shtick go a bit awry. Suddenly a great line came to life and from that moment on was presented as part of their patter.

What do you say when the electricity goes out? You forget your speech? The overhead projector blows? The building catches on fire? Someone has a heart attack in the middle of your presentation? (Of course, if you are teaching CPR this is a great opportunity; however....)

I have divided up the solutions to these and many, many other situations into over 100 potential disaster areas for presenters, trainers, teachers, and speakers.

You may never encounter 99 of the situations listed, but after reading this book, you will at least have a solution in mind if the disaster hits your talk.

I have divided each potential problem area into three sections:

1. How to prevent it from happening

2. What to do when it does happen

3. What to say when it happens (and sometimes what *not* to say)

---

*Ecclesiates 3:7

†Check the Glossary of Speaking Terms in the back of this book for the interesting origin of "off the cuff." I had a great deal of fun finding out the history of words and phrases which presenters use all the time and which we often just take for granted. I would hate for you to miss it—especially after all the research I did! Enjoy!

Whenever something is going wrong, you need to do *something else.* Simple. Many, many times in the book I suggest that the something else you try should be an audience participation and/or experiential exercise. So I have included a whole chapter of those for you to use.

Those of you who read my last book, *Secrets of Successful Speakers: How You Can Motivate, Captivate, and Persuade* (McGraw-Hill, 1993), will notice a few things that I have borrowed from there.

If you are new to the speaking platform, please don't panic as you read the contents of this book and see *all* the rotten things that can—and do—go wrong. Most audiences are on your side. They will usually forgive your mistakes, and laugh with you about them. Your foreknowledge and preparedness for those mistakes will help you create a mood of fun when *your* platform springs a leak.

So why "Lilly Walters" to write this book? You're *that good on the platform?*

Actually, yes! I'm that good at making really dumb mistakes on that platform! It was no trouble at all for me to come up with numerous rotten situations for speakers, teachers, trainers, and presenters, because I've barely survived most of them myself. But as an agent and speakers bureau executive, I have a tremendous pipeline to some of the most experienced business presenters in the world. "Experienced" doesn't just mean the top performers, experts, authors, and the like. It means people who got to be the top performers, experts, and authors because they, like the phoenix, have died on the platform and risen out of the ashes many a time, richer for the knowledge they gained from their "near-death" experience.

I found it fascinating that many came up with exactly opposite solutions to the same problem. Sometimes, the solutions suggested by speakers made me cringe. But I know these same speakers to be successful and well liked by their audiences. Which just proves it's often the attitude and delivery, rather than the words, that make the solutions presented workable.

How to Read This Book

This book is like a doctor's desk reference. If you are worried about a certain problem—becoming ill on stage, encountering a hostile audience, and so on—simply check the Table of Symptoms and go right to your special interest area. I didn't originally intend for this book to be read cover to cover, and so I was surprised that the five presenters I asked to preview this book all said, "Every presenter will want—no, will need—to read this cover to cover!"

Sometimes I've put the same line in two or three different categories because it was so perfect for those specific situations, so look in other areas rather than just the one specific to the situation. For instance, when the mic* goes out, Gene Mitchener uses "I would like to thank Radio Shack for supplying the equipment this evening." He also uses that same line when the overhead projector breaks. Some lines were good for so many different situations—like "Gee, is this *Candid Camera*, or what?"—that I decided to create a whole section called "Surefire Savers for Any Situation."

Warning, Warning, Warning

When things go wrong up there, your mind will often lock. In order to retrieve any of these great "savers," you must have them firmly nailed into your subconcious to keep that mental door from slamming shut when you need it.

So find lines that tickle your fancy and rehearse, rehearse, rehearse. To make it look like it's spontaneous and off the cuff takes a ton of practice. (Mark Twain, one of the highest-paid speakers of his era, said, "It takes me at least three weeks to prepare an impromptu speech.")

How to Deliver a "Saver" Line

All the lines in *What to Say When* are what makes this book unique; they're the toughest to come up with in a panic situation. I've done my best to compile a number of these for you in each situation.

As in my last book, *Secrets...*, I went to all kinds of professional speakers, entertainers, executive spokespeople, and others, and asked them to share their best ideas. I've even included some lines I don't think are very funny. Well, of course, some aren't supposed to be funny. But some were, and I just didn't get much of a chuckle. However, some of my friends started howling when they heard them. To each his own—so here they all are!

Just remember that all lines included here have been proved and tested under fire. It is the *way* you deliver them that will make or break you.

---

*Before you say, "Wait! That is supposed to be spelled 'mike'," see the Glossary of Speaking Terms at the back of this book.

Where humor is concerned, there are no standards—no one can say what is good or bad, although you can be sure that everyone will!
                                                        —JOHN KENNETH GALBRAITH

It takes practice to be funny—planned spontaneity. Use what is happening, when it is happening to be funny.

As Steve Allen says, "Nothing is better than the use of the unintended humor of reality."

Victor Borge says, "I just go for what the moment calls for. The natural reaction to things is the greatest humor I know of. That is the essence of humor: to grab the moment and caricature the moment."

When magical humor happens, the first time it is spontaneous, but from then on it should be prepared, shaped, and practiced to "seem" spontaneous the next time you need to use it in a similar situation.
                                                        —TERRY PAULSON

INTERRUPTIONS OR ENHANCEMENTS?
by Nate Booth of Robbins Research

If you have been on stage enough times, you have had it happen—that unexpected event that takes you by surprise! It's not a question of *if* it's going to happen. It's a question of *when* it's going to happen and, more importantly, *what it means to you* when it happens! The meaning you attach to any event in your life is going to determine your emotional reaction to the event and what you *do* in response to the unexpected event.

When it comes to unexpected events, there are two basic kinds of speakers:

- **Frank Flustered**—Frank gets upset and flustered because he views the unexpected event as an *interruption* that disrupts his presentation. The audience sees that Frank is emotionally upset about the event that "shouldn't have happened." Frank's presentation is clearly thrown off course. He may even apologize to the audience about the "unfortunate situation."

- **Oprah Opportunity**—Oprah actually gets stronger when the unexpected event happens, because she views the event as an opportunity to *enhance* her presentation! (Incidentally, Oprah Winfrey is a master of turning interruptions into opportunities.) The audience sees her resourcefulness. Oprah becomes more effective from the front of the room because she *uses* the unexpected event as an *opportunity* to inject some humor into the situation or as a chance to illustrate a point!

You may be saying to yourself, "Well this all sounds good, but how do I turn interruptions into opportunities?" Here are some steps I would recommend:

1. Walk into your programs with two beliefs in your head. *Belief One*, "When I'm on the stage, it's like life in fast forward. Unexpected events are going to happen. I *welcome* them because...." *Belief Two*, "There is always a way to turn this interruption into an opportunity that will enhance the experience I provide my audience!"

2. Within reason, construct your program to *increase* the likelihood of unexpected events happening! *Don't* give a "safe" presentation. *Don't* hide behind a lectern, reading from your notes and have no audience interaction. *Do* work from a "mind map" or with a few notes (or no notes at all)! *Do* roam around the stage with energy and purpose! (I have personally tripped over everything from electrical cords to papier-mâché rocks!) *Do* go out into the audience and connect with people! *Do* ask people questions that you have no idea of what the answer is going to be! *Do* create a lively two-way conversation with your group! *Do* take your group to the edge of the cliff and have them look over the edge! It's riskier; and it's more exciting and impactful for everyone that way! An audience once stretched by a new and positive emotional experience never returns to its original size!

3. Establish rapport with your audience up front! When you have deep rapport with your audience, you can make the stupidest mistakes; the weirdest external things can happen and your audience will still be on your side *wanting* to help you out! If you don't have that kind of rapport, your audience will leave mentally or physically when things don't go "right."

4. At the beginning of your program, *preframe* your audience (create a mindset) for the unexpected by leading people to make commitments to be playful, curious, flexible, and energized throughout your program (or throughout the multiday conference, if you are a kickoff speaker)!

5. In the beginning, create a few positive *anchors* that you can use later on in your program. An anchor is something unique that *you* do or say from the front of the room (or something that you have people do or say) that automatically puts the audience in a resourceful emotional state. Examples of anchors are a unique smile, a particular spot where you stand on stage, the word

"yes" said in a strong voice, or a clenched fist. You set the anchor by getting the audience in a peak and resourceful emotional state. Then you do or say the anchor (or have the audience do it). The anchor and the emotional state become linked in people's nervous systems! The anchor automatically fires off the emotional state!

6. If an unexpected event does happen, put a smile on your face, stand up straight and strong, and immediately ask yourself this question, "How can I use this event as an opportunity to create humor or illustrate a point?" Ask and you shall receive. You will get an answer that will enhance your program. It is also a great idea to have a few "stock" answers in your tool box.

Is It Funny? How to Make It Funny

At least 75 percent of successful humor is a matter of *delivery*, not merely material. Jack Benny was able to bring his audiences to mirthful tears, not so much by his material, but by the silence between the words he used.

> *The right word may be effective, but no word was ever as effective as a rightly timed pause.*
> —MARK TWAIN

When you are deciding which lines from this book you want as part of your personal repertoire, here is what to do. First, read them all through. Those lines that make you chuckle are the ones that are your best bet.

Then, read them again. Remember, these lines are to be *spoken*. But you're *reading*. Something gets muddled in the translation from the written word, when it flows through your brain, out into the spoken word. Sometimes, the same lines you are considering will get a great laugh if you just deliver them in a different manner.

Theater is a passionate hobby of mine. I have observed that different actors can deliver exactly the same line with hugely varying effects. If you don't "hear" a line as funny the first time you read it, read it again at least three times. Each time pretend a different one of your favorite comedians, or even a funny friend, is saying the line. You may discover a whole new humorous aspect to the line.

Take the famous Will Rogers' line "I never met a man I didn't like." Now pretend Mae West is saying the same line, or Liberace or Robin Williams. New meanings, nuances, and subplots all come to mind from the same simple line with each delivery.

Customize It to Fit Your Style and Needs

Try changing the lines around to fit your own delivery style and audience. For example, when a loud crash occurs:

I bet the next time that guy learns from his mistakes.
  —DIANNA BOOHER

If I heard a loud crash, I might deliver the same line by pretending to be horrified and making a big dramatic face, then saying, "Betcha he learned a thing or two on *that* one."

At the turn of the century Robert Frost said, "The brain is a wonderful organ; it starts working the moment you get up in the morning and does not stop until you get to the office." Fifty years later, George Jessel, the American comedian, customized that to say, "The human brain is a wonderful thing. It starts working the moment you are born, and never stops until you stand up to speak in public."

Look at lines and dialogue suggested by the various presenters, but adapt them to your style and needs.

Punch Up Your Shtick

When something goes wrong with equipment, Jeff Slutsky says, "That's the last time I get my equipment from Mattel." Jeff claims he gets a better laugh by putting the "punch" word (the funny word) at the end of the one-liner. Also, he gets a better chuckle by putting in a company, country—whatever—that obviously would do a rather mediocre job at making whatever the issue or product is. Or a company that in no way would ever make the equipment. Using the top competitor of the group you are talking to would be super. For instance, if you are talking to McDonald's, you would say, "That's the last time I get my equipment from those guys at Jack-in-the-Box." The McDonald's group will think that is a real hoot.

The difference between the right word and the almost right word is the difference between lightning and the lightning bug.

Wit is the sudden marriage of ideas which before their union were not perceived to have any relation.

—MARK TWAIN

Running Gags

You will get a great laugh if you continue a line in several situations. For instance, if you had gotten a chance to say "That's the last time I get my equipment from Mattel" earlier in the presentation, then later, if you stumble over your words, you can come back with "That's the last time I rent my lips from Mattel." Then when someone asks a question you can't answer, you can reply, "That's the last time I rent my audience members from Mattel." "Running gags" are always fun.

> *The plane of the morning speaker, Mr. T, was delayed. The first vendor's presentation required the distribution of catalogs to the retail audience, but they got lost in shipping. He said, "The catalogs must have been on the same plane as Mr. T!" Got a nice laugh.*
>
> *The next presenter didn't have his slides there in time so he used the same line, "The slides must have been on the same plane as Mr. T." Then the show promoter announced that the show programs were late and used the same line again. It's now an ongoing gag.*
>
> *During my speech I did a little routine about the importance of making commitments to our customers. I said, "To show you how much I believe in making a commitment to my customers and making good on promises... I was on the same plane as Mr. T!"*
>
> —JEFF SLUTSKY

Use Your Humor with Compassion

In all situations, avoid becoming hostile and using any of the lines in anger or with *heavy* sarcasm. Light sarcasm is fun, but it goes a long way. Whenever possible, turn the joke back onto yourself, rather than aim it at someone in the crowd. If you are going to make someone else the brunt of the joke, set it up during a break or before the presentation and *ask* the person first!

> *The real wit tells jokes to make others feel superior, while the half-wit tells them to make others feel small.*
>
> —ELMER WHEELER
> (Quoted in *Eat Dessert First,* by Steve Wilson, DPJ Enterprise, Inc., 1990)

Roger Burgraff couldn't get to the air-conditioning unit easily in one of his meetings rooms. He asked one of the attendees seated next to it if he would handle the controls. The man agreed. Dr. Burgraff said, "That way if they're not happy they can talk to you about it." A gentle titter was heard by the group. Within 2 days the sponsoring organization got a letter from that man, incensed at being made the brunt of humor.

No matter what you do, about 2 percent of your audience is going to be looking for a reason to get mad. If more than 2 percent get upset with you, change your style. It's you, not them, who's to blame. Your audience will be much more forgiving if you allow the mistake or problem to show you to be human. Laugh, smile, use a few saver lines, *fix the problem, and get on with your presentation!*

> *It's great to be great, but it's greater to be human.*
> —WILL ROGERS
> (Quoted in *Eat Dessert First*, by Steve Wilson, DPJ
> Enterprise, Inc., 1990)

> *There are all kinds of tricks to learn to help prevent problems. But the right strategy will come to you at the right time if you try to have:*
> *"A passion for your topic and a compassion for your audience."*
> —LILLY WALTERS
> (From *Secrets of Successful Speakers*, McGraw-Hill,
> 1993)

Know the Audience Before You Use the Line!

Let's say you get a heckler. So you use, "Excuse me. I do my speech the way you have sex—alone."

In almost *any* audience, somebody is going to laugh if you use that line. However, the retort will be met with varying degrees of success. In a nightclub, it's a great line. In a business afterdinner speech, you may be doing your swan song. People will still laugh, but they will immediately start in behind your back with "Well! That's certainly not appropriate for *our* group!"

I'd like to tell you just to use your own common sense—but humor is terribly difficult to judge until you drop some pretty big bombs and learn for yourself. I can tell you that when you're in doubt as to whether to use a line, it's best to err on the side of compassion and morality. (Yeah, yeah, I know. Sounds dull, but you'll get asked back more! Besides, a world with a little more compassion and morality will be no bad thing.)

Credit Where Credit Is Due

This book is a compilation of thoughts from many great minds—like mine (grinning broadly here). I have credited all the people who sent me ideas and thoughts for your use.

And the ad-libs?

Giving credit where it is due to ad-lib lines in a book like this is a Challenge, with a capital C. Some of the witty lines I have heard, and heard, and heard, from many speakers. When I asked the speakers where they heard a line first, the answer was often "Uh...gosh...um." Some would say, "I made that up, and have used it for 5 years!" Then I found out that somebody else used the exact same line 30 years earlier! Many of the books I looked at with witty ad-lib lines didn't even bother to credit anyone! "There is nothing new under the sun." So, who said it first? Whenever I know for sure, I have said so. Or, if a speaker sent it to me, I have given him or her credit. If I heard it from a ton of other speakers, I have credited it as "unknown."

For those of you who see one of your lines listed here as someone else's, or as an unknown, I do apologize. As much as I hate the idea (being a person who is paid for her words), once you have said something witty, it tends to slip into the public domain. Please let me know if you see a misquote, and we'll fix it in the next edition!

But Is Humor the Right Thing to Do When Something Goes Wrong?

I think you are on your way to making life—and the bumps in life—acceptable when you can laugh at them. Getting the audience to laugh along with you means people have now accepted the catastrophe as "all right." A bonding occurs when you laugh together. It's not *always* the right answer, but it sure feels like the right way most of the time.

> *Humor is like a needle and thread—deftly used it can patch up about everything.*
> —UNKNOWN
> (Quoted in *Eat Dessert First*, by Steve Wilson, DPJ Enterprise, Inc., 1990)

> *It is when humor restores proportion that our blind eye is open.*
> —LORRAINE KISLEY
> (Quoted in *Eat Dessert First*, by Steve Wilson, DPJ Enterprise, Incl., 1990)

But don't get so caught up in the one-liners that you forget the price you need to pay to make the presentation work—the content. That is where your main focus needs to be. Wit is the spice of the presentation, not the meat and potatoes.

Is Your Material Too Serious to Laugh About?

If your compassion for the listener is soul deep, you can use humor just about anywhere.

Humor is the hole that lets sawdust out of a stuffed shirt.
—UNKNOWN

Gene Mitchener is confined to a wheelchair. It always takes people in the audience a few minutes to know how they are supposed to react to him. He uses many little funny lines to release their apprehensions. Whenever a female introducer gives him a hug or kiss after the introduction, he snikers at the audience and says, "I'm not going to tell you what she just said! Well, OK, I guess I'll tell you. She said she loves a guy she can push around."

Dorothy and Bob DeBolt tell hilarious stories about their 19 severely disabled adopted kids—not a real funny situation. But their humor brings the message right into your soul and heart. When they're done talking, you want to run right out and adopt a disabled child. (I say this with no sarcasm—their message is delivered straight into your heart.)

I lost half of my left hand in an accident when I was 11. When people get up the courage to ask me about it, I have found my own little humorous way to diffuse their discomfort.

"Lilly, what happened to your hand?" looking sympathetically at my *left* hand.

I hold up my *right* hand. "Oh, you noticed." I begin to play with my nails on my good hand. "You know, I don't really like the polish the salon used this week either."

"Um... I meant... well... I, you see...I was talking about your, well... you know, your other hand." They apologetically sweat.

"What do you mean?"

Now they panic. "Oh, well... nothing... never mind."

About then I quizzically look down at my left hand and scream at the top of my lungs, "AHHHHH!"

They stare horror-stricken at me, pulse racing; then they realize I'm laughing. At which point they usually say something rather crude, occasionally followed by small acts of violence to my person. But at least those old endorphins are working.

Now, what do you say when....

Lilly Walters

Acknowledgments

A special thank you to five of my dear friends—Joseph M. Bradley, David R. Villanueva, Steve Gottlieb, Burt Siemens, and Beverly Smallwood—who slaved over 650 pages of very "rough" manuscript and helped me turn this book into something to be proud of! Thanks also to Betsy Brown, my editor at McGraw-Hill, who thought of me first when this project was proposed.

Although over 100 speakers gave of themselves freely to supply the material in this book, there were several who gave, gave, gave, and then gave some more: Tom Antion, Roger Langley, and Terry Paulson are chief among them.

An added note of gratitude is extended:

- To Eileen Mason, for the many excerpts from her book *Great Book of Funny Quotes*. The quotes are used here by permission of Sterling Publishing Co., Inc., 387 Park Avenue South, New York, NY; © 1993 by the Groma Group.

- To *Speaker's Idea File* (Lawrence Ragan Communications, Inc., Chicago, IL) and to *Current Comedy* (Georgetown Publishing, Washington, DC). Both publications allowed me to dip freely into their vast collection of materials for presenters.

- To Dave Enslow, who graciously supplied the wonderful cartoons at the beginning of each chapter.

- To the IES (Interactive Educational Services) volunteer teachers in America Online for their research and assistance.

Finally, special thanks to the entire reference desk team at the Glendora Public Library—especially Jill Patterson—for its selfless dedication and extra personal, friendly, and tireless support.

1 Curatives for Speech Delivery Problems

Please take a look at Chapter 6, "An Ounce of Prevention," for ideas on how to design your presentation. Most of the curatives for death on the platform lie in building a healthy presentation. But in the interest of curatives for terminal speech delivery, Nate Booth has several suggestions.

DON'T GIVE A PRESENTATION, CONDUCT A SYMPHONY
by Nate Booth of Robbins Research

Remember your three favorite movies of all time? What made them such great movies? Right now come up with at least two reasons. I'm sure there was an excellent story in each of them; and there was superb acting in them all. There is one hidden factor in almost all memorable movie experiences that most people don't realize—well-orchestrated emotional variety! To have maximum impact from the front of the room, you need to utilize the same principle!

Let's take three extremely successful movies as examples. Two of them are classics and one is more recent—*Gone with the Wind, The Sound of Music* and *Home Alone I.* Were there exciting, high-energy parts in all of them? Were there parts where the action flowed along at a moderate pace? Were there touching, highly emotional parts that moved slowly? And were these diverse parts masterfully blended together to create a rich, textured experience that kept you interested and energized?

The masters of music use well-orchestrated variety in their longer compositions as well—allegro movements to invigorate you; andante movements to depict action at an average pace, and largo movements to slow things down to convey the softer emotions. The word *movement* says it all. Movements move people in different emotional directions, depending on their pace!

As a speaker, you also need to move people to take action and the best way to do this is to conduct an energizing, impactful symphony from the stage! I personally don't think of myself as a speaker. To me, a speaker is a one-directional talker. One-directional talkers are boring and don't move people to constructive action! I am an experience inducer—a person who connects with the audience and then builds on that connection with a carefully blended symphony of emotional experience that will respectfully throw the audience all over the room to jar people out of their conditioned pattern of thought and behavior!

We have all experienced what a lack of emotional variety feels like in an audience. Remember Ms. Slam Bang Motivational Speaker who did a 3-hour, nonstop, ultra-high-energy presentation? How long did it feel "right" to you? About 20 or 30 minutes at a stretch is all most people can tolerate. It is absolutely true that most great speakers have high-energy segments in their presentations and they blend these segments with average-paced information delivery, plus role playing, writing in a participant guide, telling touching stories, and so on. They literally conduct a different symphony for each audience (depending on the outcome they want to achieve) each time they face the lights! True masters use their wealth of knowledge and experience to create a unique experience for each audience!

There are three basic segments you can use to construct an experience:

- *Visual Segments*—These are the high-energy segments. In *Home Alone,* the visual parts included the mad rush to the airport and the slapstick comedy with the two burglars. In a live audience experience, visual segments help you get people moving and excited!

- *Auditory Segments*—These are the "normally paced" segments. In *Home Alone,* the auditory parts included the boy preparing the house for the bad guys' visit. In a live audience experience, auditory segments involve presenting your "content" at a normal pace.

- *Kinesthetic Segments*—These are the touching, feeling-oriented segments. In *Home Alone,* the kinesthetic parts included the boy's loving relationship with his mother and the emotional scene with the old man across the street. In a live audience experience, kinesthetic segments include personal stories that touch the heart and awards to special people.

Variety is the spice of life. Spice up your audience experiences with a variety of emotional experiences! The audience and you will never be the same!

WHAT TO SAY WHEN
...Your Joke or Story Bombs

To Prevent It from Happening

You tell your witty joke or anecdote, you watch the audience's faces until a tiny voice in your mind screams, "Incoming!" You watch your wit crash with a big *kaboom!* Sigh. It happens to *everyone* who takes the platform. It's part of this great journey presenters are on. You just can't please all the people all the time. But you can cut down the number of bombs that hit your presentation if you just practice, practice, practice!

When you practice, here are a few tips to rehearse it "right."

- *Memorize the punch line.* (Need I say more?)
- *Make it quick!* As an exercise, *time* your humor, story, or joke. Now

do it again and force yourself to cut your story in half. You may be surprised at how much better it can be.

■ *Wait for the laugh!* Savor the moment. It takes the audience longer to process a joke than you—after all, you already know the punch line.

■ Use *humor only to make a point that people must remember.* Fortunately, the funny stuff is what people tend to remember a year from now. Unfortunately, it's *only* the funny stuff people tend to remember a year from now! So don't use humor unless you want them to remember the point made by the humor.

■ *Don't blame the audience when it doesn't work.* It's rarely the audience's fault. Go back over all the rules above.

What to Do

It's not bad if a joke or story falls flat. In fact, many presenters set up situations like this just so they can use their witty "saver" lines. Always have a few at the ready. You will find a lot of savers in this book.

But here are a few other things you can do.

Pretend it was serious!
        —PATRICIA FRIPP

If you are close enough to your audience, things don't have to be perfect. It's OK to explain when something does not go quite right.
        —W MITCHELL

I have been known to pucker my lips and imitate a bugler playing Taps.
        The way to ensure against a story bombing, though, is to make it relevant to the subject matter about which you're talking. That way, the success or failure of your anecdote is dependent not upon what kind of laugh it gets, but on how it illustrates your point—what Dr. Joel Goldman of the Humor Project calls the "haha" to "aha" connection.
        —DICK FLAVIN

Have a laugh track and play it.
        —TERRY PAULSON

What to Say

OK...here's another one you might not care for.
        —RON DENTINGER

That was a joke designed to get a silent laugh...and it worked!
        —ROGER LANGLEY

I happen to be doing subliminal humor. You may be staring, but your "liminal" thinks it's hilarious.
—UNKNOWN

That takes a while to sink in. Around 2 a.m. that's going to seem so funny that you won't be able to sleep.
—JIM MCJUNKIN

They get better.
—DOUG MALOUF

These are the jokes!

My program kind of grows on you, so apply plenty of medication—you don't want to catch it.

Have fun! Misery is optional!

You don't think that is funny? David Letterman wrote it.

Ladies and gentlemen, I don't sing or dance. This is it.

Gee, I thought that was a joke.

This is a time-released program—you'll be enjoying it later all night long.

I know it's not original. I stole it from _____, who stole it from _____, who heard it at a party with Lincoln in Washington.

It was funnier last night.

Obviously, you don't know who I think I am.
—TERRY PAULSON

Now, that was the part where you were supposed to laugh.

My last audience laughed at that.
—W MITCHELL

Don't worry...some of these are just for me!

Don't worry...I'll explain this later.

The reason I told you that story is....

Yeah, not very funny (in a serious tone). The reason we don't laugh is...
—MICHAEL PODOLINSKY

I told that joke (story) in Swahili the other day, and they laughed hysterically. Something got lost in the translation.
—TERRY BRAVERMAN

(Pull out a pen and pretend to jot down a note.) I like to keep track of the jokes that go over really big.

I'm keeping score on these gags as I go along; that joke gets about a 3. Out of 100.
—JOHN NISBET

*Look at someone in the audience whom everybody else knows and say:
"_____, that is the very last time I use your material!"*
—UNKNOWN

That joke was given to me by grandfather on his deathbed. He should have taken it with him.

I have a lot in common with the post office. My delivery is terrible too.

Fortunately I have Allstage Bad Joke Insurance.
—From *Speaker's Idea File*, Original Humor
section by Gary Apple, June 1993

Well, my Mom liked it.
—KEN BLANCHARD

Just a little joke I threw in. Guess it should have been thrown out.
—JEFF DEWAR

When my wife heard that, she said, "You'll never get a laugh with that line." I can see that all of you agree with my wife.

I've never told that story in public before. And judging by the looks on your faces, I may never tell it in public again. In fact, I'm kind of sorry I told it this time.
—GENE PERRET

That wasn't meant to make you laugh, and from your reaction, I can see I succeeded.

Services for that joke will be 2 p.m., Sunday.
—From *Current Comedy Newsletter*,
June 24, 1991

Remind me to pick up that Final Exit *book.*
—From *Current Comedy Newsletter*,
September 9, 1991

I'm a practical joker—and that was practically a joke.
—From *Current Comedy Newsletter*,
November 25, 1991

Now let's think this through. You can't be witty all the time—your response to that last joke kinda proves it.

You know, you are not going to get the audience-of-the-year award.

No, no. We need to try laughing as a team. Individually we accomplish less than working as a team, so if we all try laughing at the same time rather than individually....
—LILLY WALTERS

If silence is golden, that joke must be worth about $40,000.
—ALAN PEASE

(If only one person is laughing.) Could you run around the room and make it sound like everyone's doing it?

Thanks, Mom.

—Tom Ogden

...They Don't Applaud

To Prevent It from Happening

It's *not always bad* if people don't applaud. Sometimes they are so involved, so caught up in the message, they are mesmerized. I was in a musical called *Quilters*. One of the scenes was horrible in content and emotional feelings. It dealt with a prairie mother begging the doctor for an abortion because she was pregnant with her twelfth child, and the last one had almost killed her. She is turned away, so instead she uses an age-old potion to force the abortion. As the scene ends and the lights go out, all that is heard are her agonized screams as the potion begins to work. The audience just sat there, unable to applaud and deep in thought over the horror of the moment.

On the other hand, you can purposely set up "no applause" situations in order to promote laughter.

> *Sometimes, I set up situations at which the audience will deliberately not applaud, just so I can come back with one of my favorite saver lines. This can be done by the inflection in your voice that implies you are "going on," so people will not applaud. Then you throw the saver line and they go into hysterics.*
> —Tom Ogden

What to Do

If at the end of your presentation you *really* bombed and people are not applauding because they don't like what you did, for heaven's sake don't make cute remarks. Cut your losses and get out of there! The audience hates a cute remark, the meeting planner hates it, *I* hate it!

If people are quiet because they are "moved," you have done a terrific job. Leave them in that state, and again, move on.

If people miss an obvious "applause cue" in the middle of your talk, use one of the following saver lines under "What to Say."

> *I actually carry a prop that has APPLAUSE △ APPLAUSE △ APPLAUSE △ APPLAUSE △ written on it. I only use it when I'm telling a "groaner" type story. I also have signs that say HISS and BOO!*
> —Michael Aun

What to Say

> *It's the hills and valleys. We're in the valleys right now.*
> —Johnny Carson

It was nothing. I can tell by the applause.
—Tom Ogden

I appreciate you honoring my arrival with a moment of silence.
—John Nisbet

At 3 a.m. this is going to make you burst into delayed spontaneous applause.
—Jim McJunkin

What *Not* to Say

What are you guys, an oil painting?
I know you're out there, I can hear you breathing.
Gee, what a nice quiet place to come to rehearse.
I'm doing comedy over there and tragedy over here.
This is like entertaining a Valium tablet.
I can go over that again more slowly.
Thank you for that pathetic round of indifference.

Be very careful of insulting the audience. Humor is a fine line. It's too easy to step over it and fall off the edge.

...You Forget Your Talk or Freeze During the Talk

My first speech—a magnificent piece entitled "We Are Digging Our Graves with Our Mouths"—consisted of seven foolscap (foolproof) pages of double-spaced typed script. And I had it word perfect. The big day arrived. It was held in a country town School of Arts building—a huge corrugated iron shed with a stage 4 feet from the ground. When my name was called, there I was hanging onto my seven pages like grim death. I walked out onto the 4-foot stage and faced the audience; 200 eyes staring at me; 200 ears waiting for my words of wisdom. I neatly arranged my book on the lectern* provided and stated,
"Mr. Chairman, Ladies and Gentlemen..."

---

*Lecterns and podiums. Many people think a podium (a thing you stand on) is a lectern (the thing you put your lecture notes on)—not so! Do check the Glossary in the back of this book for the interesting history of these two words. However, 50 percent of the American public will give you a lectern if you request a podium. If you really want a podium, try asking for a dais or a riser. If you want a lectern, say lectern. That way, the people who know the correct usage of words will be impressed by your knowledge and will still get you what you want; the ones who don't know any better can remain blissful in their ignorance. Besides, you're more popular if you *don't* point out people's ignorance—especially when you are depending on those same people to make your presentation go smoothly. Otherwise, you are going to really need the parts of this book that talk about "staff sabotage"—servers who suddenly start clearing, lights that mysteriously go out, and so on.

At that precise moment somebody opened the back door of the School of Arts hall, and the next thing I remember is seeing my magnificent seven-page speech flying out into the crowd like seven magnificent birds in all directions. The next two important words to come from me: "Thank you." And so I ended my brilliant career as a public speaker.*
—Doug Malouf

When I was asked to lead a church service one Sunday in order to spare the pastor's voice for the sermon, I noticed that he had the Lord's Prayer pasted on the lectern. It is possible to forget anything apparently.
—Philip Crosby

To Prevent It from Happening

I have three times seen speakers freeze. Two of those were speakers considered by many—including myself—to be patriarchs of the speaking industry. Oddly, in both cases they looked out at the audience and said, "I'm sorry, I don't know what I'm doing here." Thinking back about those moments, I say to myself, "There but for the grace of God go I."

You will usually forget your talk for one of four reasons:

1. You are underprepared.
2. You get sidetracked from your planned talk.
3. You get stage fright and freeze.
4. You are extremely overtired or emotionally distraught.

If you don't have the time to prepare properly, use lots of notes. (Yes, I think notes are all right.) If you must use notes, try putting them into the form of a workbook or handout. Audiences like handouts—they help people retain information. Also, a handout or workbook gets you organized, on track, and safe from forgetfulness.

You get sidetracked when you don't have your objectives firmly in your mind. Go back and define exactly what you want to accomplish. (See the next section of this chapter.)

You can "freeze" and panic when you don't prepare *properly*. Seventy-five percent of your stage fright problems will be cured with proper preparation. (See the appropriate section in Chapter 6 to polish your delivery.)

Being tired, ill, or emotionally upset can be a great distraction to a speaker. (Review the appropriate sections covered later in this chapter to help deal with these issues.)

*Today Doug Malouf is one of the leading speakers in the world, author of several books on presentations, and a master at audience involvement. He says that, despite his disastrous beginning, he was so fascinated by people who *could* speak in front of groups that he launched into a self-designed study program of books and expert advice on the topic.

What to Do

- Relax.

- Say nothing. Silence is golden. Take this golden opportunity to allow people to think, while you gather your thoughts.

- Make a lightly humorous comment.

- Launch into a discussion exercise while you gather yourself together. (See Chapter 5 for examples. You will see suggestions for audience participation repeated *many* times in this book. Keeping several up your sleeve at all times is one of the most valuable tools you can have.)

Take a drink of water. You know your mind is blank—they think you are thirsty. And the longer your mind is blank, the thirstier you are!
—JOHN KINDE

I always carry one or two 3″ × 5″ cards containing an apt quotation or startling statistic relevant to the subject on which I am speaking or the audience to whom I am speaking. If I do have a memory lapse, I merely pull out one of the cards and say, "Let me digress for a moment, and share with you an interesting tidbit on this subject." You then read the "interesting tidbit" and hope that your mind kicks back in. If your mind remains blank, refer to a second card that has an outline of your presentation.

If even that fails, go to the Q&A session. Do not admit you have forgotten what you were going to say. Acknowledging this may show admirable honesty, but it also suggests you are either very nervous or, even worse, not concerned about the subject you are addressing.
—LARRY TRACY

I always carry a bunch of props that I can use in what I call "go to" situations.
—MICHAEL AUN

What to Say

Serious

Let me change the pace of the talk for a moment. Turn to the person next to you and share the single most important or impactful idea you have heard in the last month, relating to our topic today. Then I will ask you to volunteer the ideas you have collected. You have only 5 minutes for this exercise so please begin immediately. (Now, go look up your notes.)
—MICHAEL PODOLINSKY

I have something to read to you...(and then pull out your notes!).

(Restate the last thought you just shared with the audience.) In other words...

(Do an internal summary.) So far we have covered points 1, 2, and 3.

(Use the last word you spoke as a seed to ad-lib a few thoughts. If the last word was "inflation," you might continue as follows.) Inflation is one of those unpleasant realities of life we all have to deal with....
—JOHN KINDE

Humorous

Oh, my! How strange. I was just caught in a time warp, and although I'm sure you noticed nothing, the last time I spoke to you was 4 days ago. Let me check my notes....
—JOHN NISBET

I just wanted to pause a moment here in case any of you have lost your place.
—From *A Funny Thing Happened on the Way to the Boardroom*, by Michael Iapoce, Wiley, 1988

My mind is wandering and my tongue's following it!
—ALAN PEASE

I'm a bit addled. Please hold on until I get my bearings.
—DIANNA BOOHER

Sometimes silence says a lot...but not this time.

If any of you have heard me speak before, you can go on to the next thought or help me out here.

Have any of you ever had amnesia and déjà vu at the same moment? I have totally forgotten where I was going, but have been blessed by an entirely new direction.

I have a great memory, but it's short.

Some days I speak on optimal performance; other days I can't even say it.
—TERRY PAULSON

I must be getting absentminded. Whenever I complain that things aren't what they used to be, I always forget to include myself.
—GEORGE BURNS
(submitted by Terry Paulson)

Does anyone have any idea of what I could possibly be saying?!?!
—BOB BURG

(I go up to people I can tell have been laughing along with me.)
  Now I can tell you're the type that does not pay attention at these meetings! Let's test it. Where were we?
  (If they don't know.)
  See!
  (If they do know.)
  That's right!
—JIM McJUNKIN

I seem to have lost my train of thought. Train? It's more like I lost the whole railroad.
—ROGER LANGLEY

I know this speech as well as I know that my name is...ugh...
—LORIN PAULSEN

Shush! God is talking to me!
—PHIL CASS

It's just this rare disease I have. Don't worry. It affects only people who eat _____ (whatever the audience had for dinner).
—LILLY WALTERS

Is someone taking notes?
—TONY KING

I'm sorry, I did a lot of drugs as a small child. I almost overdosed on baby aspirin. I just had a flashback where I saw this great vision of St. Joseph. Wow.
—GENE MITCHENER, THE WHEELCHAIR COMIC

Let's forget the rest of the speech and continue with this fun stuff.
—MIKKI WILLIAMS

I do get ahead of myself.
—ROGER BURGRAFF

This bad memory of mine almost caused me to get a divorce, until they reminded me I wasn't married.

I'm the only person I know who can successfully plan a surprise birthday party for myself.

Once I almost figured out why I'm so absentminded—but I forgot the answer.
—Adapted from *Bigshots, Pipsqueaks and Windbags,* by Gene and Linda Perret, Prentice-Hall, 1993

Memory is the thing you forget with.
—ALEXANDER CHASE

Of all the things I've ever lost, I miss my mind the most.
—UNKNOWN

There are three things I always forget: names, faces, and—the third I can't remember.
—ANONYMOUS
(From *Great Book of Funny Quotes,* by Eileen Mason, Sterling Publishing, 1993)

The trouble with facts is that there are so many of them.

—SAMUEL McCHORD CROTHERS, AMERICAN CLER-
GYMAN, BORN 1857
(From *Great Book of Funny Quotes,* by Eileen
Mason, Sterling Publishing, 1993)

Now wait (look like you're thinking). I had a speech when I came in.
—UNKNOWN

...You Get Sidetracked in the Middle of the Talk

To Prevent It from Happening

I find there are three main reasons you might get sidetracked:

- You don't have clear objectives.
- You're not well prepared.
- You get irrelevant questions.

Your objectives will be crystal clear if you firmly establish your exact mission, develop a theme to support the mission, and simplify your presentation to three or four main points to support the mission. Make the "track" easy for you to follow, and it will be easy for the audience to follow.

Rehearse, rehearse, rehearse. (See the appropriate section of Chapter 6 to polish your delivery.)

Finally, if you get irrelevant questions, subtly steer the audience back.

The most brilliant response of successful speakers when they are asked irrelevant questions is to do these three things:

1. Answer the question.

2. Do so with respect and compassion for your audience. Remember, the audience is your customer. Treat them with care.

3. Tie the seemingly irrelevant question back into your topic.

—LILLY WALTERS
(From *Secrets of Successful Speakers,*
McGraw-Hill, 1993)

What to Do

Try, "What was I saying?"
Hey! It's honest and it works. Few people expect a speaker to be perfect.

I've never forgotten or "frozen," but I have gotten sidetracked in multiple-day workshops and have had to ask what we were doing, what I was saying before the digression. It actually works so well, sometimes I, on purpose, appear to get sidetracked as a way to wake people up and test to see if they are listening.
—MICHAEL PODOLINSKY

On one occasion I was addressing a conference consisting of 280. About 3 hours into the talk, I went off on a tangent and forgot where I was in the presentation. I threw my hands in the air, let them drop by my sides, and said exaggeratedly, "Sorry, I've completely lost the plot! Where was I?" Some 280 people were quick to put me back on the right track, and the result was that they were even more on my side than they were before. Don't be afraid to show your vulnerability.
—RON LEE

When you find yourself wandering down a side track, first check what time it is and how much time you have left. Decide what part of your planned presentation you will now cut out. *No, don't just plan on talking faster.* When you do delete something, don't make apologies to the audience for cutting something! No one knows but you what you intended to cover. I promise, the audience will immediately be disappointed if you announce that you are going to cut something. People get upset when they think you are leaving something out that you normally would have covered. So just carry on as if what you *are* doing is what you *always* intended to do.

What to Say

I do digress. Now back to…
—ROGER BURGRAFF

I sometimes digress…but you've probably guessed that by now.
—ROGER LANGLEY

Sorry, I've completely lost the plot! Where was I?
—RON LEE

If any of you have heard me speak before, please go on to my next thought and I'll catch up.
—From *A Funny Thing Happened on the Way to the Boardroom,* by Michael Iapoce, Wiley, 1988

(Look at the audience.) Now what was I telling you?
—W MITCHELL

Now where was I?

(Then turn the situation around with a remark such as) Thank heaven someone was listening!

—Tony King

The reason some people get lost in thought is that it's unfamiliar territory.

—Paul Fix, American actor and producer, born 1902

(From *Great Book of Funny Quotes,* by Eileen Mason, Sterling Publishing, 1993)

Is sloppiness in speech caused by ignorance or apathy? I don't know and I don't care.

—William Safire, American columnist and writer, born 1929

(From *Great Book of Funny Quotes,* by Eileen Mason, Sterling Publishing, 1993)

What *Not* to Say

I'm too young for Alzheimer's! (To those who have the disease—or any other disease you refer to—or to those whose loved ones are suffering, this line will not be funny.)

Now where was I? Why should I worry? You won't know. (It would be very easy for this line to backfire on you. It has to be delivered with perfect timing, and at exactly the right moment.)

...You Want to Use Notes

During my speech, if you allow me to refer to my notes, I'll permit you to refer to your watches.

—From *Current Comedy Newsletter,* November 11, 1991

The speaker had his notes (3" × 5" cards) placed neatly in a pile on the lectern. They were carefully organized, well thought out. He sneezed, his hand jarred the cards, and down they went—all 30 of them—onto the floor in a clutter.

To Prevent It from Happening

There are four ways I know of to keep notes, with good and bad attributes to each.

1. The full written text
2. Outlines

3. Mind maps

4. 3" × 5" cards

Let's take them one at a time.

The Full Written Text

If, like politicians and many executives, you never give the same speech twice, you most likely need to have the full text in front of you. You may even want to consider using a TelePrompTer (see Chapter 3).

If you use a full written text, number the pages carefully in large print (in case you drop them). For readability, use large type, bigger than 10 points (the size of this paragraph), and have it triple spaced (this page is single spaced). Don't staple the sheets together in a corner; it is too hard to lay them on the lectern. Most speakers prefer not to staple them at all. You may want to consider a three-ring binder.

> Originally Winston Churchill believed in the "I don't need notes! I rely on my extemporaneous skills" philosophy. Then he bombed doing a trade union speech—he forgot the whole thing. Thereafter, he came armed with everything written down, including pauses, pretended fumbling, anticipated "cheers," "hear, hears," "prolonged cheering," and even "standing ovations"!
>
> As he didn't have the wonderful advantage of a computer, he would dictate his presentation to a secretary. Then he would edit it with scissors and paste. Finally, the secretary would rewrite it with a special typewriter with extra large print. He always had it put into "psalm form." He read his speeches, word for word. They looked like

We shall fight on the beaches.

We shall fight on the landing grounds.

We shall fight in the fields and in the streets.

We shall fight in the hills.

We shall never surrender.

—LILLY WALTERS
(From *Secrets of Successful Speakers,*
McGraw-Hill, 1993)

Outlines

For the classic extemporaneous speech—a speech you know well, but have not memorized word for word—you might find that a simple outline, one or two sheets, is the most effective way to keep notes.

Some speakers use color coding. I know one who uses one color to highlight the main thoughts—the points the presenter absolutely can't pass by. A second color sets off the humor story that helps to substantiate a main point. A third color pinpoints the audience participation exercise. If you find yourself running out of time, you simply skip the colors you don't need.

Mind Maps

If I'm concerned about having too much to say or what to cover in a speech, I organize it by mind-mapping the material. I put the topic or theme in the middle of the page, then brainstorm everything I can think of about that topic. I write just a word or so that represents each of those thoughts. I put little squiggles around each word, just for fun. I then look at the thoughts and number each one in the way I might use them. I don't draw pictures or get elaborate in terms of colors—my wife Marge does like to organize her talks that way."

—KEN BLANCHARD
(Quoted in *Secrets of Successful Speakers,* by
Lilly Walters, McGraw-Hill, 1993

You can also mind-map with drawings. As you mull over what you might want to speak on, you draw little stick drawings on a clean sheet of paper that represent the concept you are thinking of. Just plop them down as they occur to you. Don't analyze or organize; just place them or the page. If you are lucky, you may have computer art and a simple drawing program to help you think. Remember, the quality of the drawing has nothing to do with a mind map.

Let's say you've been asked to give a spirit-raising talk to get everyone cheered up in these tough times of downsizing and stretching the budget. As you think about what you might talk on, you start plopping some of the ideas down as shown in Fig. 1-1.

All these bits of art represent your key thoughts in speaking to the group mentioned above. After giving it a good think, you can start to make lines and connections, perhaps ending up with a finished product like the one shown in Fig. 1-2.

A mind map won't mean much to anyone—except the person who doodled it. The pattern and fabric of what concepts need to be covered, and when they need to be covered, are crystal clear to the presenter who created the mind map.

Perhaps mind mapping will work for you.

3" × 5" Cards

My mother used index cards for years. She kept them by categories: sales, customer service, and so on. Before she gave a speech, she

Figure 1-1. Preliminary mind map created from existing drawings.

would pull out only the cards that applied to the ideas she was developing. She liked to put a simple picture on the card that reminded her of the story she would tell, kind of an early version of mind mapping.

The good news about 3″ × 5″ cards is that they are easy to organize. The bad news is that they are much too easy to drop when you're in the middle of your speech!

If you want to use them, punch a hole in the upper left corner. Once you get them organized in the manner you want, bind them together with a large key ring or loop of twine. Then if you drop them, you can easily scoop them up, and they will still be in order.

I don't think it makes a bit of difference if you use notes or not. The difference comes when you hide behind the notes and avoid the audience. Do what you need to do to get the message into your listeners' minds and hearts. The magic is in the way you mix flexibility and spontaneity with the memorability of a good structure.

Figure 1-2. Finished mind map.

...You Run Out of Time

To Prevent It from Happening

Organized material is delivered more quickly and is received with more clarity. Practice your material in "real time." Actually give your presentation out loud, and time it.

Timing Devices

Buy a watch with a large face and place it on the lectern. If you wear your watch, slip it around so the face is on the inside of your wrist. It is much less obvious to the audience when you are checking the time. Or wear a timing device that you can preprogram, like a pager, to buzz or zap you at crucial moments. (Well, I guess pagers don't really zap you. Maybe "jiggle you" is a better way to put it.) If your speech is to be 30 minutes and you want to know when the halfway mark is reached, you preprogram the device to buzz or jiggle at the 15-minute mark. You might want to be buzzed again when you only have 5 minutes left.

Human Timers

I always have a human timer stand in the back of the room and give me the halfway mark, a 10-minute warning, and a time-out signal. I train the timer to keep trying each signal until he or she sees me nod slightly. Otherwise the timer will just assume I have seen the signal. Often my adrenaline has me soaring so high I would barely notice the building fall down around me. You need to encourage timers to be persistent and aggressive.

What to Do

If you are conducting an interactive exercise, or something else that requires feedback, it's best just to tell people what they learned as opposed to having them discuss it. They will learn more if you allow them to discuss the concept, but discussion takes more time.

In longer sessions, remember that small groups (two or three people—dyads or triads) can get through an exercise quicker than bigger groups. As you see time running out, cut discussion groups down to smaller sizes. Whatever you do, don't apologize for running out of time; it makes the audience focus on the "great stuff" they are missing.

I don't say anything, I just cut to the close.
—W Mitchell

Always remember that the audience doesn't know what you're going to say until you've said it. If you leave something out, they'll never know. Your speech does not have to be delivered exactly as you planned.
— JOHN KINDE

Always finish on time, even if those ahead of you have taken more than their share. It is better to have them begging for more than blaming you for being late.
— PHILIP CROSBY

What to Say

First of all, let me tell you my lite speech has been word-reduced and contains no cholesterol.
— TERRY PAULSON

I'm going to keep my comments brief because I believe in getting right to the point...and my babysitter has to be home by ten.
— From *Speaker's Idea File*, May 1993

Last night I tried to eliminate anything in my speech that seemed in any way dull. So in conclusion...
— From *Using Humor in Business Speaking*, by Michael Iapoce (submitted by Terry Paulson)

I'm sorry, but it looks like I have a surplus of speech and a deficit of time.
— ROGER LANGLEY

I need to go. They don't even know I left the hospital.
— GENE MITCHENER, THE WHEELCHAIR COMIC

...You Go Overtime

I lost the World Championship of Public Speaking for Toastmasters International in Toronto, Canada, in 1977 for going 8 seconds over my time limit. I was disqualified. When you do something dumb like that, the first thing you do is have a "pity party." Quick show of hands: How many of you here today know what a "pity party" is? There I was in the Toronto International Airport, sitting on my suitcase, feeling sorry for myself...as my plane taxied off without me. I came back one year later in Vancouver, British Columbia, and won the World Championship of Public Speaking in 1978. It's interesting, did you know you have to go through Toronto to get to Vancouver?
— MICHAEL AUN

Ever since I was little, my mother has taken me to hear great speakers (many of whom she was sharing the platform with). One time we went to hear a speaker who—although I was too little to understand—was known for being loooonnnng-winded. Right before he started, he removed his watch from his pocket and placed it on the lectern. I asked Mom, "What does that mean?" She leaned over and whispered to me, "Unfortunately, honey, in this case, it doesn't mean a thing."

> *After a speaker had talked loud and long, he asked the audience if there were any questions. A hand shot up. The speaker nodded.*
>   *"What time is it?" asked the man.*
> —LARRY WILDE
> (From *Library of Laughter*, Jester Press, 1988)

To Prevent It from Happening

Don't go overtime! I wish I could leave it at that. But sometimes you are forced to go over. (See the preceding section for prevention techniques.)

What to Do

As soon as you see that you are going overtime, cut to your close. Don't make excuses; don't comment. Just cut, close, and vacate the platform.

> *I ask for their patience for my windup.*
> —ROGER BURGRAFF

What to Say

Serious

> *I know our time is up, but I want to leave you with this last 3-minute story.*
> *(This lets them know I acknowledge that we are having time problems.)*
> —W MITCHELL

> *When you are with people you enjoy, it's easy to lose track of time and that's what I did tonight.*
> —ROGER LANGLEY

> *Time marches on, and so do I.*
> *Time flies when you're with good people.*
> —DEANNA JEAN BROWN

Humorous

> *Well, _____ said that I could take as long as I wanted for this speech, but that you would all be leaving at _____. Guess I'm 'bout done now!*
> —UNKNOWN

I apologize for running overtime. I got one of those new metric watches.
I'm sorry I've exceeded my time...my hourglass must have sprung a leak.
—ROGER LANGLEY

There must be something to reincarnation. It's hard to believe I could get this far behind in one lifetime.
—LEONARD RYZMAN

I see we have run out of time before I have run out of things to say—that's what you get when your speaker is a manic expressive.
—LILLY WALTERS

Can you stay an extra minute or is your mother picking you up?
—HERMINE HILTON

...You Are Forced to Start the Talk Late (Your Time Is Cut)

To Prevent It from Happening

If you are the only event on the program, starting late isn't a big deal. Of course, if the audience has somewhere else to go—like home and to sleep—they will begin slipping out the back before you get a chance to talk. Unless you are in charge of the event, there is nothing you can or should do to prevent it from going over. All you can do is repair the damage of the others.

What to Do

There are two choices:

1. Cut your talk short to bring the program back on schedule.

2. Go ahead and give the full talk you prepared, and let the entire rest of the event be off schedule too.

In private, before you go on, ask the people in charge what you should do. If they graciously say, "Oh, take the full allotted time. It's our fault after all," graciously remind them what that will do to the rest of their program. Tell them you don't mind cutting your talk short—it's up to them.

Now this next part takes some considering. Occasionally, once the organizers have made their final decision on what to do and have told me privately, I again ask the person in charge in front of the audience. When I am told publicly to cut my hour talk down to 15 minutes, everyone will realize that there is a challenge to the schedule and that I am being very sensitive to their needs. On the other hand, mentioning in public that a scheduling problem exists implies a fault with the organizers. This may set a bad tone for your presentation. If you just deliver the shortened talk and make no comment on it in public, the whole event might be a better experience for everyone. You will need to make that decision for yourself when the time comes, depending on the situation.

> *I was about to do a 75-minute stress program and right before I went on I was told to cut it to 45 minutes. I made a mistake that no one with my experience should ever make. I tried to give a 75-minute program in 45 minutes. Did not work. I should have cut more than half the content out and made it into a relaxed 45-minute session.*
> —CHRIS HEGARTY

> *I find that, even if the talk is going well, your audience appreciates getting out on time. And—though it wasn't your fault you started speaking late—if you go overtime, you're the one who is speaking when the time runs out, so you will get some of the blame. That's life, speakers!*
> —ANITA CHEEK MILNER

What to Say

> *My grandmother used to say a late start means a happy ending. I'm confident Grandma will be proved right tonight.*

> *I believe in starting on time, but if you can't start on time, the next best thing is to start late.*
> —ROGER LANGLEY

> *Sorry I'm late. My company is cutting back and made me travel on United...United Van Lines.*
> —From *Current Comedy Newsletter*,
> July 15, 1991

> *Sorry I'm late. Today's presentation is so sedating, I had to get it approved by the FDA.*
> —From *Current Comedy Newsletter*,
> September 9, 1991

> *Some things never change. Especially traffic lights when you're in a hurry.*
> —From *Current Comedy Newsletter*,
> November 11, 1991

> *Sorry I'm late. I waited at the airport for hours until someone told me that Pan Am was out of business.*

> *Sorry I'm late. I circled the parking lot for an hour. There were plenty of spaces. I was just scared to come in.*
> —From *Current Comedy Newsletter*,
> December 23, 1991

Sorry we've gone so late. We've had more delays than a shuttle launch.
—From *Current Comedy Newsletter*,
August 12, 1991

I know it's getting late. The program is like the Energizer bunny—it keeps going, and going, and going…

I hope we break for dinner soon. This microphone is starting to look a lot like an ice cream cone.
—From *Current Comedy Newsletter*,
October 7, 1991

I guess this puts me in competition with David Letterman.
—TERRY BRAVERMAN

Everyone here looks so fashionable, it seems only proper that we should begin fashionably late.

Those "Exit" signs are starting to look mighty tempting.

They say "better late than never." But by the end of this program you may feel otherwise.
—From *Speaker's Idea File*, Original Humor
section by Gary Apple, September 1993

What *Not* to Say

I had been under the impression that I was supposed to speak here after dinner on _____, and not at breakfast the next morning.

…You Arrive Late

Don't!! After 12 years of doing this full time, if I'm not there 1–3 hours early, I believe I'm late. One time, I got there just in time when a contract was prepared for me while I was overseas and it clearly stated I was to speak after lunch. I arrived 3 hours early for lunch and 4 hours early for my talk on this Sunday morning to find out the talk was supposed to be after brunch. They had just concluded their business and were about to dismiss the group without me as I walked in the room. The Chair started reading my introduction as I took off my coat. I had no time to set up my wireless mic so I took out my spare handheld hardwire mic and 50 feet of mic cord, walked up to the lectern as he completed my intro. As the applause died down, I unplugged the lectern mic, connected my mic and 50 feet of cord, and said, "Now when I say I'm glad to be here, I'm really glad to be here." It was one of the best talks I've ever given and it could have been a disaster!
—MICHAEL PODOLINSKY

Arriving late is not fashionable—it's rude. Lateness rarely becomes a problem if you make it part of your schedule to arrive early and mingle with the guests, or at least check in with your hosts. If nothing else, arriv-

ing early is good for the blood pressure of the person who booked you. Arriving early allows you to find the room where you are speaking and check out the arrangements. You may not be able to do anything about them, but at least you won't be surprised.
                                    —Anita Cheek Milner

To Prevent It from Happening

- Always arrive early. The people planning the event should find you there when they arrive.

- Don't take the last flight into an area. Even if you are going to be 8 hours early, don't take the last flight. If anything should happen to that flight, you will have no way to arrive at all!

What to Do

- Find out from the event planners how long they want you to speak. They may still want you to present for the full time, or they may want you to cut the time to get them back on track.

- Calm yourself before you go on. You will no doubt be rattled that you are late. Leave your frustrations in the wings; you have a job to do.

- Don't blame others—even if it is clearly their fault and not yours. Accusations at this point will only make the audience angry at you. Just leave matters alone.

- Apologize sincerely to the audience for being late, possibly follow up with a humorous line, and quickly move right into your presentation.

What to Say

Serious

(Tie what they are feeling into your presentation) We are starting _____ minutes later than we planned. What emotions are you experiencing at this moment because of that? Take a moment and analyze your feelings (wait, have them share). Now, this applies to my topic this way...
                                    —Lilly Walters

Humorous

Last time I'm taking Greyhound.
                                    —W Mitchell

It's not really me that's late; it's the others who are always in a hurry.
                                    —Marilyn Monroe, American actress, born **1926**
                                    (From *Great Book of Funny Quotes*, by Eileen
                                    Mason, Sterling Publishing, 1993)

Don't pay the ransom! I've escaped!
                    —ED McMANUS, THE JOKESMITH

I've been on the road longer than asphalt.
                    —TERRY BRAVERMAN

Sorry I'm late. I couldn't find a parking place and it took me quite awhile to sell my car.

So in conclusion.
                    —TERRY PAULSON

Sorry I'm late...so much for my New Year's resolution.
                    —From *Speaker's Idea File,* Original Humor
                    section by Gary Apple, premier issue

Forgive me for being late. I'm humiliated. I feel like a pair of brown shoes in a world of tuxedos.
                    —GEORGE GOBEL (SUBMITTED BY ROGER LANGLEY)

My sundial broke.

My sundial needs batteries.

I was on Chicago time (or whatever your hometown time is, or executive time, or presidential time).
                    —DEANNA JEAN BROWN

...They Ask You to Go an Extra 30 Minutes

To Prevent It from Happening

Being asked to go *even longer* than planned will be a very rare problem! But it might happen. *Don't try to prevent it from happening.* Always have something extra you can do.

What to Do

Try an audience participation exercise. Organize people into discussion groups.

I have developed an expanding/contracting type of presentation. I list the points of my presentation with two or three stories and hooks that make each point. This way I am able to add and subtract depending on the time constraints.

Audience involvement is another great way to stretch the time. I just ask if people have had any bad experiences about the topic of the day, then

I sit back and collect all kinds of great material for my next talk!
—Max Hitchins

Review major points of the presentation with new stories.
—Deanna Jean Brown

What to Say

I always cleverly leave extra time at the end of my presentations to give my audiences a chance to ask for my autograph. No one ever has yet.
—John Nisbet

You want me to go an extra 30 minutes? That's practically a half-hour!
—Roger Langley

Now I have time to share with you some of the juicy details.
—Deanna Jean Brown

...You Run Out of Things to Say Before the Time Allotted Is Finished

As far as I know, no one has ever complained about a presentation being too short.
—Philip Crosby

To Prevent It from Happening

Always prepare twice the material you will need. This will take care of your stage fright and better position you as an expert on the topic.

What to Do

Launch into a discussion exercise. (See Chapter 5 for examples.)

Particularly when an audience has been remote or cool and I have unconsciously talked faster in order to get it over with, I try to have one or two really funny short stories for my conclusion. Though it takes courage, I try to make myself go ahead and use them and get out of there, even if I've run short. It's hard to find any audience that doesn't appreciate a shorter rather than longer speech. Of course, the meeting planner often doesn't feel that way, but then you have to tell him or her you did what you felt from years of experience that the audience liked best. And then you just don't go back there again.
—Hope Mihalap

What to Say

Serious

> *(I do a short exercise in which people discuss what they have gotten out of the event.)*
>
> *Write down one thing you're going to do differently after our experience here today.*
>
> *(Then I may ask a volunteer to share with the group.)*
> —Roger Burgraff

> *Let me change the pace of the talk for a moment. Turn to the person next to you and share the single most important or impactful idea you have heard in the last month, relating to our topic today. Then I will ask you to volunteer the ideas you have collected. You have only 5 minutes for this exercise so please begin immediately. (Now go to the restroom or plan another group exercise.)*
> —Michael Podolinsky

> *(Make an excuse.)*
>
> *I was asked to finish early because of traffic (it being Friday, questions afterward, and so on).*
> —Roger Burgraff

Humorous

> *Well, I see I gave you a 5-minute refund on your investment of time.*
> —Dianna Booher

> *Blessed is he who, having nothing to say, refrains from giving wordy evidence of the fact.*
>
> —Anonymous
> (From *Great Book of Funny Quotes*, by Eileen Mason, Sterling Publishing, 1993)

> *Parkinson said speeches expand to fill the time allotted and this proves it...by being the exception.*
> —Roger Langley

...You Realize You Have Not Been Given the Correct Information About the Audience

To Prevent It from Happening

- Ask former attendees.

- Interview current attendees.

- Interview some of the other presenters for the event.

- Interview former presenters to this same group.

- Interview whoever is planning the event.

- Interview whoever planned the event last time.

- Prepare a preprogram questionnaire (see Fig. 1-3) and send it to some of the people listed above. This may be a real time saver and facilitate getting answers.

> *Make sure that when you discuss what you are to cover, you have the top executive and the meeting planner in on the discussion. Get them both to agree to the three things they want your presentation to accomplish. I also ask them to "be my partner on this; meet with me at the break to see if we are still on track and to give me new direction if needed."*
> —CHRIS HEGARTY

What to Do

Always be gracious and warm when you realize what has happened. Seriously consider not mentioning it at all. Do the best you can to deliver what the group you *are* addressing *does* want to hear.

If time allows, break the audience into discussion groups. Give them 5 minutes to come up with the three things they hope you will cover. Then, when they share these things with you, try to throw them back out as discussion questions.

What to Say

Serious

> *You're not the audience I expected and I'm not the speaker you anticipated, but maybe we can still share information and learn from each other.*
> —ROGER LANGLEY

Humorous

> *I just realized we are all victims of a scheduling mix-up. I feel like the Pope at a Baptist Convention.*

> *I understand your confusion and please understand mine. It's like going to a restaurant, ordering a steak, and getting an omelet. There's nothing wrong with an omelet, but it sure doesn't taste anything like a steak.*

> *A mix-up like this is like turning on your TV to watch the Super Bowl and getting the ballet. Both require fancy footwork, but somehow it's just not the same.*

> *I suddenly realized I'm in the right place with the wrong message.*

> *It's unfortunate my schedule got mixed up, but appearing before you has been a learning experience. Now I know how a chicken feels when introduced to Colonel Sanders.*

Figure 1-3. Sending out a preprogram questionnaire can help you analyze your audience's needs, wants, capacities, and attitudes.

Preprogram Questionnaire

Dottie Walters' presentation to your group is on _____.
We need your help! Dottie would like to meet your needs specifically with her presentation. Please take a few moments to give us the answers we need.

We have filled out the answers to the questions below to the best of our knowledge. Please double-check our answers and make additions and corrections. Fill in the questions we left blank—we were uncertain of this information and thought it best for you to provide it for us.

PLEASE: Send any printed information on your group that may help. Corporate reports? News publications? Etc.

Return this questionnaire to Dottie Walters, P.O. Box 1120, Glendora, CA 91740 no later than _____. If you have any questions, call 818-335-8069.

BACKGROUND INFORMATION

Presentation title _____ Date _____

Time frame?   Start time_____ End time____ Any breaks?____

What happens just before Dottie speaks? _____

What happens right after she speaks? _____

Appropriate dress code for presentation _____

Conference theme _____

Specific purpose of this meeting (awards banquet, annual meeting, etc.)

_____

Specific objectives for Dottie's presentation _____

Sensitive issues that should be avoided _____

Introducer's name_____ Phone _____

Is there any publicity work Dottie can do for you while she is at your event? Radio or TV? _____

_____

(Continued)

Figure 1-3. (*Continued*) Sending out a preprogram questionnaire can help you analyze your audience's needs, wants, capacities, and attitudes.

Who are the other speakers on the program?

Speaker _____ Topic_____

Speaker _____ Topic_____

Speaker _____ Topic_____

Speaker _____ Topic_____

What speakers have you used in the past who covered topics related to the material Dottie will be doing for you? _____

_____

What did you like and/or dislike? Omit their names if you would like, but do comment on the material they used! _____

_____

Three main movers and shakers of your group who will be in Dottie's audience. We would like to contact them for more research information on your group.

1. _____ Phone_____

2. _____ Phone_____

3. _____ Phone_____

What would make Dottie's presentation meaningful for your group?

_____

TELL US ABOUT THE AUDIENCE

Number attending _____ Percentage of male to female_____

Spouses coming _____ Average age_____

Annual average income _____ Income range_____

Educational background_____

Major job responsibilities of audience _____

Problems? _____

Challenges?_____

Breakthroughs? _____

What separates your high-performance people from the others? _____

_____

TELL US ABOUT YOUR INDUSTRY

Problems? _____

Challenges?_____

Breakthroughs? _____

TELL US ABOUT YOUR ORGANIZATION

Problems? _____

Challenges?_____

Breakthroughs? _____

Significant events (mergers, relocations, etc.) _____

Will Dottie's presentation be taped?_____

If you wish Dottie to make her educational materials available so that your audience may continue the learning process at home, there are two ways this can be arranged. Please check the one that is the most appropriate for your group.

A. __Group purchase in advance for each attendee, at wholesale.

B. __Materials made available at the back of the room after the presentation.

If you checked "B," please make sure that

1. Nothing will be happening after her presentation for at least 20 minutes.
2. A table will be made available for her to place her materials by the exit door.
3. Someone from your group will be available to assist with sales.

TRAVEL INFORMATION

Location of presentation, venue name _____

Address_____ Phone _____

Location at the site, room rate, etc. _____

(Continued)

Figure 1-3. (*Continued*) Sending out a preprogram questionnaire can help you analyze your audience's needs, wants, capacities, and attitudes.

Airport to arrive at _____

How will Dottie be transported from the airport to your site?

Taxi? _____ Car rental? _____ Pickup person? _____

Pickup person's name _____ Phone_____

If an emergency occurs on the way to the site, who would an alternate contact be if you are unavailable? _____

Name _____

Business phone _____ Home phone_____

This is embarrassing. It's as bad as the time I gave a talk on birth control to the College of Cardinals.

I feel like Burt Reynolds at Loni Anderson's family reunion.
                                                —ROGER LANGLEY

What *Not* to Say

You know, they told me you were all the pro-_____. This is not my fault. I don't know what to say to the anti-_____.

...You Are into Your Story and Realize the Speaker Before You Has Already Told It

Jeff Dewar was speaking to Lockheed Corporation at its Los Angeles headquarters. He was going over his famous statistics, which he has packaged as "What Does 99.9% Quality Mean to You?" He says that if any of the following situations operated at a 99.9 percent level of quality it would mean: "One hour of unsafe drinking water each month!" "Your heart would fail to beat 32,000 times per year." "Some 22,000 checks would be deducted from the wrong bank account each day." The list goes on. This set of stats is so much fun it has been published in over 100 newspapers around the country. Usually this part of his talk is a big hit, but at Lockheed that day it fell flat. One of the attendees told Jeff afterward, "Sure seems like everybody is quoting those

99.9 percent statistics." Swelling with pride Jeff said, "Really? And where did you hear them before?"

"Oh, the speaker this morning. He said *he* came up with them *too*." Not fun.

I spoke to the event planner about it later and he told me, "Oh, those aren't Jeff's! I've heard all kinds of speakers use those."

So Jeff fell flat because the audience had heard the other speaker first and thought Jeff was the one lying about who originated the statistics.

Really, not fun.

> *It's happened to me too. I get up to talk and people quote our "Rock"— you might have heard it: "Rule #1—Customers are always right. Rule #2—If they are ever wrong, reread Rule #1." I'll be talking to the people at breakfast before I speak and they'll say, "Oh, yeah, the speaker yesterday told us all about you. She said...." Then they'll repeat our "Rock," or stories about me. I have to rush in and change my slides around.*
> —Stew Leonard, Jr.
> (From *Secrets of Successful Speakers,* by Lilly
> Walters, McGraw-Hill, 1993)

To Prevent It from Happening

Make a list of your key stories and jokes, and go over them with the event planner. You can then drop the stories that have already been used. That way, even if another speaker mentions them, the person in charge will know they were yours to begin with.

However, the planner may not attend every session before you and often may not know which stories have been told.

What to Do

Watch and feel the audience. If you see people slyly looking at one another, chances are something is wrong. Very casually stop, keep the mood you are trying to create in your voice and mannerisms, and ask, "Have you heard this before?" Let people tell you. Encourage them to tell you what some other speaker said, and then have them relate what they learned. Turn it into a group sharing moment. It can be very powerful.

Do not say anything about the other presenter using your material, unless you deliver it as a compliment! Even though you may been grinding your teeth in frustration, you will only seem weak if you whine about it.

What to Say

Serious

> *Have you heard this before?*
> *Tell me what it meant to you. (Keep pausing to let people respond.)*
> *Anyone else experience a different lesson? What did it mean to you? How might you apply those lessons?*
> *(After people are done sharing, sum up with the message you intended to make in the first place.)*
> *Yes, what a wonderful message on life that story tells! For me, it helps me to remember...*
> *I am so honored that _____ (name of the presenter who used your story) likes my story.*
> —LILLY WALTERS

> *OK—you've obviously heard this story before. Let's see if you can make up a new ending. Take 60 seconds, and with the people on either side of you, see what you can come up with.*
> *(Then have just a few of them share.)*
> —DEANNA BERG

Humorous

> *How many of you know the punch line to this story? Good. I was just checking to see if you paid attention to the previous speaker.*
> —ROGER LANGLEY

> *I told _____ I'd be happy to present a short review quiz for those of you who need it.*
> —MARIAN WOODALL

...You Stumble over the Pronunciation of a Name or Word

What to Do

It's only mispronouncing people's names that will get you into serious trouble. The audience will just get a good laugh if you mispronounce something else. If you're holding a training session in which you often call on people, you will get to slaughter their names only two or three times before they lose their good humor. If I'm having a hard time with someone's name, I write the phonetic spelling down on a sheet of paper on the lectern. I make a big show of saying, "I can get this!" The next few times I call on that person, I make a big deal out of making a mad dash for the lectern, staring at the paper, mouthing the pronunciation, then setting the paper down as if nothing had happened and saying, "Why, yes, _____, you had a comment?"

What to Say

Later on I'll pass out printed translations of that sentence.

(End with a Swedish garble.)

To help you, the rest of my speech will be dubbed in English.

Some days I speak on optimal performance; other days I can't even say it.
>   —TERRY PAULSON

I speak in a high-pitch reverse, as though I'm backing up a tape in fast rewind speed.
>   —BOB BURG

I hold that a man has as much right to spell a word as it is pronounced as he has to pronounce it the way it ain't spelled.
>   —JOSH BILLINGS, COMIC WRITER, 1818–1885*

I have a high-strung tongue.
>   —TERRY BRAVERMAN

I just spent $1000 on my eyes, and now my mouth's not working.
>   —ALAN PEASE

Sorry, these are rented lips.

Sorry, it's my first day with a new mouth.

My next speech will be dubbed in English.
>   —From *A Funny Thing Happened on the Way to the Boardroom,* by Michael Iapoce, Wiley, 1988

Wow, I seem to be rejecting that tongue transplant.
>   —JOHN NISBET

I got my tongue caught in my eyetooth and I couldn't see what I was saying.

I just washed my tongue and I can't do a thing with it.
>   —TOM OGDEN

Sure, that's easy for me to say.
>   —JEFF SALTZMAN

Wow! The last time something like that came out of my mouth, I was in a dental chair!
>   —NATE BOOTH

My lips just took a short vacation.

---

*Josh Billings' humor depended chiefly on misspellings, bad grammar, and crackerbarrel philosophy. *Josh Billings' Farmer's Alminax* was published in 1874.

How do you say thee name? Let me count the ways!

What's in a name? A rose by any other name would smell as sweet...but at least I can pronounce "rose."
—Tom Antion

Talking's fun when you get the hang of it.
—Phil Cass

(Indicating my teeth are false—or loose.) You just can't buy these things at Kmart!
—George Goldtrap

(Pointing to teeth.) You just can't get 'em by mail. You really have to see the dentist in person.
—Steve Gottlieb

These new plastic tongues are no good.
—Roger Langley

...You Trip on the Way to the Lectern

To Prevent It from Happening

Before you stand up to walk to the lectern, take a deep breath, get "centered," then stand up and walk. Go slow. Your adrenaline is running at a much, *much* faster pace than your listeners'. So although you feel like you are *crawling* slowly to the lectern, they are seeing you scurry along at a good clip.

What to Do

So you trip. You know, no one *really* minds that you trip. Chevy Chase made a career out it. People mind if you get hurt. They mind if you seem upset or angry. Just be lighthearted about it and it will more than likely set the stage for a great presentation. People like you better when you're human and have faults—especially if you are able to laugh at your own faults.

Turn it into a gag, overstate it. Make it so big that the audience thinks it's so exaggerated, it must be part of the act.
—Ron Lee

What to Say

I also do magic tricks.

It took years of finishing school to learn to do that.

I had a good trip. See you next fall.

I'm the only speaker who can fall up a set of steps.

Is there a doctor in the house?

All that money I spent at Arthur Murray's was a waste.

OK. Who planted the banana peel?

I used to be too humble to stumble.

Give me an inch and I'll take a fall.

(Sing) Blow the man down matey, blow the man down...
—From *One-Liners for Disaster*, by Tom
Antion, Anchor Publishing, 1993

Tah dah! (Put you hands in the air as if you planned it.)
—TERRY PAULSON

I keep taking these shoes back and asking for ones with a longer string between them.

Aren't you glad vaudeville's back?
—LILLY WALTERS

Did you notice the word "graceful" wasn't in my introduction?
—TERRY BRAVERMAN

I think I may have stumbled onto something back there.

I don't believe I'll make a return trip.

Like our LSD guru Tim Leary used to say: "That was some trip."
—ROGER LANGLEY

Thank you. That was my impersonation of Chevy Chase (or Gerald Ford, Dick Van Dyke, John Ritter, Evel Knievel).
—JOHN NISBET

Hey, it's an acquired skill.

—BOB BURG

Practice, practice, practice.
—JIM MCJUNKIN

I'm a trained professional. Don't try this at home.
—From *Current Comedy Newsletter*,
August 12, 1991

That's a strange place to put a speed bump.
—From *Current Comedy Newsletter*,
August 19, 1991

No good being a klutz unless you can demonstrate it once in a while!
So, let me tell you how things are going at charm school.
                                             —Steve Gottlieb

...You Sweat

To Prevent It from Happening

Remember the movie *Broadcast News,* with Albert Brooks? One day Albert's character finally gets his big chance to anchor the news. In front of the camera his body goes crazy. He can barely see from the sweat pouring down his face and into his eyes.

Yes, it can happen to anyone, even you. (Please, not me!) It might happen for several reasons:

1 It's hot. If so, everyone else is sweating too, and nobody really cares. (See the "hot room" section in Chapter 3.)

2. You're physically ill. (See the section on illness later in this chapter.)

3. You're having a nervous attack. Now *this* you can do something about. Extreme nervousness will hit you when you think are bombing. Just retreat to material you are 100 percent comfortable with. If it is going to be your first time up there, you will cure 75 percent of your fears through rehearsal and preparation.

What to Do

Break people up into discussion groups (see Chapter 5). While they are talking among themselves, calm down. Go over your notes and cut the things you are not comfortable about. Firmly think of the three things you want people to take home. Go back into the speech with those in mind. Don't worry about the presentation being too short; they'll rarely complain about that.

What to Say

I have nothing to offer but blood, toil, tears, and sweat.
                                             —Winston Churchill

---

(I have a shaved head—no, not bald I have to explain to everyone—and I'm almost 50 years old.) Gosh it's hot here. Here I am, only 29 years old, and I'm in the midst of puberty. It may be all right for you to perspire, but when I sweat it gets a running start—I have a waterfall down the front of my face.
                                             —Jim McJunkin

What dreadful hot weather we have! It keeps me in a continual state of inelegance.
—JANE AUSTEN

Please excuse me. As the good book says, "The spirit is willing, but the flesh is weak."
—ROGER LANGLEY

There must be something very sensual about speaking in front of this audience. This doesn't normally happen to me.
—TERRY BRAVERMAN

...Your Feet Hurt

To Prevent It from Happening

Normally, your feet go on strike when you are doing a program of several hours. Although your feet may hurt in a shorter session, your adrenaline will carry you through and you most likely won't notice. I was once in a musical in which I had to do 2 hours barefoot. No problem until I pulled a tendon in my foot and it kept screaming at me when I stepped on it. But every time a cue came for me to go on, I forgot everything but the show. I was not being brave. The pain just went away while I was performing; waiting in the wings again was another story.

However, if your doggies are barking at the end of an 8-hour session, the old adrenaline rush that carried you that far is pretty much gone. So some smarter tactics—other than relying solely on enthusiasm—are a super idea. One obvious strategy is to wear comfortable shoes—ladies. Yes, ladies. We are worse for wanting to show off a nice thin (looking) calf—which is why some masochist invented high heels. The downward slant of the foot makes the calf ever so much more attractive. But, if at the end of 8 hours, people are still thinking about your calves and not your content, you might as well try a new career.

Wear shoes you know you can wear all day—low heels with good support and padding. (Running shoes would be great if they passed the dress code. No, they don't.) *Never* present or perform in new shoes, unless you are going to be seated for the whole presentation! Try them out someplace else, and make sure to wear them for the same amount of time you will be standing on them when you present.

What to Do

Go into the restroom (see below for ways to exit) and run the water as hot as you can get it. Take your shoes, one at a time, and let the water totally saturate the inside and outside of the leather. Make the wetting even, or the shoes will look wet. Shake them off and use a paper or cloth towel to dry them a bit. Now put the wet (and yes, squishy) shoes on your feet and go back to work. The wetness is soothing to your feet. Also, the hot water loosens the leather, which helps combat the chafing. As the leather dries, it conforms to *your* foot, not the foot of some model back at the shoe factory. Because you carefully wet the whole shoe, it will just appear darker in color, not wet to the audience. This can't be very good for the longevity of your shoes. But your performance, and your lack of pain, are more important than a few months knocked off your shoes' life. Better the shoes' early demise than your feet!

I hesitate to mention this, but when I went to Australia, guess who used brand new shoes for her full-day program? Yeah, yeah, yeah—I told you, that's why they asked me to write this book. I've done plenty of dumb things. Within the first hour of the seminar I did a section on how important it is to be physically comfortable in order to teach well. Well, my footsies were hurting big time already! Inspiration hit. I said, "The most important thing is for you to let go of worrying about how audiences think of *you!* You need to concentrate on *them!* If your shoes hurt, get rid of them!" I then kicked my shoes off with a great show and said with deep sincerity, "*They* are not important," pointing at the shoes. "The audience, its needs and wants, is what matters. That is what you are there for." I saw all their eyes glaze as they filled with inspiration. I'm thinking, "Whoa, *that* stays in."

I did the entire rest of the day barefoot.

What to Say

(Make a big show of dramatic limping.) It is better to die on your feet than to live on your knees!

Thank goodness I don't have my brains in my feet. (Look at an audience member and say) Never mind, don't say it.
—Lilly Walters

...You're Wearing a Cast

In the book *How to Hold Your Audience with Humor**, Gene Perret tells about a brilliant opening by Phyllis Diller. She was addressing an audience in Las Vegas, and because of a minor injury, her arm was in a

---

*This excellent book is now out of print. But Perret has others, equally good, available at local bookstores.

cast. "I'd like to begin with a public service announcement: If there is anyone here who has just bought the new book *The Joy of Sex,* there is a misprint on page 206."

To Prevent It from Happening

Well, take life a little slower.

What to Do

Ask your doctor for a cast with the least restriction of your movements. Don't let the cast upset you. If it doesn't bother you, it won't bother the audience. There are speakers with all kinds of movement disabilities who do a tremendous job of captivating an audience.

Ask the audience for help if you need it. If you need assistance in turning lights on and off, moving packages, whatever, just let others know. People love to help a speaker in this way. You will quite endear yourself to them. (You might want to consider having a fake cast made just for this purpose! Sorry, just kidding.)

What to Say

Now what's wrong with this picture?
—LILLY WALTERS

I'd like to begin with a public service announcement: If there is anyone here who has just bought the new book The Joy of Sex, there is a misprint on page 206.
—PHYLLIS DILLER

I got the bill for my surgery. Now I know what those doctors were wearing masks for.

—JAMES BOREN, AMERICAN TEACHER AND WRITER, BORN 1925
(From *Great Book of Funny Quotes,* by Eileen Mason, Sterling Publishing, 1993)

I just got back from India, where they still have the caste system.
—ROGER LANGLEY

...You Cough, Sneeze, Have a Hoarse Throat, Pass Gas

To Prevent It from Happening

I used to suffer fairly often from a hoarse throat and/or laryngitis. No more, though. Some years ago I gave up coffee, tea, and soft drinks. I now

drink six to ten cups of hot spring water a day, and I haven't had a frog in my throat or any other trouble since then. Not only that, I get plenty of rest going back and forth to the bathroom all day.
—Dɪᴄᴋ Fʟᴀᴠɪɴ

I always carry a lozenge in case my voice gets raspy.
—Vɪɴᴄᴇɴᴛ Bᴜɢʟɪᴏsɪ

PROTECTION OF THE VOICE
by Roger Burgraff

- Prior to speaking:

  Reduce or eliminate the use of coffee and tea.
  Stay away from smokers.
  Avoid dairy products.

- Pitch too high, or pitch too low—abusive to the voice and the listener's ear. Find the medium range that is comfortable for you.

- Slowing the pace helps your voice relax and lowers the pitch slightly.

- If speaking at an all-day seminar, try not to speak at lunch break. Instead, give your voice a break.

- When necessary, clear your throat *gently.* Begin clearing with a hum.

- Develop a sense of "openness" of voice to help relax it.

- For sore throat: try a salt water gargle. Lozenges are all right, but they may make you override the pain and fool you into overusing the voice when it requires rest.

- If your voice is raspy for 10 days or more and you don't have a cold or flu, see an ENT (ear, nose, throat) doctor. Ask for a direct laryngoscopy (a look at your vocal mechanism, with the use of a mirror).

- The voice likes wet and warm. I usually avoid heavily iced water and use instead cool to tepid water. Lemon water is all right if you enjoy it, but it's the water itself that is important.

- For help on voice evaluation, contact American Speech and Language Hearing Association, 10801 Rockville Pike, Rockville, MD 20852; phone: 301-897-5700.

Copyright by Roger Burgraff, 1992; from *Secrets of Successful Speakers*, by Lilly Walters, McGraw-Hill, 1993.

What to Say

I feel like the guy who worked for the state on a road construction crew. He showed up to work one day with laryngitis; the foreman sent him up the road to warn motorists that the road was partially blocked because of construction. He flagged down the first car and whispered to the driver, "There's a state road construction crew up ahead."

The driver whispered back, "That's OK. I'll drive by quietly so I won't wake them up."
—DICK FLAVIN

Now it is my turn for a demonstration of human frailty.
—DEANNA JEAN BROWN

Please excuse me...I sound like the car I used to drive in high school.
—ROGER LANGLEY

You may have noticed I'm coughing (sneezing, sniffing, and so on) a little. Please forgive me, as I'm just recovering from the Bubonic Plague." (Malaria's also good, as is South American Jungle Lizard Bamboo Fever.)

(Try relating it back to the topic.) You need to increase your _____ sales, and I'm just sick about it.
—JOHN NISBET

I've got a frog in my throat—first bite I've had since breakfast.
—GEORGE GOLDTRAP

I've got to get that fixed.
—TOM ANTION

God bless me! Lord knows he had to hear that!
—ALAN PARISSE

I had a friend who died from a sneeze (cough) like that. Of course, he was standing in his neighbor's bedroom closet at the time.
—CHARLES JARVIS

I think I'm allergic to you people.

I think I'm allergic to _____ (whatever the big issue is that they are all talking about).

(Burp or belch.) Ah, yes! (Grab a pen and pretend to write on something.) Pay gas bill.

God bless me. Did you know the reason we give this good wish is because a sneeze is a little death? Everything stops in your body when you sneeze—just like it did for my talk.
—LILLY WALTERS

This is fairly important stuff. It's nothing to sneeze at!
                                        —RON DENTINGER

I will speak only 15 minutes at most because of my throat. Your chairman threatens to cut it.
                                        —LARRY WILDE
                                        (From *Library of Laughter,* Jester Press, 1988)

(You pass gas.) Now that moves us to the topic of nonverbal communication.
                                        —TERRY PAULSON

...You Get Really Ill Before or During the Talk

Jim McJunkin was giving a presentation in Mexico City when, 10 minutes into his speech, Montezuma's revenge caught up with him big time. He quickly excused the audience for a break and made a mad dash for the restroom. Everything he had consumed in the past 2 days decided to leave his body: "Two exits, no waiting."

After about 10 minutes of noisy trauma, Jim decided he felt well enough to continue and dashed back to the meeting room. At his waist was the control and battery pack to the wireless microphone he was wearing. He smiled at the audience as he reached down to turn the mic back on. His smile froze in place. His eyes slid from the audience to the controls, realization dawned. He slowly brought his eyes back up to the audience and noted that everyone was a lovely shade of forest green.

He smiled at the squeamish crowd and said, not knowing what else to do, "Well, anyone ready for lunch? I'm buyin'."

To Prevent It from Happening

"The show must go on—my public needs me!" Nonsense! *Call it off.* All those people who are going to be annoyed that you didn't take care of yourself and cancel will be *more* angry if you go on stage ill and don't perform well. But they will *really* detest you if you are one of those sorts who goes on and makes a big deal about gasping behind the scenes, with an "I *have* to go on—it may kill me, but what choice do I have?" attitude. If you're that sick, *call it off!*

Having said that, I know of very few actors or presenters—including myself—who don't force themselves to go on with show. Some have even dropped down dead—literally—in the middle of the show.

If you feel you can go on, without damaging yourself, and without making everyone around you irked with your dramatic self-sacrifice...

Now, wait a minute. That's not very nice. This person is giving his or her all to make the show go on. Don't you think people are a bit more sympathetic and caring than that?

No. Well, OK, yes, sometimes. But audiences want competence in their presenters. Part of competence is getting to the presentation in good shape emotionally and physically. I've been through this dramatic self-sacrifice routine several times with other speakers and actors. The sick person is rarely very popular a week after the "episode." It is usually assumed that the illness was psychosomatic. According to statistics, 85 percent of all illness is. Of course, if you are prone to psychosomatic illness, you are at this moment irked at me yourself.

If your illness is psychosomatic, then your subconscious is telling you it does not want to be involved in *something* that is going on in your life. Often the stress and fears of preparing for a presentation will bring on illness. Your subconscious is trying to give you an out. Often, if you rehearse and prepare enough, you will find your health returning. If your illness is brought on by your fear of the audience, once you get on stage and get the presentation under way, it will pass.

Actual illness is usually nature's way of saying, "You have abused your immune system—*take a rest!*" If you have a real bug and overcome the symptoms with drugs so you can do the presentation, you are just postponing your body's revenge. Once you get off that stage, have a bed ready to crash in. You're going to need it.

Know thyself! If you have the tiniest tendency to get a nervous stomach, don't eat before you talk. Many speakers, my mother among them, cannot eat before a speech. They walk around the room and talk to the audience members instead. To prevent illness, pace yourself as well as you can when you prepare for the presentation.

What to Do

If you can perform fairly well with medication (and you have asked for, and are following, your doctor's advice), then you have a choice to make. Don't go on because the audience "needs you." Rubbish! Do it because we presenters and actors have ego and self-esteem needs that feed on the adulation of the crowd. The truth is we would rather be sick on stage than healthy at home.

Whatever the cause of your illness, if you decide to go on, you may need to combat the symptoms. Carry a small arsenal of drugs with you at all times. Just to be on the safe side, I keep over-the-counter remedies for nausea, coughing, runny nose, and headache in my purse when I'm presenting. (Yes, I'm one of those who gets a psychosomatic cold if someone says a cross word to me.)

I had a light case of flu during a theater performance in which I had to sing, dance, and act up a storm for $2\frac{1}{2}$ hours. I have a 32-ounce insulated "sipper" bottle I use when I do full-day seminars. (It looks tacky, but using a straw doesn't take my lipstick off the way drinking out of a cup does—a good tip for giving a presentation or a theater performance.) I filled my sipper with hot water and two packages of one of those remedies that you make into a hot tea for coughing, sneezing, fever, sore throat, and so on. It was great. Hot water relieves a bunch of flu and cold symptoms anyway. I sipped it all through the show and was able to perform just fine. But make sure that whatever you use is the "daytime" version. You don't want to get drowsy up there.

The audience will react to the situation as you do. If you are miserable—and let people know—they will be unhappy. If you are miserable—but silly and comedic about it—you will be endearing and doted upon.

What to Say

Serious

(If I have to leave the platform I usually get people into a quick exercise.) Pair up with someone and in the next 3 minutes share the most important point you got out of the last hour or segment and how you intend to apply it.
—Roger Burgraff

Something I had for lunch seems to be disagreeing with me; give me a few minutes out of the room if you don't mind, and while I'm gone turn to the person on your right and describe the most embarrassing thing that ever happened to you. When I get back, I'll ask to hear a couple of them.

(If people refuse to respond positively to anything as open and good-natured as this, then they're a lost cause and you don't need to go back there again for love or money.)
—Hope Mihalap

Humorous

(Make a great show of blowing your nose—with lots dramatic honking and snorting. When you're done, look at the audience, panting and weaving.)

Yes! A lesser man would be dead! But I'm going to stick this out till the end—which we'll pray is not before I finish my talk.

(Pretend you are going to sneeze and blow again, walking toward the people in front.)

Ah...Ah...

(By this time they should be screaming and you can go on with your talk.)
—Jim McJunkin

(I relate how concerned my wife is about my health.)
  She stays on my case about my weight and cholesterol. I tell her not to sweat it. I'm well insured. In fact, I'm my best client.
  (I own an insurance agency.)
  In fact, I don't have any problems that death ain't going to clear up. I tell my wife, honey, you have three responsibilities. Number one—wear black. Number two—keep your head down at the funeral. Number three—try to look sad. Let's face it. It's tough feeling real bad knowing you're going to be in the chips in 3 weeks.
  —MICHAEL AUN

OK, I'm dangerously ill now. What's the difference? My friends tell me I'm usually dangerously well!
  —LILLY WALTERS

It's amazing what you catch on airlines these days.
  —W MITCHELL

Never go to a doctor whose office plants have died.
  —ERMA BOMBECK

I enjoy convalescence. It is the part that makes the illness worthwhile.
  —GEORGE BERNARD SHAW

You'll have to forgive me, I haven't been myself today....I know some people are hoping I'll stay that way!
  —LEONARD RYZMAN

...You Need to Use the Restroom While You Are Talking

I heard Bill Gove ask Cavett Robert [two of the patriarchs of the professional speaking industry] the most important thing he'd learned as a platform speaker. Cavett replied, "Go to the bathroom before you talk."
  —TERRY PAULSON

To Prevent It from Happening

Don't drink too much water. Your throat needs the moisture, but you can get the moisture by sipping hot tea or water. You are less likely to consume gallons of a very hot drink. Often it is just your nerves telling you to drink. Do deep-breathing exercises instead.

  Soda, tea, and coffee all have diuretic effects—use caution in how much you consume.

Nerves often affect your bowels and bladder. Make sure you allow a few minutes right before you go on for a quick bathroom break. I always do this myself. One time my announcer didn't notice I wasn't in the room and went right ahead, "...and please help me welcome Lilly Walters!"

Thunderous applause...applause dies down...quizzical looks...frantic looks...nervous titters. I walk in and sit down to finish my dessert and wonder why everyone is staring at me.

What to Do

If it happens in the middle of a talk, call a break or send people into a discussion group. (See Chapter 5 for examples.) Then duck out to fix the problem. They really think *you* are very eloquent when *they* get to talk.

Don't call attention to the fact that you need to use the restroom—just go!

What to Say

Please break into groups of three and discuss these crucial issues. (As you run for the door!)
> —Jeff Saltzman

Let's take a 5-minute break while I go find the rest of my notes.
> —Philip Crosby

...You Need to Go on When Your Heart Is Heavy

What to Do About It

You must step into the hearts of the audience. Focus on their needs. Be like the English and carry on.
> —Dottie Walters

My longtime girlfriend Lou Ann Morell died of cancer in 1985, and I was deeply grieving her for several years after that time. Most of my day was spent in thoughts of Lou Ann, of how much I missed her, of how I wasn't sure that my life was worth living without her. Sometimes doing a presentation was a great "escape" from those feelings for me; other times, I felt as though my life's work of teaching adults how to be more playful was completely irrelevant work, when compared to the great pain that was the reality of my waking life.

The turning point professionally for me came after Lou Ann's death, when I was scheduled to give a presentation to the Texas Society of

Association Executives (TSAE). Just before my presentation was to begin, the association gave its award for Member of the Year to one of the association executives—I believe she was the head of the Texas Library Association. In the middle of her acceptance speech, this association executive unexpectedly ripped off her wig, stood bareheaded in front of her audience, and talked to us about her own treatment and recovery from cancer.

It was a dramatic and an emotionally powerful moment, and the audience reacted with great respect and love for her. In my talk that followed hers, I suddenly felt liberated from having to stick to my "topic"—it was obvious to me that she had opened the door for me to share with the audience the story of my own life as the surviving partner of a cancer patient. And so I talked that day about Lou Ann, and about her great love of life, and how she faced the surety of her own approaching death with the same joy and passion with which she faced the rest of her life. I shared with the Texas group how some of my friends had tried to console me by saying that "Lou Ann was like a hummingbird—flitting from one of life's pleasures to the next; she lived a whole lifetime of experience in her 33 years!" My response, I told the audience, was that of course she had lived her life like a hummingbird, but that didn't necessarily dull the pain of her early death for me, because "who would mind having a 70- or 80-year-old hummingbird flying around the house with you?"

After that first experience with the TSAE, in many of my presentations I began to talk about Lou Ann's death and how it affected me. I believe that it gave an added depth to my presentation—that people could see that I was not just advocating that they have some lightweight "fun" in their lives, but that the upbeat way in which Lou Ann loved both her life and her death showed that fun and play could give an added resource to people during the difficult times in their lives, as well as in the fortunate times.

My advice to other speakers who are dealing with the pain of death or divorce in their lives is to be "real" on the platform, to tell the truth, and to see if you can use the truth of your own experience to help draw a map into the unknown for the members of your audience. The irony of someone like me whose topic is "Fun and Play at Work" suddenly talking about death in the middle of my presentation was not lost on me—but I believe that if you are in a place of deep mourning, then you will not be "present" for your presentation if you do not speak from your present time reality. And an experience of death was the reality of what was happening for me at that time. Incorporating the truth of my personal life into my professional work made both of them feel like a richer and a much more meaningful experience for me.

—**Matt Weinstein**

Tell the truth about it—if it is something unresolved that everyone can relate to. Carl Rogers, the famous psychologist, gave a speech to a large conference I attended a week or two after his wife died. He spent the first 5 or 10 minutes talking about his grief and his loneliness. He talked from the heart. We were all deeply moved by his open self-disclosure. At the end of his draining about his wife, he transitioned into his regular speech and we were with him every step of the way.

If the heavy heart is from something more transitory and less severe—a child getting expelled from school, let's say—I would go inside myself and say a little prayer, remind myself of my higher purpose for being there, and visualize the positive outcome I am there to create.

The prayer I use is

Father/Mother God, I

ask just now to be surrounded,

filled and protected with the white light of your Holy Spirit.

I ask that I be given the inner strength and guidance to say only that which

is for the highest good of all concerned.

I thank you for this opportunity to be of service.

And so it is. Amen.

I then visualize everyone in the audience being moved to act by my speech or seminar. I visualize a standing ovation and people wanting to buy my books and tapes for further reinforcement and to share with their families.

—JACK CANFIELD

My father died the day before—I couldn't get out of the speech; they were depending on me.

I didn't know what to do. But my mother said, "Your father was so proud about your career as a speaker. Your father would have wanted you to do the speech."

I wore a black ribbon on my lapel. But I never told the audience or the client why.

About 60 minutes before I went on, I visualized myself doing the speech. I heard the applause and laughter where it was supposed to be. I emptied my mind and focused on the talk.

—JEFF SLUTSKY

I was doing a musical. A 20-year-old girl came in before the show obviously very upset. I went over to her and said, "What's the matter, Nora?"

I gave her plenty of time and finally she said, "My mother died yesterday." Then after another long silence, "...I just don't think it's right for me to perform now. It seems disrespectful." She didn't seem like she was ready to be held or hugged; she was very controlled.

So I just thought about it, then said, "Did your mother ever come to see you perform?"

"Yes, always."

"Oh, but she didn't approve? She wasn't proud of you?"

This shocked her. She started to cry, and then I held her. When she was ready, I asked, "What would have made Mom feel best?"

Nora gave an excellent performance that evening.

If you decide to make a disclosure on the platform, don't do it without some thought. Think for a moment: What do you want the people in your audience to know, feel, or do differently after they hear your disclosure? What part of your discourse is relevant to their learning the objectives that you have set? Try to give them what *they* need. Doing so will be tremendously difficult. If you suddenly feel you cannot go on unless you unburden yourself, the disclosure will be something to heal you, not necessarily them—and you have a responsibility to the audience. But in order to serve them, you must also be responsive to your own heart's needs. So if you must disclose your pain, take a moment to do so. The messages to be learned from your pain can assist others. Maybe you can all grow a bit together.

"Now remember, there's no such thing as a bad audience."

2 Antidotes to Audience Problems

WHAT TO SAY WHEN
...They Cough, Sneeze, Belch, Pass Wind

The art of acting consists in keeping people from coughing.
—SIR RALPH RICHARDSON

To Prevent It from Happening

If all your listeners are coughing or sneezing repeatedly—usually combined with wiggling around—chances are they are *under*impressed with your presentation. Of course, the entire audience may have been hit with a plague—possible, not real probable. My vote says they're bored.

If just one or two people are coughing or sniffling, chances are they are ill.

What to Do

If it's just one person and is chronic, and if it *is* annoying you or the others, call a quick break or go into a group discussion exercise. The person may be relieved for a chance to duck out. Before you start back up, take the person aside and ask what you can do to help. Be solicitous. Suggest that he or she sit in the back until the symptoms subside.

> *Be sympathetic; let the audience be annoyed. This is the old "good cop, bad cop" script. If you reverse it and act uncaring, the audience will move over and be defensive of the person who is ill. Don't let this happen.*
> —DOTTIE WALTERS

If the whole group is getting restless, switch tactics. What you are currently doing is not working.

- Switch to your best material.
- Go into a participative exercise.
- Let the audience leave early.

If it's just a one-time cougher or sneezer, you can have some fun with them.

What to Say

For Sneezing

> *God bless you! Lord knows he heard you!*
> —ALAN PARISSE

> *Gesundheit. I'm glad I'm not the only one who does that.*
> —W MITCHELL

> *(Offer them a tissue or handkerchief.) Remember me? I always seem to sit in front of you at the theater.*
> —RON LEE

(The first time) Bless you.
(The second time) Bless you.
(The third time) From here on out consider yourself blessed!
                                      —Bob Burg

This is fairly important stuff. It's nothing to sneeze at!
                                      —Ron Dentinger

For Sneezing or Coughing

Are you OK? No sense both of us dying.

Bless you. Would you like a drink of water? A shot of penicillin?
                                      —Roger Langley

I had a friend who died from a sneeze (cough) like that. Of course, he was standing in his neighbor's bedroom closet at the time.
                                      —Charles Jarvis

I've had all kinds of audiences before, but this is the first one that's been allergic to me!
                                      —Dick Flavin

For Belching and Passing Gas

Please be careful of calling attention to anyone passing gas! Do it only if it is obvious that the entire room has heard the noise, and the "offender" is aware of that fact. Then your humor can help relieve this person's embarrassment.

Critics!
                                      —Tom Ogden

(Audience member passes gas.) Now that moves us to the topic of nonverbal communication.
                                      —Terry Paulson

Was that an accident or an opinion?
                                      —Alan Pease

...An Audience Member Becomes Seriously Ill

As I made my opening remarks, a lady in the front row had an attack of some kind and the ushers escorted her, kicking and agitated, in front of my audience. I said, "I have got to get some new material."
                                      —Art Linkletter

In one of my sessions, a guy laughed so hard he fell backward, then just lay there! I called for a break. The guy was on the ground; people were trying to give him a heart massage and breathing in his mouth. I said, "Is there a doctor in the house? Call for a doctor from my office!" It took us about 45 minutes to an hour to realize he'd died. His friends said, "Well, that's the way he would have wanted to go, laughing with his friends." What else could you do? I just ended the program there.
—ALAN PEASE

To Prevent It from Happening

You can't prevent illness from happening, but you can be prepared. As a leader *before the event ever gets started,* you need take into account the fact that it could happen. Know what the venue's emergency procedures are and assign an assistant to help you.

What to Do

Always assume it is a serious, life-threatening emergency. If an emergency occurs, immediately send your assistant for help. If the audience member is just joking, he or she will quickly let you know it's a gag. The rest of the audience is looking to you for leadership. Ask if anyone in the group is a doctor or nurse and request that the rest remain seated calmly.

Call over the mic for a doctor; direct that help to where the person is. Announce an immediate break in the program for 10 minutes. Go directly to the person and offer aid, and solace. A number of strong people will follow you. Take the person's hand, as you would a member of your family's. As soon as help arrives and the person is removed from the room, call for the audience to return. Then lead a moment of silent prayer and proceed.
—DOTTIE WALTERS

Most speakers know that there is nothing you can do here but stop your talk immediately. What most speakers don't realize, however, is that they also need to ask the audience if it is OK to continue once the situation is under control.
I had a woman pass out at a program in a hospital setting, and none of the medical personnel in the audience would do anything until I asked them to get the paramedics. Because of the tension of the situation and my topic of humor, I could not start again until I asked the audience if I could go on.
—ALLEN KLEIN

When things are under control or the person has been taken out of the room, start over, repeating or summarizing your last paragraph in order to let people recall where you were in the talk.
—PERRY BIDDLE, JR.

What to Say

All the lines below are for you to use *after* the ill person has been taken from the room, you have seen that he or she is being taken care of, and you have asked for and gained permission from the audience to go ahead. Be careful of your delivery and make sure that people know you are concerned.

> *I hope that was not just an excuse to get out of listening to the rest of my talk.*
> —W MITCHELL

> *I think she (he) heard me speak before.*
> —LILLY WALTERS

> *I hope it wasn't something I said.*
> *I didn't realize I was that bad.*
> *I don't usually have that effect on people.*
> —TONY KING

> *(Affecting a radio announcer's voice.) We now return to our previously scheduled program, in progress.*
> —DICK FLAVIN

...The Whole Audience Is Ill (or Hung Over)

To Prevent It from Happening

When you can, schedule events to discourage excessive alcohol consumption. If you have "social" hours in the evening, plan an activity.

Alcohol acts as a sedative, dulling the mind and blocking its ability to process information. Hard alcohol has become less and less popular at meetings and seminars. More often, light wine and nonalcoholic drinks are served.

Snacks that are high in fat, protein, starch, and B vitamins—such as cheese and crackers—help attendees metabolize the alcohol.

Drinking makes listeners even more thirsty. Serve tall, cool glasses of water with lime or lemon slices close to the bar. Often people will grab these instead of a second alcoholic drink.

> *I ask for lots of extra tomato juice and lemon to be made available. I also start off with a higher level of involvement exercise than I would normally use. I might use an exercise which has people imagine both a negative and a positive state and muscle test each other in pairs.*
> —CHRIS HEGARTY

Make the content light. Make sure there will be lots of water and coffee.
—**Marilyn Wheeler**

When we anticipate the audience will be extra tired, we schedule the meeting to start an hour or so later in the morning. We still deliver the same-length program, but just start it later. Everyone is very appreciative.
—**Don Dewar**

What to Do

Be as high-energy as possible.

Suggest to the meeting planner that we cut it short.
—**Patricia Fripp**

Speak softly—no lectern pounding. Forget about motivating, teaching, or changing their minds about anything. Don't make them move around. I switch to long humorous stories that vaguely illustrate my points. (Try to become as much like Garrison Keillor as possible.) Depending on the group, I might also try imagery or hypnosis. Overall try for passive rather than active involvement.
—**Albert Bernstein**

When I feel that I am not connecting, I immediately tell myself to love them anyhow. I used to get up-tight and try harder. I don't do that now. They have their reasons. Sometimes they are tired, disappointed in the conference in general, unhappy with the lodging facilities, the prices, the food....So they hold back on the speaker too. I eyeball them, tell them my truth, love them, and eventually we end up in a great place.
—**Rosita Perez**

What to Say

Serious

I want you to touch yourselves...now thunder in your outdoor voices: "I am AWAKE!" (Wait for them to repeat, then...)
   Do you want to triple your income and double your time off? (Wait for them to respond, then...)
   If so, you must be 100 percent "present time" and available! Sit enthusiastically upright in your seats! You give me all you got and I'll give you all I got. You have what it takes to be here and learn. You're too good not to give me your absolute best. You can sleep next week!
   (Then I lead them in exhilarating stretches, hand-clapping, shouting, and spirit-elevating techniques.)
—**Mark Victor Hansen**

Humorous

Swear...I'll never do it again!
—**Patricia Fripp**

*While last night I regretted not staying at the party with all of you, today I
know I made the right decision by...(grimacing)...looking into your faces!*
                                                              —Chris Hegarty

...The Audience Doesn't
Care About Your Talk
(No Interest)

*An optimist is any speaker who looks out over the audience with their
heads bowed and their eyes closed—and thinks they are praying.*
                                          —Robert Orben, humor consultant
                                     (From *Sharing Ideas*, February–March 1989)

If people don't care, they have a lack of interest in your topic. This is
not the same as them not wanting to be there—which means their attitude is bad. People's interest in a topic can affect their attitude. The
home owners association of a housing project located next door to a
proposed nuclear waste dump site may have a rotten attitude toward
you if you're presenting in favor of the dump site. But it *will* have a
very keen, even savage interest!

To Prevent It from Happening

Find out before the program what their projected attitude will be. Use
a preprogram questionnaire. (See Fig. 1-3 in Chapter 1.)

Interest can be adjusted by finding out how you can make your
topic benefit the listeners, then giving them lots of those benefits up
front. Once you get them listening, you can bring them around to the
purpose of the presentation. Try taking a survey before the event that
implies their ideas will be incorporated and their needs met at the
meeting...and incorporate them!

Look carefully at your presentation. Think in their terms. What is in
your topic for them? What results of following your advice can they
get excited about? Put all those things in the first few minutes of your
presentation. Close the presentation by restating those things again.

What to Do

If you are in the middle of the talk and you realize they are uninterested, try an audience participation device. I suggest a "T diagram." (See
the instructions in Chapter 5.)

*The value of any speaker is measured by what learned experience he or she
has to share with the audience. But often the audience is skeptical about*

their own ability to accomplish the positive changes you "the expert" are suggesting. While they are in their "But will it work for me?" mode, if you can give them some examples to try that will show them on-the-spot results, their excitement over their own success will be infectious. So give them something new that they can do and while they are actually cheering for themselves, it's you who'll be getting the standing ovation!
—HERMINE HILTON

I was speaking in Africa on goal setting. I was about 5 minutes into a 4-hour seminar when a woman raised her hand and said, "Mr. McJunkin. You don't understand our situation here. We work 12 hours a day, 6 days a week; then we go home to take care of our families. Our men and children will not help us, so we have a full-time job there too. We have no time for anything but work and work."

I was stopped for a minute; then I just nodded and said, "Then let's forget this." I threw my notes into the air. I walked up to someone in the front and said, "Let's talk about you. What challenges are you facing today?"

It was one of the best presentations I've ever given.
—JIM MCJUNKIN

What to Say

Serious

Stop everything you are doing. Now think. What are you feeling? Why? (Give them 20 seconds.)

Pick a group leader. I want you to come up with three reasons that this topic is foolish, or has no value to you.

(After they have done that, it should take at least 3 minutes, maybe more.)

Now come up with three ways this information might have been valuable if only.

(Give them another 3 minutes.)

All right, now let's share how the information could have been valuable.

(Many, of course, are going to say that what you are telling them is valuable and why. You will also get good ideas why it's off the mark and you can fix it right there.)
—LILLY WALTERS

In today's quickly changing business environment, we can change our ways, or we can update our résumés. The strategies we are going to discuss in a few moments will give you the strategies you need to excel in this quickly changing environment.
—JEFF DEWAR

Humorous

If you think this is dull...you should see my diary.
—RON DENTINGER

I bought some furniture the other day and got a 60-day, no-interest loan. I didn't know I could get a 60-minute, no-interest talk.
—Tom Antion

...The Audience Doesn't Want to Be There (Bad Attitude)

Did someone force these people to attend? Did a manager imply to them that they were inept at their jobs and in desperate need of hearing your presentation? You can bet their attitude is going to be bad.

To Prevent It from Happening

Do your research to find out what their attitude will be. As in the preceding section, take a survey before the event that implies their ideas will be incorporated and their needs met at your presentation. Then do it.

What to Do

Don't acknowledge the bad attitude. Ignore it. Right at the beginning, tell people how honored you are to be asked to present to them. Let them know that they have been "chosen" to attend. They are the sort of "superior" personnel the company is willing to invest money in. If you feel them start to loosen up, go on; if not, try Dr. Ken Blanchard's advice.

> *I was talking to a group once; I was getting no energy back from them. So I stopped the talk and said, "Let me give you a little feedback. Who cut off your nerve endings? I feel like I'm doing all the work. Something is going on here. Is there anybody willing to share what is going on here?" They told me they were forced to go to these seminars every year and nothing ever happened to them; seminars were just a waste of time as far as they were concerned. They would rather be back at work. So I told them to go back to work. "There is no point in being here if you can't focus in." A few went back. But the rest who stayed were ready to learn, or at least shocked into giving me a chance.*
>
> *Warren Earhart had a great saying: "Life which you resist, persists." If something is bothering you and you don't deal with it, it does not go away; you just gunnysack it. But it prevents you from taking in new stuff. The same is true for your audience members.*
>
> *When I work with government groups, I say, "Look, before we get started I want to take about 10 minutes and break you into groups. Let's play*

'Ain't It Awful!' I want you to tell me all the things that are awful about being in the government that I ought to know." You see, they are all sitting there bitching about me: "He doesn't know about us." "He doesn't understand our problems."

John Jones—a wonderful trainer—has a wonderful statement, "When in doubt, confront. When all else fails, try honesty." So first try perhaps, "What's going on here?" to confront the issue. If that doesn't work, try honestly telling them how you feel, "I'm feeling very uncomfortable."

—KEN BLANCHARD
(Quoted in *Secrets of Successful Speakers*, by
Lilly Walters, McGraw-Hill, 1993)

What to Say

Serious

I am so honored to be asked to speak to you today. It cost a great deal of money to bring me here. You may note that your group did not send everyone to attend today—only those they are willing to invest in. That says quite a lot about the caliber of people sitting here with me today.

—LILLY WALTERS

Everybody wants to go to heaven, but nobody wants to die.

—JIMMY CALANO

Humorous

Some of you must feel like a fig in molasses. You didn't want to be here, but you have to stick around.

—ROGER LANGLEY

I am acquainted with audiences that want to be somewhere else—I speak in prisons from time to time.

There are three times a man goes to church without his consent: to be baptized, to be married, and to be buried! You may wish you could be somewhere else right now. I'll be finished soon and you can go.

—PERRY BIDDLE, JR.

...The Audience Has Just Had Bad News or Is Depressed

To Prevent It from Happening

The points raised in the two previous sections, "...The Audience Doesn't Care About Your Talk" and "...The Audience Doesn't Want to Be There," can also apply to this situation.

Well, it's why professional speakers are brought in, to take the tough hits.
—CHRIS HEGARTY

What to Do

If the bad news is on their minds, you must acknowledge it and give them a chance to let it go.

- Shift their thoughts to the happy times.
- Try to tailor your remarks as strategies to deal with the bad news.

> *I was speaking on the topic of "Humor and Healing" for the hospice leaders and volunteers. That week one of the key volunteers lost her husband to cancer. She was asked to say a couple of words before I spoke. Her tears and her story touched everyone, including me. Her grief was so strong, my introducer got up and said, "I just can't go on. Here's Dr. Paulson." She wiped her eyes as she handed me the microphone. I looked out at a sea of tears and I was supposed to talk on humor. I looked at her and said, "You've touched me as you have all of us. Your experience makes me think of my wife and how I would feel if it were her that had died. I don't know what I would have said, but I do know that one of the strengths I would hold onto would be my memories of her, not the bad memories but happy and joyful moments that we had together. You see, we laugh a lot together." She smiled and shared a funny memory of her husband. We all laughed, and with that permission and transition, my program was off and running for a healing look at laughter.*
> —TERRY PAULSON

What to Say

Serious

> *(Try a mind exercise; speak slowly and calmly.)*
> Close your eyes. Take a deep breath—inhale, hold...exhale. Now keep doing that over and over slowly, inhale, hold...exhale. Think back to a moment in your life that caused you the most tranquillity, warmth, and happiness. How did that make your hands feel? (pause) How did that make your chest feel? (pause) How did you see yourself in your mind? (pause) How did your feet feel? (pause) What did your face do? (pause) Let that same feeling come into your face now. (pause) Let that same feeling throw light into your mind. (pause) The room here is much brighter now. (pause) Open your eyes and look. (pause)
> Now, the next point I want to make today is...
> (and go right on.)
> —LILLY WALTERS

I understand the news of the last few days has not all been pleasant. But the secret to being a competent executive is to constantly learn new skills, even if you don't get to use them here. What we will discuss today will help you to aid you, wherever you are.
—CHRIS HEGARTY

Humorous

Be very careful of using humor until people know how deeply you feel for them about the bad news.

...The Audience Has Just Had Good News

To Prevent It from Happening

Oddly enough, you *do* want to prevent people from getting some tidbit of really exciting news right before or after you speak. They will lose focus on what you would like them to learn, and think only of the good news. If the introducer announces that the group has just won the Lotto and then follows with "Oh, yeah, and here is our speaker on 'Time Management in the 1990s,'" you will have one heck of a time bringing the group back to your topic.

What to Do

Whenever possible, control the "announcements" that people will hear before and after your talk.

On the other hand, you may be able to work *some* of their good news into your presentation. If you can find a way to use the "good news" to make your point, you will be well ahead. W Mitchell was speaking in Australia, where the rugby team had just won a huge championship against New Zealand. There is a *major* standing rivalry between the two countries. He started off with how glad he was to be in Australia, then added: "But I am so sad. I just left New Zealand. What a lovely country! Wonderful food and people. Oh, and their fantastic countryside. Their businesses are all flourishing...." By this time the Aussies were starting to squirm and roll their eyes. "Yes, what a great country, all those wonderful things it has to boast about...including the *second* best rugby team in the world." They were on their feet cheering.

Be aware of what "buzz" is in the air before you speak. Quickly think of ways to apply what people are thinking about to what you want them to learn.

What to Say

Serious

What a day! To have accomplished _____ (the good news), I was thinking of how you could apply the lessons those people (or you) must have learned to _____ (your topic). Take the next 30 seconds and just think about that; maybe jot down a few ideas.
—LILLY WALTERS

Humorous

I have bad news for all you pessimists in the audience.
—From *Current Comedy Newsletter,*
November 25, 1991

...You Lose Control of a Wildly Enthusiastic Crowd

Dr. Edson Bueno is president of the second largest (and fastest-growing) insurance company in South America. He has a year-end celebration every year for his entire team of collaborators (they don't like to be called employees). The third year it was held, I was invited down to help fine-tune his address. The speech was one of the best. Edson is wonderfully dynamic. He implemented some new ideas to help bring his already very enthusiastic collaborators to a higher level of exultation during their party (they also don't like to call it the "Year-End Annual Meeting"). They had bags of streamers and confetti on the tables, and wonderful music playing with a great dance beat. Edson had preplanned for a few of the guests to be up on the stage, just clapping, dancing, and celebrating, as most of the attendees arrived. It was a wonderful emotional high for everyone.

Halfway through the 2½-hour program, Edson was introduced. The members of the audience went wild (he is extremely popular with them). He went into his dynamic, poignant, and thought-provoking speech. Unfortunately, the mic system was malfunctioning—about a third of the group couldn't hear him. Also, by this time people were so excited and aflame that they couldn't do anything other than hoot and yell and have a good time. So the party just went on, oblivious of Edson's message, but cheering wildly anyway.

So much for the best-laid plans.

To Prevent It from Happening

Structure your program with people's moods in mind. You may *want* them in an emotional, enthusiastic, screaming, yelling high. Fine. Just figure out what you are going to do with it once you get it.

Know which points of your speech are going to generate the most emotion. Plan for laughter or interruptions. Don't get so caught up in the audience's reaction to you that you forget where you are. Regaining control is often simply a matter of pausing long enough for the audience to catch their breath. Make sure you're ready to continue once you've regained control.
—SCOTT PATON

What to Do

Don't get angry. Laugh and have a good time with the others as you think of ways to bring them back into control.

Usually there are a few up front still listening to you. Make a motion to them as if enjoining them to help you. Put your finger to your lips and go, "Shhhhhhh," encouraging those watching you to do the same. As others start to pay attention, encourage them to do the same. Make a game of it, conducting the volume high and low on the "shhhhing." Soon the whole audience will be following your lead, as you direct everyone to sit, and then go on with the talk.

I use the "prescribe the symptom" method from hypnosis. So, if they are speaking loudly I would say, "OK, everyone stand up! Now talk as loudly as you can!" They would get louder, then laugh and come back to me.

Do anything that they are not expecting—drop something, stand on a chair.
—DEANNA BERG

Be clear in your expectations up front, then get them to agree to the rules before you launch into an exercise.
—CHRIS HEGARTY

Taking a break works best. All seminars need smoking/drinking/potty breaks. Smile (never look frustrated or show your dismay at your loss of control) and say something like: "OK, let's take a little break; the restrooms are down the hall and drinking fountains and snack machines are in the lobby; all smoking is outside." This will allow you to break up the crowd and regroup. After 5 minutes or so you should detect a lull. Ask someone to go retrieve the stragglers and start over.

If you cannot take a break (say, you just took one), then note that most rowdy crowds are influenced by one or two instigating members. Locate and isolate the overly zealous folks. Ask them a question or have them come up to the stage for a demo. Without a leader the crowd normally loses momentum.

If you do not detect a crowd instigator, try directing the audience's attention to another topic. Humans are curious creatures. Bait the crowd with a curiosity question such as: "Who can tell me what this is?" Pull out an item from your props or briefcase, or simply point to something in the room such as a painting. This will buy you about 10 seconds of control in which to change gears and regain attention.

In each case, try not to lose control again, as regaining control becomes more difficult each successive time.

—DAVID R. VILLANUEVA

What to Say

Serious

(I learned this from Bob Pike of Creative Training Techniques.)
Clap once if you can hear my voice.
(You clap yourself and some of the others will clap also.)
Clap twice if you hear my voice.
(You clap twice. Usually all will be clapping and have refocused back up front.)

—LORNA RILEY

Humorous

Don't let me interrupt!

—GEORGE GOLDTRAP

(If you are doing a good job this will happen often, so with a big smile I blow a whistle, then say...)
At the beginning I couldn't get you to talk! Now I can't get you to stop!

—CHRIS HEGARTY

I'm not sure, but I think I started losing control of this group last Tuesday.

—STEVE GOTTLIEB

...Hostiles and Critics Are in Your Audience

Churchill was once asked, "Doesn't it thrill you to know that every time you make a speech the hall is packed to overflowing?"

"It's quite flattering," replied Sir Winston. "But whenever I feel that way I always remember that if, instead of making a political speech, I was being hanged, the crowd would be twice as big."

—LARRY WILDE
(From *Library of Laughter*, Jester Press, 1988)

To Prevent It from Happening

This will be no great surprise to those of you who know me, but I'm rather opinionated. Voicing my opinions, in less than diplomatic terms, has ever been one of my weaknesses. When I was in my teens, I remember Dad consoling me when I had ruffled some feathers in an association I belonged to.

"Dad, I don't understand why they are reacting like this!"

"Honey, if you are the kind of person who *does* things, people will criticize you. They rarely take shots at people who are holding still."

Over the fireplace in Fred Astaire's Beverly Hills home was a yellowed MGM interoffice studio memo—a souvenir of the dancer's first screen test. Dated 1933 and sent by the testing director to his superior, it read: "Fred Astaire. Can't act. Slightly bald. Can dance a little."

If you decide to take the platform, you will be criticized. You are the sort of person who *does* things. You will also be adored. It all just goes with the territory. Some audiences will be better, or worse, than others. Do your homework before the event. Find out what the mood of the crowd will be. Are people angry? Why? Are they uninterested in the topic?

Attitude can be adjusted with humor. Interest can be adjusted with benefits.

Where there is much desire to learn, there of necessity will be much arguing, much writing, many opinions; for opinions in good men is but knowledge in the making.

—JOHN MILTON

If I know that they will be hostile, I identify three or four people in the audience who are perceived to be leaders, and spend time with them beforehand. Then I can call on them during the program for support if I need to, such as "George, come on up here, let's do an exercise" or "Pete, what do you think of that?" It's always worked, even among a group of Russian managers in St. Petersburg. I asked the translator to identify the leaders ahead of time and gave them cigarettes. They did their work when hostility arose. When the group sees that their leaders support, they follow along.

—JANET LAPP

Don't "pull rank"—imply you know more than they do—especially when you do; it's the best way to lose an audience!

—ALBERT BERNSTEIN

What to Do

Anger is a low brain function. Let's hope you are giving the kind of presentation that will bring people into a higher brain function.

1. Start your presentation from their side of the argument. Give them the impression that you agree with them. There is always *something* about either side of an issue you can agree with.

2. Phrase your comments in such a way as to downplay the things you don't agree with and accentuate the things you do agree with.

3. Break people into groups and let them come up with 10 solutions to the problem. Often, thinking of other ways that a challenge can be met will bring people to a higher level of reasoning and help them see more sides of an issue.

4. If possible, meet with the members who are the angriest and keep incorporating their ideas into the presentations, giving them credit.

5. Get them laughing. Take out all those "ethnic" joke books. "How many _____ does it take to change a light bulb?" You plug in the things they are angry at. If they are angry about a safety regulation, you would say, "How many safety officers does it take...."

Be careful if there are two sides to the argument and both sides are present. Find things they are both willing to take pot shots at and target those things in your humor. If they are angry about the budget, instead of attacking management or whoever set the budget, take shots at the political system that made the situation occur in the first place.

You never need to continue with a presentation that's threatening or useless. Just stop, say you respect that people don't want to be there, and offer to stick around for questions. That's perfectly all right.

I remember watching a videotape of Don Jacobs, a San Francisco psychologist and hypnotist, who was able to tame wild horses simply by hypnotizing himself. I encountered a very hostile group once. Here are the tactics I used to bring people around:

- *I stayed centered.*
- *I openly acknowledged their anger.*
- *I sided with them when I could and spoke in terms that identified me with them (their language).*
- *On the first challenge from the group, I set clear limits, such as "You're ticked off—that makes sense. However, speaking like that puts us both down and it won't work. Let's figure out another way." By the time you've lost control, you've probably also lost respect.*
- *I used their anger as energy, and told them how positive it was and how they could use it better.*
  —Janet Lapp

The biggest mistake people make is to escalate the conflict by using comedian heckler lines. These just fan the flames of hostility.

Instead, use conflict management techniques. One approach is to poke fun at yourself to derail the conflict. By making fun of yourself, you give the audience something they can agree with you about. And the conflict goes off-line for a moment. This gives you an opportunity to repair the relationship.

Another approach is the distraction technique. You say something so off the wall that people cease their hostile behavior while they process it. Again, it gives you an opening to change the tone of the relationship.

And, when nothing else works, try paradoxical intervention. You reframe the situation in a way that makes it seem like you want the audience to be hostile. This really screws them up; because if you do this properly, it means that the more they hoot and deride you, the more successful you are. So the audience now has two choices: they continue their hostility and make you successful or they shut up because they don't want to make you successful. The speaker wins either way.

—MALCOLM KUSHNER

I was addressing a class when suddenly I heard the crinkling of a cola can. It was a slow, drawn-out...crinkle...crinkle...crinkle...going for a couple of minutes. The young man who was doing it was a trainer from that same soda company. It really annoyed me; it seemed like he was doing it deliberately. I was talking about group dynamics and the different types of personalities. On a whim, I was inspired to say, "Somebody here in the class is helping me set up the scenario for this type of problem." I smiled and said, "Does anyone know who I'm talking about?" They all turned and pointed to the young man from the cola company, thinking that he was working with me. Then I asked the group, "Now if you had someone in your class who was making some kind of distraction, what are different ways you can handle that?" So the class got involved. Finally, I thanked this guy and said, "Tom, really appreciate you helping me set this one up," and winked at him.

After the class was over he came to me and said, "I gotta admit, I was doing that to irritate you, to see if you'd let me get away with it or not. I know it was stupid. You really let me off the hook. I appreciate that."

—DON DEWAR

I call a break. Then I speak privately to the individual, being sure to keep my comments focused on facts rather than opinions. Additionally, I support her right to her opinion, and my right to maintain a constructive learning environment. The point is to see different as just different, not wrong.

—LENORA BILLINGS-HARRIS

I let them talk. I then try to draw my conclusions out of bits and pieces of what they say. Then they can learn something and still feel it is their idea. Good questions for you to ask are ones that elicit their values and goals related to the subject.

—ALBERT BERNSTEIN

If you have a moderator, it is his or her responsibility to maintain order. If, however, the moderator is unable, or unwilling, to exert control, then the speaker should seize the initiative, using the "volume advantage" provided by the microphone.
　　　　　　　　　　　　　　　　　　　　　—LARRY TRACY

Whenever I get very depressed with those who would take me down, I like to read from a famous presidential speech.

Far better it is to dare mighty things, to win glorious triumphs, even though checkered by failure, than to take rank with those poor spirits who neither enjoy much nor suffer much. Because they live in the gray twilight that knows not victory nor defeat.
　　　　　　　　　　　　　　　　—TEDDY ROOSEVELT
　　　　　　　　　　　　　　　(Speech before the Hamilton Club, Chicago,
　　　　　　　　　　　　　　　April 10, 1899)

What to Say

Serious

Thank you for your input. Would you please stay afterward to talk about this?
　　(Then move to another part of the stage.)
　　Let's move on. I have so much I want to give you today!
　　　　　　　　　　　　　　　　　—DOTTIE WALTERS

He is venting his frustration because he expects me to do something about it. That's a step in the right direction.
　　　　　　　　—BILL CLINTON, PRESIDENT OF THE UNITED STATES

(Simply be silent, look at the audience for at least 60 seconds, and then take the microphone and speak very loudly.)
　　I appreciate that there is some unhappiness in the room, and I honor your feelings. However because our purpose today is _____ (state your purpose), we're going to be moving on with the program.
　　(Then simply take charge and forcefully go on talking in the program. Whoever is not listening, or is talking, will simply back down as you assert your own personal power.)
　　　　　　　　　　　　　　　　　　—LEE MILTEER

It's obvious to me that you and I see the world very differently. I know I can live with that; I hope you can too.
　　　　　　　　　　　　　　　　—CHRIS HEGARTY

The communication technique we are learning is not an easy one to implement under pressure, or when emotions are high, as you have just seen. We all must practice it continuously. Let's take a stretch break for 7 minutes, and then get back on course when we return.
　　　　　　　　　　　　　　—LENORA BILLINGS-HARRIS

Neil Young wrote in one of his earliest songs, "All you critics alone, you're no better than me for what you've shown."
—JIMMY CALANO

Do you think your boss paid all that money to send you here to straighten me out?
—PHILIP CROSBY

I know what I have been presenting has not been received very well thus far. I think there is merit in what I was saying and would like to open discussion with you to see how we should proceed. If we could start back up now, I'd like to have some feedback so that we can tailor the remainder of the time so that everyone will derive some benefit. What comments do you have on my presentation thus far?"
—DAVE CAREY

(Use a standing microphone in the audience and ask people to line up and respond to questions.)
 What do you think is the most important thing for someone to know about _____ (the topic)?
 What is the best lesson you have learned during your years of experience with _____ (the topic)?
 If you were speaking today, what advice or information would you give your audience?
—DEANNA BERG

For now, could we just agree to disagree on this point?
—TOM ANTION

I appreciate your asking me about it—and I want to explain.
—HILLARY RODHAM CLINTON
(Press conference on the Whitewater affair, April 1994)

Humorous

Don't make me get up!
—GENE MITCHENER, THE WHEELCHAIR COMIC

Many people today are Catholic because their fathers were Catholic. Many other people today are Protestant...simply because their fathers were Catholic.
 (Substitute the group that people are mad at for "Catholic," and substitute what the majority of the them are for "Protestant." Thus, if you are addressing a group of factory workers who are mad at environmental engineers, you might say: "Many people today are environmental engineers because their fathers were environmental engineers. Many other people today are factory workers...simply because their fathers were environmental engineers.")
—UNKNOWN

If honest disagreement is healthy, you must be a real health nut.
                                        —ROGER LANGLEY

(In response to a crude or four-letter word.)

You're not alone in your opinion. My ex-husband (wife) feels exactly the same way!

Lots of other people feel the way you do. Like my teenage son when I won't let him use the car.

I understand what it's like to feel frustrated and angry...I live with a teenager.

[When they tell me I don't understand _____ (minority group).] That's true. But then, I don't understand white people either. You know how crazy they are!
                                        —DEANNA JEAN BROWN

Now isn't that special (or a blessing)? Thank you for sharing.

You're hoping the rest of this meeting will be at least as good.
                                        —LILLY WALTERS

I'll try the Johnny Carson curse lines: "May the Merrill Lynch bull leave a portfolio on your rug" or "May an 80-year-old onion farmer give you mouth-to-mouth resuscitation when you are napping on the beach."
                                        —TERRY PAULSON

I'd like you to meet my opponent's campaign manager.
                                        —W MITCHELL

Just my luck—the light at the end of the tunnel was a locomotive.

The ability to be cool under fire is such a great skill. I wish I had it.
                                        —TERRY PAULSON

The only impartiality possible to the human mind is that which arises from understanding neither side of the case.
                                        —LORD GORDON HEWART, ENGLISH JURIST,
                                        BORN **1870**
                                        (From *Great Book of Funny Quotes,* by Eileen
                                        Mason, Sterling Publishing, 1993)

A critic is a man created to praise greater men than himself, but he is never able to find them.
                                        —RICHARD LE GALLIENNE, ENGLISH POET,
                                        BORN **1866**
                                        (From *Great Book of Funny Quotes,* by Eileen
                                        Mason, Sterling Publishing, 1993)

If I ever wanted a brain transplant, I'd use a sportswriter because I'd want one that had never been used.

(You can substitute for "sportswriter" any group or industry that the audience is angry at.)
—NORM VAN BROCKLIN, AMERICAN FOOTBALL
PLAYER, BORN 1926
(From *Great Book of Funny Quotes*, by Eileen
Mason, Sterling Publishing, 1993)

(Fill in the blank with the group's particular nemesis.) If all _____s were laid end to end...it wouldn't be a bad idea.

I'm 100 percent sure your idea has merit—well, maybe 90 percent sure. Come to think of it, maybe only 5 percent. We need to talk.
—LILLY WALTERS

Look, if you don't mind, you're shaking up some of the audience and waking up the rest.
—LEONARD RYZMAN

Please, friends—I'm a speaker, not a referee.

I love to see a good fight, but I'd rather see it on ESPN than in my audience.

Please, guys—give me a break. If my teacher finds out about this, I'll get kicked out of mediation school.

Please stop that. You're giving me flashbacks of me and my wife fighting over the remote control.

Did you ever see a grown speaker cry?
—TOM ANTION

...The Audience Starts Arguing with One Another in the Middle of Your Presentation

What to Do

WORKING WITH A HOSTILE SITUATION
by Somers White, Master Negotiator

Don't rush to solve the problem. Before you decide what to do, evaluate the problem, establish objectives, and develop strategies. There are as many ways to solve the problem as there are personalities.

(Continued)

Evaluate

- Why are they angry?

- How deep is their anger? Are they mildly grieved about the parking lot maintenance, or do you have a Palestinian and an Israeli? Do you know who they are, and the level of their problem? It will be best to get the argument stopped.

- What are the worst possible consequences of this dispute? Could blows be thrown or just harsh language used?

- If they have been drinking, the situation is more volatile and can quickly escalate and possibly get completely out of hand. It is easier to stop it earlier rather than later.

- Does continuation of this discussion make the points you are trying to make in the presentation? Or will continuation pull the topic too far away from the point you want to make? When the program is over, will the audience remember you and your concepts or the problem people? The choice is yours.

Establish Objectives

- Solve the problem: Depending on the situation, you may want to silence the arguers and avoid a repeat, perhaps by getting rid of them. For some reason you may want the disagreement to continue, but probably not. The focus should be on you and your presentation. Be careful about getting in the middle of the argument, for many reasons, including the fact that you may not be able to get out. You never win in a spitting contest with a skunk.

- Don't anger them more and escalate the situation.

- It is easy to say or do something that will make the audience rally to one or both of the people and become antagonistic toward you. Be careful.

- Draw attention back to yourself.

- Get your presentation back on track.

- Make the audience comfortable and ready to start learning again.

Develop Strategies

- Humor will help break the tension, but don't let either one of the people arguing feel humiliated. Direct the humor, not at them, but at something else. Don't cause either to lose face.

- You might ask the planners to come to the front. Then you say, "We seem to have a problem. Will you see that these people are taken care of?" Let them take care of their own people as they think best.

- To get the arguers out of the room, you first need to call attention back to yourself. I would stand on a chair in the front of the of the room and ask, "Ladies and gentlemen, may I have your attention? How many of you would like to see these two continue their discussion in here?" I would then wait for them to respond. "How many of you would like to see them *resolve* this outside this room?" Once they answer, I say to the arguers, "Sir, what is your name? Madam, what is your name?" Then I address them by name. "Our best thoughts are with you as you two work this out." I turn to the head planner and say, " _____, please help them find a good place outside to work this out." There is more power in the 50 or 400 people in your audience than just you standing up there asking the disrupters to leave. This strategy makes you simply a conduit to carry out the audience's wishes.

- To make your listeners comfortable and ready to start learning again, you may need to allow them "time to grieve," depending on the level of disruption and its emotional impact on the audience. One option is to say, "Let's stop for a moment and see what was going on with these two." Perhaps you may want to ask questions of individual members of the audience. See if you can find a way to relate a point they come up with back into points you are going to make later. Say, "Yes, as a matter of fact we are going to cover that exact point in a few minutes." Try to help relieve their stress with humor. "But, before we go on, let me tell you a story about...."

When working with a hostile situation, remember:

1. Sound calm. Lower your voice an octave and speak slowly.
2. Use a diversion to draw the audience's attention back to you. Stand on a chair, ring a bell, blow a whistle.
3. Get the disruptive people silenced or out of the room.
4. Smile.

What to Say

Serious

(Use the old "Shhhhh," with finger to lips.) This is wonderful! You all have so many good ideas. Will you hold those questions and comments until we come to the Q&A? Thank you!
                                                        —DOTTIE WALTERS

I apologize if my skills as a speaker don't match your ability to listen. I need to be more sensitive.
                                                        —ROGER LANGLEY

Humorous

Before using any humorous lines, carefully read Somers White's advice under "What to Do."

Well, well, well. We're just all getting along like brothers here...like Cain and Abel.
I feel like I'm refereeing a war here. Who wants to wear the blue and who gets the gray?
                                                        —LILLY WALTERS

Oh, great! Now I have the audience heckling the audience.
Don't make me get up and come back there.
                                        —GENE MITCHENER, THE WHEELCHAIR COMIC

Two farmers each claimed they owned a certain cow. While one pulled on its head, the other on its tail, the cow was milked by a lawyer.
                                        —JEWISH PARABLE
                                        (From *Great Book of Funny Quotes*, by Eileen
                                        Mason, Sterling Publishing, 1993)

Many a man's tongue has broken his nose.
                                        —ANONYMOUS
                                        (From *Great Book of Funny Quotes*, by Eileen
                                        Mason, Sterling Publishing, 1993)

Feel free to talk among yourselves while I'm up here.
Thanks, Mom (Dad)!
                                        —From *A Funny Thing Happened on the Way to
                                        the Boardroom*, by Michael Iapoce, Wiley,
                                        1988

(Being a magician, I always have a bag of props, one of which is a bull whip. I crack it and say...)
    Now, don't make me use this!

(Over the years I have used the same line with equal success holding a Fisher-Price chainsaw, and a sci-fi ray gun.)
—Tom Ogden

Did my mother-in-law invite you people here?
—Lorin Paulsen

Please, sir(s), this is a conference, not Wrestlemania.
—From *Speaker's Idea File,* Original Humor
section by Gary Apple, August 1993

...Ill-Mannered Louts Invade Your Presentation

To Prevent It from Happening

If you single out and then try to nail a heckler—as he or she justly deserves for interrupting the presentation—*you will be the bad guy.* No matter how much the audience agrees with you that the twit is wrong and you are right, the "twit" is still a member of the peer group—you are the outsider.

Develop strategies to deal with heckling before the event. My favorite strategy is to ask the meeting planners to be ready to help. But be very careful in the way you request their help. Always tell them a disruption is very unlikely to happen in *their* group. They don't want to think that you have a negative picture of them. Explain: "In the very *unlikely* event that someone might be a tiny bit—*silly*—at your banquet tonight, I need you to be prepared to help me. Just be ready to go to the heckler and say, 'You have a message' or 'You have a phone call.' Please *get hecklers out* of the room and deal with them kindly—but firmly—outside."

What to Do

It is much better to come up with a way to get the heckler out of your room than to use one-liners. As Joey Bishop said, "No matter how many witty lines you have for hecklers, they can always come back with just one more...'Oh yeah!'"

Do not use off-color, nightclub humor unless you're in a nightclub. Avoid lines like "Excuse me, I do my speech the way you obviously have sex...alone."

Although a gentle and clean joke or two in your pocket is a good idea, it's not your *best* strategy. Try walking over to the troublemaker. Put your hand on his or her shoulder, and keep right on going. If you make eye contact, just smile. Usually the heckler will pull out of his or her haze and realize something else is going on that's worth paying attention to.

Don't mistake a legitimate skeptic for a heckler. The way you handle yourself is more important than how you handle the heckler. Be fair, be firm, and end the heckling quickly. For example, "It's obvious you and I see things very differently. I can live with that! And I hope you can too!"
—CHRIS HEGARTY

I turn to the people with him and say, "Is he with you?" or "Did you all come on the same bus?" That will usually get the others with the heckler to quiet him down. If that does not work, I walk off the stage, walk up to him, and say, "That's a great line, incoherent, but a great line." Over the audience's laughter, I turn off the mic and say in his ear, "You must be quiet, you are disrupting the group." Then I smile at him and walk away. Ninety-nine percent of the time it works, and the audience thinks I have just been gracious.
—TOM OGDEN

Ask the heckler to identify himself and his company. They usually prefer to be anonymous.
—JUDI MOREO

Usually I let them rant until the crowd boos them down.
I always try to answer the heckler seriously—when I can.
—JACK ANDERSON

Realize they are part of your audience. Love them all. Dolly Parton said, "If you love the rainbow, you gotta be prepared to put up with the rain."
—DOTTIE WALTERS

Slightly drunk people all at one table misbehave by scowling at me, looking at their watches, waving napkins at me to stop, getting up and leaving, and so on. If they made more noise about it, the rest of the audience would see and possibly censure them, which would make it much easier for me. But if they sit toward the back of the room and I am the only one who can see them, I try desperately not to look at them, focusing instead on smiling people at other tables. This is one of the hardest things in the world to do, but I don't know an alternative. Because if you call attention to them in an effort to make them behave, you are always the one who ends up looking awkward, foolish, or prima donna-ish.
—HOPE MIHALAP

Often people will come up to you and say that they can't hear because a small group behind them is chatting and giggling while the presentation is going on.
I first ask the whole group—without picking on the noisemaking group—to please hold their comments down until the breaks. If that doesn't work, I

actually go to the noisy group while the others are busy and ask them to tone it down.

Sometimes just walking over and standing next to the noisemakers will make the entire group turn and look at them, and that forces them to be quiet.
                    —ROGER BURGRAFF

What to Say

I think the party you're looking for is down the hall.
                    —W MITCHELL

Steroids?
                    —TOM OGDEN

I do a single.
                    —ROGER BURGRAFF

A fellow in the front row says he'll trade seats with you.
                    —ROGER LANGLEY

I'd like to help you out. Just tell me which way you came in.
                    —LEONARD RYZMAN

Oh, good, another speaker. I was afraid that I was going to have to do this alone.
                    —RON DENTINGER

Dad (Mom), I told you to stay in the car!
                    —PHIL CASS

Remember the days when alcoholics wanted to stay anonymous?

Throw your keys to someone in the front row and say, "Start my car" (as if to make a fast getaway).

I can't believe that out of 2 million sperm cells you were the fastest swimmer.

When you use those microwave ovens, you're supposed to keep the door shut.
                    —TERRY BREWER

The worst thing about some men is that when they are not drunk, they're sober.
                    —WILLIAM BUTLER YEATS, IRISH POET, BORN **1865**
                    (From *Great Book of Funny Quotes*, by Eileen
                    Mason, Sterling Publishing, 1993)

You have the right to remain silent.
                    —JACK ANDERSON

This convention is operating like a well-oiled machine—and I can tell a lot of you are well-oiled.
—From *Speaker's Idea File*, May 1993

Remember, a closed mouth gathers no feet.

You know, drinking does relieve you of stress. Keep it up and it will also relieve you of your spouse, your house, and all your cars.

I suppose if the Good Lord didn't want us to drink he would have made it easier to swallow celery.
—Adapted from *Bigshots, Pipsqueaks and Windbags*, by Gene and Linda Perret, Prentice-Hall, 1993

Sir? Excuse me, I work alone!

Let's play a little game. Only the person with the microphone gets to speak.

Now, now, your part doesn't have any lines.
—UNKNOWN

Please, please. The group rules are that only one person at a time is permitted to make a fool of himself. Right now it's my turn.

Based on the evidence, I know you'll acquit yourself equally when your turn comes.

(Ask the heckler where he works.) Good, because tomorrow I'm going to go over there and bother you while you're working.
—DICK FLAVIN

Can you hear me? (After the heckler responds in the affirmative, I look at him disapprovingly and add) Because I can hear you too!

That's funny, I didn't know _____ (the local bar or pub) closed as early as this.
—IAN HAMILTON

What Not to Say

Excuse me! I do my speech the way you obviously have sex...alone!

I wish I had a lower IQ so I could appreciate that.

Sir, I'm getting paid to make a fool of myself. What's your excuse?

Why don't you stand up against the wall? That's plastered too!

Madam, I only have these fifteen minutes to earn my living. You have all night.

...People Make Sexual Innuendos to You During (or After) the Presentation

To Prevent It from Happening

Do you *want* to prevent it from happening? It depends on the image you're trying to portray. At least 75 percent of all nightclub humor is sexual. In a business setting, especially in today's environment of sexual harassment—alleged, actual, and the fears thereof—it's a good idea to practice safe speak. (OK, it was a cheap laugh, but the temptation was just too *alluring*.)

My mother, Dottie Walters, was a pioneer of women in sales and sales management. She wrote the first book ever by a woman for women in sales: *Never Underestimate the Selling Power of a Woman*. A woman competing in a sales environment had it even harder in my mother's day than she does now. Women like my mother took the sneers and the knocks until they proved to the world that woman could make it in a "man's world." Her advice to women who are met with sexual comments is just to be like Caesar's wife—above reproach. Hmm. Well, it works for her.

What to Do

During the Q&A, one of my speakers, a strikingly lovely woman, was suddenly asked, "So, how are ya in bed?!" I was sitting in the back of the room, about two seats away from the rather drunk man who had made the comment. This management group had paid our Speakers Bureau handsomely to bring the woman in, and I was truly tempted to dump my peaches flambé over his head! The speaker—luckily—handled the situation with more professionalism than that. The audience was mainly laughing. She just smiled, looked a trifle confused but totally professional and absolutely nonhostile, and asked the CEO who was seated on the dais next to her lectern, "What was that? I didn't catch that last question."

The CEO just gritted his teeth and looked down. She shrugged lightly, looked at the person next to the CEO, and tried again, "I didn't quite hear that last question." Well, there was no way this guy was going to enlighten her when the CEO wouldn't. He wisely mirrored the CEO's "eyes on the table, gritted teeth" look. She gave each of them a bemused look, shrugged, looked at someone else who had raised a hand earlier, and said, "You had a question?" And on they went.

I think you are safest just to laugh at sexual innuendo from the platform, if it's light and meant to be in fun. If it begins to get ugly, try some of the strategies mentioned earlier for handling "ill-mannered louts" who invade your presentation.

Many people seem to "get off" on the idea that they can make you lose your composure and distract you. They try to "come on" to you. I just give them a sarcastic grin, turn the other cheek, and keep going.
        —SHERRY KINISON, GOSPEL SINGER

I demurely smile and usually laugh, letting people know I know they must be kidding.
        —MARK SANBORN

Become deaf. Ignore them. Carry on.
        —DOTTIE WALTERS

What to Say

(In response to any comment that has "score" in it, like "Yo baby, wanna score.") Ah! A fellow music lover!

Long time at sea sailor?
        —LILLY WALTERS

Thank you darling! Means the operation was a success!

(In response to any "Show us your _____," direct your comment to a man close by on the platform, as if the heckler meant the other person all along.) Ah, come on, John! He wants to see your _____. Yours are cute, don't be bashful.
        —MICHELE BLOOD

Would you mind repeating that? (Often hecklers don't have the grit to say it again.)
        —BRAD PLUMB

My husband is not that open-minded.

(If comment is flattering.) Gee that's nice; I'll write that down in my journal. When I get angry at my husband, I can always pull it out to check and see what my options are.
        —DIANNA BOOHER

Now, now, don't you think that's a bit foul-mouthed for a fair-minded kinda guy like you?
        —ROGER LANGLEY

...The Heckler Is a 2-Year-Old

To Prevent It from Happening

If you notice that someone is going to bring a small child into your audience, go up and speak with the adult before the presentation. Avoid any tone of condescension or sarcasm. Simply discuss strategies if the child get bored and restless. This lets the caretaker know that he or she will be expected to deal with the situation.

What to Do

One pastor I know just stops talking until the child stops. The parent is humiliated and embarrassed and takes the child out of the room. (I think this is a great way to ensure that your audience dislike you, but it does cure the problem of a disruptive child.)

Break the group into pairs to discuss some aspect of your talk. Go up to the caretaker of the child and ask for assistance with something—something that will take you out of earshot of the others. Then ask the person to take the child out. But express your deep concern that the caretaker will miss the talk. Offer to call personally to discuss the issues. Or offer a gift of a tape of the talk, a copy of your notes from the day—whatever you might have—to help the caretaker gain some of the information you wanted to convey in your presentation.

If there is a soundproof "tech booth," ask the caretaker and the child to go there to watch and listen.

> *It is very touchy dealing with babies. You can come across as cold and uncaring. If it becomes annoying, ask a committee or staff person to offer assistance to the lady by taking the baby out of the room. The mother wants to listen to your presentation also.*
> —FLORENCE LITTAUER

WORKING WITH YOUNG, DISRUPTIVE CHILDREN IN YOUR AUDIENCE
by Ralph Archbold

The situation with a youngster disrupting your program is one of the most difficult to handle. The best way is not to let it happen in the first place. If you arrive for your meeting and there is an adult with a child there, you might want to talk to the child and find out the child's name.

(Continued)

You could then suggest to the parent that the child might be bored and would be happier in another location. Sometimes this might even work.

If the child ends up attending your presentation and interrupting it, you must be very careful. *The audience's sympathy can easily* lie with the "cute" child. I have found a couple of things that work sometimes. Since I have found the child's name out before the meeting, I can either call for a short stretch break or get the audience started in an exercise of some sort, and while they are busy I can walk over to the child.

The next step depends upon the age of the child. If it is a crying baby, going to the mother and suggesting that the child might be more comfortable in another location may be an option. If the child is a toddler and you have anticipated this possibility, you can reach into your bag of tricks and offer the child something to occupy the time. Always use the child's name and sympathize with the difficulty of having to be there. (Remember the child would much rather be outside playing.) You can carry a few small toys with you. (Not too small. A choking child might be a pleasant thought during the interruption but will definitely not be a crowd pleaser.) A little box of Legos purchased in Kmart is great.

If the child is older and you can go over very close to the child, it will often work to have a little talk with him or her. Be sure you do it while the audience is distracted with some sort of an activity and then have a frank talk with the child. Explain that you expect him or her to help you with good behavior during the program. Also explain the options of finding a nearby place or back of the room to play or read quietly or risk having you stop the program in the middle and embarrassing the child in front of *all these people.* If the child says he doesn't have anything to read, pull out some carefully selected reading material geared to a youth. Since the offending youth is more likely to be a boy, a sports-oriented book or even comic book may work.

If this situation happens to you when you are before a large audience, you are probably better off ignoring the disturbance and hoping the responsible adult is adult enough to take care of the situation.

To sum up, it always is better to have a plan prepared and the tools to put it into action. If nothing works, it is also important to realize that the sympathies of the audience are with you as soon as the cuteness of the child wears off. It also helps to be glad you don't have that child in your family and then make sure that you don't let any of yours become "that child" in another situation.

Remember that by confronting the child in front of a listening audience, you risk making yourself the villain. Also remember that a child listens and is more likely to respond favorably if you know his or her name. Loss of anonymity will make the *child* less daring and possibly less defiant.

You also can tell an anecdote, the moral of which might inspire a responsible adult to take control:

"I recently saw a cartoon which I found very amusing. It was from the comic strip which is one of my favorites, Calvin and Hobbes. Calvin is a typical adventurous boy and Hobbes is the stuffed tiger who, to Calvin, is not only his favorite friend but comes to life and interacts with him.

"In this particular strip Calvin is at school (without Hobbes) and closes up his book saying, 'That's it! I'm through learning today.' As he starts to leave the classroom he meets the unmovable object…his teacher. The next scene shows him back at his desk with a disgusted look on his face as he says: 'I think I'm a better judge of when I'm through.' I think it is obvious to many of you that our young friend has decided he has learned enough today. Since I know *you* don't want to miss what is coming next, perhaps someone can find some better location for this future tycoon of industry."

Make sure to say this sort of thing with *lots* of laughter and caring in your voice so you don't humiliate the parents. Then you can either call for a short stretch break or continue on with the program. In any event, good luck and may it never happen to you as it did to me.

When my son was about 4 years old, I took him to one of my speeches and he sat right in the middle of the front row (where I could get to him if there was a problem). Just as I was coming to a great inspirational close to a 45-minute speech, my darling son stood up on his chair and, stretching out his arms, entertained the audience with a huge audible yawn, totally destroying the dramatic conclusion of my previous 44 minutes. The only thing I could do was to introduce him to the audience and admit he was mine. They thought it was great. And to tell the truth, when he turned to the audience and bowed to them I thought it was too.

P.S. I didn't take him along again. It wasn't that cute!

Copyright 1993 by Ralph Archbold.

What to Say

Serious

It's OK. I'm glad both of you are here. It is better to build a child than to repair an adult.
—LILLY WALTERS

I am a parent of a 3-year-old myself. I appreciate your commitment to wanting to be here to learn and grow. However, it seems like your child's _____ (shouting, crying, fighting) is beginning to be a distraction for the rest of us. What do you think we should do?
—JACK CANFIELD

Humorous

I love kids. I could even eat a whole one right now.
—PHIL CASS

I don't mind if you interject, as long as Dad (Mom) isn't a ventriloquist.
—LEONARD RYZMAN

Oh, great. I'm being heckled by a 2-year-old! (Sigh.)
—GENE MITCHENER, THE WHEELCHAIR COMIC

My sentiments exactly.
—ALAN PEASE

I've often said the same thing myself!
—STEVE GOTTLIEB

How come that kid is so smart?
—TONY KING

Where are you W.C. Fields when I need you?
—LORIN PAULSEN

(If baby is crying) I see he heartily disagrees.
—DIANNA BOOHER

What *Not* to Say

Can I hold the little horror?
I know baby talk. He says he wants to go outside.
Ah, what a cute kid...must be Don Rickles' kid.

...You Don't Want to Answer the Question

To Prevent It from Happening

If there are questions about your topic that you do not want to answer—and you know what they are—plan your strategy. There are several clever ways to get around answering something.

What to Do

■ Make a joke, and go right on to the right questions. Sometimes the humor distracts people from the question.

> *During the presidential debates between Reagan and Mondale, Reagan came up with a classic line. One of his speech coaches, Roger Ailes,* knew the other side was bound to bring up the age issue. He helped Reagan with a terrific comeback.*
>
> *Sure enough, the inevitable question came up. Did he feel "the age issue was going to be a problem"?*
>
> *He confidently replied, "I want you to know that I will not make age an issue of this campaign. I am not going to exploit—for political purposes— my opponent's youth and inexperience."*
>
> *Many agree the campaign was won from that comment on.*
> —LILLY WALTERS
> (From *Secrets of Successful Speakers,*
> McGraw-Hill, 1993)

■ About halfway through your program, give people a few minutes to reflect. In groups of two to six, have them come up with questions that they would like you to answer. This approach actually ensures that you will get a much higher grade of question, since people answer many of the questions among themselves during their discussion. Ask them to write each question on a separate sheet of paper. Then have all the papers collected. During the break, go over the questions and pick out the ones you *want* to answer. You can even put in questions which they didn't think to ask but which show you off nicely. You then conveniently run out of time before you get to the questions you do not want to answer.

Is this ethical?

I never said this was going to be a book on ethics. It's more of a survival manual.

■ Instead of giving a direct answer, reply by describing a process. For example, I was once asked, "Miss Walters, I heard it said that you are cold-hearted when speakers call you to get advice on how they can obtain bookings from your Speakers Bureau. Is this true?"

I replied with, "Well, I hope not. I always tell every speaker who asks me that my Bureau currently tracks over 20,000 speakers. It is impossible for one agent to obtain bookings for that many speakers. I also say that I would be glad to give them 5 minutes of advice, but

*Author of *You Are the Message—Secrets of the Master Communicator,* Dow Jones-Irwin, 1988.

if they really want to know how to stand out in the crowd I suggest they read the book Dottie and I wrote, *Speak and Grow Rich*—it took us 3 years to come up with the answers. Before most speakers can expect to get paid to speak, they need to plan on giving at least 100 speeches free."

I have not really answered the question: Am I being "cold-hearted"? It is an unanswerable question. To some, I must seem that way; to me, I'm just trying to be truthful. So, instead of trying to confront the "cold-hearted" part of the question, I answer it with the process of what I do when a new speaker calls me.

Answer with a process.

For example, as a lawyer, I have often been asked, "Mr. Walters, are we going to win or lose this case?" I reply: "Well, first, we are going to file the case. I will argue with _____. The other side might say _____. Our strengths are _____."

I never really answer the question, because there isn't a true answer to give—other than "I don't know," which would just make the questioner upset.
                                                            —R. MICHAEL WALTERS

Be sure to thank the questioner —people ask questions mainly so they get noticed, so notice them by thanking them for the question. Then invite responses from the audience.
                                                            —TONY KING

What to Say

Serious

The answer is rather long and complicated. Please see me after the presentation. (People almost never come up and ask again.)

(If you really don't want to answer the question, reply very seriously and with no condescension in your voice.) I see, what you really mean is _____ (rephrase the question to be one you want to answer).
                                                            —R. MICHAEL WALTERS

You know people ask me that a lot and there's no easy answer. But if your question is...da, de da, de da... (go on and ask yourself a question that you are comfortable answering.)

I'm interested in knowing why you ask it.
                                                            —GERALD C. MEYERS

I think the reason you are asking that is much more important than any answer I could give. Would you share your reasons for asking that question with us?

(Nodding sagely) Often the question is more important than the answer. (Let them think about that in utter silence—pause—and move on to the next question.)

—Lilly Walters

A question like that deserves a more comprehensive answer than I'm prepared to give at this time.

—Roger Langley

Well, how would you answer that? (Usually they just want the opportunity to talk.)

Why is that important to you? (This gives you an idea of what they really want to know.)

I want to make sure I understand that question. Let's get together and clarify it at the break, then we'll cover it after with the whole group.

I don't want to give you a simple answer to what is obviously an important question to you. Let's you and I talk about that at the break (or after the program).

That's a question I cover in my other programs. We just don't have time to cover it today.

Hold on to that; we'll get back to it later. (Then at the very end of the day.) We didn't have time to cover that. Why don't you stay and we'll talk about it?

(They usually won't stay.)

—John Patrick Dolan

Please see me after the program on that one!

Make a note of that question and if it isn't answered by the end of the program, please ask it again!

I don't know the answer. Is there anyone in the audience who does?

—Chris Hegarty

Humorous

Better to remain silent and be thought a fool than to speak out and remove all doubt.

—Abraham Lincoln

I'm glad this question came up, in a way, because there are so many different ways to answer it that one of them is bound to be right.

—Robert Benchley, American actor and
humorist, born **1889**
(From *Great Book of Funny Quotes*, by Eileen
Mason, Sterling Publishing, 1993)

Thank you very much. (And go right on.)

—Bob Burg

Well, we've just run out of time!
(Smile and make a motion as if to leave the podium. After the laugh, mock a brow mop, then)
    My wife told me not to come tonight.
    (Move on to the next question.)
                        —GERALD C. MEYERS

(I repeat the question they have asked, smile, and throw it back. For example, if they said, "How are you in bed?")
    How are you in bed? Hum? (With a smile) Next question, please.
    (Things are very funny when repeated verbatim.)
                  —GENE MITCHENER, THE WHEELCHAIR COMIC

Someone in the audience asked me that same question just last week. And I'm going to dodge it the same way I did them.
                  —From *Speaker's Idea File,* Original
                    Humor section by Gary Apple,
                    September 1993

I'll have to take that up with my therapist.

That is far too profound a question for a speaker to answer.
                  —HOWARD K. SMITH
                  (Submitted by Terry Paulson)

Everything I say is right—much of it is factual—none of it is politically correct.
                —R. MICHAEL WALTERS

Please save your questions until I'm finished and well on my way home.
                —From *Current Comedy Newsletter,*
                  June 24, 1991

You know, my grandmother always used to say, "It's always darkest right after they turn off the lights." (Move on quickly before they realize you didn't say a thing!)
                —LILLY WALTERS

...You Don't Know the Answers to Their Questions

To Prevent It from Happening

Prepare twice the material you will need to present that day. Be an expert!

What to Do

This is really not so much to worry over. No one has all the answers. Besides, as a whole, human beings really don't like people who seem to "have all the answers."

■ When I don't know an answer, I do a great deal with silly facial expressions and body language. Sometimes I stare at the person asking, let my mouth hang open slightly, and make a panicked face that says "I have no clue to the answer." Sometimes I start toward the person who asked in an I'm-going-to-strangle-you manner, then as if I just got a sudden inspiration, I say sweetly, "Thank you for sharing.... Next question?" and pretend that I'm moving on. As the audience laughs, I go back and joke with the person who asked: "Where did you think of that? I'm supposed to be the expert here, and I have no clue to that one! Anybody else know?" If anyone does know the answer, I'll say, "Gee, good thing they paid me before they knew how much smarter you guys are than I am." If no one knows, "Well, at least we can all feel undereducated together."

■ If it is a question you really should know the answer to, ask the questioner—while the whole audience is listening—to write it on the back of a business card. Announce: "I will call you within 2 weeks with the answer." Then do it. If you're the expert, you should have those answers. This approach also lets your listeners know that you care about their learning and receiving all the information they wanted from you.

■ If you are one of the high-tech types doing longer sessions, you might consider plugging your laptop computer into the phone in the meeting room to access your "information service." (There are many around now, such as Prodigy, CompuServe, and America OnLine.) You might be able to do a fast search during a break.

■ If it is a question you really should not be expected to ever know the answer to, just tell the audience "I don't know" with a smile and a shrug, and move on.

> *I'll usually confess when I know little or nothing about a topic. The audience can usually see through you anyway, so you come off as being more honest and up front about it.*
> —GENE PERRET

What to Say

Serious

> *Great question! This time I want to hear the ideas some of you have on the subject. Who would like to contribute an idea?*

(By the time two or three suggestions are given, and you comment on them, you will come up with a closing comment of your own.)
                                                     —DOTTIE WALTERS

First I'd like to hear your answer.
                                                     —ROGER LANGLEY

I don't know, but _____ is where I suggest you look for the answer.
                                                     —ROGER BURGRAFF

Humorous

I take note of the fact that the heart of the issue, in the final analysis... escapes me!
                                                     —LORIN PAULSEN

That will teach me.
                                                     —DOUG MALOUF

You can't scare me...I have children!
                                                     —UNKNOWN

An interesting question. Does anyone have an interesting answer?
                                                     —GEORGE GOLDTRAP

I used to have all the answers; now I don't even know the questions.
                                                     —EILEEN MASON

Can you rephrase that question? Rephrase it into something I can answer.
                                                     —From *Current Comedy Newsletter,*
                                                        September 23, 1991

I'm going to give you a straight answer. Straight from my notes over here.
                                                     —From *Current Comedy Newsletter,*
                                                        October 21, 1991

Now for my humility act.
                                                     —DEANNA JEAN BROWN

That's an excellent question. I wish I had an excellent answer.
                                                     —ROGER LANGLEY

Eighty percent of what I have say on this topic is incisive, innovative, and intelligent. And 20 percent of it is pure baloney. The only problem is I can never tell which is which.

You can ask me anything at all about this. If I know the answer, I'll glad-

ly give it to you. If I don't know the answer, I'll generally give you one anyway.

—GENE PERRET

They say you get smarter when you realize how much you don't know. I think I'm turning into a genius fast.

_____ planted you here, didn't he (she)?

Interesting point of view. Hum. Now let's take that core concept and grow with it.

—LILLY WALTERS

You know, I'm an expert in this field and I have an answer to every question. One of those answers is...I don't know.

—R. MICHAEL WALTERS

There has been an alarming increase in the number of things I know nothing about.

—ASHLEIGH BRILLIANT
(Submitted by Terry Paulson)

I'm the world's authority on absolutely everything—except that.

—PATRICIA FRIPP

Between my Dad and me, we knew everything. Unfortunately, that's one of the things he knew.

—BOB WALTERS

Please ask me that question at the break—and I'll avoid answering it then too!

That question leaves me dangling 'twixt heaven and earth in an ecstasy of esoteric sublimity!

—STEVE GOTTLIEB

Oh, sure, show the rest of us up. I'll bet you're the type that actually tries to solve problems instead of just complaining about them!

—Adapted from *Bigshots, Pipsqueaks, and Windbags*, by Gene and Linda Perret, Prentice-Hall, 1993

Are you a plant? (Not like flora, but like have you been planted?)

That's my sixth-grade teacher. She's (he's) been following me around for years asking me these kinds of questions.

—W MITCHELL

That's a good question. (Pause.) Are there any other questions?

—RON DENTINGER

That actually is a two-part question. Unfortunately, I can't answer either part.

—From *Speaker's Idea File*, Original Humor
section by Gary Apple, September 1993

...They Won't Ask Any Questions

If you have a great ending, they are just too emotionally moved to think about asking you questions....
  'Course, if you bomb the same thing happens.
—Jim McJunkin

To Prevent It from Happening

Plant questions. Once you get the ball rolling, the others will follow.

What to Do

Rather than say, "Are there any questions?" I always break the audience into small subgroups and ask them to come up with questions. After they talk among themselves, I ask them to share a few of these questions with the entire audience. Under this method, people often answer each other's questions. So the questions that finally get to you are usually quite insightful—maybe even too hard for you to answer (see "...You Don't Know the Answer to Their Questions").

It happens often (I hope because they are spellbound).
  I usually make a few jokes until the first ones ask a question, then the dam opens and they all start asking questions.
  I usually have at least a full hour of questions from my audiences.
—Jack Anderson
(From *Secrets of Successful Speakers*, by Lilly
Walters, McGraw-Hill, 1993)

"Right up front...I often will state a thought and leave it incomplete, and indicate with my hands I want them to finish it by filling in the word. They do so immediately. That sets the tone for a give-and-take that is automatic—and exhilarating!
—Rosita Perez
(From *Secrets of Successful Speakers*, by Lilly
Walters, McGraw-Hill, 1993)

If the audience has no questions, ask people to write down three questions first and then discuss their questions with a partner. Then have them ask their rehearsed questions of you.

The worst thing to do is to ask, "Do you have any questions?" The answer is usually silence. Instead, ask them what three things bother them the most about X, what three frustrations they've had with Y, what three things make for good Z, and so on. If they still don't respond, go back and ask them to write their three thoughts down. Then ask them to share what they've written. If they still are not sharing, then give them the opportunity to share by going around the room in sequence and asking people to share one of their thoughts or ideas, or questions they've written down.

—MICHAEL PODOLINSKY

As you begin the question section, step forward to the front of the stage, raise your arm, smile, and say, "Ready for your great questions!" Then up jumps your helper, and you are off and running.

Another approach is to use some humor. You might say, "That reminds me of a lady who asked me a question about love. I told her, 'If love is the answer, would you redefine the question?'"

—DOTTIE WALTERS

I was presenting on the topic of "Employee Involvement Teams" to a group of supervisors, managers, staff people, and others. The very top guy of this electronics company was dead set against the company bringing in any kind of employee involvement teams. I knew from having talked to the human resources people that this guy was going to be their major roadblock. All the way through my 4-hour presentation he kept making it very clear where he stood. I normally reserve the last hour for getting people to ask questions. At my call for questions, there was dead silence—everyone was intimidated by this manager. I'd never had that happen before.

I said, "Well, I know that you have questions. What I want you to do is tear off a blank paper from the pad in front of you. Write a minimum of one question—you can write more, but I want at least one." Please do not sign your name to them. This gave people a way to express themselves, while not setting themselves up as a target for their manager's wrath when he got them out of this meeting. People began writing furiously. I collected all the questions and answered every one.

I thought it was a lost cause. But 3 days later that same manager decided to initiate the program. From the questions that his people had asked, he saw the enthusiasm and the value of this type of program.

—DON DEWAR

What to Say

Serious

(Ask the group to come up with questions.) What questions came to mind while I was talking? Please come up with three or four questions that you wish I would have covered more clearly.

(With a lightly humorous attitude.) Let's talk about what you would like to talk about. I will stand here and stare at you while you bring it up.
—PHILIP CROSBY

A question I'm often asked is...

(Make sure to ask yourself a question you can answer well.)
—ROGER BURGRAFF

Humorous

Is there anyone in the room who would like to ask the first question? (Silence) OK. Is there anyone in the room who would like to ask the second question?
—ALLEN KLEIN

Looks like the question-and-answer session is going to be brief today.

After living with a 2-year-old, you don't know how wonderful it is not to hear someone ask, "Why?"
—ROGER LANGLEY

If I don't get any questions now, I have to start over from the beginning.
—LORIN PAULSEN

Are there any answers out there?
—TERRY PAULSON

Glad to see you aren't a group that rushes into things.

Great to see a discerning audience that doesn't speak without careful thought.
—LEONARD RYZMAN

Don't be embarrassed to ask the simplest, most basic questions—those are the ones I'll be able to answer.
—From *Speaker's Idea File,* Original Humor
section by Gary Apple, September 1993

If I can throw any obscurity on the subject, let me know.
—JAMES JOYCE, IRISH NOVELIST AND POET, BORN **1882**
(From *Great Book of Funny Quotes,* by Eileen
Mason, Sterling Publishing, 1993)

Dare to be naive.
—R. BUCKMINSTER FULLER, AMERICAN ENGINEER
AND PHILOSOPHER, BORN **1895**
(From *Great Book of Funny Quotes,* by Eileen
Mason, Sterling Publishing, 1993)

(Look worried.) Now this was the audience participation portion of the program. They paid me extra for this and I already used the money to buy _____ (whatever is being sold at their meeting or through their group).

(Try for a Rod Serling demeanor and stroll calmly toward a light switch.) Come with me on a journey beyond sight and sound. A speaker asks a question—or has she? Perhaps she has entered...the Twilight Zone. (By now you are at the light switch. Flip it on and off a few times, humming the Twilight Zone theme.)

(Look scared.) This is very scary. An entire audience that knows the topic better than I do.

—Lilly Walters

Does anybody have a question? (Then, raising your own hand) I do! (Ask yourself the first question, which of course you then answer.)
—Barry Eigen

(Pick one person in the audience. Have him repeat after you the question that you want asked, and then say) Thank you, sir. I was hoping someone would ask that!
—Mikki Williams

I came with all the answers.

—W Mitchell

You might as well ask me for my opinion. I'm going to give it you anyway!

I know what I'm talking about. But if I don't, that won't stop me!

I actually have a photographic mind...underdeveloped, but photographic.

I can explain little-known facts to you in such a way that you will immediately understand why they were little-known in the first place.

Really, I'm versatile. I can make an ass of myself on any subject.
—Adapted from *Bigshots, Pipsqueaks and Windbags*, by Gene and Linda Perret, Prentice-Hall, 1993

If you promise to remain this quiet, you all can come up to my room for a drink later.
—Ron Dentinger

What *Not* to Say

Looks like everybody knows everything.

Oh, come on! What are you guys, an audience or an oil painting?

I've given presentations in morgues where they asked more questions than you guys!

...You Can't Hear the Question

To Prevent It from Happening

Check out your room well before the event starts. Have an assistant stand in several spots in the room and talk to you to test the sound levels. Sometimes, because of the way a room is constructed, a person who is closer is actually harder to hear than someone farther away. Rearrange the room so you have an optimum balance between you hearing them and them hearing you.

If you are presenting to a large audience—600 and over—it won't matter how you set up the room. You will barely be able to hear people even if they scream, which is awkward for everyone and impossible for some. In this case, you will need microphones set up in the house. Have someone travel through the audience with a wireless mic and approach each person with a raised hand. Or have mics set up on stands at strategic locations around the room and encourage attendees who wish to ask questions to form lines behind the mics.

What to Do

Stop the program and ask people to submit their questions in writing. Give them a few minutes. Then you and/or your assistants can gather the questions. Or have assistants go out into the audience, write down the questions, and bring them to you. As you answer one question, the assistants quietly gather more.

If you don't have assistants—or if you prefer—go out into the audience yourself. Walk right up to the person so you can hear the question. If you can't hear a question, then neither can some people in your audience. Make sure you repeat the question into the microphone once you figure it out.

What to Say

Serious

I'm sorry, I can't hear your questions, and I very much want to! Please, take 2 minutes and write your question on a blank piece of paper. I will send someone around to collect them. Then I can answer them all from up here into the mic so you can all hear.
                                                                    —LILLY WALTERS

Humorous

I'm sorry—my hearing is not what it used to be. I had three sons going through puberty at the same time.
                                                                    —JIM MCJUNKIN

...Someone Asks a Question That You Already Answered

To Prevent It from Happening

Unless you don't allow questions, it will happen to you.

What to Do

- Do not comment on the fact that you already answered the question. Don't embarrass the person asking.
- Simply rephrase the answer you already gave.
- Open the question up to the audience, and let people comment.

What to Say

Serious

Ah, obviously a question that is on everyone's mind tonight. Let's get some feedback from the rest of you. What do you think about _____?

Well, what I mentioned before about _____ also applies here. (Restate your response even though it is exactly the same thing.)
—LILLY WALTERS

Humorous

Déjà vu! (The rest of the audience who realizes will giggle, but you go right on to answer the question seriously.)
—LILLY WALTERS

...You Don't Understand the Question

To Prevent It from Happening

When I speak in other countries—heck, in states other than my home state of California—I have on several occasions found myself staring at someone and thinking, *I know that was English. I wonder what he said?* The dialects and colloquialisms within a single country can addle the brain. African audiences typically speak several languages, with English as possibly their third or fourth. So the way they phrase ideas in English often sounds odd to my ear.

If you are worried that misunderstanding might be a problem, hire an assistant who is versatile in your language (and dialect) and that of your audience. Also, doing a little research about the audience's perceptions of your culture can help you develop some "savers" unique to your situation. (See also the sections below on presenting to people for whom English is a second or third language and presenting to a culture or country other than your own.)

Of course, the misunderstanding might not be a dialect issue. A member of your audience may have a speaking disability.

What to Do

Be careful not to embarrass people! Take the burden of misunderstanding upon yourself. I always get a good laugh by saying, "I need an interpreter. Does anyone here speak _____? I then use a less-than-flattering word that their culture uses to describe my culture. For example, if I was presenting in Mexico, as a white Anglo I might say, "Does anyone here speak *Gringo?*" If you are not from the south of the USA, but you are presenting there, you might try, "Does anyone here speak *Yankee?*" (assuming you are a Yank, of course!)

Never say, "I can't *understand* you." Instead say, "I'm sorry, *I can't hear* you," even if you can hear. This puts the burden of the misunderstanding at your doorstep and helps the questioner save face. Ask someone else in the audience to repeat the question for you. The second person may be someone you are able to understand.

Sometimes people ask questions in jargon exclusive to their industry—or noninclusive of your education. This always makes me feel awkward, since I hate to admit I don't know what the heck someone is talking about! But often there is no choice. Just put on a big smile and ask the questioner to bring it down a level or two. If you don't understand the question, chances are a good part of the audience won't either. All of them will appreciate your having the question repeated in simpler language.

What to Say

Serious

> *I'm sorry, I can't hear you. Can one of you sitting closer by repeat that question for me?*
> —LILLY WALTERS

Humorous

> *(Use your best robotic accent with lots of sign language.) Big words, small brain. Repeat please. Use small words for small brain.*
>
> *Would one of you translate that into Californian, please? (Substitute the area, company, or career you are from and so on.)*

(Use the following only if people are throwing out jargon or big words. Do not use it if someone has a foreign accent or speech disorder.) Have you traveled far to visit our planet? Is your ship in orbit? Take me to your leader!
—Lilly Walters

Sorry? (Wait for them to repeat.) I heard you, I was just sorry.
—Phil Cass

Socrates said we should question everything, so I'm going to question your question. What did you say?

Whaaaat?

I know there's a question in there someplace, but I'll be darned if I can find it.

Could you give us the Reader's Digest version please?

That's more question than I've got answers for.
—Roger Langley

What *Not* to Say

Look, no one here understands that. Quit showing off.

...You Lose the Meaning When Working Through a Translator

Judi Moreo was presenting in Japan with a translator. She told a humorous 1-minute story that made the point of her talk splendidly. Then she waited for the translator. The translator retold the story in about nine words, and the audience laughed hysterically. After the talk, hoping to edit her story to have the same great impact each time, she asked the translator how he created such a stirring effect in so few words! He said, "Well, I didn't think they would understand the joke, so I just said, 'She is trying to be humorous. Americans do this when they speak—laugh.'"

I hit the translation wall as I prepared to give my seminar "Secrets of Successful Speakers and Trainers" in Rio. I do several "games" and fun experiential exercises and use odd props, such as potatoes, string, beach balls, ropes, and washers.

Teresa, the assistant assigned to "make sure everything is just perfect for Lilly," called me. English is her third language, and it's my first—and sadly, my only—so we had a few linguistic challenges.

"Lilly, we do not have 'washer' for each person. We do not understand."

"Ah, just ask the person who repairs your office; he will know what a washer is."

"Then we will not need. We are having meeting in hotel; if anything breaks, hotel will fix."

Now I'm stuck. "Never mind. I'll bring the washers."

"Lilly, this list says 'string.' String is the same as rope?"

"Well, rope is thicker. String is skinny. You know, like you use to fly a kite."

"Pardon? What is 'kite'?"

"Wait, I have my *Português Dicionârio*...kite. Then I said very proudly and loudly, "*Paragaio!* We need the kind of rope you use for a *paragaio*."

"*Paragaio!*" She sounded dumbfounded. I was rather proud, thinking she must be awed at my remarkable use of her language.

I listened to a rapid conversation among the entire staff in the background. Finally Teresa came back on the line, very confused. "Lilly, you want to have animals in your class?"

"Uh, never mind. I'll bring the string." It turns out *paragaio* is also the name for a parrot.

To Prevent It from Happening

Always assume that people will understand only about 40 percent of what you are telling them. Cut your material in half. Tell them everything twice, using two separate ways to deliver the information.

Go over your jokes ahead of time with the translator. He or she will let you know what works, or how to rephrase it so it works.

Speak very slowly. English uses fewer words to convey concepts than do other languages. So it is hard for a translator to keep up. A simultaneous translator is about 10 words behind a speaker.

My first experience with simultaneous translation was, again, in Rio de Janeiro. Two people repeated my words in Portuguese just after I said them. We all had hearing devices on, so as I was talking, I was also listening to the Portuguese translation in my ear. Most Americans speak fairly fast—I speak especially fast. This means translators just can't get all the words in and must paraphrase things. I had to go very slowly—for me, with lots of dramatic pauses. Day One of my seminar is about 50 percent lecture, 50 percent audience exercises. Although it was successful, by comparison, Day Two—which is 90 percent audience exercises—was a raging triumph. The experience brought home to me the limitations of one-way communication, especially in a multicultural environment, and just how important audience exercises are.

Avoid reading materials out loud in English while audiences read along in their language. Instead, ask a volunteer to read, in the audience's language, from the handouts and workbook you have sent ahead to be translated.

Translators will often request a written transcript of your presentation ahead of the event. I think it's more effective to sit down with them once you get there and explain the conceptual meaning of what you are trying to say, rather than the literal meaning, which often does not translate well—especially in the case of humorous remarks.
—MIKKI WILLIAMS

With simultaneous translators rehearse all your jokes and punch-line stories ahead of time. Don't be surprised, though, if people laugh when they shouldn't and don't laugh when they should. Stay loose and move ahead with a smile.
—PAUL DINSMORE

(Always be careful of idioms.) My worst slip was to say that a person's elevator did not go all the way to the top. They had no idea what I meant.

Several times during the presentation I ask them to tell me what we have agreed on.
—PHILIP CROSBY

...English Is Their Second or Third Language
To Prevent It from Happening

---

10 TIPS FOR PRESENTING TO CROSS-CULTURAL AUDIENCES
by Marcy Huber, President of The Center of Language Training

1. *Speak slowly, simplify your language, and enunciate well, but never, never talk down to them.*

2. *Pause while speaking.* Don't be afraid of silence; Americans think they have to talk all the time, but people from other cultures are used to silence. Japanese businessmen can't understand how Americans can talk and think at the same time! (Guess what? They can't!)

3. *Idioms can be confusing.* We use so many idioms, and people whose first language is not English tend to take them literally. A woman in a seminar came up to me and said her boss asked her to "touch base" at 11:30. It was then 11:20, and she asked me if I knew where the base was. Was it inside or outside?

(Continued)

The American idiom for doing something exactly right is "He hit the nail on the head!" The Japanese idiom is, "The nail that sticks out gets hit." (The group is more important than the individual.) We have totally opposite approaches to the same nail!

4. *Avoid idiomatic verbs.* Are you aware of how many idiomatic verbs we use in everyday communication? One workshop participant flipped open his notebook and said his boss asked him, "Will you go ahead with this project if I go over once more how to go about it?" He gave me a blank look and said, "Please translate. I know what 'go' means, but this doesn't make sense."

5. *Be aware of humor.* Humor doesn't translate well. Check with the meeting planner to find out who will be in your audience, and then try out your humor with some people from that culture first. Plays-on-words are not understood, because they are usually taken literally.

6. *Sarcasm is rarely understood.* One computer programmer told me he would *never* understand Americans. His computer had gone down the day before, and he lost half of the program he was writing. When he told his boss, she said, "Wonderful! You just made my day."

7. *Many Asian cultures are very uncomfortable with direct eye contact.* Try to pick out the Americans in the audience and look at them, or look at the walls, or hold your handouts and stare at them.

8. *Often people from other cultures will show little reaction as we speak.* We feel as if we are talking to a stone wall. We have no way of knowing if we are "getting through," and may never know! Whatever happens, never, never get angry or talk down to the audience. Statements such as "Yoohoo, is anyone out there?" are totally inappropriate, and you can be sure the audience will now "tune you out" if they were listening before.

9. *Questioning the presenter is almost impossible for people from some cultures.* They have been taught to respect authority, and you are the authority. They won't ask questions for two reasons. One, they don't want to look stupid in front of their colleagues, and two, it is conceivable that you might not know the answer, and then *you* would "lose face" or be embarrassed in front of the audience.

> If you are unsure if your message is being understood, ask people to form small groups and discuss specific points or write the information you have just presented in order of importance for them. Then, as you circulate among the groups, you will invariably find they do have questions and you can answer them in a "safe" way. Another possibility is to have cards available so they can write their questions.
>
> 10. *Be yourself. Be natural and sincere.* Your sincerity will be very evident to the audience, and will persuade them to your point of view even though they may *understand* every word you said.
>
> From *Secrets of Successful Speakers* by Lilly Walters, McGraw-Hill, 1993.

Speak to the heart—the universal language. Go slower. Speak clearly. Smile.
—DOTTIE WALTERS

Music is the universal language of mankind.
—HENRY WADSWORTH LONGFELLOW

When speaking to people who speak English as a second language, it's always helpful to have a few one-liners in their language ready so that, when needed, they can roll "trippingly" off the tongue.

In Taiwan, before an audience of thousands, I once had a great use for a line borrowed from comedian Don Rickles which I had thought to prelearn in Chinese. When a 7-foot-plus giant, a Chinese soldier, approached the stage with a camera, leaned in, and proceeded to just stand there and click away, I put my nose to his camera and delightfully surprised the audience by whispering loudly in Chinese, "Will you please get your foot off my stage." Thousands cheered and my translated one-liner earned me very positive front-page coverage in the next day's news.
—HERMINE HILTON

Use stacks and stacks of pictures.
—DOUG MALOUF

Use graphics.
—TONY KING

I find I do more body language and facial expressions. Crossing my eyes, silly faces with odd lifted eyebrows; I wring my coat in a huge overdramatic comedic gesture in the front as if in fear. Smiling and laughter translate perfectly.
—JIM MCJUNKIN

What to Say

Serious

Your _____ *(whatever your language is) is so much better than my*
_____ *(their language), please help me when I come to a word that*
we don't know.
> —W MITCHELL

Humorous

I really admire those who speak two languages. I'm still having difficulty
with one—my own.
> —DIANNA BOOHER

I can identify with your problems with the English language. After all,
I'm from Boston.
> —DICK FLAVIN

English is like such a bother. Why, in California we haven't spoken it in
years.

Before joining you here today, I studied elementary _____ (their lan-
guage) diligently. It didn't occur to me that none of you would speak ele-
mentary _____ .
> —LILLY WALTERS

...Presenting to a Culture
(or Country) Other Than
Your Own

When asked what he thought of Western civilization, Indian leader
Mahatma Gandhi replied, "I think it would be a good idea."

On my first speaking tour of the United States, I found out, the hard way,
that American humor is not like Australian and English humor, which is
largely based on irreverence. I was addressing a group, and one partici-
pant mentioned the name of a town, and everyone laughed heartily. I said,
"I'm the new boy. What's so funny about that town?"
"It's a boring place."
I came back with, "Oh, yes, that's right. I stayed in a hotel there once
and it was boring. In fact, I sent out for another Bible."
Not a breath.
I thought, "That line always works well in Australia; why didn't it
work here?"
The penny dropped. "Of course, this is Jacksonville, right in the heart of
the Bible Belt!" Then I made the appropriate mental erasure.

Know the audience before you use the line!
I was addressing a conference of funeral directors and was advised not to make any spontaneously "funny" remarks about their profession, so I behaved quite conservatively.
Instead, I created a situation which encouraged them to give feedback that allowed them to see and express the humorous side of their business. The result was that the 1-hour presentation turned into a self-generated feel-good session, showing that no subject is too serious for humor.
　　　　　　　　　　　　　　　　　　—Ron Lee

To Prevent It from Happening

Don't try to tailor your remarks to the other culture.

What!

That's right. If you are Armenian, and they know that coming in, they are expecting an Armenian, with Armenian mannerisms and outlooks. Give your presentation the way you are strongest at delivering it. Don't change *all* your stories and illustrations because you are afraid they will never have heard of them. Just start it off with, "In Armenia (or wherever you are from) we have a famous story...."

However, adding or changing a few examples so they are about your audience's current or past history shows people that you did some research and are interested in them. This is a very endearing quality in any culture.

Do be sensitive to their culture. Research like crazy. When I did my seminar in Brazil, I used my on-line computer service to pull up the electronic encyclopedia entries on Brazil and all the current news articles. A Culture-gram (available from any library) is a quick and insightful look at any national or ethnic group. For example, the Culture-gram on Brazil told me that the "OK" hand sign we use all the time in the USA is very crude and rude in Brazil...that you should always bring a small gift when going to someone's home...that it is much more acceptable for men to make comments on the anatomy of a female walking past than it is in the USA.

Before I got there, I went through my 2-day seminar and made a list of all the jokes and anecdotes. As soon as I arrived, I spoke with the translator and tried them out on her. Some we cut; some we changed to fit. I do a magic trick with a rope to make a point. As the trick finished and they were all giving the typical "How did do she do that?" look, I said with a mock African accent, "*Mocumba!*" They howled.

The owner of the company exclaimed, "Where did you learn this word?"

"Why, in Brazil, of course." They howled again—too funny.

Now, if you are not Brazilian, you are thinking, "I don't get it." (I gotta tell you this was their attitude on *most* of my other jokes.) But they laughed because *Mocumba* is an African religion, very prevalent in Brazil, that is well known for using witchcraft. If a Brazilian had used the same line, it might have fallen flat. That an American knew about it and was being silly with it really gave them a chuckle.

Watch their eyes and their expressions closely. When they have a tiny frown, stop the program and ask questions, "Did I say it wrong?" They will hasten to reassure you, and let you know what their confusion really is. You need to do this right from the start. It sets the mood of you being very anxious to help them through the language barriers.

Be careful of analogies and idiomatic expressions. I witnessed an American friend slowly die in a presentation in Vienna as he used baseball expression to explain his point. When he perceived the audience was not following him, he used more and more such analogies thinking that this would make things clearer. He died with microphone in hand. If you use analogies, weed out those that are not part of the local culture.

—Paul Dinsmore

What to Say

In all the following statements, substitute your home state or region for "California."

Serious

We are going to have a problem with language today. You all speak English; unfortunately, we haven't spoken English in California for years. So, when I start using words and phrases you are not 100 percent certain of, please stop me. Everyone else in the room will be grateful.

—Lilly Walters

Humorous

(Exaggerated sigh, wiping the forehead.) That is really funny in California.

OK, that was a joke. We need to have an agreement so my feelings don't get hurt. I'll hold up this cue card when you're supposed to laugh—not that anyone laughs back in California either. But at least my feelings won't be hurt!

(You can have a good time holding up the sign at obvious wrong moments.)

—Lilly Walters

...They Yell, "I Can't Hear You!"

To Prevent It from Happening

Do a mic and room check before the presentation starts.

What to Do

- If it is something that can be fixed, stop and wait for the tech people to do so.
- Launch into a discussion exercise (see Chapter 6 for examples) while the problem gets fixed.
- If it looks like it is not going to get fixed, get the attendees to pick up their chairs and move as close as possible to you.
- If that's not possible, move out into the audience.
- If only one person is having a problem, suggest that he or she move up closer. Do *not* say, "Are you hard of hearing?" Just say, "Well, come on up here then."

What to Say

Serious

I'm sorry! Some of the areas in this room do seem to absorb the sound. Please, move up here.
—LILLY WALTERS

Humorous

That may be a good thing.
—DOUG MALOUF

What I said was, people who shout at the podium are oversexed.
—JEFF SLUTSKY

Well I can hear you!
—JIMMY CALANO

There's a guy up front who says he can hear me fine (pause)...and he'd like to switch seats with you.
—RON DENTINGER

(Shout) Is this (silently mouth a few words) better?

Is there an audio doctor in the house?

Is anyone here an M.D.—microphone doctor?
—ROGER LANGLEY

What *Not* to Say

Oh, are you hard of hearing? Why don't you move up closer?

...Members of Your Audience Are Physically Disabled

I was speaking to a group for a division of rehabilitation services. I said, "Everyone stand up." Two of them didn't. I smiled and said, "Hey, stand up!" They looked amused and said, "We can't." It was then I finally noticed they were seated in wheelchairs.

I'm a great deal more careful now.

—DEANNA BERG

The most embarrassing speech of my life occurred right here in my hometown—Glendora. I disobeyed all my own advice to others, and paid the price. I got a call from a civic group that supported the blind community asking me to donate my time to do a keynote speech. I looked at my calendar. The meeting was just a few days before I was going to Africa to present—the perfect chance for me to practice some new things and help a good cause. "Well, my topic is 'Secrets of Successful Speakers—How You Can Motivate, Captivate, and Persuade.'"

"Oh, that would be perfect!"

"OK, then. I would be delighted to speak for you!"

The day comes. About 60 minutes before I was to drive the few blocks to the event, I called the meeting planner. "I just wanted to check in. And by the way, what are you hoping your members will gain from my presentation today?"

This made her very confused. "I don't understand."

I tried again. "What message do you want me convey to your group about presentation skills?"

"Well, whatever you normally do."

Realizing I was not communicating well, I searched some more. "Well, uh, yes...let's see. How will your people use the information I will present tonight? Do they give talks in the community about vision impairment? Maybe to raise money for your group?"

Now she was clearly alarmed. "Oh, no! They would never do that! We are all retired."

I was very unclear why being retired had anything to do with restricting civic involvement, but now *I* was in a panic, realizing I should have had this talk the day she asked me to speak, not 60 minutes before I was to walk in their door! "Yes, er, I see." Trying to think fast, I added, "Tell me, why did you want me to speak today?"

Now she seemed to relax. "Oh well, we have a speaker every month, you know."

Oh, boy. By this time I was rather nervous. Still, thinking she had to be wrong—these people must have *some* need to talk about their group to the community—I got in the car and went down, feeling very frustrated that I—the big expert on presentations—had forgotten to do my homework!

I got there early, as I always try to do, and watched people arrive. Then it hit me. This was not a "support" group as I had pictured. It was a group of nonsighted people, mostly over 75. When you get in a panic, you have two choices: You can freeze and just muddle your way though with great ineptitude. Or you can open your heart and mind to the audience and its needs—allow the spirit to fill you with enthusiasm for people's wants. Which approach do you suppose I took?

You got it, I panicked! I kept thinking, "I have an hour to talk to people who have no hint of interest in what I have to say!" I jumped into the talk with that idea clearly in mind. I thought, "OK, I'll do lots of participatory stuff." I launched into a group activity that needed three volunteers. Up they came, with their seeing-eye dogs. I beat myself up thinking, "What an idiot! I didn't even ask how nonsighted people are supposed to get to the front of the room!" Anyway, they made it up there, and I started the exercise. Then it hit me, "This exercise will make sense to people only if they can *see* it! Oh, brother!" So I quickly started explaining, "Now imagine that...." Then I had the volunteers explain what they had felt and learned during the exercise. The point, of course, is that there are hundreds of other exercises I *could* have used.

I kept trying to make my points apply to communicating in general, instead of presenting to crowds. The shift worked fairly well—but not half as well as if I had *prepared* my talk that way for them from the start. At the end I wanted to crawl out. "Geez! How could I have been so stupid!" The meeting planner came up to me, thanking me warmly. I thought, "Well, at least she is trying to be kind."

"And you were one of our best speakers ever!" she concluded. "No one fell asleep this time."

Ah, fame...

To Prevent It from Happening

What you want to prevent from happening is your own foolishness and stupidity. Always find out who you are presenting for—in plenty of time to suit your material and style to the audience's needs, whatever they are! Some of their needs may relate to disabilities, or to content, or even to a slight change in your speaking style. But that's why *you* get asked to present, because you are supposed to be smart enough to ask and alter accordingly. (Yes, I'm talking to myself here too! I'm still beating myself up about being insensitive to that audience's needs.)

It will be a rare audience that does not have some people with a disability of some kind. Fifty percent of almost every audience you address will be hard of hearing. Even if people do not have a movement disability that is easy to spot, like crutches or a wheelchair, they may still have other movement restrictions that might need your assistance.

> *If there is a need to refer to persons with disabilities, the speaker should learn the "correct" or "accepted" terminology. "Handicapped" is out, though I still hear it often. "Disabled" displays less insensitivity, but is fast becoming unacceptable when used as an adjective —e.g., "disabled person." The politically correct expression is "persons with disabilities" as indicated in the Americans with Disabilities Act. Though terms such as "visually challenged" and "physically challenged" are used, they are more often used by persons who are not so challenged. Those that I know who are completely without sight have no problem saying they are blind. If they can see some, they refer to themselves as being "visually impaired." As a blind person, I think "visually challenged" is rather cutesy and prefer to be called "blind" or "visually impaired."*
>
> —DANA LaMON

What to Do

Take a careful look around the room. Watch people as they come in. Note who might need assistance and go up and speak to them privately and frankly.

> *The challenge is you do not want to point at someone and say, "You are disabled." There are lots of us are who are disabled: Some of us are in mental wheelchairs, some of us are in physical ones.*
> *The biggest mistake is dancing around people with disabilities.*
> *If you notice someone can't stand and you have just asked them all to stand, just come right out and say, "If you can't stand, do this from your seats."*
> —W MITCHELL

> *I don't do anything that might make a disabled person feel singled out or different. I always try to make eye contact with as many people as possible*

in my audiences. However, I always make a special effort with any physi-cally disabled people. Many people—because they feel unsure of how to treat the disabled—don't look directly into their eyes. With my eye con-tact I make sure they know that I know they are real and important.
                                                            —TOM OGDEN

Physical Disabilities

I approach people privately and ask how I can make them more comfort-able. A pillow on the table? A pillow on another chair? Women in casts often appreciate being given a blanket to cover their leg—often they can't get into pants with a leg cast and modesty prevents them from putting the casted leg up on another chair where it would be more comfortable. I always offer to get water or coffee, and ask others with that person's group to assist.

Also be sensitive to people who have Ace wraps.
                                                            —ROGER BURGRAFF

Visual Disabilities

As a blind member of the audience, I am bothered by the speaker's sin-gling me out as the reason for making adjustments to his or her presenta-tion. A speaker who recognizes that he or she must modify the presenta-tion for his or her listener who cannot see, ought not to announce such. Do not say, "For Dana's sake I'll describe the...." The description of an action or a visual aid to accommodate the member of the audience who cannot see should be incorporated as part of the presentation without ref-erence.

There is no need to hold back on the use of terms such as "look," "see," and "watch" just because a speaker addresses persons with visual impair-ments.
                                                            —DANA LaMON

A blind person in my audience pointed out—at the first break—that it was very unhelpful when I said things like "Look at the diagram on page 2" or "As you can see by the illustration..." I would give the conclusion without saying what it was. Now I try to be very aware of sight-disabled people. I describe what illustrations look like: "As you can see from this circle that has been divided into six sections...."

If they bring a dog, I always ask how I can assist with the dog—water, food, and so on. Once a dog gave a huge noisy yawn that gave me the opportunity for some great laugh lines.
                                                            —ROGER BURGRAFF

Hearing Disabilities

Hearing-disabled people will usually let you know. They need to be seated up front, on their "good side." They usually know what they need and take care of it. Once someone came in late and needed to sit up front,

which he let me know about at the break. Since the seats in front were all taken, I got the hotel staff to bring in an extra table.
                    —Roger Burgraff

From my experience as the executive director of a counseling center for the disabled, from conducting hearings as an administrative law judge, and from speaking to audiences which include persons with hearing impairments, I have learned three important considerations. First, the speaker must always face a person who relies on lip reading for communication. Second, the speaker must talk at a moderate rate (about 125 words a minute) to facilitate lip reading, or for translation into sign language. Third, breaks should be taken at least at 45-minute intervals to allow the interpreter a chance to rest his or her arms.
                    —Dana LaMon

...You Say or Do Something Really Embarrassing (the Faux Pas)

Nick Carter, vice president of Communication Research of Nightingale–Conant Corporation, was speaking for Land O'Lakes in Minnesota. His subject was the wonderful 16-billion-cell computer sitting between the ears of every human being. To make his point, he went over to a man whom everyone in his audience of 200 could see. He had a particularly thick head of healthy-looking hair.

To make his point about the power of the brain he said, "Do you realize it would take a computer the size of a two-story building covering the whole state of Texas to duplicate what you have here between your ears?"

He grabbed the man's beautiful hair and said, "Do you realize, under this hair..." and into his hand came the most perfect, thick wig the world has ever seen.*

To Prevent It from Happening

Always ask permission of your volunteers if you plan to touch an audience member. Since most of your ad-libs should be well rehearsed, you should have a very good idea of what you want to do and the sort of person you want to do it with.

---

*From *Sharing Ideas* newsmagazine, February–March 1988, page 6. Royal Publishing, Glendora, CA.

During my talk, I usually do a bit where I put makeup on a bald man's head. I always obtain clandestine permission from my "victim" when no one else is looking. As everyone files in and socializes, I check the crowd for a good potential "head." Once I spot my candidate, I go up to him quietly and say, "Can I speak to you privately for a minute?" Then I have him follow me out of the room. I carefully explain that I need a nice "shiny" head. "Do you know of anyone in the group who doesn't mind getting poked fun at?" This gives my confidant an option to volunteer himself, which is of course what I'm hoping he will do, or at least to suggest someone else. My candidates almost always want to volunteer themselves. "OK," I say conspiratorially, "but don't let anyone else in on it!"

One night I was careless. I was doing a dinner talk for an aerospace company's monthly meeting. I asked the CEO and his wife whom I should use. They said, "Oh, use Harry! He is bald and he's a kidder, he'll love it!" Guess what? Harry was one of those who gives it out but can't take it. He was not amused—like no kidding. Like the whole audience was stunned at his response—as was my stomach. It took a great deal of effort to get the talk back on track.

Two years later the same company—surprisingly—invited me back. I asked the same CEO about Harry. "You know, Lilly, it's sad. He's never come back to a single meeting since then." Great. Just what you want to hear. Your insensitivity has caused someone to be hurt for over 2 years! Then the CEO added, "We wanted to thank you; we're glad he's gone."

Well, the point is still valid. Even though I managed to get rid of a problem for the company, I think I must have hurt his feelings rather badly. So for heaven's sake, *ask* before you bring the spotlight over anyone in your audience.

What to Do

Whatever insensitivity you stumble into, the first thing to do is apologize. Stop what you are doing and make the point verbally. If people are offended, it is your fault. Occasionally a light bit of humor can help, but only if it is coupled with humility and an apology. Then move on. Don't dwell on it, or people will just grow more offended.

You must be the first one to acknowledge your mistake. If someone else does, you will look foolish for one of two reasons:

1. *If you are too dumb to realize you made a mistake, you look bad.*
2. *If you don't mention it first, it will look like you are trying to hide it and fool the audience.*

—Tom Antion

Apologize sincerely. Move to another part of the stage and begin a new subject quickly.

Make up your mind to think of the audience and their feelings first. As Marlene Dietrich said, "The average man is more interested in a woman who is interested in him, than he is in a woman with beautiful legs." Same with an audience. The important thing is that you care about them.
—DOTTIE WALTERS

A faux pas can sometimes be to your advantage, especially if it makes the audience laugh. Here's your chance to laugh at yourself or express shock at yourself in a funny or theatrical tone.
—HOPE MIHALAP

Focus on your message, not your mistakes.
—DICK FLAVIN

What to Say

Serious

I'm very sorry. Please, let me try that again.
—LILLY WALTERS

Humorous

(In shaky tones, as in a horror movie, or any funny manner that comes naturally to you.) What did I say?!
—LILLY WALTERS

Forgive me, everybody. I had no idea my mind was so warped and twisted.
—HOPE MIHALAP

I can still hear the last words my wife said to me as I left the house. She said, "Try not to make a fool of yourself." You can see obviously that I never listen to my wife.
—GENE PERRET

Sorry, it must be the steroids.
—TOM OGDEN

That's the last time I'm going to let anyone hypnotize me.
—W MITCHELL

When I make a faux pas, it's a magnum cum laude faux pas.

I realize you can never get the toothpaste back into the tube, but please accept my apology. That's not what I meant to say.
—ROGER LANGLEY

I knew these $50 teeth would get me into trouble!
                              —PHILIP CROSBY

I certainly put my foot in my mouth on that one. I'm getting used to it. Lately I've started using Odor Eaters as a breath freshener.

Guess I put my foot in my mouth that time...too bad I didn't put it in far enough to shut me up.

When I said that, I guess you were wondering what was on my mind, if you will allow the overstatement?

I am invited to speak at some of greatest meetings in the world—once.
                              —LILLY WALTERS

A man must pay the fiddler; in my case it so happened that a whole symphony orchestra often has to be subsidized.
                              —JOHN BARRYMORE

You'll have to forgive me. That is only the first mistake I've made...in the last 10 seconds.

If I ever do that again, you all should put me out of my misery.

I can't believe I said (did) that. Who would like to come up here and smack me?
                              —TOM ANTION

We learn from our mistakes. For instance, I'm learning that I make a lot of mistakes.
                              —From *Speaker's Idea File,* Original Humor
                              section by Gary Apple, May 1993

What *Not* to Say

I'm sorry! I didn't realize you were so sensitive.

...You Misquote—and Get Caught!

Stealing someone else's words frequently spares the embarrassment of eating your own.
                              —PETER ANDERSON, AMERICAN LAWYER, BORN **1940**
                              (From *Great Book of Funny Quotes,* by Eileen
                              Mason, Sterling Publishing, 1993)

To Prevent It from Happening

Do your homework! If you are not sure, start with, "As a wise person once said...."

What to Do

As a credible expert, you need to know who said what. If your listeners catch you with a bit of information that is wrong, they begin to wonder if all your information is bogus. You need to let them know that you will immediately get to the bottom of the issue and track down the true source of the information. Ask the person who contradicted you to write down the disputed point on the back of a business card and give it to you. Get it from the person right then, in front of the rest of the audience. Thank that person for pointing out the conflict and telling you about it. State publicly that you will call the person within 2 weeks with the correct information. Then do it. You don't want to be caught again.

Dr. Terry Paulson, who is quoted extensively throughout my books, maintains records of what he calls "keepers." Whenever he hears or reads something noteworthy, he puts it in his computer. When he sent me material for this book, he was one of the few who had documented exactly where he heard or obtained the information, down to the page number. Impressive.

What to Say

Serious

Really? I have always seen it attributed to _____. Please write down the way (or person) you think it is on the back of your business card. Give it to me now. Thank you for pointing this out. I may have been saying it wrong for years! I will call you within 2 weeks with verification on who really originated this information.
—LILLY WALTERS

Humorous

I've been on the road, and I got my mental wires crossed. Thank you for catching that! Would you like a job proofreading my material?
—DOTTIE WALTERS

Don't tell fish stories where the people know you, particularly, don't tell them where they know the fish!
—MARK TWAIN
(Submitted by Terry Paulson)

Well, that's what I would have said if I was him.
—ROGER LANGLEY

What *Not* to Say

Oh, they all look alike to me.

No, I'm sure you are wrong.

...You Plagiarize—and Get Caught!

The only "ism" Hollywood believes in is plagiarism.
                    —Dorothy Parker

If you steal from one author it's plagiarism; if you steal from many it's research.
                    —Wilson Mizner, American dramatist,
                    1876–1933

To Prevent It from Happening

It sounds so harsh when you say "plagiarism." Plagiarism is a bad thing. I'm a good person. I don't do bad things; therefore I'm just...just borrowing, or maybe showing off the research I've done.

If the author of that research were sitting in your audience, would he or she feel the same way?

It is just too easy to acquire other people's material. The more you use it, the more you begin to believe it is your own!

> *Cavett Robert's immortal rule:*
> *First time the speaker says it: As Lilly Walters says, "quote."*
> *Second time the speaker says it: As someone once said, "quote."*
> *Third time the speaker says it: As I always say, "quote."*
> *Notice I attributed that because I believe Cavett coined it and it's a specific quote. Otherwise, I wouldn't.*
> *I try to do to others' quotes as I would want them to do unto mine. That's Longfellow's rule.*
> > —Dr. Layne Longfellow
> > (From *Secrets of Successful Speakers*, by Lilly Walters, McGraw-Hill, 1993)

The best thing to do is use your own original material. When you use other people's material, try to credit the source. On the other hand, if you credit every source on every point, you give a speech of footnotes with no continuity at all! But the longer you study a topic, the more original insight you will bring to it.

What to Do

Since we know it will never really be plagiarism but just an honest mistake, see the section preceding this one on misquoting and getting caught! The same strategies apply.

What to Say

Serious

> *I've said that for so long, it has begun to feel like my own! Of course, you are right, that was originally said by....*
> —LILLY WALTERS

Humorous

> *Is he still copying my stuff?*
> —LILLY WALTERS

> *I should have listened to Shakespeare, who said, "neither a borrower nor a lender be." I guess I borrowed too much!*
> —ROGER LANGLEY

What *Not* to Say

> *I only steal from the best.*
> *No, I said that. He (she) took it from me.*

...You Go to Jail for Using Music in Your Talk

OK. So I exaggerated slightly. I wanted to make sure you read this section. You won't go to jail, but you will get one heck of a fine if you use music that you don't own or that is not in the public domain. Music is a fun and wonderful addition to a talk. For example, "Greensleeves" and "Home on the Range," songs that were written years ago, are in the public domain. You can use those yourself. If you put on a tape of Roy Rogers singing "Home on the Range," you may get sued. Roy's singing is not in the public domain, nor is the work of the backup singers or the arranger of that particular rendition of the song.

To Prevent It from Happening

You can:

- Pay ASCAP or BMI for the rights to use the songs—either the tapes of others singing, or the songs you want to sing or play yourself.
- Use public domain songs and play or sing them yourself.

■ Use a public domain song and pay a starving artist to make a tape of it for you. Have a contract with the artist that you will pay a one-time fee and no royalties. Then you own the piece and others will have to pay you to use your rendition of the song.

...You Ask Them to Read Something, Then Realize They Can't Read!

To Prevent It from Happening

Never, ever ask a specific person to read—and for that matter to stand, to write on the flipchart, or to answer a question. Ask for volunteers. You can never tell when you will have physically disabled people, limited-English speakers, or nonreaders in your audience. It may feel like an eternity before someone gets up the courage to do what you want—but wait, somebody will volunteer eventually.

What to Do

Find a way to help people "save face." Pretend there is something else wrong. Make up an excuse for the situation, not the person.

What to Say

I'm sorry, I can be so rude! I should have asked if you had your reading glasses with you. Could someone else read that please?

The light is terrible in this part of the room. Can any of you see better over there?

Wait! I've skipped ahead of myself. Before we read that, I want you to discuss in small groups the two most important reasons for....(Name the issue discussed in the item you were about to have that person read.) Please take only 2 minutes; go ahead. (Don't go back and have anyone read the passage except you.)
　　　　　　　　　　　　　　　　　　　　—Lilly Walters

Wait a moment! They can't hear in the back. Let me read it so the audience can hear it properly.
　　　　　　　　　　　　　　　　　　　　—Tony King

I felt the same way the first time I saw that passage. Let me help you with it.
　　　　　　　　　　　　　　　　　　　　—Roger Langley

...You Are Speaking to an "Empty House"

To Prevent It from Happening

Meeting planners usually err on the side of thinking there will be more people attending than really show up. If it happens, there is not much you can do about it. You can check with the event planner the day before and see how attendance is coming along. If the planner knows ahead that it will be light, suggest switching to another room.

What to Do

Having the room switched to a smaller one at the last minute is deadly difficult. So you might get stuck presenting to a small crowd in a big room. It's awful. You will see six rows of empty seats in the front and people standing in the back. People just have phobia about sitting in the front, which makes speaking to a small crowd even worse.

Try to get a last-minute approximation of how many people are actually going to be in the room. If the house is light, take the excess chairs out in the back of the room and stack them in a corner. If tables are used, get these moved out also. If the chairs are stationary, as in a theater, rope off the entrances to the rear aisles; you can also use masking tape to do this. Set out handout materials in the front only. It also helps if you have assistants who actually escort people to their seats—and put them right in front.

Call everyone down front. Take your mic off, grab a chair, and sit down. Ask people to form a circle with their chairs and hold the presentation that way. Avoid making excuses like, "Well, I don't know why the rest aren't here." Just go on as if that's the way you planned it all along.

> *If your audience is smaller than you expected (I don't mean short people, I mean fewer people), do not punish those who do attend. Don't comment on the small crowd, or make any remarks that would cause the people in attendance to wish they, too, had gone somewhere else. Make them feel welcome and give your usual wonderful presentation, so they will spread the word about what a great talk the others missed.*
>
> —ANITA CHEEK MILNER

What to Say

Serious

> *We always try to have a bigger room than you might think is best. I'm going to have you do several interactive exercises and we need this extra space.*
> —LILLY WALTERS

Humorous

(Get excited and say) Wow, this is great! Elvis used to buy out the house like this. One of you must be really famous. This is great!
—GENE MITCHENER, THE WHEELCHAIR COMIC

I'm glad we have so much room in here, 'cause after that big dinner, I'm getting stouter by the minute.
—ROGER LANGLEY

If we start now we can make everyone else feel guilty for coming late.
—From *Laughter Works*, Vol. 1, January 1989

What *Not* to Say

Interest rates are down. In fact, interest seems to be down here, too.

Who told everyone I was the speaker?

Either I'm not popular or this flu epidemic is worse than I thought.

I'm not surprised that so many seats are empty. What surprises me is that the rest of you are [still] here.

...The Audience Members Arrive Late During Your Talk

To Prevent It from Happening

Audience members may have legitimate excuses for arriving late—weather, transportation problems, other sessions running over, and so on. There is not much you can do to prevent this. You can try to soften the impact of the disruption as people arrive late. If they are all arriving late, you need to deal with the issue of whether those in charge want you to extend the stop time of your presentation or to cut your talk short.

What to Do

Just before the Broadway opening of *Anything Goes*, Cole Porter decided against having an opening chorus—a standard convention of the time—and insisted on placing the show's biggest hit, "I Get a Kick Out of You," within the first 5 minutes of the first scene. It seems that his society friends thought it was amusing to drift into the theater 15 or 20 minutes after the curtain had gone up so that all their friends could observe what they were wearing. Because Porter regarded such behavior as rude, to audience and actors alike, he warned his friends for weeks before the opening that they had better arrive on time, or they would miss the big song: with a wry smirk, he added that they never forgave him.*

I thank them for coming, and encourage them to come right in front. I tell them there are lottery tickets under the front seats.
                                                                          —W MITCHELL

What to Say

(In a cute manner) Did you bring a note from home?
                                                                          —MIKKI WILLIAMS

Gee, everyone in the room just sang a song. Now it's your turn...
                                                                          —JIMMY CALANO

I'm sorry. The meeting's started and we've already elected new officers. (pause) Congratulations!

Good, now we can start.

Good, we thought you'd never get here.
                                                                          —TOM OGDEN

Why were you late? You'll have to clean all the erasers after class.
                                                                          —TOM ANTION

Oh great, I have to start all over again (sigh)! Hi, my name is Gene Mitchener and this morning (repeat the first few sentences).

Excuse me. Could you just look at someone's notes?
                                                                          —GENE MITCHENER, THE WHEELCHAIR COMIC

Since everyone is obviously watching the person coming in late anyway, I finish the line I am on and say, "And that concludes today's seminar."
                                                                          —JEFF SLUTSKY

What *Not* to Say

Get a seat, we're just doing a session on time management.

Come in! We've been waiting for you. You haven't missed much!

---

*From "Some Words About *Anything Goes*," by Miles Kreuger, in the liner notes for the John McGlinn, EMI Records, Ltd. recording of *Anything Goes*, p. 17, 1989.

...They Don't Want to Come Back—or Come Back Late— After Breaks

To Prevent It from Happening

First, why does it happen? Either you have gotten people so high that they are talking excitedly in the halls (which is a wonderful thing!) or you have bored them so that they dread coming back in (which is a bad thing!). Or perhaps you have trained them that start times are not important. If they are bored, quickly find ways of getting them excited again. If they are excited, rejoice! But do get them back in there. If they are perpetual stragglers, look in a mirror. If you start the meeting 10 minutes late, you've just taught them that timing is not important to you. If you wait for them to come back from a break, you are reinforcing their opinion. You are also telling the ones who are on time that they are being silly to rush back.

About 3 weeks into most theater productions I have acted in, the directors start getting frustrated that people are not on time. But from day 1 these same directors would be chatting and organizing materials at the announced start time. Thirty minutes later we would get under way. It doesn't take long to teach people what to expect from you.

What to Do

- Set clear expectations. Tell people exactly how much time they have for the breaks.

- Start precisely when you say you will. After the first break, you will teach people by example that they must get back in the room on time.

- Appoint a hall monitor. If there is a natural leader, or even a big mouth, just assign this person as Roundup Chairperson (or some other silly name).

- Whistle. Carry a big whistle in your kit and blow it when you need people back in.

- Play music. Teach them early on that when the music starts, it's time to return to the room. Bring a tape player and some nice music that complements your topic.

- Look at stragglers when they come in late. Just glance at your watch with a very slight frown, and go right on.

  Piece of cake. I carry a small microphone that I ripped off from my 10-year-old. Attached to the mic is a siren that sounds like an ambulance. I blow the siren and announce that it's time to get back to work. I may even wear my "drill sergeant" hat or my "firefighter" hat to let them know I'm rescuing them.

—MICHAEL AUN

I just clap my hands real loud and ask for their attention. Then I ask them all to please come back in the room. I inform them that we'll be starting in X number of minutes. Sometimes, if the group is small enough, I go around and touch people on the shoulder and ask them to please reenter the room.

I always start each session with several overheads of cartoons and a moving story from my book Chicken Soup for the Soul. *People always rush back because they enjoy the beginning of each session. I also start when I say I will so people get used to being on time. Also, when I start with some cartoons and a story, people who straggle in don't miss valuable content.*

—JACK CANFIELD

I tell participants, "Time is money." Synchronize watches. When and if they come back from break on time, then I give the first ones dollar bills. I sometimes offer penny candy. I have also given fake coins to be turned in for a door prize at the end.

—LORNA RILEY

The best technique I have found is to have the people in charge of the meeting go out and tell the audience that we will be starting in 3 minutes. When it is time to start, simply get on stage and start talking. What will happen is people feel like they're missing things and will instead return immediately to the room.

—LEE MILTEER

Sometimes I use a fun type of game or puzzle. I let them know there will a prize for the first group finished. There is team pressure to be the first ones back to get the exercise done, since they can't do it without all the members of their team. I put the exercises on the tables while they are at break.

—MIKKI WILLIAMS

Begin telling a very interesting story to the few who have come back. This tends to make others feel they are missing something.

Have a great attention-getting overhead that can begin conversation and questions.

—MARILYN WHEELER

What to Say

Serious

(I use the cliff-hanger approach.) We have just talked about _____ (your topic), but the real secret I will give you immediately after this

*break. When you hear this whistle, you have 60 seconds to go before I give
the secret.*
                              —CHRIS HEGARTY

Humorous

*I know we are all having great fun on this break and the sooner we can get
started in here the sooner we'll be able to get to the next break.*
                              —DAVID CAREY

Last one back in will tell the rest of us an appropriate joke.
                              —MARILYN WHEELER

(Go out to where they are milling around.) He's starting! He's starting!

Two-minute warning! He's starting in 2 minutes.
                              —NATE BOOTH

If you don't come back right now, I swear I'll start singing.

My feelings are hurt. You're having so much fun without me.

*I think I dropped a $100 bill in here. Would you come in and help me find
it?*

*I'm sure you are all discussing how much you are enjoying my seminar.
C'mon in and I'll give you some more to enjoy.*

*I'm so flattered you are having such a good time talking about me. I'm
just afraid to hear what you are saying.*
                              —TOM ANTION

---

*Welcome back. You'll be pleased to know that while you were out, I man-
aged to think of something more to say.*
                              —From *Current Comedy Newsletter,*
                                December 23, 1991

...An Unexpected Event
Leads to a Long Break in
the Action

To Prevent It from Happening

Almost anything can cause an unexpected pause in the action. After
all, this is a whole book of things that can cause an interruption. Plan
for as many of them as you can. Rejoice when they don't happen!

What to Do

If the break was more than 60 seconds:

1. Address the situation as appropriate. Each predicament has its own coping strategies. Review the various headings in this book.

2. People will use you to gauge how they should react. If you are angry, they will be too.

3. Allow them to vent their feelings and frustrations if the situation warrants it.

4. Recap what you had covered before the interruption. Then carry on.

Restart at the same energy level as the group. On a scale of 1 to 10, with 1 being no energy and 10 being totally energized and passionate, restart at a level 5 if the group is a level 5. It doesn't make any difference if they were a level 8 before the unexpected event. After you get down to their level and reconnect, you can move them back to level 8!
—NATE BOOTH

What to Say

See additional sections that discuss *specific* unexpected events that lead to a long break in the action.

Serious

Close your eyes. Now think, "What do I want to accomplish today?" (Wait 15 seconds.) Open your eyes. Now, focus on those goals as we continue with...
—LILLY WALTERS

Humorous

And now, back to our regularly scheduled program.
—LILLY WALTERS

...You Want to Get a Standing Ovation

What to Do

Play the national anthem.
—PATRICIA FRIPP

My mother says a standing ovation always starts on the left, toward the front, then works into the rest of the audience. She looks right at that first person who stands, gestures toward the person to draw the rest of the audience's notice, and says, "Oh, thank you!" That usually gets more of them on their feet.

I always go for the standing ovation. A great speaker and poet showed me the greatest tip to get one. She says to the audience, "I want to do one last thing before we close. Why don't you all stand up. Put your right hand on your left shoulder, and your left hand on your right shoulder. Give yourself a hug, you are very special people. Now, go out into the world and make a difference!" They are already on their feet, you have your Standing O!

> —KEN BLANCHARD
> (From *Secrets of Successful Speakers*, by Lilly
> Walters, McGraw-Hill, 1993)

I've watched Danielle Kennedy use a song to close. She says, "I don't worry about a standing ovation. I tell everybody to stand up at the end and sing."

> —MIKKI WILLIAMS

For a standing ovation, close your program with a great heart story.
Then take a bow with your head down, then way up and your arms out-stretched up, then out to them.

> —DOTTIE WALTERS

At the beginning of a session I often talk about our minds getting locked into a position without us realizing it. I tell the audience that I can lock them into their seats right at this moment without using ropes or binds. Naturally, most of them doubt this! I ask them to sit upright in their chairs with their backs against the support and their feet in front of them. Then I invite them to stand, without bending forward or moving their feet. It can't be done. At the end of my session I take them back to this example...but this time I ask them to bend their backs slightly and see what can be achieved with a small adjustment. This brings them to their feet. I say thank you for being a great audience and they are already on their feet, ready to give me a standing ovation.

> —MAX HITCHINS

By the way, the greatest compliment for a banquet speaker is not the standing ovation. It's when the banquet employees linger by the door, listening to your talk.

> —ANITA CHEEK MILNER

What to Say

Now if I could get you all to stand up, please? Hold your hands out in front of you about 2 feet apart. When I say "Thank you," bring them together very quickly and repeat that movement several times very loudly. Thank you.

> —GENE MITCHENER, THE WHEELCHAIR COMIC

(As I'm wrapping up I sometimes say) Before I close for my standing ovation....

> —MIKKI WILLIAMS

What *Not* to Say

It's my birthday and I've never had a standing ovation.

You know, my poor little disabled son, Johnny—gee, his one real joy is to hear all about his Dad's performances. Every night when I come home from a show I go right up to little Johnny, seated in his wheelchair by our feeble fire. Johnny looks at me with adoration and says, "Did they like you, Dad? Did they applaud? Did they give you a standing ovation?" Don't make me lie to little Johnny.

In closing, I wanted to share with you that today is the anniversary of my father's death—just last year. He never got to see me perform. His dearest dream was to see me get a standing ovation. Maybe you all will join me on this anniversary and think good thoughts of Dad.

Actually, you might try some of these—but *only* in a highly comedic, totally tongue-in-cheek manner.

...The "Stars" in Your Audience Think They Know More Than You Do

These "stars" will sneak into your audiences. Whatever you say, they have a *witty* thought to add—or a *small* correction, an *interesting* anecdote—at least in their eyes. The problem is not just the disruption of the agenda. It's what happens in your mind—especially if they are making some pretty good points! You start to wonder, "The whole audience thinks this person knows more than I do!"

To Prevent It from Happening

You can't prevent it; you can correct it.

What to Do

If you ask the stars to "knock it off," your authority and *pathos** with the group will diminish. On the other hand, if you allow them to keep on going, you may need to rent the room for an extra day. But if the interruption is pulling the presentation too far out of the pattern you need for your message to penetrate, you need to get it stopped.

- If the information is good, rejoice.
- Don't embarrass the "star performer."

*From the Greek word meaning to suffer, used now to indicate feeling and compassion.

- Move the whole group into a quick 5-minute exercise, and take that person aside. First, thank him or her for participating. Then ask that person to help you encourage the others to participate.

Ask the entire group to write down two ideas. Then call on specific people whom you notice are writing, but who have not yet participated as much as the others. Go up to these potential "stars" at the break and give them the chance to talk and tell their stories. It's how they learn.
—TERRY PAULSON
(Quoted in *Secrets of Successful Speakers,* by
Lilly Walters, McGraw-Hill, 1993)

Ask five people who either contributed the most or are very knowledgeable to come up front to form a "panel" to share their wisdom with the group. It compliments them. It is less threatening in a group panel for people to share. It affords a lot of audience participation. If the audience has no questions, ask people to write down three questions first and discuss their questions with a partner next to them. Then have them ask the panel. Instant program up to an hour in length!
—MICHAEL PODOLINSKY

What to Say

(Take the "star" aside quietly in private, where none of the other audience members can hear you.)
You are so much more comfortable in voicing your opinion than the others here. I need your help to get them talking. For the next 2 hours let's try this: Don't volunteer an answer unless I look at you and put my hand in my pocket—like this. Then, if you know the answer, help me out. Maybe that way these others won't be so embarrassed. Someone of your abilities can be a bit intimidating to others.
—LILLY WALTERS

(Take the "star" aside quietly in private, where none of the other audience members can hear you.)
It is a delight to get people to participate as wholeheartedly as you do. However, when there is an obvious leader, like you, the others just sit back and are content to let you lead. I need to find ways to bring them out of their shells, and get involved. So, when I notice that they are retreating again, I'm going to give you a secret hand signal, which will be your cue to hold in any comment. Eventually they will get involved. I appreciate your help. Between the two of us, we will be able to get them learning.
—TERRY PAULSON
(Quoted in *Secrets of Successful Speakers,* by
Lilly Walters, McGraw-Hill, 1993)

As _____ knows well from his years of great experience...
(Acknowledge the "star" directly. People only want recognition.)
—DOTTIE WALTERS

...The Audience Really Does Know More Than You

To Prevent It from Happening

If you don't know anything about the topic, decline the invitation to speak to the group. However, you may know quite a bit about the topic and find out later that the audience happens to know more.

Send out a preprogram questionnaire. (See Figure 1-3 in Chapter 1.) Interview the attendees. At least you will then know what you are up against. But make sure your presentation has been advertised as either a "workshop" or a "discussion." Then instead of your trying to give people things they have never heard—which is almost impossible, anyway—you become a facilitator of their sharing of the pooled information.

What to Do

There is no reason you can't present to a group that knows more than you.

- Be delighted and excited that everyone is there; it brings just that much more information to the group.

- Don't bluster your way through. Don't try to pretend you know something when you don't.

- Encourage people to share information with the group.

What to Say

In groups of _____, identify three companies that are successful at _____ and the reasons for it. (You move out of the role of expert speaker and into the role of facilitator.)
—JEFF DEWAR

It's a privilege to address such a group of experts. In fact, many of you may be wondering why I'm even here today. After all, most of you have forgotten more about _____ (the topic) than I'll ever know. And that's exactly why I'm here—to refresh your memories. We're going to review the basics today.

Presenting to a group of experts like this reminds me of that old story about the Johnstown flood survivor who later died and went to heaven. He was going on and on about the Johnstown flood. He told God that he wanted to give a speech about it because he was an expert on floods and was sure that everyone in heaven would be fascinated to hear him speak about it. God said, "OK, but don't forget—Noah will be sitting in the first row."
—MALCOLM KUSHNER

I realize that all of you have much more information on this subject than I do. However, everything is not going well at this time, so perhaps we could examine the situation from the viewpoint of one who is not so well informed.

All of you understand the business completely, but the company is losing market share. Let's look at it from another platform.
—PHILIP CROSBY

You know, speaking to you this morning makes me feel like a high school football coach making a presentation to the NFL coaching staff. The interesting thing is, I've learned that the more skilled and capable people are, the more they are in search of any good ideas that will aid them in their pursuit of competence. And in that light, I make my presentation.

This is indeed a rare occasion for a speaker. Your program chairperson could easily put on a blindfold, reach into the audience, and upgrade the program by picking any person at random. But as I stand before all of you who have had such eminent success, it is a given that you are all looking for ideas to get even better.

I'd like you to know that in all the areas I cover today, you are free to ask any questions you like. There will be no question you could possibly ask that I don't have an answer for (pause) though one of my most frequent answers may be "I don't know." So, since I don't need to have the answer, you are free to ask any question you like! I think someone in this audience will have the answer.

—CHRIS HEGARTY

As I look out at the incredible pool of knowledge assembled here, I am reminded of George Bernard Shaw's words, "I am not a teacher: only a fellow traveler of whom you asked the way. I pointed ahead—ahead of myself as well as of you."
—LILLY WALTERS

...Someone Starts Giving a Speech in the Middle of Your Speech

It may happen for many reasons. You may have someone who uses your presentation as a soap box for a pet project. But you may also have someone who is just oblivious.

To Prevent It from Happening

Unless you are the kind of presenter who discourages feedback from the audience, you will have a problem on occasion with your time being invaded by others.

What to Do

What you do depends on the attendee who is creating the problem. If he or she is taking over and discoursing on a topic that has nothing to do with you, you must bring the subject back on track. No matter how much the audience dislikes the interrupter, you need to remain the benign monarch, not the harsh dictator. The members of the audience have given you power over them; you are in a privileged position. If you abuse that position to "slap" the interrupter down—no matter how justified the slapping down—they will think poorly of you in the long run. Instead, be gentle, be firm, but get your group back on track.

If the interrupter is simply oblivious, you must be extra careful. One man has now come to my full-day session "Secrets of Successful Speakers: How You Can Motivate, Captivate, and Persuade," *three* times. Normally that would be nice, but this person comes because he can't remember that he has been there before, even though we gently remind him each time he signs up. This attendee is loud, opinionated, and verbose, and unfortunately he does not have a good grasp of what the heck I'm talking about.

I am lucky to have had this experience so I can speak to you about it with conviction. I began to notice that the audience was much more frustrated by the interrupter than I was. Every time he would talk (trust me, this was often), the others would shift around in their chairs and roll their eyes. I began to wait for this attendee to say a sentence and at the first possible breath, I would break in with a smile and redirect us back to the subject at hand. The trick was trying to find a segue from his rambling back to what I was talking about. By the third time this person came to one of my sessions, I had become pretty good at the old segue shuffle, which gave me a chance to be more objective. When I felt my frustration starting to rise, I would smile and say to myself, "We are all here together. When do we start working on finding out how to care for one another? If not me who? If not now when?"

Search for your own affirmations to calm yourself when it happens to you.

I strongly believe that there are times when it's important to let someone in the audience get his or her message out. If that person can hurt you after the session, by stirring up frustration with "Ah, see? She never lets anyone else say anything," remove eye contact from the individual and never make eye contact again. Removing eye contact is key; most troublesome individuals will lose steam quickly when the speaker is not looking at them.

—Marian Woodall

When people begin to give a speech inside your program, you must learn to interrupt. Look for a good summary statement from their message. Interrupt with, "I think that is a good point. As _____ (the interrupter) says, we all need to _____ (his or her point). In fact that point moves us beautifully into _____ (another). If you interrupt, you must continue talking even if your interrupters try to get on with their point. They will stop if you keep going. You can sometimes talk to them during the break to thank them for their contributions and let them know how much material there is to cover.

—TERRY PAULSON

When someone gets on a soapbox during a Q&A session, the worst thing I can do is start to argue, because that undermines my credibility. If an audience member goes ballistic, I calmly walk away from the podium and take a seat in the audience. I cradle my face in my hand, and sort of squish my cheek up into my eye in a comic caricature. Eventually the "offending" member realizes, "Oh, I guess I'm out of line, ain't I?" Then I say in a whimsical manner, "Gee, and I was gonna start taking notes. OK, where were we? Oh, yes."

—DAVID R. VILLANUEVA

If you can't get a word in edgewise, try leading applause for this person. The others should join right in, because they are probably tired of the monologue, too. Usually only a few members of the audience can even hear what that person is saying, so they are really anxious to get back to your program. I've only used this technique once, in desperation, but it did the trick.

—ANITA CHEEK MILNER

What to Say

Serious

I think that is a good point. As _____ says we all need to _____ (point). In fact his point moves us beautifully into...

—TERRY PAULSON

(Wait for the interrupter to take a breath, and say with a big smile) Yes, indeed. Now back to...

Let me stop you there. I need to clarify. See, what I meant to direct our conversation to was...(go right back to your topic).

Wait a second. Let's talk about that during the break. (Smile) Now, as I was saying...

—LILLY WALTERS

(Wait for the speaker to take a breath and then quickly plunge in with) That's a great story. Does anyone else have a question?

—SCOTT PATON

(I start talking while they are talking and say something like) That's a very good point and I can see that you have considerable background on it. Suppose you and I discuss it after this session. Does anyone else have any questions?

(Or, hopefully I have noticed someone else who was going to ask a question and I will turn to that person and say) I believe you had a question. What were you going to say?
—DAVE CAREY

You've got some really great ideas. Can we talk about them at the break? I might want to include some of them in my next talk.

Let's hear a round of applause for _____ because of his (her) enthusiasm for this subject.

I really want to hear more about your thoughts on this, but in the interest of time we must move on so I can get all the material covered. Thank you for your input.
—TOM ANTION

Humorous

I thought for sure I was the speaker and you all were the audience.
—TOM ANTION

Sir (madam), everybody here wants to have the chance to throw hard questions at me, and I don't think you should have all the fun.
—LARRY TRACY

What *Not* to Say

Wouldn't you know it? I just got a note that there is a phone call for you in the hall!

Look, they paid me to make the speech. Do you mind?

That's not what our topic is today. Please let's try to stick to the topic!

...Someone Else in the Audience Answers a Question Directed to You
To Prevent It from Happening

You can't prevent it; you can correct it if it becomes an ongoing problem.

What to Do

As long as "second guessing" is not a chronic problem, just laugh about it or make a joke. It's an opportunity for some silliness and it encourages the mood of sharing. It's also a good sign that people are attentive and learning.

If it is a chronic problem, apply many of the same strategies that you use to deal with hecklers. Try walking over to the person. (People are easier to control if you are next to them.) Try actually touching the person by gently putting your hand on his or her shoulder.

What to Say

Serious

Thank you. Would you give us your name and company name, please? Now, let's consult the questioner: "Does Mr. (Ms.) _____'s response satisfy your question? (If yes, move on. If not, you answer.)
—PAUL DINSMORE

Good answer! And here is another idea!
—DOTTIE WALTERS

Humorous

Thank you. I've appointed this gentleman (or lady) to answer all questions.
—TERRY BRAVERMAN

Oh, ventriloquism.
—TOM OGDEN

(I look at the person who answered and reply with a little routine I memorized from Fireside Theatre about a mock game show host announcing prizes to a contestant. I speak very fast, as in a Federal Express commercial.)
That's absolutely right! Johnny, let's tell him exactly what he won!
Well, Jeff, he won 2 full pounds of Chef Anton's Southern-Fried Grits, toasted to golden perfection, cubed, reheated, and returned to water. And look at this—close the door and the light stays on! Now back to you, Jeff."
"Thanks, Johnny."
—JEFF SLUTSKY

Thank you, Jim! We rehearsed that all night.
—JIM McJUNKIN

What *Not* to Say

I do a single.
You have the right to remain silent.
Remember, a closed mouth gathers no feet.

Sir (Madam)? Excuse me, I work alone!

Let's play a little game. Only the person with the microphone gets to speak.

Now, now, your part doesn't have any lines.

...You Disagree with Your Audience

> *There is only one thing a philosopher can be relied on to do, and that is to contradict other philosophers.*
> —WILLIAM JAMES, AMERICAN PHILOSOPHER, BORN 1842
> (From *Great Book of Funny Quotes,* by Eileen Mason, Sterling Publishing, 1993)

> *He who speaks the truth should have one foot in the stirrup.*
> —HINDI SAYING
> (From *Great Book of Funny Quotes,* by Eileen Mason, Sterling Publishing, 1993)

> *When you accept our views, we shall be in full agreement with you.*
> —MOSHE DAYAN, ISRAELI STATESMAN, BORN 1915
> (From *Great Book of Funny Quotes,* by Eileen Mason, Sterling Publishing, 1993)

To Prevent It from Happening

You can't avoid it. If you are communicating, and you are human— chances are you qualify on both of those—*sometimes* you are going to disagree with some of your audience members.

Try to come prepared with answers to difficult questions.

What to Do

To avoid conflict, try to find those gems in whatever people are saying that you can agree with. On the TV the other day I heard an officer being interviewed about a military maneuver in Somalia. The interviewer asked, "Is it true you killed women and children today?" The officer replied, "Today, we were able to stop the attacking forces that were firing on our troops."

> *The bible says, "Agree with your adversary early." The minute you agree, people let their guard down.*
> —DOTTIE WALTERS

Answer with a process. For example, you are asked, "Mr. Walters, are we going to win or lose this case?" You answer them with "Well, first, we are going to file the case. I will argue with _____, they might say _____. Our strengths are _____." You never really answered, because there wasn't really a true answer to give them, other than "I don't know," which would just make them upset.
                                          —R. Michael Walters

---

During my lectures on the Kennedy assassination, there usually are some "conspiracy theorists" in the audience who vehemently oppose my anti-conspiracy position. Instead of an ad hominem attack on the person asking the question, I respond on the merits of the point in question.
                                          —Vincent Bugliosi

What to Say

Serious

I see I'm in the vast minority here. Please indulge me while I present the opposing view.
                                          —Dianna Booher

(Make sure to "make them right" when they give an answer.) That could be right.

There are a lot of people who would agree with that.
                                          —Terry Paulson

Can we agree to disagree agreeably?

There is such strength in diversity.

I can see how you might think (feel) that way.
                                          —Roger Burgraff

I can see how you might think that way, but perhaps you didn't know that...
                                          —Dottie Walters

One of the great things about being adults is that each of us can have our own opinions.
                                          —Doug Malouf

A wise person once said, "It is far better to debate a question without settling it than to settle a question without debating it."
                                          —Unknown

Humorous

I'm sure your idea has merit...come to think of it, I'm not sure at all.
                                          —Roger Langley

What can I say? Save time...see it my way.

Your reasoning is silly, illogical, irrational, and it's beginning to make sense.
—TERRY PAULSON

Now I know what it feels like to be in a minority. (Use only if it is true.)
I'm willing to be converted.
If I were in your shoes, I'd feel (think) exactly the same way.
—DEANNA JEAN BROWN

...Your Temper Is About to Explode

Father Michael Mulvaney, a speaker and counselor on self-esteem, traveled a great distance at his own expense to do a talk for a high school group. (A nightmare in itself. High school students are either the most fabulous audiences in the world, or they are hell!) That day the group seemed antsy and inattentive. One small clique in the back had a girl who was so rude that she had her back turned to Father Mulvaney as she blithely went on with her own conversation! Finally, this kind and good— but very tired and frustrated man—singled out the girl with her back to him, and in a stern tone said, "Look, I've traveled a long way just to be with you today. I deserve to be treated with some respect. You can at least give me the courtesy to turn around and look at me! You have no right to be so rude." The girl was very embarrassed and distressed to be singled out. With tears of humiliation and shame in her eyes she said, "Father, I'm so sorry! But these are our deaf students, and I was translating your talk for them." As you can imagine, he wanted to drop through a hole in the ground and never reappear.
—From *Secrets of Successful Speakers,* by Lilly Walters, McGraw-Hill, 1993

To Prevent It from Happening

Prepare your presentation well. Think of all those touchy areas that might set off your temper. Stockpile witty and lighthearted remarks to deal with them.

What to Do

Focus on the members in the audience that need you, and that want you. Fill your mind with thoughts of them and there is no room left to worry about anything else.

If you must express your anger and frustration, try humorous exaggeration of *your* feelings rather than a scathing description of their character and personality. For example, you might say, "If that PA system goes off one more time, I am going to lead us all in a riot in the lobby! We can start a bonfire and shout rude things about the voice on the box! Then we can all rip off our clothes and run screaming through the halls! That'll teach 'em!"

Take whatever it is that is making you angry and express it in non-hurtful ways. You can often diffuse your anger this way. The outrageous absurdity of your comments makes them giggle. This is especially important if it is a person in your audience that is frustrating you! Don't attack their self-esteem by such statements as, "You are so irresponsible" or "You are so thoughtless."

He who laughs, lasts.
> —MARY PETTIBONE POOLE
> (From *Great Book of Funny Quotes,* by Eileen Mason, Sterling Publishing, 1993)

Speak when you are angry and you'll make the best speech you'll ever regret.
> —AMBROSE BIERCE, AMERICAN JOURNALIST, BORN **1842**
> (From *Great Book of Funny Quotes,* by Eileen Mason, Sterling Publishing, 1993)

I have noticed that nothing I never said ever did me any harm.
> —CALVIN COOLIDGE, AMERICAN LAWYER AND THIRTIETH PRESIDENT OF THE UNITED STATES, BORN **1872**
> (From *Great Book of Funny Quotes,* by Eileen Mason, Sterling Publishing, 1993)

Impelled by a state of mind which is destined not to last, we make our irrevocable decisions.
> —MARCEL PROUST, FRENCH NOVELIST, BORN **1871**
> (From *Great Book of Funny Quotes,* by Eileen Mason, Sterling Publishing, 1993)

People who fly into a rage seldom make a smooth landing.
> —ANONYMOUS
> (From *Great Book of Funny Quotes,* by Eileen Mason, Sterling Publishing, 1993)

Recognize that some people are placed on this earth to irritate you. When they're bugging you, just say to yourself, "He's only doing his job!"
> —MORRIS MASSEY

What to Say

Let's take 5 minutes. In groups of _____, see if you can come up with three solutions to _____ (the situation that is getting you hot).
   (While they discuss it, you cool off, and try to find some solutions on your own.)
                                              —LILLY WALTERS

(In a small group, among your own people, if someone is hassling you unnecessarily, or just being a jerk) Listen, before I come unglued here...
                                              —JIMMY CALANO

What *Not* to Say

I can't believe this. It makes me so mad.

I'm the expert here; just take my word for it.

If I wanted to be nagged, I'd go back to my wife (husband)!

...The Audience Has Gathered into "Cliques"

Participants will feel less intimidated to express themselves freely and experience new things if you break them out of their normal groups (family, work groups, friends, and so on). However, breaking up traditional cliques is initially intimidating and takes a bit of perseverance on your part. Yet in longer presentations, you should find ways to do it.

To Prevent It from Happening

All you have to do is break the whole group up at the outset. This can be done as people arrive, or it can be done once or many times during your program as a part of "the experience" you provide. I often break groups apart three times a day: once when they arrive, once after lunch, and once at the final break.

What to Do

A variety of networking, ice-breaking, and learning experiences are available, depending on the mission of the presentation. For example:

- As people come in the door, assign seating. One way is to have them pick a number out of a hat. Those numbers correspond to numbers you have placed at the tables.

- Have a group exercise in progress. As people come in, assign each one to a separate group. As the people arrive in the morning for my full-day sessions, I like to use a hidden message game. (For full instructions, see Chapter 5.)

- Tom Ogden teaches several seminars that revolve around magic, including "The Magic of Creativity" and "Teaching and Training with Magic." He breaks up the groups as they arrive by giving them an exercise. He teaches the first four arrivals a simple magic trick that any young child could do; each person has a special trick to learn. Then he sends each person to his or her own corner of the room. As new people arrive, they are sent to a corner to learn only that person's trick. Soon the room is divided into four equal parties.

- Assign a number to each table, and then ask people to move to their table. You coordinate it this way: Once the whole group has been seated, have them count off from, say, one to ten. The first person in the first row says, "one," the second person says, "two"—all the way to "ten." You keep going around the room, but start counting over at one. Then you say, "This is table 1; all the ones go here. This is table 2; all the twos come here."

- At a certain point in the program, have people stand up and find one person in the room they have not yet spoken with. Have them share something with that person—one great thing they have learned or one thing they plan to apply tomorrow. After they do that, tell them to go into groups of three, and share something else—again you need to say what that something is. Keep doing this until you have as many subgroups as can sit at your tables—usually two to six people per table, depending on the way you set up the room. Have them sit down at their tables.

- Assign groups by the colors on the covers of your handouts or workbooks. (Of course, you have all materials printed with this in mind.)

> Sometimes I break people into groups by gender. This changes the dynamic and gives them a chance to address issues they may not normally feel comfortable sharing in front of the other gender. Or the changed dynamic just brings out different issues.
> —MICHAEL PODOLINSKY

> If it is a business group, first I try to mix them by keeping the same level of people (say, VPs) together. I make an exception if the high-level people are "people-oriented." If they are the aloof types, I find ways to slowly work them into group exercise.
>
> I preprint out my computer cards. Each card has a number of things on it.

Maybe animals, colors, fruits, automobiles. I figure out ahead how many groups and how many people I want in each subgroup. Then I say, "OK, all the tigers go over there, lions over there," and so on.
                                    —DAVE CAREY

What to Say

(I use frequent, short dyad exercises that I introduce with humor.) "I want each of you to pick a partner you do not directly work with. I consider people you know well as 'used' people. Those of you who are assertive will get to pick; those who are left wandering around I will pair up. Find a partner!" (Not only will you have good participation, you will initiate more team-expanding contact and notice an immediate increase in audience energy and comfort.)
                                    —TERRY PAULSON

(Put colored dots on people's name tags as they check in, either randomly or alphabetically.) "All the blues to go over here, the reds over there," and so on.
                                    —BRAD PLUMB

...The Audience Starts Walking Out Before You Are Done

Humorist Art Gliner was introduced by the president of the company and began his opening remarks to the board members by telling them what he was going to cover. Then a man in the front interrupted. He stood up and said, "I don't think I want to waste my time with this stuff. I don't think the others here want to waste their time either. I have better things to do, and so do they!"

With that, all the board members got up in apparent disgust, and marched out of the room. There Gliner stood, looking at the president, and gasping. Then he noticed that the president was laughing. Just then a head appeared in the door and a deep voice said, "Can we come back in now?"

It was all a hoax! He said it got him wondering what he would have done if they hadn't been kidding.*

---

*From *Sharing Ideas* newsmagazine, February–March 1988, Royal Publishing, Glendora, CA.

SPEAKER: *Did you notice how my voice filled the town hall?*

SPOUSE: *Yes, in fact, I noticed several people leave to make room for it.*
           —LARRY WILDE
           (From *Library of Laughter*, Jester Press, 1988)

Don't be bothered unnecessarily by walkouts. Two percent of the people in your audience won't like you anyway, so just tell yourself those are the ones who are leaving. Sometimes people leave and then come back. I always tell myself that they went to the bathroom, not that they just had to return to see if I was as awful as they had thought. I have had people walk out and make it a point later to tell me they had something else they had to take care of. Some people just want to get out early and get a good place in the banquet room or beat the rush out of the parking lot. Every speaker has walkouts.
           —ANITA CHEEK MILNER

To Prevent It from Happening

Of course, people *may* just be going to the restroom. But if they start leaving en masse, you're in trouble. Generally when people walk out, it is because of a prior commitment. Often the event has just been poorly planned and buses are leaving to take the group somewhere else. Weeks before your talk ask the person who planned the event if there is anything going on after your presentation that might conflict. If there is, suggest that you cut yours short. You can also plan for a group activity at the point where some will be leaving. Announce at the beginning that you will break at _____ to give those who need to go to the _____ an opportunity to leave.

What to Do

If they are all walking about because they have another event, cut to your close. Leave them with the three points you hope they will remember and say good-bye.

If they are walking out because they are bored, the only reasonable alternative is for you to panic and shoot yourself in the foot. That always grabs their attention. (For my analytical readers, that was *sarcasm*.) Try changing your tactics dramatically. If you are lecturing, switch to a group exercise, a video, film, slides—anything that will switch tracks.

Three words for you: Cut it short.
           —DOUG MALOUF

Generally, I won't highlight people walking out on me. I prefer to ignore it because it's not a positive and sometimes the people have to leave and

are already embarrassed enough. However, if I know it's not going to embarrass either them or me, I might say something.
—GENE PERRET

What to Say

Serious

I know many of you need to leave at _____ (the time). We will be doing a discussion exercise at exactly that moment. So those of you who must go, leave then. I won't let you be late! Promise. (Once the others leave, get everyone to move down closer to you.)
—LILLY WALTERS

Humorous

No, wait! I won't use any of that material that _____ (a bigwig in the group) told me to!
—LILLY WALTERS

How about that. The speaker before me was so bad that in the middle of my talk people are walking out on him.

Honest to God, sir, I get better.
—GENE PERRET

(If just one is getting up to leave, pretend that you don't notice.) Could I get one of you gentlemen (ladies) to get up and leave the room right away? (Notice the one who is leaving.) Oh, thank you! You guys are quick.
—GENE MITCHENER, THE WHEELCHAIR COMIC

Excuse me! There is a penalty for early withdrawal!
—ALAN PEASE

(In a stage whisper) Now we can talk about them.
—MICHAEL IAPOCE

(In a belligerent tone of rage, I race toward them and say) Where do you think you are going? (When the shocked departers turn and look at me, I break into a big, sincere smile) If you're coming back, I'll wait for you.

Don't worry, I've got a wireless on. I'll just tag along.

(Fall down on your knees in a theatrical overdramatized comedic manner, sobbing) Please! Don't go! I'll get better!

(After they leave, say in a sinister, foreboding voice) I can't stop you from leaving during my presentation, but I will make fun of you! (From that point on, if people try to sneak out, I let them leave in peace. This can be risky! Handle it with care.)
—MARK SANBORN

Good, I thought they'd never leave.
                    —Tom Ogden

I see my time is running out—along with a good part of my audience.
                    —From *Current Comedy Newsletter,*
                    December 23, 1991

What *Not* to Say

We didn't need them anyway.
People can be so rude!

...Audience Members Walk Around During Your Talk

To Prevent It from Happening

Why would people be walking around? Either because they are bored or because they have other business to attend to. There are three ways to prepare against boredom: rehearse, rehearse, and rehearse. If people are walking around because they have other business, the task is more difficult. People usually will not be that rude if they can avoid it.

What to Do

Call a quick group exercise while you find out from the event planner what the problem is and try to get it fixed.

What to Say

This is great! It's been years since I played musical chairs!
The speaker is supposed to walk his talk—not the audience.
                    —Tom Antion

What *Not* to Say

I hope we're not interrupting your walk?
Would you mind sitting down, please?

...Audience Members Are Too Shy to Volunteer

To Prevent It from Happening

Set a mood of fun; encourage participation.

What to Do

It usually takes a great deal of time for the first few people to volunteer. Just wait and smile. Usually someone will eventually come up. Be cautious about saying "I need a volunteer." It just feels scary somehow.

Start small and build up. During the first group exercises have people remain seated, with only light participation. As you progress, ask people to do more—perhaps stand to do the exercises or move around.

First ask them a series of questions where they have to raise their hands— a series of questions that are innocent and that they can feel comfortable in answering. "How many people are here from Kansas? How many people here have children? How many people are grandparents? How many people here graduated from college?" Then say, "I need a couple of volunteers. How many would be interested in volunteering?" Typically you will have a greater potential for response because the fear of raising their hand isn't there any more—the fear of volunteering maybe, but not of raising their hand.
—BRAD PLUMB

I always give prizes away, from the first few minutes on—candies, little toys that make the points I want to. This encourages them to volunteer.

(If members of the audience know each other) Now I need a volunteer. You pick the person who is most creative (or whatever the topic is on the day). (I let them choose and push someone up to me.)
—DEANNA BERG

Use of the term "role-play" tends to be a turnoff for potential volunteers. They immediately think, "I can't act!" Words like "opportunity to practice" or "practice exercise" work better for me.
—BEVERLY SMALLWOOD

I often need volunteers to work with me one on one during presentations, especially to demonstrate some communication techniques. I've usually asked people to think of something to say or contribute before we have our "interaction." I've also explained the task completely so they know exactly what's being asked of them, not just a blind "I need a volunteer." I ask for volunteers by saying, "There's someone here who would be willing to discuss that with me." Then waiting.

The wait is probably most important. Allow people to consider it, then volunteer. Wait up to 10 seconds. If nobody volunteers, I've usually established eye contact with one or two people who have smiled at me, made an aside to their neighbor, or in some other way signaled that they do have something to discuss; they're just a little reluctant to volunteer. I usually come off the platform, approach them, extend my hand palm out and say,

"Thanks for volunteering. Please come up." A good 99 percent of the time they graciously agree.

There have been only a couple of times that people did not agree. I let them off the hook quickly. Each time, someone else who had finally gotten up the courage volunteered right away in another part of the audience.
—BOB TREADWAY

What to Say

Serious

I need someone's help for this next part.

This next part I cannot do alone. Would one of you help me?
—LILLY WALTERS

(Hold up a copy of one of your books or tapes, and say) The wonderful person who comes to help with this role-play will win a copy of my book, 14 Reasons Corporate Speeches Don't Get the Job Done.
—MARIAN WOODALL

Humorous

Put your right hand in the air. (The person does so.) Yes, you may come up on the stage...give him a nice hand!
—PHIL CASS

I need a volunteer...someone's who's a good sport. OK, I'll take a bad sport.

I need a volunteer...someone with an open mind. OK, I'll take a Democrat (Republican).
—ROGER LANGLEY

I really need a volunteer to write on this for me. My handwriting looks like graffiti.
—LILLY WALTERS

It's a shame we have so many troubled kids writing graffiti. Judging by their illegible scrawl, they would probably have made great doctors.
—From *Speaker's Idea File*, Original Humor
section by Gary Apple, June 1993

What *Not* to Say

Oh, come on. We don't have all day.

It's all right, I won't bite.

...Your Audience Is Nodding in the Afternoon Slump

To Prevent It from Happening

When possible, ask for your program to be scheduled in the morning. Often, you will have no choice but to present in the afternoon. If you do, look over your material. Use all the bits that make people think, do, and act. If possible, do not lecture for more than 10 minutes at a time. Keep switching tracks. For example, do 10 minutes, then use an audience participation device, run a short video, then go back to 10 minutes of lecture. Discussion groups will keep people alert for up to 60 minutes, but a 45-minute limit is safer.

> *First, I maneuver it so I don't present then [afternoons]. Second, if I do, I talk to the meeting planner about a lighter, lower-fat lunch. And third, not everyone slumps in the afternoon.*
>
> *It's a mistake to always assume that dragging audiences always need to be energized with activity. Many Europeans can't work until around 4:00 p.m. Honor that. Let them drag or slump if they want and need to. It's actually a very receptive period if you use it. Give them content they need to hear in a hypnotic-like fashion. They will hear the material at several levels. More than once, when my audiences have clearly outdone themselves and were very tired but well meaning, I have conducted a meditation-like exercise wherein some people went to sleep and others were deeply relaxed. They emerged in about 15 minutes feeling terrific, refreshed, and ready to go. These were senior executives of a large bank.*
>
> —JANET LAPP

> 1. *I encourage attendees to eat a light vegetarian or fruit lunch.*
> 2. *I give them specific luncheon homework to do with another participant.*
> 3. *I literally have them run around the room at 2:45 p.m.*
>
> —MARK VICTOR HANSEN

What to Do

If you are following another speaker in afternoon session, and you must lecture, you are in trouble. Do something that will make them move. Once I was stuck with this situation. The introducer said, "...and please help me welcome Lilly Walters!" I walked up to the introducer, shook his hand, then turned around and walked away to another brightly lit spot in the *back* of the room. That got them all to sit up a bit. I said, "Please stand up." They all did. "Now stretch your hands over your head. Now to the side, now the other side. Twist to the left, twist to the right. Now grab your chair and do two mediocre knee bends! Great, since you've got your hands on your chair, pick it up and move it around. I'm going to speak from back here." They were totally awake now and curious. They figured either that I had no clue how a presentation was supposed to be given or that whatever I was going to do next would be terribly original and innovative. At least they were listening.

Bob Pike, of Creative Training Techniques, actually does a brief and simple hypnosis exercise when people come back from lunch.

To deal with afternoon slump time, I do several things:

- *Prepare a very funny opening.*

- *Perform a magic trick. (I could start with my ropes instead of end with them.)*

- *Trip on my way up to the stage and then comment on my clumsiness. "I've heard that we only use 15 percent of our brain's capacity. I'd like to know what happened to my other 85 percent."*

- *Create a highly interactive session. To get the blood going, I sometimes use the element of competition with a prize for the winning team, or perhaps give a quiz that they can take in teams.*

  —Jeff Dewar

I plan very interactive sessions so they have to get on their feet frequently. Also, I change the media often—from overhead, to slides, to paper and pencil.

  —Dianna Booher

I like shoulder rubdowns. Simply ask the group to stand and face the center aisle. Have people place their hands on the shoulders of the person in front of them and give a good rubdown. This has always worked for me, no matter what the audience. I would, however, be aware of the sensitivity of one person touching another. I always pull an audience member up on the platform and illustrate by giving a shoulder rub. Be sure to clear this with your meeting planner in advance. The way I typically handle it is to tell the planner, "Many things can go wrong during a program—from microphones dying to equipment breaking down. If that happens, is it OK for me to use a filler like a 'rubdown' till we can correct our problem?" They have always said yes, and I've never had anything but compliments and sincere thanks.

  —Michael Aun

I get them up and moving or interacting with each other in pairs or small groups at least once every 30 minutes. The process can be as simple as a 1-minute thumb-wrestling contest with someone the same size as you, or as complicated as a small group process that lasts 8 or 10 minutes.

I also use a lot more humor, jokes, overheads of cartoons, and humorous stories. I've even asked the audience to share some of their best jokes.

I have tried to become a master of 1- to 5-minute energizers. I think every speaker should have at least 20 to sprinkle throughout a presentation. I try to make them relevant to the content I'm teaching.
                                                        —Jack Canfield

Blood sugar peaks around 90 minutes after a meal, so the greatest challenge is around 2 p.m. I usually do something physical around then, once taking the audience out of the meeting room completely on a learning assignment.
    Regardless of the content or audience, I shift attention every 3 to 5 minutes. In a "fresher" time of day, I could let the energy "waves" drag out to every 8 to 10 minutes. By waves, I mean the peak of humor or activity and the valley of a transformational story.
                                                        —Janet Lapp

What to Say

Humorous

(Surprise them with a loud noisemaker.) Aha! I just wanted to see if you were still awake.
(Lead them in a quick lap around the building or hallway.)
Wouldn't it be nice if we could all take an afternoon nap like we did when we were kids?
(Lead them in a cheer.) Two bits, four bits, six bits a dollar. All for _____ (company name, sports team, etc.) stand up and holler. Yeah!
                                                        —Tom Antion

This is the Teflon hour, when nothing sticks.
                                                        —Janet Lapp

...Someone Falls Asleep During Your Presentation

To Prevent It from Happening

You have 20 minutes to give a straight lecture before the human mind will wander. I try to switch horses every 20 minutes in the morning, and every 10 minutes in the afternoon. Meaning, I try to switch from straight lecture to anything else. This tends to help keep people awake.

If people often fall asleep during your presentations, you need to take a serious look at pizzazzing up your style. Move more when you present. Speak less and do things that allow people to talk to one another. "If you always do what you've always done, you always get what you've always got." So, you *gotta* change something. Consider using a speech, humor, or magic consultant to assist you in spicing up your talk. (See Chapter 6, "An Ounce of Prevention," for examples.)

But just because people are sleeping doesn't mean you are boring. They may suffer from a sleeping disorder, have been on a plane all night, or have undergone a terrible emotional trauma that has left them drained and worn out. They may even have had a quiet heart attack or stroke and be in serious need of medical attention. Be alert to what is happening in your audience.

What to Do

Raise your voice. Walk closer to them. If that doesn't work, break the whole audience into an audience participation exercise and find out what the problem is.

—Don Dewar

Be careful when trying to wake people up. You need to be warm and sensitive to them and to the possibility that they may be in an emotional or a serious physical crisis that is causing them to sleep—or to appear to be asleep. Go to them while the rest of group is distracted with an activity and gently try to wake them. If they are just tired, quietly (so no one else can hear) suggest that they find a place to sleep.

At the first opportunity, call for a break. Quietly go the sleeping person and wake him or her up. "Excuse me, did you know you were sleeping? Are you all right? Do you need assistance?" The shock of being awakened by the presenter will usually be enough to keep the sleeper alert for the rest of your presentation. If not, the sleeper will probably leave.

—Scott Paton

I had a night-shift participant nod off in a full-day program. He started to snore. Since he had co-workers in the room going through the program, we made it a team project. At the suggestion of one of the members, we changed the clock and quickly left the room. We had the secretary ring the room. The words that we heard through the door when he thought he had slept through the rest of the day cannot be repeated for your book. The laugh tied us all together and helped him stay awake.

—Terry Paulson

When someone is sleeping in the audience, if possible I move toward that person, and I usually raise the level of my voice. As a general rule in consulting and training work, at the very beginning of the day during the "administrivia" comments (introductions, schedule overview, where the restrooms are, etc.), I also talk about their being free to stand up, move about, get coffee, and so on. Therefore, if someone dozes, I can say something like "John, please feel free to get a cup of coffee. The next couple of points are going to be critical."

—Dave Carey

What to Say

Serious

(If members of the audience tell me that someone is asleep) It's all right. His subconscious will hear what he needs to learn.
—DEANNA BERG

Humorous

Don't feel bad (for going to sleep). You couldn't help it. I've been practicing subliminal hypnotism and I guess I am better than I thought.

In Japan closing the eyes is a sign of extreme attention. I'm glad you are (were) so engrossed in my talk.

I don't mind your sleeping; your snoring is prohibited.

Why is it that she is sleeping and I'm having the nightmare?

You're not sleeping, you're dreaming about how you are going to use my material, right?

If I had known that this would happen, I would have given out pillows instead of handouts.

You were so excited about coming to my session you couldn't sleep last night, right?
—TOM ANTION

(Do a takeoff on the radio giveaways.) Oh, too bad. I had a special prize for the second person who fell asleep.
—MARIAN WOODALL

What *Not* to Say

He's sleeping! Hey! One of you guys sitting next to him, just shake him.

Some people are so rude.

Do you think you could manage to stay awake for the rest of the talk?

...You Are Much Older Than Your Audience

To Prevent It from Happening

Is age important? Well, maybe. You must answer that. For me, it does not matter how much older or younger the audience is. Now, if people are smarter than I am, I need to plan a different strategy. But it is important to decide just how you feel about the "age gap."

If you've matched your topic to the audience interests and your own credibility as a speaker, you're OK—for example, an 80-year-old retired train engineer is speaking to a group of 30-year-old railroad buffs about the good old days of railroading.

—MALCOLM KUSHNER

What to Do

I tell them an anecdote from my life at their age, something amusing and in which I did not cover myself with glory.
—PHILIP CROSBY

What to Say

Serious

I am not here to teach you, tell you, or lecture you. I wish to share with you some ideas that will help you not make the same mistakes as I've made.

—DOUG MALOUF

George Bernard Shaw said, "I am not a teacher: only a fellow traveler of whom you asked the way. I pointed ahead—ahead of myself as well as of you."

—LILLY WALTERS

Humorous

I'm now chronologically advantaged.
—TERRY PAULSON

I refuse to allow my opponent's youth and inexperience to be an issue in this campaign.
—PRESIDENT RONALD REAGAN

In preparing to speak to you today, I tried to remember what I felt about _____ (the topic) when I was your age. Unfortunately, I couldn't remember that far back.
—MALCOLM KUSHNER

Wait till you get to be 70 as a speaker. Everything you say will remind you of something else.
—LOWELL THOMAS
(Submitted by Terry Paulson)

We're only young once, but with humor, we can be immature forever.
—ART GLINER
(Submitted by Terry Paulson from *Laughter Works*, Vol. 1, January 1989)

You know, I have discovered people my age should say little and listen a lot. We're too young to call ourselves wise, and too old to resist the temptation.
—GERALD C. MEYERS

They tell you that you'll lose your mind when you grow older. What they don't tell you is that you won't miss it very much.
—MALCOLM COWLEY, AMERICAN SOCIAL HISTORIAN, BORN **1898**
(From *Great Book of Funny Quotes,* by Eileen Mason, Sterling Publishing, 1993)

...You Are Much Younger Than Your Audience

To Prevent It from Happening

Chances are you don't need to. I have worked with many speakers who feel inadequate because they are younger than their audiences. Please keep in mind that you would not have been asked to present if the event planners thought you were "too young." The only one who thinks you are "too" young is probably you.

What to Do

Don't try to overcompensate and "act" older. It shows as an "act." Just be you. If you are young—or just feel young—then act the way you feel. Audiences will like you more for being happy with who you are, than if you act like something you are not.

(To help develop an affinity with an older audience) I get out from behind the lectern, which I prefer anyway, and start out with a story of when I had a memory loss. I use my grandchildren in stories.
—PHILIP CROSBY

What to Say

I know I'm young, but I'm as old as I can be for my age.
—TERRY PAULSON

I am not young enough to know everything.
—JAMES BARRIE, SCOTTISH PLAYWRIGHT AND NOVELIST, BORN **1860**
(From *Great Book of Funny Quotes,* by Eileen Mason, Sterling Publishing, 1993)

...You Just Can't Think of a Witty Retort

To Prevent It from Happening

Ad-libs are supposed to be spontaneous—a *few* really are. The really brilliant ones are practiced, rehearsed, and drilled until they are a part of the presenter's subconscious. Take time with this book. Use a highlighter and mark all your favorites, then find ways to use them in conversations until they become part of your own personal psyche.

What to Do

You may want to keep this book with you on the platform and make a great show of looking dumbfounded, grabbing the book, and madly looking up an "ad-lib." That in itself would get a great laugh.

You can always fall back on the Jack Benny "look." Eyes a bit wide, just stare for a long, uncomfortable silence and slowly bring your hand to your chin. Support the elbow of the arm holding your chin with your other hand, and just stare some more. Silence can be one of the funniest and most eloquent things you can do.

What to Say

Start with "Well, as Aristotle said...," then lie about the quote. Say whatever you need to say—like, "Well, as Aristotle said, 'Never argue with men in blue ties on Tuesdays.'" Either the audience will know you are kidding, or Aristotle, Mark Twain, Will Rogers, or whomever you used, will get the credit—or the blame. Either way, your speech or presentation goes on.

> *You have quite the ear for a quick retort—like Van Gogh.*
> —Lilly Walters

> *Some days it just doesn't pay to get up.*
> —Roger Langley

> *OK. Wise guy in the front wipes out _____ (magician, humorist, speaker) with _____ (witty remark, quick retort, joke). Yep, the crowd has turned ugly. (Then turn to someone else in the audience, pointing) But you didn't have to change too much, did you?!*
> —Phil Cass

You are the eyelash in the eyeball of my existence!
—ANITA CHEEK MILNER

That statement leaves me dangling 'twixt heaven and earth in an ecstasy of esoteric sublimity!
—STEVE GOTTLIEB

"Remember Our Motto! Expect the Unexpected!"

3 Room and Equipment Afflictions

Several of my meeting planners asked me to tell presenters to please, *please,* practice with the equipment before they use it. Even very experienced presenters are really pretty rotten at using equipment in a smooth and easy manner. Videotape yourself using the equipment. Take serious notice of how you stumble over the cords, put things in upside down, scurry around back and forth.

Most presenters need to rely on *some* equipment—lights and mic at a minimum. Other presenters like the higher-tech equipment—videos, computer simulators, and so on. Whatever equipment you prefer, find ways of using it effortlessly. Remember, though, that no matter how much you practice, equipment breaks. Be ready to carry on in a light-hearted manner. Audiences hate to see you display your temper.

> *In 1992, I was one of several speakers at a women's conference. The keynoter was one of the big names in the speaking profession, highly respected and successful.*
>
> *At the start of his presentation, there was a bit of trouble with the sound system. It was minor, but recurring, and each time it seemed to be fixed, it happened again.*
>
> *After about six times, the speaker displayed a brief flash of temper. It was fleeting and certainly understandable, but it did not go unnoticed by the audience. There were some quiet murmurings, and the woman next to me leaned over and made an unfavorable comment about the speaker.*
>
> *Because he was so polished and professional, he had little trouble "getting" the audience again, but I've never forgotten the incident. For those of us who have less experience handling an audience, such a flare-up of temperament could be fatal.*
>
> —ANITA CHEEK MILNER

WHAT TO SAY WHEN

...The Mic Acts Up

I don't know a speaker who *doesn't* have a horror story about the mic acting up. My most embarrassing was when I was singing the national anthem for a horse show in a huge oblong stadium. I had to keep circling slowly to take in the entire audience. I always do my darndest to be expressive. I like lots of gestures and poignant, meaningful expressions. (OK, so the ham in me comes out.) I always start with, "Ladies and gentlemen, won't you please help me sing our national anthem." I did that, and with grand, sweeping expressions and gestures went on, "Oh say, can you see, by the dawn's early light...." I thought it odd that out of 800 people hardly anyone was joining in; in fact, they looked horribly confused. Unbeknownst to me, the mic cut out at "by the dawn's early...." There I was pantomiming my guts out to 800 people. The announcer decided to help me out and began singing into her mic. "The Star Spangled Banner" is a challenging piece, and unfortunately, the announcer was one of those singers who was not up to the challenge. After a few words, she realized her mistake and stopped, but the audience must have thought it was me and figured the sponsors just hadn't had the budget for a singer who could come close to the pitch in which the accompaniment was being played in or a singer who knew all the words—not a pretty picture.

I was working on a shortwave walkie-talkie radio microphone broadcasting to a loudspeaker system. Right in the middle of my remarks about my grandmother's funeral we picked up an announcement from a local radio station through my mic—advertising a fertilizer sale!

—ART LINKLETTER

On a convention stage before an enormous audience in Australia, smack in the middle of my presentation, the PA system blasted out with the music of Mick Jagger and the Rolling Stones, who were performing in another part of the building. Without missing a beat I began to dance, had the audience clap along, and kept their attention until the problem was fixed and the Stones stopped rolling.

—HERMINE HILTON

As Gene Roddenberry's lecture agent, I often traveled with him as "road manager," "show producer," and so on. We were in Minneapolis doing "The World of Star Trek with Gene Roddenberry" show. On this night we had about 6,500 patrons. This show requires excellent AV and sound equipment. About 5 minutes into the program the sound and all the AV equipment went out.

After another 5 minutes the crowd started to get restless. I asked three stagehands to remove part of the floor in front of the stage. Under the floor was ice. In a three-piece suit, and with Mr. Roddenberry yelling encouragement from the stage, I proceeded to present the worst ice-skating demonstration in the annals of skating history. Thankfully, it got some laughs. At 15 minutes without sound we heard that welcome crackle of the speaker turning on. The show is still OK! I was glad, Mr. Roddenberry was glad, and the audience was relieved (not to have to watch me anymore!). I enjoyed the skating, but felt I should keep my day job.

—DAN SAVAGE

To Prevent It from Happening

Always have a sound check. Always ask for an additional mic to be set up, tested, live, ready, and right there on the podium someplace where you can easily grab it. If the first one breaks down, go to the second.

I was doing a keynote in Washington. I carefully tested the mic with the tech guy. The first speaker went on. We all had dinner, the local band did two numbers, everything was amplified just fine. I went on—dead mic. They couldn't get it back up, so on I went. Big mistake. Fifty percent of the attendees couldn't hear me and were irked that the *supposed* know-all expert on presentation skills would be so daft as not to check her mic. (Yes, that is exactly what one of them said on his rating sheet!)

What to Do

If the mics are totally out before you go on, and the audience is over 100 classroom style or 500 theater style, don't go on. If you bellow, you will barely be able to be heard in a house that size. In a house larger than that, there will be no way your voice will carry. I'm a professional singer, my forte is "loud" à la Ethel Merman, but there is no way I'd be able to pull it off.

Have the event planners announce what is happening and ask for the audience's patience. Stay off the stage or you will become the target of the audience's frustration. If the folks in charge *insist* you go on without a mic, have them make an announcement that graciously lets the audience know you are doing what has been requested of you: "We are having technical difficulties with our sound system. We have asked Miss Walters to make a 'valiant effort' to try to bellow her presentation, which she has graciously agreed to do. If possible, please move down closer." Or you may be able to move out closer to the audience to help with the sound problems.

If the sound goes out after you have begun your talk—assuming you forgot to have that second mic ready for you—get the tech crew on it. Yell a few self-abasing "saver" lines to show how good-natured you are, and launch into an audience participation exercise while the sound gets fixed. Try to wait until the mics are up before you go back on.

It's tempting in the middle of a microphone disaster to deflect blame to any target you can find. When in pain, we want to find someone to blame. Some speakers rail at the audio people, others glare at the meeting planner or logistics team. Still others pout before the audience in a personalized version of "Poor me!" Avoid the blame frame!

Use your positive energy to pull your audience to you as your support team works to correct the problem. The audio people already feel bad enough; don't add to it. You want them putting their energy into fixing the problem, not getting even with you for making them look bad. The pros in any leadership role take more than their share of the blame and less than their share of the credit.

Learn an important lesson early—never blame people from the platform, even if you must confront them privately later. Remember, everyone makes mistakes, and some staging problems are no one's fault! They just happen!

—Terry Paulson
(From *Microphone Man,* copyright by Terry Paulson)

About 3 years ago, I was with a group of 2200 businesspeople and the sound system went out! I have a pretty strong voice, but I couldn't project to the back of the room. After it was apparent that it wasn't going to be a "quick fix," I called for an unplanned 20-minute break.

When the group got back together, the energy of the room had fallen and their attention level was definitely lower. I started out by saying, "What just happened is a great illustration of what we were just talking about! Sometimes in life when you're rolling along, something happens that's not your fault. And it throws you off course a little or a lot! The question is not whether these things are going to happen, it's a question of how you respond when they do happen.

"Do you all remember how you felt as a group just before the sound system went down? Let's all stand up and move our bodies around a little. Now turn to your neighbor and do 5 seconds of your best Three Stooges imitation." The audience did it and was laughing like crazy! Then I said, "When life crashes a tree on the road to your success, what are the best things to do? Pull the tree off the road, put a smile on your face, take steps to minimize the chances of it happening again, and keep on truckin' down the road! You have all done a fantastic job of doing just that right now!"

Then I picked up right where we left off. The event was not an interruption. It was an opportunity to enhance my program by using a real-life experience!

—NATE BOOTH

I always carry my own portable public address system in my trunk to cope with this situation and I've used it three times. Each time I've earned the undying gratitude of the host.

—TONY KING

Scott McKain exhibited the best example of dealing with mic problems that I have ever seen. He was speaking to 23,000 people—the Future Farmers of America. Many mics were being used that day: mics in the audience for the kids to ask questions from, one on the lectern. The technical people would switch the juice to the mic being used for that particular presentation. For Scott's presentation the introducer used the lectern mic and Scott walked up with his handheld wireless. The kids were thrilled and excited; they screamed a standing ovation as he came on. He raised the mic to his mouth—nothing. He figured he couldn't just stand there like a dummy and pantomime, so without skipping a beat, he went across to the lectern and started doing his presentation. But what no one realized was that through the whole time he's tapping his wireless mic held down at his side, so he hears through the sound system when the handheld goes hot, he heard his tapping—I'm sure no one else recognized it because he stopped the tapping and switched to the wireless and moved out onto the middle of the stage.

—BRAD PLUMB

What to Say

...For Microphone Feedback Problems

Now that I have your attention.

—DOUG MALOUF

Is that feedback, or is Clinton playing that saxophone again?
—From *Speaker's Idea File*, Original Humor
section by Gary Apple, premier issue

If you think that was annoying, wait till you hear my speech!
—From *Current Comedy Newsletter*,
July 29, 1991

This mic is haunted by the Ghost of Boring Speeches Past.
—From *Current Comedy Newsletter*,
November 25, 1991

I haven't heard a shriek like that since

...I got my last real estate tax bill.
...I dropped a 90-pound barbell on my lifting partner's foot.

So much for my imitation of

...two tomcats fighting for the affection of the only female in sight.
...hitting the brakes on a speeding locomotive.
...a bull elephant's mating call.

If I could hit a note like that, I'd be singing at the Met.

If you want to know what I said the last time I spoke to the IRS, that was it.

Come in Tokyo. Come in Tokyo. You can tell I saw too many World War II movies.

Could have been worse. I could have done my fingernails on a chalkboard routine.

There you have the note, now let's all sing...

What is that song? I'm tone-deaf.

Wasn't that the latest hit song by...
—ART GLINER

Oh, God is listening!
—ANONYMOUS

You can't scare me...I have children!
—UNKNOWN

Any of you who have teenagers will be used to this!
—NATE BOOTH

That must have been my lunch.
—ALAN PEASE

(Once, every time I approached the microphone, it would whistle shrilly. I'd step back, then approach it again, and it would whistle again. Finally,

the caretaker turned it down and I could safely approach it.) That's what happens when you can't get home and shower before giving a talk.
—Gene Perret

Stand back! Don't touch me! I may be radioactive!
—Unknown

Ah, the wonders of modern technology.
I see the techno-gremlins are operating again.
—Roger Burgraff

I said in the key of "C."
You rang?
I dare you to say that again.
Where does it hurt, dear?
(Exaggerated James Cagney) You dirty squealer.
(While rubbing the jaw) Ouch! That one melted my fillings!
(Haughtily) How rude! (Or) Really!
You've heard of Snow White and the Seven Dwarfs? This is Squeaky.
—Roger Langley

That concludes the musical portion of the program.
—From *A Funny Thing Happened on the Way to the Boardroom,* by Michael Iapoce, Wiley, 1988

A little more feedback, please!
Don't worry, it's only the fire alarm.
—R. Michael Walters

This is the portion of my presentation where I do my elephant impression.
I'll bet you never heard anyone clear their throat like that before.
Don't worry. I pass out earplugs at all my talks. If I don't, someone else will.
If you think that's bad, wait until I start singing.
Is there an ear, nose, and throat specialist in the crowd? You'll have plenty of business tonight if this keeps up.
The microphone and I are squealing with delight because we are both happy to be here.
For those of you who can still hear, welcome...
Squeal comes from the Latin word squeal-en, which means—you will look like a big dummy before you start your talk.
—From *One Liners for Disaster,* by Tom Antion, Anchor Publishing, 1993

Stare cautiously to the left while listening to the microphone buzz; pause and blink your eyes slowly. Then say in hushed, concerned tones, "Whatever it is, it's getting closer!"

Is this microphone mating season or something?

You know, I'm actually starting to like it.

OK, you win! (looking up as if talking to the sound) Microphone, you take the parts; I'll take melody.

Obviously, someone in the control room has already heard me before.

(Get down on your knees and pray, lifting the microphone to the heavens as for a blessing.) "All right, God, I'll change the subject!"

Facing the microphone, say "Prepare to die."
                                    —TERRY PAULSON
                                    (From *Microphone Man,* copyright by Terry
                                    L. Paulson, reprinted with permission)

Don't be alarmed, this is only a test.

(Looking at the mic as if trying to understand why it is treating you so poorly) Haven't I told you I love you?
                                    —TERRY PAULSON

Was it as good for you as it was for me?
                                    —STEVE GOTTLIEB

(Since the government has been caught more than once eavesdropping on me, I like to say) It's nice to speak into a microphone you can actually see!
                                    —JACK ANDERSON

...If the Microphone Goes Dead

The microphone once failed on Winston Churchill during an important speech. With a dramatic gesture he flung the dead mic to the ground, where it smashed in pieces. Then he thundered: "Now that we have exhausted the sources of science, we shall fall back upon Mother Nature!"

(Indicate mic) A microphone for Marcel Marceau (or Harpo Marx).
                                    —TOM OGDEN

(Tap on the mic—then ask) Is anyone at home?

How many of you in the back of the room read lips?
                                    —TERRY PAULSON

This mic reminds me of my brother-in-law—neither works.
—ROGER LANGLEY

I'd like to thank Radio Shack for providing the sound equipment this evening.
—GENE MITCHENER, THE WHEELCHAIR COMIC

That's the last time I get my equipment from Mattel.
—JEFF SLUTSKY

That idea was so powerful that it blew out this entire sound system! I would circle it if I were you!
—NATE BOOTH

(Move your lips and use gestures but say nothing.)

(Put your ear to the mic, listen intently, then ask) Is there a mortician in the house?

I think it's terminal.

Mike! Mike! Are you all right?

No need for both of us dying.

Welcome to pantomime theater.
—ROGER LANGLEY

(I gesticulate and move my lips silently and say) It's OK—I started in silent films.
—TERRY BRAVERMAN

(Put your ear to the mic, like you are trying listen to it, and say) It sounds OK to me.

(When they can't hear you at all, move your lips in a very pronounced way, wave your arms around, and when the mic goes back on, say) Well, that was the part you all came here for.

(If the floor is carpeted and the mic is totally dead, throw it in a hopeless gesture and look comically helpless.)
—R. MICHAEL WALTERS

...The Mic Stand Needs to Be Adjusted

To Prevent It from Happening

Before the event, adjust the mic stand to your height. But chances are always good that if *anyone* uses the mic before you, it will be adjusted to another height. Practice adjusting the mic you will be using so you won't feel like a buffoon when you have to readjust it as you step up on stage.

What to Do

Adjust the mic. Be calm. Make a funny. Go on with your talk.

What to Say

(My boss used this 20 years ago: Put the lavaliere way too low on your tie or blouse. As the audience encourages you to move it up higher and higher) What! Are you trying to strangle me?
—JIMMY CALANO

(When the mic slowly collapses, I pretend that I didn't notice it and just keep talking as I follow it down.)
—JIM McJUNKIN

Either I have to shrink (or grow) or this mic stand needs adjusting.
—ROGER LANGLEY

How many speakers does it take to adjust a mic stand?

When I first started speaking I thought I was supposed to get a technician to do this...I guess I was right.

For tall speakers:

I know you all want to ask me "How's the weather up here?" Well, it's calm now, but when I start talking it gets awfully windy.

I'm thankful this mic stand can rise to the occasion. I hope I can too.

This mic stand is like a variable rate mortgage. The higher it goes the less you get for your money.

Please don't hate me because I'm tall.

When are they going to put motors on these things—like those fancy lecterns.

For short speakers: (Stand on toes or jump, say one word at top of each jump) I'm...so...happy...to...be...here...
—TOM ANTION

I'll just shift this over here. (As you run your hands over your hips) It makes me feel fat.
—PHIL CASS

I had a chance to be taller when I was young. I turned it down.
—BARRY EIGEN

A $3.5 million hotel and a mic stand from Kmart.
—AL LAMPKIN

See the end of this chapter for good all-purpose savers for any technical or mechanical problem.

...The TelePrompTer Acts Up

President Clinton was speaking about health care reform. Unfortunately, the prompter was displaying the wrong speech! Luckily he had the correct speech on paper in front of him. He calmly had Vice President Gore check on the problem and just carried on.

A prompter works like a heads-up display in a jet fighter. You can look at the audience, yet still see your text in your sight line. If you never give the same speech twice, and you don't have time to thoroughly rehearse your talk, it is the best solution to help you appear more natural. It does not block the audience's view of you; in fact, the prompter is practically invisible to the audience. To bring one to a presentation, with the operators, only costs about $500 (going upward depending on rehearsal time).

In spite of the trouble Clinton had, prompters have a good track record of being reliable.

To Prevent It from Happening

However, to prevent disaster, don't go out on a stage with a prompter until you have had a dress rehearsal! Practice several times at your home or office with a prompter if possible. Days before the event, make sure the text on the screen will be easy to read: nice large type.

You actually create the text yourself, on your own word processor. The operator uses your disk and converts it into the prompt format. So make sure you don't do any editing after submitting your disk, unless you have discussed it with the planners.

Always have a hard copy of your notes on the lectern with you. Turn the pages as you deliver the talk, even though you are not looking at them. That way, if there is a problem with the prompter, you won't have to go searching for your place in your hard copy.

What to Do

Calmly find your place on your hard copy and carry on. Your listeners can't tell if the prompter is working or not. The only way they will know there is a problem is if you call their attention to it. There are very few instances when distracting their concentration from your topic is a good idea.

...The Electricity Fails and the Lights Go Off

What to Do

Immediately make a joke. Follow that by asking the people seated next to doors to open them—if they feel they can do so safely. Also, ask those next to curtained windows to open the curtains. Point out that venues almost always have auxiliary power, and the backup system should be up in a few minutes. While you are trying to find more light by opening doors and windows, make a few more jokes.

It's a good idea to keep a little flashlight in your emergency kit. As you are making jokes, grab it and shine it at the windows and doors that you want people to open. Once you have a tad more light so that people are not frightened or claustrophobic, go on with the talk. Or get people out of the room and into a sunlit area. If you are presenting in the evening, your best bet will be to wait with your flashlight and continue your talk to keep people's minds off the darkness.

What to Say

...While It Is Dark

Serious

> *(Pretend it is part of your presentation) Now, I have asked that the lights be turned out because I want you to think back on your own experiences. What lessons have you learned about _____ (your topic)?*
> —LILLY WALTERS

Humorous

> *Did the power just go out, or do I have a brain tumor?*
> —JEFF SLUTSKY

> *I'm still up here.*
>
> *Looks like the power company was serious when they said "final notice"!*
> —ROGER LANGLEY

We are going on a journey beyond sight and sound. The next stop, the Twilight Zone.

Toto? I don't think we're in Kansas anymore.

In the words of the immortal poet, Lord Tennyson, "Honor the Light Brigade." Let's add a thought or two about launching the charge now...please.
—LILLY WALTERS

I know you are out there, I can hear you breathing.
—DOUG MALOUF

Now, lets all join hands and communicate with the living.
—LORIN PAULSEN

(Yell) Could I get someone to turn off all the electricity? Thank you. (Then go on as if it was planned.)
—GENE MITCHENER, THE WHEELCHAIR COMIC

Oh, oh. I've offended someone.
—ROGER BURGRAFF

I think we ought to pass the hat and pay that bill.
—GEORGE GOLDTRAP

I was going to talk about the myth of perfection, but I guess I've already taken care of that.
—TERRY PAULSON
(From *Microphone Man,* copyright by Terry
L. Paulson, reprinted with permission)

I guess I'll have to donate a portion of my fee to the electric company.

The caterer will be here shortly with carrots for everyone.

I guess God tried to hit me with a lightning bolt, but hit your electric box instead.

I hope my talk hasn't left you in the dark.

It appears that I need to shed some more light on this subject.

Since you're all sleeping anyway, I decided to turn off the lights.

This is carrying energy conservation too far.
—From *One Liners for Disaster,* by Tom Antion,
Anchor Publishing, 1993

(I put my hand in my pocket like I'm searching for money, start to walk away from the mic, and say) Excuse me. I better go pay the light bill.
—TERRY BRAVERMAN

OK, now I am going to talk about black humor.
—Allen Klein

Keep your hands to yourself.
I didn't know this was going to be a seance.
—W Mitchell

A line from Robert Orben: "At last. The tunnel at the end of the light."
—Michael Podolinsky

I forgot to mention we have a curfew tonight.
—From *A Funny Thing Happened on the Way
to the Boardroom,* by Michael Iapoce, Wiley,
1988

...When the Lights Come Back On

(Affecting the voice of a radio announcer) We now return to our previously scheduled program, in progress.
—Dick Flavin

...The Lighting Is Terrible (People Can't See You)

To Prevent It from Happening

Check out the room before you speak. Often the track lighting can be adjusted to shine on the spot you are going to speak from.

I rarely speak from the spot where the lectern is set up. For some odd reason whoever sets up rooms insists on putting the lectern in that one special corner with the worst light.

Before you go on, stand right in the middle of the audience seating, and look at the dais area. What will people see? Often (all *too* often) there are lights set into the wall, right behind where you will stand, that will shine in their eyes when they try to look at you. Have someone unscrew these lights for you. It may make your corner even darker, but it will be easier for the audience to look at you.

What to Do

See if the track lighting in the ceiling can be adjusted before you go on. If you can, take the mic and move to a lighted spot. If the mic won't reach and the crowd is small, consider doing the presentation without the mic.

If the room has both house lights (lighting in the audience area) and stage lights (lights that hit the platform) and only the stage lighting is bad, ask to see what it all looks like with the house lights up (when the house lights are turned on higher). You may find lighting that is hitting an aisle area. Go stand out there. Just keep turning around so you make eye contact with the entire group.

I walk over to the corner of the stage and crouch to see the audience. This usually gets the administration to cooperate.
—PHILIP CROSBY

What to Say

(Lights flicker) I forgot to mention that this convention has a curfew.
—TERRY PAULSON

Anybody bring a flashlight?
—W MITCHELL

You'd think that a $40 million hotel could spend a dollar for a light bulb so we could see each other.
—ART LINKLETTER

That's it, close your eyes.
—LILLY WALTERS

This light reminds me of the last time I was mistaken for Tom Cruise (Christie Brinkley).
—LEONARD RYZMAN

Hello out there!
—GEORGE GOLDTRAP

I'm sorry about the lighting. I can see you—'course some of you may be sorry you can see me.
—ROGER LANGLEY

Can we have the amber and the opalescence turned up, please? Let's just kick in the follow spot. (Of course, nothing happens.) Thank you! That's much better.
—GENE MITCHENER, THE WHEELCHAIR COMIC

I've actually arranged this lighting—my wrinkles always look better in the dark.
—ART GLINER

What *Not* to Say

The black hole of Calcutta had it easy!

I'm sorry for the lack of professionalism on the part of the hotel (management) in setting up the lighting.

...You're Blinded by the Light

Gene Mitchener, the Wheelchair Comic, got one of his first big breaks when he was asked to open for a famous international musical celebrity. His big moment finally came. Excited, he rolled out onto the stage. Now, before Gene gets going into his talk, audiences always feel a bit awkward about how they are supposed to react to him. Once he is with them for about 5 minutes, he has them rolling.

So, out he rolled into the blinding stage lights. The audience hushed, not sure what to make of this newcomer. On he moved, thrilled, excited, terrified about this wonderful opportunity he was about to embark on...and rolled right over the edge of the stage and down the 5-foot drop into the orchestra pit! The lights were so glaring that Gene was too blinded to see the edge of the stage. Now the audience was really confused.

As he lay down there in the pit, with a few bones cracked and in a great deal of pain, he thought, "No! My first big break is *not* going to end this way!" He was still wired for sound so he shouted out, "Live from New York! It's Saturday Night!"

The crowd was hysterical; people thought he did it on purpose. The stagehands quickly got him back on stage. After the show, it was Gene who signed the most autographs.

To Prevent It from Happening

If you are performing for a big crowd—1000 or more—you are going to need good lighting. For some staging people, this means a bright stage and a dark house. For the audience, this creates the best dramatic affect. For you, this will mean being unable to see the audience, or the edge of the stage. You *must* practice in it.

Many speakers just won't allow that kind of lighting. You can't imagine a Billy Graham or Robert Schuller performing in a dark house. Try to talk the staging and production coordinator into keeping the house lights up for your presentation. If the house lights are on, you will be able to see the audience's eyes.

What to Do

If the production people refuse to turn the house lights up, you will not be able to see the edge of the stage. Be careful! You can still be dramatic, but stay away from the edge. Even if you can't see your listeners, tell your mind that you can. See them, feel them. They are there—make contact with your mind.

However, sometimes production people say they will turn up the lights, but then just forget. If so, calmly stand there and ask them to turn the house lights up.

What to Say

I have seen lighting like this once before. Yeah. It was at the Nuremberg Trials.
—STEVE ALLEN

(If the follow spot is after you) I feel like a moth up here.
—PHIL CASS

...and the Lord said, "Let there be light!" But let's not overdo it! That's some light. I confess, I confess.
—ROGER LANGLEY

I know you're out there. I can hear you—can't see you, but I can hear you.
—JIM MCJUNKIN

...The Lighting Is So Bad You Can't See Your Notes

I have spoken in some places where the lighting was so bad I couldn't see my notes. There should be a light on the lectern or right overhead.
—VINCENT BUGLIOSI

To Prevent It from Happening

- Always arrive early, before the crowd comes. Check out where you will speak.

- Request a well-lighted lectern.

- Bring a flashlight.

- Try not to use notes.

What to Do

Call a 5-minute discussion exercise while you try to fix the problem. If possible, move the lectern to a lighted spot in the room. Ask if more lighting can be brought up in the house.

Take your flashlight out of your emergency kit and use it. Place it on the lectern so it faces away from the audience and preferably is hidden from view by the lip of the lectern. This is a desperate last resort. If you use a flashlight and you need to hold it, people will see only the flashlight and be totally distracted by it.

What to Say

Ah, well—$16 million for a hotel and not $1 for a light bulb!
                                        —ART LINKLETTER

...The Room Is Too Hot

To Prevent It from Happening

The room will always seem colder when it is empty. As it fills with people, the temperature rises. Each person is actually a tiny, powerful heater. The larger the crowd, the warmer the room gets. It is much better if the room seems cold to you when you first come in. If it seems hot, immediately ask the venue management to adjust the air-conditioning. If it seems cold, leave it alone.

Ask where the air-conditioning controls are. One in a hundred will be accessible to you, but you may get lucky. At least you can find out before the event what the procedure is for adjusting the temperature.

What to Do

- Ask your assistant to go and get the air adjusted.
- Suggest that people throw business decorum to the wind and take off their coats.
- Consider opening the windows and/or the doors.
- Consider moving your session to another room, maybe even outside. (This is usually feasible only for a small group.)

What to Say

Serious

(Pretend it is part of your presentation.) Now, I have asked that the room be set this hot because I want you to experience some things. In groups of

_____, *discuss what you have experienced and how it applies to*
_____ *(the topic of the day).*
   (Try to find ways to adjust the air while people are talking. When you
start again) Now, in the same groups, come up with a list of three positive
ways this applies to _____ *(your topic) and three negative ways.*
(Continue trying to fix the air conditioning!)
—LILLY WALTERS

Humorous

(Get the appropriate names out of the program or from the meeting plan-
ner.) I would like to thank _____ *for supplying the wonderful pro-*
grams today, _____ *for organizing the door prizes, and* _____
(the CEO, or a competing company, or any person or group that has been
picked on at this event) for especially supplying—just for us today—the
thermostats.
—LILLY WALTERS

Is there any extra charge for this sauna?
—W MITCHELL

Must have been some members of Congress in here earlier.

Think of this as good training for your next trek across the Gobi Desert.
Too bad we can't get a tan too.
—ART GLINER

I tried to lower the thermostat—but it's already melted.
—From A Funny Thing Happened on the Way to
the Boardroom, by Michael Iapoce, Wiley,
1988

It's a jungle out there. And it feels like a jungle in here, too.
—From Current Comedy Newsletter,
June 24, 1991

America is a melting pot—and we're doing our share of melting in here,
too.
—From Current Comedy Newsletter,
December 9, 1991

Is it always this cold in here?

This room is soooo hot...(Wait for, or encourage, the "How hot is it?")
This room is so hot my pitcher of water almost caught on fire.
—ROGER LANGLEY

I know I'm full of hot air, but this is ridiculous.

I knew this was a hot topic—I didn't know it was this hot!
—TOM ANTION

We have added a slight special surcharge onto your hotel bill for the use of this sauna.

You've heard of sleep learning, you've heard of mind-mapping, well, _____ (the group's leader) is experimenting with a new theory called heat learning.
                                                    —LILLY WALTERS

Since the air conditioning isn't working, I'll keep my remarks brief. The last thing we need is more hot air.
                                                    —TERRY PAULSON

The thermostat was installed by a Swedish masseuse!
                                                    —GEORGE GOLDTRAP

Putting ten people in a medium-sized room will raise the room's temperature one degree an hour. (Two people and their lawyers in court can raise it a degree a minute.)
                                —From *Great Book of Funny Quotes*, by Eileen
                                  Mason, Sterling Publishing, 1993

What Not to Say

It is like a steam bath in here.

It is not my fault.

I'm sorry, I know you hate this as much as I do.

...The Room Is Too Cold

To Prevent It from Happening

Read the previous section on a room that is too hot.

What to Do

Read the previous section on a room that is too hot. Remember that if a room is cold when empty, it should be just perfect when it fills with people.

What to Say

Serious

The person next to you is so cold, he needs a little neck massage.
                                                    —DOUG MALOUF

(Pretend it is part of your presentation.) Now, I have asked that the room be set this cold because I want you to experience some things. In groups of _____ (size), discuss what you have experienced.

(When you start again) Now, in the same groups, come up with a list of three positive ways this applies to _____ (your topic) and three negative ways.

(While all this is going on, you keep trying to fix the air conditioning!)
                    —Lilly Walters

The best way I know to warm up a room like this is to fill it with laughter. So, on the count of three...

                    —Art Gliner

Humorous

Kind of hot in here, isn't it?

The manager gave the janitor orders: "Don't fire the furnace until you see the blue of their noses!"
                    —Roger Langley

Don't you love when they tell you: "Don't touch the thermostat! It's there for a reason." I don't know what that is, but there is a reason.
                    —Terry Paulson

Have they had trouble keeping you guys awake in other meetings?
                    —W Mitchell

Did we set the thermostats on Siberia?
                    —Lilly Walters

For handouts today we are passing out thermal blankets.

Frostbite presentation pamphlets will be available at the back of the room.

Don't worry. When I start talking, the room will heat up quickly.
                    —Tom Antion

Wish I had stayed home and killed hogs!
                    —George Goldtrap

I asked the janitor to turn on some heat—but he said he had to go feed the polar bears.
                    —From *A Funny Thing Happened on the Way to the Boardroom*, by Michael Iapoce, Wiley, 1988

As the first speaker, it's up to me to break the ice. In this case, literally.

Jack Frost is nipping at my notes.

We've been asked to keep the temperature low because Mrs. Paul (and her fish sticks) is (are) in the audience.
                    —From *Current Comedy Newsletter*, November 25, 1991

It's sure cold in here. And it's only going to get worse once I start speak-
ing and the wind chill factor takes effect.
                                —From *Current Comedy Newsletter*,
                                    December 9, 1991

...The Room Is Too Small,
Packed Too Tight, Set Up
Wrong, Not Enough Chairs

They put me in an L-shaped room. I told them, "This won't work! Don't
you understand? The half seated in the other part of the room won't be
able to see me!"
    "Really?" It honestly had not occurred to them.
    They put me in the corner of the L—the only spot in the room with no
light at all. So they had a drunk man sit in front of me with a wavering
flashlight shining up into my nostrils. I looked like the ghoul from hell! I
kept saying to myself, "This too shall pass...I'm a professional, I can han-
dle this. This too shall pass...I'm a professional, I can handle this...."
                                —BILL WOLFF

Mark Mayfield was speaking at a banquet for high school shop teachers.
At the last minute the planners realized they needed more seats at the
head table, which was set up on a 6-inch riser. Instead of putting up a
larger riser, the hotel just set up more seats at the table. Everyone up there
was real—real—tight. What the hotel staff hadn't taken into considera-
tion was that a couple of the people were rather large and took up more
than their allotted space. As people were jockeying for position, one guy
moved over and fell right off the side! As he was falling off, he grabbed the
tablecloth, at which point all the glasses and silver start falling into peo-
ple's laps. So people quickly moved backward and three more fell off the
back. Luckily no one was hurt, but the place was up for grabs.
    Once order was restored, the evening went on with the awards, one of
which was for going a whole year without an "accident" or "injury."
They had an Olympic theme for their event, so when the man came up to
get the award he stood on a pedestal—where the ceiling fan whacked him
in the head! And then they announced it was time for the speakers to go
on. The next day the newspaper had a picture of this man holding his
Safety Award plaque in one hand and his bleeding head in the other.
                                —BRAD PLUMB

To Prevent It from Happening

Submit a seating chart to the event coordinator weeks in advance.
Always bring an extra copy in the hopes you will be there early
enough to fix problems that come up.

My needs are very simple. For my full-day sessions I submit the room setup in Figure 3-1. For my shorter presentations (20 to 90 minutes), I submit this request:

> For audiences of over 50 people, please provide a lavaliere, lapel wireless microphone (preferred); a long-cord lapel microphone is acceptable; if neither is available, a handheld microphone, detachable from the lectern, with a long cord will do. Lilly will also need a lectern to set props with a glass of water; a table for her books and products next to the coffee table in her room (if one is provided) or by the main exit door; two assistants. Please set up the lectern in the portion of the room with the most light.

Room Setup

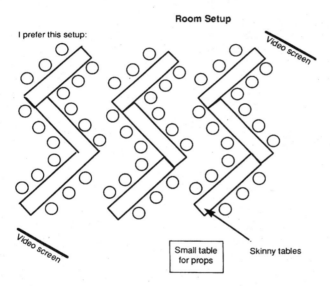

I prefer this setup:

Video screen

Video screen

Small table for props

Skinny tables

If your room <u>will not</u> allow for the setup above, either of these are acceptable:

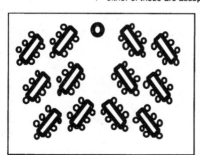
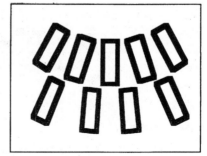

Figure 3-1. Example of a room seating chart that the presenter should provide to the event coordinator.

What to Do

If the seating arrangement is really horrid, then fix it. Just have each attendee grab a chair and move it. Don't make a fuss; do it with a smile.

Consider moving yourself. You may be able just to move to the back, side, or even the middle of the room to deliver your presentation. Calmly do it. People will never know you hadn't planned it that way all along.

What to Say

Serious

(Pretend it is part of your presentation.) Now, I have asked that the room be set up this way because I want you to experience some things. In groups of _____ (size), discuss what you have experienced.

(When you start again) Now, in the same groups, come up with a list of three positive ways this applies to _____ (your topic) and three negative ways.

(While all this is going on, you keep trying to fix the seating!)
—LILLY WALTERS

Humorous

The next time you open a tin of sardines, you now know how they feel.
—DOUG MALOUF

I must be a big hit.
—W MITCHELL

Einstein said space and time are expanding, but apparently not fast enough.
—ROGER LANGLEY

I guess the bar was closed.
—LILLY WALTERS

Don't worry too much if you don't have a chair right now. They tend to open up real quickly during my presentations!
—NATE BOOTH

The economy is shrinking—and so are these meeting rooms.
—From *Current Comedy Newsletter,*
June 10, 1991

What *Not* to Say

Someone should talk to the committee that set up this room. I know it was a committee—only a committee could come up with something this inappropriate.

...The Lectern Is Inappropriate for Your Speech

You'd be surprised how often you find poor lecterns. I always ask the sponsor for a lectern that is wide enough for two legal-size pages to be set side by side. Otherwise, after I speak from each page, I have to pick up my stack of pages with one hand. Though small, this is an unnecessary interruption.

The incline on the lectern should be just slightly up from the body— sometimes, if it is too steep you have to find something to put at the bottom to prevent your papers from falling off the lectern.

—VINCENT BUGLIOSI

To Prevent It from Happening

Make sure to include all your room requirements on your equipment needs list. Always send a list with your room and audiovisual needs. Make sure it is very clear. Jeff Dewar uses wording like this:

Cordless mic preferred, neck-hanging type lavaliere with long cord acceptable; 35mm carousel slide projector (tested) with remote control, extension cord, and screen. Please note: Extension cord for slide projector remote device must reach from the projector to the lectern (standard cords are usually too short).

W Mitchell and Gene Mitchener both speak from their wheelchairs. They always send their unique requirements—a ramp, no lectern, wireless lavaliere microphone—with the initial contract. But they always arrive early to make sure it has all been set up right.

If the size of the lectern is a perpetual challenge to you, consider not using a lectern. My brother, R. Michael Walters, an attorney, speaks on "Dealing with Difficult People." He says you need to revert to the oldest laws of all to deal with people—the laws of human nature. The first thing to do when you are confronted with an angry customer or irritable client is to get on the same side of the counter or table as he or she is. The ancient laws of human nature say that is where a friend is. Only the enemy hides behind the barriers.

If you are comfortable enough and your presentation is one you give often enough to allow you familiarity with the material, get out from behind barriers like lecterns.

The whole idea is to shorten, even eliminate, the distance between you and your audience. You want them to identify with you.

—DAVE CAREY

What to Do

If the lectern is wrong, don't be too big of a pain in the side to the people planning the event. Well before the audience comes in the room, again ask them nicely if it would be a hassle to change it. If it is, just let it go. Both W Mitchell and Gene Mitchener have faced situations where no ramp was provided for their wheelchairs. They had to be carried on stage rather than get there under their own power, which could and would be humiliating to people with a lesser sense of self-worth—and a lesser sense of humor. But they just did what needed to be done.

Try turning the lectern sideways. You can then be seen fully by the audience.

What to Say

I think I'll just wait until after I speak to get behind this thing. In case you throw things.
—Roger Langley

...If the Lectern Is Too High

I had a chance to be taller when I was young. I turned it down.
—Barry Eigen

I'm not short. I just wear special shoes.
—Ron Lee

You may wonder about the size of this lectern. It's called a coffin-style lectern. It's perfect for speakers like me who have occasion to give jokes immediate burial!
—Art Gliner

I'm not short. I'm vertically challenged. I'm not fat either—just horizontally challenged.
—R. Michael Walters

(Stand on toes or jump, say one word at top of each jump) I'm...so... happy...to...be...here...
—Tom Antion

I used to be taller, but they kept asking me for an idea off the top of my head....
—Jeff Slutsky

...The Overhead or Slide Projector Acts Up

Overhead slides are the easiest of the professional visual-aid options to use. Everybody uses them! But it's hard to stand out and be unusual if you use "plain old overheads." On the other hand, they are quick and inexpensive. Almost everyone has a copy machine, and that's all it takes to make an overhead slide. Next to a flipchart, they are the easiest to prepare. They give you greater control than 35mm slides, because you can easily decide not to show "the next few" if you get rushed for time, and no one but you knows the difference. Anything that can be photocopied can be turned into a colorful transparency. I have heard many people say that a color overhead provides greater retention than a clear overhead.

The drawbacks to overhead slides are that they can easily be dropped and get out of order. Also, if your presentation does not allow for keeping them in a set order, it will be awkward shuffling through them.

Computers can now be tied right into the overhead using LCD projection devices. As the audience makes suggestions and changes, you push a button and there it is on the screen.

To Prevent It from Happening

- Always test your equipment.
- Always bring an extra bulb.
- Always assume the projector is going to break anyway.

What to Do

There are a lot of speakers out there who use the A/V (audiovisual) as a crutch. They crumble if there is a problem with it. They are not used to members of the audience looking them in the eye—they are used to them looking at the charts on the wall, or the slides, while they stand in the dark. They had darn well better learn their shtick with people looking at them in the face.
—BRAD PLUMB

I try to buy the audiovisual person time to fix the problem. I get the audience members to give one another a back rub if the problem is minor. If there is no A/V man present, I'll have them break into groups of four and discuss the point we're currently making while I fix the A/V problem.
—MICHAEL AUN

The audience members should never know there is a "problem." If you cannot seek help without them knowing what is going on, then act as if using your overhead was a teeny, tiny portion of your presentation, really of very little significance—regardless of how desperately important the slides really are to your presentation. Then you must just carry on.

Do not explain what each slide looked like. *Do not* say, "Well, if you could have seen the next slide it would have looked like...." Just give the presentation without making reference to the slides. "Talk" the message that is on the slides—don't refer to the slides if they are not there.

What to Say

Humorous

I'd like to thank Radio Shack for providing the equipment this evening.
—GENE MITCHENER, THE WHEELCHAIR COMIC

(I sometimes pick on the A/V guy while he is fixing the problem.) You buy them books...you send them to school...and this is what your kids do to you.
—MICHAEL AUN

I am more high fashion than high tech.*
—PATRICIA FRIPP

Was this machine provided by the low bidder?
—ED McMANUS, THE JOKESMITH

This must be one of the those old wood-burning models.
—ROGER LANGLEY

This machine was working fine this morning. Wait a minute! I wondered why that NBC news crew was lurking about.
—From *Speaker's Idea File*, May 1993

(Use this one only if you never hope to work for a competitor.) This _____ (broken or malfunctioning item) must have been made by _____ (competing company).
—From *One Liners for Disaster*, by Tom Antion, Anchor Publishing, 1993

(I hold the tiny overhead or slide up in the air and say) This is where I was going to show you a visual. Well, here it is.
—ALLEN KLEIN

Once again, a technical challenge!
—ROGER BURGRAFF

Some projectors are better than others. This is one of the others.
—LEONARD RYZMAN

---

*Patricia Fripp is a very sophisticated, fashionable dresser who uses references about her image a great deal in her talk—with excellent effect.

...The Light Goes Out in the Projector

To Prevent It from Happening

Always carry a spare bulb and practice how to put it in quickly.

What to Do

Make a joke as you casually and calmly put your spare bulb in. At the break, see about getting *another* extra bulb for when your spare one gives up the ghost!

What to Say

Overriding principle according to Nathan Hale—I will only regret it if I have but one bulb to lose for my audience.

This is the first time I have been brighter than my equipment.

I don't understand. I left this thing on day and night for 6 days to make sure the bulb worked.

(Talk to projector lovingly while patting it) Now, don't be shy. These nice people really want to see you. (Sternly) And so do I.

(Wave hand in front of the lens) Wake up in there. Yoo hoo. Wake up.

I have a joke. How many projectors does it take to mess up one presentation?

Patrick Henry said, "Give me liberty or give me a light bulb."

Does anyone (in the audience) happen to have a (long description, recited quickly) quartz, 2-prong, model 921 EYB, 125-volt, 250-watt overhead projector lamp on them?

These overheads (slides) are a little darker than I expected.

(Refer to blank screen) Can everyone see this in the back—or front—or anywhere?

(Refer to blank screen) Don't you enjoy the vivid colors of my visuals?

(Pretend to find a service tag and pretend to read) Last serviced by Thomas Edison.

—From *One Liners for Disaster,* by Tom Antion,
Anchor Publishing, 1993

I do my best work in the dark.

Is there a boy scout in the house?
—ROGER LANGLEY

I know what you're thinking, "How many speakers does it take to change a light bulb?"
—ED MCMANUS, THE JOKESMITH

...The Slides Are In Upside Down

To Prevent It from Happening

Always test your equipment, in the room where the presentation will be, with the equipment that is being supplied. Some slide projectors flip your slides to view them—so even though you have placed them the way you do *every* time, they will be upside down when viewed.

Always beware of audiovisual people who don't want to let you test your slides. These are the first people who will have them in upside down.

What to Do

Make a lighthearted comment and turn the slide or overhead around. If the entire slide carousel is improperly inserted in the projector, make a lighthearted comment and ask your assistant to fix the problem while you go on with the show. Try to stand in a part of the room that will pull people's attention away from the screen and from the assistant fixing the slides.

If you don't have an assistant, launch into an audience participation exercise. (See Chapter 5.) Simply carry on as if it was always your intention to do the audience participation exercise. Then calmly flip the slides over.

What to Say

This slide looks good no matter how you look at it.

I'll get another one; this one must be defective.

I have reversed my position on this issue.

I really want you to try to understand my position on this.

Maybe if I turn the screen over, you'll be able to see this one better.

It was really difficult to take this picture.

If this slide doesn't confuse you, then you'll love the rest of my presentation.

This is my favorite slide, and I didn't want anyone else to see it.

This slide holds a very special position in my carousel.
—From *One Liners for Disaster*, by Tom Antion, Anchor Publishing, 1993

I'm sorry. Sometimes I just love to stand on my head to take photos.
—GENE MITCHENER, THE WHEELCHAIR COMIC

Now what's wrong with this picture?
—LILLY WALTERS

That means we'll stand on our head to get your business!
—ED McMANUS, THE JOKESMITH

Now, if you would all please stand on your heads.
—ROGER LANGLEY

What *Not* to Say

Look, I need to fix this, so I want you to...(Just launch into the exercise; don't emphasize the problem.)

Please don't watch my assistant fix the slide carousel; just look over here at me. (That is the best way to ensure they will look at your assistant.)

...Your Highlighter Runs Out of Ink

To Prevent It from Happening

Carry a spare highlighter in your emergency kit. Always ask the venue if they keep spares (in addition to the one you carry). Chances are several pens will go out before you get done with your talk.

What to Do

- Make a lighthearted comment and grab one of your spares.

- If you don't have any more spares, make a lighthearted comment and stop using the flipcharts.

- Launch into a group discussion exercise while you go find another marker.

- Don't make any kind of comment about it being a *problem*. Carry on as if you never really intended to use the marker in the first place.

What to Say

Now what's wrong with this picture?
—LILLY WALTERS

This is the dry part of my presentation.
I'm out of ink. I'll be back in a wink. ("K" words are funny.)

I wish I'd bought the extended warranty on this.

Does anyone know where I can get this serviced?

Old speakers never die. Their highlighter just fades off into the sunset.

No comment.

—From *One Liners for Disaster*, by Tom Antion,
Anchor Publishing, 1993

The magic has gone out of my marker.
—ROGER LANGLEY

Just teasing.

—DOUG MALOUF

What *Not* to Say

_____, I thought you would have checked this before the meeting.

...You Have Lots of Handouts to Pass Out

A handout is an excellent way to summarize all that information that you know they will never remember if you just tell them.

To Prevent It from Happening

My mother specializes in seminars on the topic "Speak and Grow Rich" (the title of the book she and I coauthored). It's a high-cost seminar with a small audience. (Normally, 10 to 20 people attend.) She passes out about 30 handouts as the day progresses. This would be daunting to most presenters, but she handles it rather simply. She has a thin accordion folder for each handout, clearly labeled. When she decides on a new handout for her seminar, her assistant back at her office makes 100 copies and puts them in a new folder. These folders all go in a box and the box follows her to the seminar. She has all the folders in order. She just grabs the first one when she is ready for it, hands it to a person in front and says, "Take one and pass it." The last person at the back walks the folder up to her when it has made its rounds, and it goes in the back of the box. This would be a disaster in a big group, but it is simplicity itself for Mom.

You can also have the handouts percolated into one big handout, a workbook. Have them at each person's place before the presentation begins, or hand them to people as they walk in the door.

Tip: Do not say, "Oh, I have included that in the appendix at the back of the handout; you can look at it later." Every person will stop listening to you and turn to the handout and look. Instead say, "Yes, I have complete details on that. I will see that you have them by the end of the day." At the end of day, you point out all the stuff in the appendix.

I always pass out the handouts before the audience enters. If you keep people very involved, they won't riffle through them.

—Deanna Berg

The best method is to put your handouts on a table outside the main entrance to the room. Put up a big cardboard sign saying something like:

Easy Money Seminar Students
Welcome!!
Please take a blue sheet

If you deal with more expensive reproduction items such as workbooks, have a helper stand by the door and hand out books to people as they enter. Or give them out at the registration desk. If you need to give handouts during a seminar, put them on a table and have people retrieve their own, one table or section at a time.

—David R. Villanueva

What to Do

Sometimes you just don't want people to have the handouts until a certain spot in your talk. Get the audience to help you. Hide them somewhere in the audience in small bundles of 10 or 20. Perhaps put one set under each table, or under the end of the chair in each row. Then ask people to pass them out at the appropriate moment. Don't make reference to the handouts until that moment.

What to Say

In my normal job as a beggar I'm usually asking for handouts, but today I'm giving them out.

—Tom Antion

(As you hand them out) I don't want you to say you've taken nothing away from my presentation!

—Lilly Walters

(If it looks like people are going to start riffling through the predistributed handouts) Raise your hands. Now, repeat after me, "I promise not to read the handouts until we get to that part of my presentation."

—Deanna Berg

I've been handing out a lot of awful programs...er, an awful lot of programs.

— PHIL CASS

...You Run Out of Handouts

Always have enough for each person in the audience. "Pretty basic," you're thinking. "Of course, I will." Well, I did a dinner keynote for an aerospace company in the great northwest of the United States. I don't normally use a handout for a dinner, but they requested that I prepare one, and it certainly never hurts to have an outline which everyone can use to follow along. So I sent the aerospace folks the master, and they had it duplicated in their facility. As we sat down to dinner I asked my host, "Where are the handouts?"

"Oh, I put one at each table in case anyone wants one."

One? I thought. Why only one? How do I have a whole table use one? Oh well, you must make do. As I gave the talk, I casually mentioned, "There is a handout at each table in case anyone wants one."

On their rating sheets, *several* people complained about how unprofessional I was not to have supplied them *all* with the handouts. Ah well...life on the platform.

To Prevent It from Happening

If you are going to use handouts, make sure each person has one. Always have about 10 percent over the estimated number of attendees, but, just in case, know where the copy machine is and have an assistant at the ready.

What to Do

If you realize you don't have enough handouts for everyone, try one of these strategies:

- Don't use them at all.
- Do without them until your assistant can get copies made.
- Set the ones you do have back at the exit doors. As a closing statement say, "For those of you who want more information, there are some handouts by the exit door." Not everyone will take one, so with luck there will be enough.
- Assign one handout to every two people. Make sure you use this as an exercise somehow—by discussing what people have to do to make sharing a handout work.

Whichever strategy you decide on, *don't* mention that you are short on handouts. No one needs to know but you!

This has happened to me when more people are "shooed in the door" than we expected.

I deal with this from the left brain–right brain aspect. Ask for hands raised on "Who keeps organized files and/or alphabetizes their refrigerator items?" "Who has at least one unlabeled box from a previous office or house move still unopened?"

Then ask the "unopened box" people to give their materials to the "organized file" people.

The "file" people will not gain anything from the experience if they don't have a workbook or handout in hand, and the "box" people are secretly happy with the freedom of no materials. (If you notice, the "box" people in any group rarely fill in anything they're asked to, and would be just as happy with plain paper and some colored markers. So carry those!) This can be a great way of bringing a group together, whether they know one another or not. I'm very right-brained, and so I announce that I'm probably going to drive the "file" people crazy and they will need the materials to keep me on track. In fact, one of the "file" people usually becomes a self-appointed "keeper" of what I say. That shows we all need each other's talents!
—Kristin Koeppl

What to Say

Serious

You may have noticed there are not enough handouts for each of you to have your own. You will need to share _____ per handout. There are several reasons for this. I want you to tell me at least one of those reasons by the end of the session.
—Lilly Walters

Humorous

And for the rest of you, we'll pretend we are in high school. Just look at the other person's paper—and cheat!
—Gene Mitchener, The Wheelchair Comic

Will all those who have handouts please raise your hands? OK, handouts. Now the left outs.

There are two kinds of people here today. Those of you who took handouts and the Republicans.

Those of you who didn't get a handout look at it this way: You won't have to hold it, carry it back to your room, pack it, carry it home, leave it around for a week, then have your spouse throw it out! Not having this handout will save you a lot of work and aggravation—and it could save your marriage!
—Roger Langley

---

*I feel a little bit like General Custer. I just didn't realize there would be so
darn many of you.*
                                        —Gene Perret

---

*Our copier has good days and bad days. Guess what it had when I did
these copies?*

*There are 40 people in the room; we have only 30 handouts. It is time to
start saving some trees.*
                                        —Doug Malouf

These are limited-edition handouts.

What a great opportunity to sit close and network!

My dog ate my handouts.

Send me your business card—and $2500—and I'll send you one.
                                        —Ton Antion

---

*What, we ran out of notebooks? Fantastic. We get to play musical note-
books. Everybody stand up. When I start the music, we move around the
room and when the music stops you sit down (pause with look). Just kidding! Does anyone have a buddy here who would be willing to share a
handout and make a copy? If not, does anyone have a clean copy we could
get copied during the break? If not, give me your card. I'll send you a copy
and you get a benefit—a reminder 2 weeks from now.*
                                        —Terry Paulson

What *Not* to Say

I'm sorry. I told _____ to make enough for everyone.

I don't know how this happens.

Just try to make the best of it.

...You Can't Find the Prop,
Visual, or Document

To Prevent It from Happening

Try one, or several, of the following ideas.

- Color-coordinate your materials.

- Rehearse your presentation, with all your props, materials, and
  equipment.

- Take time before the audience enters to arrange your materials carefully.

- Keep your materials simple, use fewer "things"—less is better.

- Launch the audience into a discussion exercise amongst themselves
  while you try to find the missing item.

What to Do

No one but you knows what you were planning on covering and how you planned on presenting it. Just carry on with a smile on your face. Consider using other media to make your point. For example, go to the flipchart and make a simple drawing of the concept you were trying to convey (via slide or prop) to your listeners.

What to Say

My dog ate my _____ (visual/paper/etc.).

I had it here just a month ago.

Just give me a few hours. I'll find it.

(Pull out any piece of paper. Pretend it is a note to you.) Dear (your name): I borrowed that (visual/paper/etc.). I knew you wouldn't mind. Signed (college roommate or any individual, not in attendance, who is significant to the group).

Is there a magician in the house that can make my _____ (visual/ paper/etc.) reappear?

—From *One Liners for Disaster,* by Tom Antion, Anchor Publishing, 1993

I will get this organized when I grow up.
—Doug Malouf

This you've got to see—the invisible visual.
—Roger Langley

...You Drop Your Prop, Visual, or Document

To Prevent It from Happening

Rehearse with all your props and materials before the event. When your adrenaline kicks in, you may zoom in a fumble-finger mode. Practicing with your props is a great antidote for nerves.

What to Do

Make a funny, pick up what you dropped, and carry on. Don't let it throw you. They will love you more if you display some basic human frailties, like dropping stuff once in awhile. They like to know you are just an average guy who makes a boo-boo now and again.

What to Say

Hey, it's an acquired skill.
                                        —BOB BURG

Let me stop and do a stretching exercise. I do this to stay in shape.
                            —W MITCHELL

This information is too hot to handle.
                                    —ROGER LANGLEY

That's the first time I dropped that...again.
                            —JOHN KINDE

(Substitute an actual object for the word "item" in all the following.)

That item must have been nervous.
I must be so boring that that item tried to commit suicide.
I guess that item disagreed with my last point.
Is that item the signal that I have talked too long?
I hope my point hits as hard as that item just did.

(Look upward and hold your hands as if you were praying.)
I swear I didn't make up that last point.
If it wasn't for gravity, that would never have happened.
I'm going to pretend that didn't happen.
(Like Clint Eastwood) Go ahead. Break my day.
I was just trying to wake you up.
                            —From *One Liners for Disaster*, by Tom Antion,
                            Anchor Publishing, 1993

I bet you're wondering why I'm so disorganized. Picture this. I'm driving here, the radio going, and BOMB! Into the back of my car, a meteorite crashes and messes up my stuff!
   No? You're not buyin' that? OK, how about this one? It was a land mine. No, OK how about...
                            —JIM MCJUNKIN

You know, creative people have a hard time finding things (smile). So, we need a team exercise: you find it. (And they come right up and find it!)
                            —DEANNA BERG

A few years ago there was reference to one prominent public speaker who—it was said—couldn't chew gum and talk at the same time. Well, I've just discovered I can't give a speech and handle my notes (slides, whatever) at the same time.
                            —STEVE ALLEN
                            (From *How to Make a Speech*, McGraw-Hill,
                            1986)

I'm just checking to see if gravity is still working.
—ALLEN KLEIN

...Someone Hands You a Piece of Paper

To Prevent It from Happening

Some event planners are new at holding meetings. They have no idea that you might not appreciate knowing that interesting bit of trivia they hand you in a note—right in the middle of your talk! Before your talk, nicely ask them to please refrain from interrupting you in any way, except to give you your timing signals from the back of the house.

What to Do

If you do receive a note, it will usually say that you are running over-time, or offer some other kind of bad news. Either way, you don't want the audience to know what is going on. So make a joke about it (see below), and find a way to deal with the item in question without involving the audience. Perhaps have people go into a discussion exercise to gain the few minutes you need to deal with the situation.

What to Say

(Using the name of one of the attendees) Jane Smith, your baby-sitter called. She wants to know the number of the fire department.
—R. MICHAEL WALTERS

(Wink at them) Just a note from the President.
—JIMMY CALANO

(Using the name of one of the attendees) Mark Jones, never mind about moving your car out of the way of the painters. Oh, and they said to tell you the color really matches pretty darn good.
—LILLY WALTERS

Will the owner of a 1984 lime-green Yugo please report to the parking lot to move your car? The head valet says it's embarrassing the management.
—TOM OGDEN

(Call out in horror) What do you mean I've been served?!

(As if reading aloud) Don't forget to pick up milk and bread.

Oh, good news. It's my psychiatrist report. He says I don't have an inferiority complex. I'm just inferior.
—TOM ANTION

*(To the person who handed you the note) Would you please call them back
and tell them their check is in the mail?*
                                                    —RON DENTINGER

Just what I need—a new joke.
(Open it.) "Don't look down, but your fly…"
                                                    —ROGER LANGLEY

…Someone Misses a Cue

To Prevent It from Happening

Always try to have a rehearsal with your support crew. How often
does it happen that you are *able* to have a rehearsal in an average business meeting? Almost never. But it's a great idea—not feasible, but
great.

What you can do is have sheet of paper with the exact cues of who
does what when. See Figure 3-2 for an example. You can write this sort
of script for your entire presentation. If you need three support people—one on lights, one on video, and one on sound—then each one
needs a copy of the script with his or her part highlighted.

When feasible, walk people through how their machines work.
Don't show them; let them do it and you watch. Start with the equipment being all the way off, and have them bring it all the way back on,
then all the way off again. Don't think because it is just too simple for
words that you need not be bothered wasting words on it. The one
time you stand up there at the height of a dramatic moment and wait

---

**(Lilly will tell story of small child called Bob. Last two sentences
are:)**

As Winston Churchill said, "Never, never give in. Never give in."

(Lights begin to dim; hit PLAY on video.)

"Never, never, never, never—in nothing great or small, large or
petty—never give in except to convictions of honor and good sense."

(Lights full dark; video is playing.)

Figure 3-2. Sample rehearsal script.

for something to happen that just doesn't happen, you will learn this lesson way down deep!

What to Do

During a musical theater production of *Little Mermaid*, I was doing a monologue on stage. My character was the narrator of the show. I was supposed to throw a line and Neptune was to start yelling backstage in a frenzy. I threw the line—poignant silence. I put my hand to my ear and said, "Uh, Oh! Did you all hear that? Neptune is really mad now!" OK, the audience bought it. Right then the next character was supposed to come skipping along the stage in front of me. Nothing. Neptune was then supposed to start yelling—again. Still nothing. There I was looking at 500 faithful little kids and their parents who just *knew* everything was going as planned.

Talk about an adrenaline rush. I just kept up with "Do you hear how mad Neptune is?" Then I talked about the other character and how I had heard just a few minutes before that—and I proceeded to describe what the audience would have learned had the actor shown up as he was supposed to! By that time, whatever problems were occurring backstage got patched up, and we moved on to the next scene. The audience never knew. That's the magic of theater—that "willing suspension of disbelief." Whatever goes wrong, just carry on as if you planned it that way all along.

Your audience should never sense if there is a problem. If the lights go out at an obvious wrong spot, or the video starts playing something when it's not supposed to, the only cover you can have is to have a good time with it. The audience will respond to any catastrophe with the same attitude you do. Laugh inside and out, and so will they.

What to Say

The strange thing is she (he) was the only one who showed up at rehearsal.
—GENE PERRET

In rehearsal we got it just right.
—W MITCHELL

Were we ever married?
Did you marry my ex-wife?
—JIM McJUNKIN

_____, my mind is on lunch too! Let's try it again!
—DOTTIE WALTERS

...Servers Start Clearing the Room While You Are Talking

When a humorist began his presentation to a prestigious meeting, a waitress at the end of the head table began picking up soiled plates. She stacked them vigorously on top of one another. Three thousand eyes left the speaker, turned fascinated to the waitress. Oblivious to everything, she doggedly continued stacking. The racket made speaking impossible. The humorist turned and looked at her, swiveled to the audience with a broad, sweeping gesture, and yelled over the din, "Have you all met my wife?" The audience howled.*

To Prevent It from Happening

Several days before the event, mention to the event planners that your presentation will be more effective if no one serves or clears while you are speaking. If they agree, an hour before your presentation go to the head server and confirm that no one will be serving or clearing while you speak. Event planners often get busy and just forget to mention it to the serving staff.

> *The greatest compliment for a banquet speaker is not the standing ovation. It's when the banquet employees linger by the door, listening to your talk.*
>
> —ANITA CHEEK MILNER

What to Do

Launch into a discussion exercise. (See Chapter 5 for examples.) Then go quietly up to the servers and ask them to wait until you are done speaking before you continue.

> *"Hey, could I have another helping of this cake when you come back in?"*
>
> *If I can, with humor, attract the server over to me, I might whisper to him or her—while the audience laughs at the cake line—"Would you mind asking them to stop clearing until I'm finished?" But I would never make this demand to a server or anyone else in a loud voice in front of the audience. It doesn't pay to embarrass people who probably didn't know they were doing something wrong.*
>
> —HOPE MIHALAP

*From *Sharing Ideas* newsmagazine, February–March 1988, Royal Publishing, Glendora, CA.

What to Say

(Start to help clear the table with noise while you speak. Look at the server and with a sweeping gesture say to the audience) Have you all met my wife (mother, father, husband)?
—TERRY PAULSON

Well, they're right on time, and you can see that they are energetic about doing their work.
—W MITCHELL

When I first started speaking, I wasn't very good. The meeting planner told me to shut up and sit down because I was interrupting the busboys.
—TOM ANTION

Pleadingly, "Mom!"
Make him finish his vegetables.
Oh, is the dishwasher leaving early tonight?
Just stack them and we'll wash them later.
He handles china like he was Russian.
—ROGER LANGLEY

My! He (she) has a lot of energy; makes me feel like a snail on Valium!
—JEFF DEWAR

I'd like to introduce my wife. We have an agreement: I speak and she clears.
—ANONYMOUS

What *Not* to Say

Look, you can't have a speaker and you guys clearing at the same time. Would you mind not doing that now?

I'm sure it would be better if you did that later.

Let's take a vote. Those of you who think it is a bad idea to have these people clearing the tables, raise your hands.

...Repair People Are Walking Around During Your Talk

To Prevent It from Happening

Ask the management of the venue to keep the repair people out of your event. Unfortunately, it is going to happen anyway. Sometimes there is something going on in another part of the venue that makes it imperative for them to get into your room while you are talking.

What to Do

If your group is small, consider moving into another room—maybe even to the hallway, or outside for a change of scene—while the repair people use your room as needed. Or launch the audience into a discussion exercise while you see what the problem is. Then make a decision to clear the room, postpone your meeting, or come to a compromise.

What to Say

While the repair people are here, let's all repair to the next room.
—ROGER LANGLEY

Some speakers will go to any length to steal my material.
—TERRY BRAVERMAN

(To the repair person) You don't fool me. I know who you are! Those guys at _____ (rival company or division) will go to any lengths to find out what we're doing over here!
—LILLY WALTERS

When you're through here, I'd like you to go out to my car and change the oil and rotate the tires.
—LORIN PAULSEN

...A Photographer Is Taking Pictures During Your Talk

To Prevent It from Happening

Usually photographers are easy to get along with. They take a shot or two and they are gone. *Sometimes* they can be a bother.

I ask the sponsor to tell the photographer to take pictures for only a minute or so at the beginning of a speech. Without this request, sometimes the photographer moves about and continues to take photographs for 10, 15, 20 minutes or longer into my presentation. I've even had photographers come up onto the stage and move around me to get a better shot. You look out at the audience and see their heads moving back and forth following the photographer. No matter who or how good the speaker is, the audience will follow the "moving object"—the photographer! It can be a tremendous distraction.

—VINCENT BUGLIOSI

What to Do

I like to stop and pose and do something silly. It is always is good for a "cheap laugh." If the photographer is getting to be too much of a good thing, just nicely tell her or him that it is enough. If the photographer persists, leave it alone. Do not make a scene or get angry; it only makes you look bad.

Launch the audience into a discussion exercise. While people are talking, you can take the event planners aside and ask them what they would like you to do. Explain that you are feeling distracted by the photographer. Chances are the photographer is part of their peer group, or even a friend. You don't want to make this person look bad in any way.

Pause in midsentence and pose a dramatic "speaker" gesture. Carry a magician's "electric deck" which enables you to cascade the cards from one hand to the other. When the photographer's flash goes off, you can stop the cascade in midair—the cards are tied together!
—JOHN KINDE

I have my own camera ready and get ready to take a photo of the photographer.
—ALAN PEASE

What to Say

Wait! Let's get a better pose. (Then stand like Washington crossing the Delaware with a dramatic hand gesture. It always gets a laugh.)
—MICHAEL PODOLINSKY

I saw a sign for photographers at a convention. It read: "Speakers should be shot as they approach the platform."
—TOM ANTION

(Turn to your photographer, smile, wave, and say) Hi, Ma!
—ALLEN KLEIN

Next week's issue of People?
Oh, the price of stardom!
—W MITCHELL

If you are trying to shoot some candid pictures, get ready for a real candid one—now! (Then stick out your tongue at the camera!)
—ART LINKLETTER

Try to make me look like Paul Newman, will you?
—GENE PERRET

(I stop, smile, pose, and say) Great. I want 25 wallets, and two 8-by-10s.
—JEFF SLUTSKY

Can you send a dozen of those to my spouse?

(With a sultry overtone) You want a good shot baby? (Turn your back to the audience and mock fumble with your clothes as if unzipping or unbuttoning something, giving the illusion you are going to be crude. Then whirl back around with a red clown nose on.)

I saw _____ (CEO, or president of the group) tell this guy (the photographer) to shoot the speaker as he approached the lectern. No don't! I'm leaving! (Start to run off.)
                                                        —LILLY WALTERS

I'm very photogenic. Last month I made the centerfold for Field & Stream magazine.
                                                  —TERRY BRAVERMAN

What *Not* to Say

I think this photographer is distracting the audience and me.

I'm sorry, you need to stop that. You are distracting me.

Speaking of "shooting for a living," can we shoot this guy?

Wait. Here take this one! (Grab some person and kiss her (him) on the cheek. Then say to the photographer in a to-be-overheard "conspiratorial whisper") OK, 50:50 split on the blackmail money!

...The Audience Is Distracted by Something Else in the Room

I was once speaking to a group of 300 women in a ballroom that had a window located near the top of the ceiling. Perhaps it led to a room where lighting or sound could be adjusted. Much to the audience's surprise (and mine!) a mustached gentleman interrupted my presentation when he leaned out of the window into the ballroom and started fussing with some equipment near the ceiling. Needless to say, some of the audience participants were distracted by his commotion, so I stopped and said: "God, is that you? (Pause) I didn't know you had a mustache—and I didn't know you were a man—but thanks for the assistance!"
                                                        —LORNA RILEY

To Prevent It from Happening

Before the crowd comes in, walk into the area where people will be seated—and sit! What will they see?

- Unscrew the lights on the walls behind where you will stand.
- Cover or take down distracting pictures.
- Close all the curtains behind where you will stand.

Stand in the part of the room that has the best lighting and the fewest distractions (behind you). Unfortunately, a single spot rarely has both, so you will need to choose. I prefer the spot with the fewest distractions. Also consider where noise will be coming from outside the room. Place the audience as far as possible away from that spot. You may need to be in the noisy spot—but better you than your listeners.

What to Do

A woman asked me how to handle the following: She was teaching an accounting class; next door was a sports bar with a big-screen TV. Some of her students had begun watching it, getting excited, drinking beer, and being rowdy in her class. I told her that she needed to acknowledge what was going on. For example: "Many of you need to be here for this information. Some of you would rather be in the bar—I don't blame you. If I didn't have to work, I would probably want to be watching the game too. You have my full permission if you want to watch the football game to leave now. However, if you stay, I ask that you respect the others who need this information."

With this statement, she would have acknowledged what was going on and given people a chance to leave. Also, the people who wanted to be there would have been on her side. If the others remained rowdy after that, they would have turned around and stared at them.
—Patricia Fripp

Launch into a discussion exercise while you try to fix the problem. Or have people pick up their chairs and face another direction in the room.

What to Say

Never thought I'd be upstaged by a _____.
—Tom Antion

No one is listening to me. Déjà vu! It's just like marriage.
—Jim McJunkin

It seems all I have left of your attention is the tension part.
—Art Gliner

...There's a Sudden Boom, Bang, or Crash from Outside the Room

To Prevent It from Happening

The three most common sources of noise are the kitchen, construction, and another meeting. If it is just a one-time bang, have fun with it and move on. If it is going to be a perpetual problem, see the following section on continuous loud noises.

What to Do

Be silly and have fun. This is a great opportunity to show off your versatility and spontaneity by carefully having a few "ad-libs" at the ready.

What to Say

Well, the 6:12 is right on time!
—W MITCHELL

That's what we do to people who won't applaud.
—LORIN PAULSEN

They have got to do something about the termites here.
—ART LINKLETTER

(Look suspiciously in the direction of the sound, then with a cunning and knowing look, say in a loud stage whisper) Rats!!
—LILLY WALTERS

(I just give it a "Jack Benny" look and don't say anything.)
—PHILIP CROSBY

I hope that wasn't my dessert.
—From *A Funny Thing Happened on the Way to the Boardroom,* by Michael Iapoce, Wiley, 1988

That was a sign from God to let you know how important this next part is.
—JIM McJUNKIN

Well! If that's the way you feel.
—ROGER LANGLEY

You can't scare me...I have children!
— UNKNOWN

And stay out!

(Bell sounds) Somebody tried to get over the wall.
— GEORGE GOLDTRAP

(As though talking to God) Was it something I said?
— IAN HAMILTON

(Look disgusted, turn to your audience, and very quickly, in a conspiratorial whisper, say)
When I say three, take your fists and give one big bang on your tables. Ready? One, two, three!
(Run over to the wall where the noise came from, place your ear against it and pretend to be listening intently, then stand up, smile, heave a big sigh of relief and say)
I think we scared it off.
— LILLY WALTERS

God must be throwing lightning bolts at me.

I always like to start off with a bang.

I'm flattered. You ordered fireworks for me.

Was that a real noise or was it Memorex?
— From *One Liners for Disaster,* by Tom Antion,
Anchor Publishing, 1993

I bet the next time that guy learns from his mistakes.
— DIANNA BOOHER

Last time I heard a crash that loud, my investments dropped 55 percent!

(If a glass breaks) Mazel tov!
— JEFF SLUTSKY

(With a shocked and innocent look) Did I do that?

The Almighty has spoken.

I knew the Turks would find me. (But of course only a Greek—like me— could get away with that one.)
— HOPE MIHALAP

Where was I? I lost my place when that waiter lost his balance.
— From *Current Comedy Newsletter,*
August 12, 1991

...Continuous Loud Noises
Interrupt from Outside
Your Room

> *Once I was talking to a business audience when I was nearly drowned out by the sound of people running across the roof of the ballroom. I said: "Stock market must be down; the jumpers are out!"*
> —ED MCMANUS, THE JOKESMITH

> *I was doing a stress management seminar in Johannesburg. There was a revival meeting in the adjacent room which got louder as the day went on. By 4:00 p.m., "My Achy Breaky Heart" was resounding through my seminar walls. I was shouting at the top of my lungs, when finally I said, "One of the best stress releases is dancing. So let's all dance!" I shouted to people (with what was left of my vocal cords) to come and address their questions and concerns to me individually. In a friendly—and loud— voice, I closed the seminar. I received very high marks for dealing with adversity and stress with humor.*
> —CHÉRIE CARTER-SCOTT

To Prevent It from Happening

If it is a one-time kaboom, see the preceding section on sudden noises.

- Check out the location of the kitchen, construction sites, and other meetings. Where is the bar? Does it have a band, DJ, or other loud entertainment? If you have control over which room will be used for your event, choose carefully. Do a reconnaissance of the venue.

- What else is scheduled in the room adjoining yours? Unfortunately, even if nothing is scheduled when you book the room, the adjacent room may be rented out at the last minute for the final competition of the national high school marching bands.

- If your event uses more than one room (like an area for registration and an area for setups), put the presentation area in the middle of your other rooms. They will act as a buffer.

- If you use only one room, ask the venue people for the quietest one. They will almost always say, "Oh, they all are quiet." (You might get lucky and have them fess up to which is quietest.) Just counter with, "We must have a room that is quiet. We will be writing a clause for nonpayment into the contract if there is too much noise. So why don't you show me which room is farthest off the beaten path and most likely to be quiet?" Use your own wits. Look for rooms in corners. Some rooms are set aside, with no other rooms on either side of them. Try for those.

■ Ask the venue manager to stop the work of what you view to be a potential noisy situation (construction, serving, cleaning) during your session. If that is not possible, find out what times the noisy folks are going to be working and consider moving your group for a "field trip" of some kind during that time.

Try for a room with fixed interior walls. Tell them your meeting is going to be very noisy and you will need to be well away from the others.
—DEANNA BERG

Most noise comes in the form of trains, planes, automobiles, restaurants/ kitchens, and, most loudly, children. Be aware of these facts. Sites near airports will be convenient but not suitable for speaking, which requires tranquility. Likewise, sites near railways or freeways will have a noise problem. Make sure the room is not near the building's kitchen or eating facilities, since the clanking and chatter inherent to these operations will surely yield an undesirable impact. And, as much as we adore kids being kids, playgrounds, day care rooms, and other kiddy hangouts will most certainly wreak havoc on any presentation that requires concentration. Avoid first-floor rooms if possible, because most conventional high-activity rooms are located on ground level and low-frequency sound waves are conducive to surface propagation. Lastly, make sure the room you book is larger than the surrounding rooms. That way any noise you generate should outweigh that of the neighboring rooms.
—DAVID R. VILLANUEVA

What to Do

Launch into a discussion exercise while you try to fix the noise problem. Consider moving the group to another spot—outside, in the lobby, by the pool, and so on. If that is impossible, turn the volume up on your mic.

Rather than have to go through the whole speech with the distraction, in front of the audience I say, "Whoever is in charge, would you please see what you can do about the noise coming from the adjacent room?"
—VINCENT BUGLIOSI

Jackie Mayer was speaking at a college. The room was next to the kitchen. For some reason, the kids cleaning up were banging and crashing the dishes. No one in the room got up to take care of it. So Jackie calmly excused herself, left the room, went into the kitchen, told them to be quiet, and came back. It was a matter of regaining control.
—BRAD PLUMB

I work with Tony Robbins. I believe that he is the most impactful and effective person that I have ever seen on stage. He does a three-day program called "Date with Destiny." The event site was very close to a train station. Trains would come into the station about every hour and blow their whistles as they entered and left. To some people, this would have been an interruption. Tony turned it into an enhancement by having people stand up and cheer wildly every time they heard the whistle. After a few train stops, the whistle became the signal—the anchor—for total enthusiasm!

—NATE BOOTH

What to Say

Serious

(Initiate a discussion session.)
With two of your neighbors seated next to you, share the worst (best) experience you ever had dealing with _____ (your topic). In other words, work in groups of three. You have five minutes. Go.
(Then dash off and try to fix the trouble.)

Humorous

(Ask someone.) Please go tell those guys that we are sick and tired of them of them having all that fun out there, while we're in here having our meeting! So either they should have less fun out there or come in with us!

—W MITCHELL

There's a feeding frenzy out there.
They're making fools of themselves out there. Would someone go out there and tell them that's our job!

—TERRY PAULSON

...Something Drops, Breaks, or Falls Inside Your Meeting Room

Gene Harrison, a retired marine colonel, was addressing a state chapter of the Painting and Decorating Contractors Association. He spoke from the head table. In back of the lectern was suspended a huge banner. Just as he reached his conclusion, the banner came floating down off the wall, covering him, the lectern, the mic, and half of the head table. After a few moments of recovery, they all emerged. Harrison picked up the mic and concluded with, "Doctors bury their mistakes, architects cover theirs with ivy. It appears that painting and decorating contractors conclude by draping theirs with a banner!"*

*From *Sharing Ideas* newsmagazine, February–March 1988, Royal Publishing, Glendora, CA.

I was on the stage talking with a group of 250 health care professionals. I was jumping around on stage and the already wobbly double flipchart I was using tumbled over with a resounding crash! I turned around, looked at the prostrate flipchart and said, "Boy, that must have been a powerful idea!" The audience cracked up and I kept right on going!

—NATE BOOTH

To Prevent It from Happening

Play with your flipcharts and any other equipment that isn't nailed to the floor. Find out what all their little foibles are. Other than that, pray that the venue construction staff and management staff put the room together nicely.

What to Do

You do need to take a moment to deal with whatever boomed, smashed, or crashed. We have been trained since childhood to "clean that up." Your audience will be very focused on whatever fell rather than on you. So take a minute, calmly check it out, sigh, make a funny, fix what broke or set it aside, and go on. This will give the audience license to attend to your words again.

What to Say

Humor can't fix everything.

I would fix this, but the only thing I learned in shop class was how to call for estimates.

That's what I get for buying this at a flea market.

I'll fix this right up. Just give me a hammer.

Does anyone have some superglue?

Does anyone have a dollar bill on them? (If possible, go into the audience in search of a dollar bill, apparently to fix the broken item.) It won't fix this, but maybe I can bribe someone to get me another one.

We really didn't need that major portion of my presentation, (say with sarcasm) did we?

All great speakers have a plan. Unfortunately, I don't. No. I'm just kidding....(Go to your alternate plan—and you had better have one.)

I know it's time for a break, but this is ridiculous.

This item just took a break, so why don't we take one too. Let's resume at...

Just when I was smokin' this darn thing gets broken. Let's _____
(take a break, shift gears, etc.).
> —From *One Liners for Disaster*, by Tom Antion,
> Anchor Publishing, 1993

Boy, that must have been a powerful idea!
> —NATE BOOTH

In this business all you need is one lucky break...and that wasn't it.
> —ROGER LANGLEY

(When someone drops something) Just put that down anywhere.
> —TOM OGDEN

...An Announcement or Music Comes Unexpectedly over the PA System

To Prevent It from Happening

You want to be able to get *some* messages from the PA (public address system)—like "Excuse me, we've had a bomb threat, depart immediately!" You don't want an annoyed voice blaring into your room, "There is no parking in the yellow zone!" Or the sounds of Elvis yodeling "Ain't Nothin' but a Hound Dog." Ask the caretaker or maintenance person (whomever you can find) about the system at the venue, what you can expect, and how to control it.

> *Music or PA should be taken care of before you get up, or by indicating that you intend not to get up.*
> —PHILIP CROSBY

What to Do

If it is an emergency message, deal with it calmly. If you are asked to evacuate, calmly reinforce the request to the audience members and get them to do as the announcement requested. Always ask them to help others in the room who might have a movement disability.

If it is a nuisance announcement, make a joke about it. Lightly ask one of your assistants to see about getting the PA turned off, and carry on. If you don't have an assistant, launch into a group exercise. (See Chapter 5 for examples.) Then find out how to solve the problem.

What to Say

Serious

> *(If it is an emergency, say in a very calm voice) All right, we have all heard the request. Please calmly pick up your belongings and we will all*

go meet at _____ (new site). If people near you have a movement disability, please help them out too. Let's go.
— LILLY WALTERS

Humorous

(If the room is low enough and you know where the PA speaker is, quickly pull a chair over to it, stand on the chair, and yell into the box) Stop that!

Pay no attention to that voice behind the curtain!
— LILLY WALTERS

May I quote you?

I couldn't have said it better.

You don't say!

Once more with feeling!

Lately I've been hearing voices, and I'm worried.
— ROGER LANGLEY

There is nothing like a bit of competition.
— DOUG MALOUF

Now that was exactly my thought!
— ALAN PEASE

Big Brother has a message.
— DIANNA BOOHER

The special-effects people are at it again. I told them to join in when they heard something particularly interesting. Obviously, they liked the last point a lot...
— PAUL DINSMORE

There is a definite message here for me.
— DOUG MALOUF

...For Unexpected Music

(Sing) Hark, the herald angels sing.

That's music to my ears.

Would you please turn down your Walkmans?
— TOM ANTION

OK, someone wants me to sing. Let me warn you, if anyone here has perfect pitch, this is going to hurt a little.

(In Chinese philosophy style) Confucius say, "He who makes music in class, stay after school to face same."
— TERRY PAULSON

Well on that note...

If there are any savage beasts in here, I hope that calmed you.

They're playing our song.

Shall we dance?

Whatever happened to the big bands?

(Listen intently for a few seconds, then say) What music?

I said hum a few bars.

—ROGER LANGLEY

...Someone's Pager or Personal Phone Goes Off

Dr. Neil Baum, a urologist from New Orleans, conducts seminars for physicians on how to run a more efficient medical practice. With a room full of doctors he gets at least three to four beepers going off at different times during a seminar, so it is important for him to have some ad-libs because he knows it's going to happen. He had me sit in on his seminar so I could critique him, and I gave him a great ad-lib during the break.

Early in his talk he discusses how to deal effectively with patients who call doctors on personal time for nonemergency situations. The most common one is asking the doctor to call in a chronic prescription refill when they knew a week before they were going to run out. Dr. Baum tells his audience that when "Mrs. Smith" calls him on his beeper he says, "You know where I am right now? I am at the zoo with my family. Now you knew a few days ago that you were running out and you could have called me during office hours to fill it. I'll tell you what. I'll call it in just this one time if you promise that in the future you'll call me when I'm in the office. OK?" And Neil really stresses "just this one time."

Then the next time a beeper goes off in his seminar, he looks at that doctor and says, "Be sure to let them know you'll do it just this one time!" Gets a big laugh. It works so well he offered me a free vasectomy.

—JEFF SLUTSKY

To Prevent It from Happening

In the first few minutes of your talk, ask your attendees to please turn off their pagers and phones. Or to give them to your assistant, who will handle the calls. Use stick-on labels to tag each pager or phone so there is no mixup, and note on the tag where that person will be sitting. Have your assistant ask the attendees how they want their pages and calls handled: Do they want the phone answered and a message taken? Should the calls go unanswered? Are they expecting an emergency call? Should your assistant call them out of the meeting if it comes in?

What to Do

Make a joke and carry on. By the second call to the same person, try staring and raising your eyebrows—but with a smile.

> *In Australia one man in the front row of a rally accepted three phone calls during my speech. I just walked to the other side so I would take the attention with me.*
> —PATRICIA FRIPP

In the rare event that a person receives two or more calls, launch the audience into a discussion exercise while you try to fix the problem. Ask the person to step outside your meeting room for a moment, and politely request that he or she sit in the back of the room near an open door for the remainder of your talk and then step out of the room when a telephone call comes in. Also ask the person to turn the ringer down on the phone.

> *If continued audible paging becomes a problem in that it keeps interrupting your speech, simply stop your speech, sigh deeply, and look directly at the person fingering the pager. Try not to look indignant—use a puppy dog type of expression—and follow the person's movement all the way to the door and/or the phone booth. This will encourage others to deselect their pagers.*
>
> *If a person receives a call on a portable phone and then begins to chat during your speech, just stop. Look at the person and all eyes will come to bear likewise.*
>
> *These tactics are not to be used in a hostile or rude manner. The intent is to make the group more sensitive to being disruptive and to instill a sense of cooperation and consideration.*
> —DAVID R. VILLANUEVA

What to Say

Serious

> *(After you have launched a break or a discussion exercise, subtly gesture to the person to follow you out of the room, then say, with true concern and caring)*
>
> *I know you must have some emergency you are handling. Is there any way we can help you with whatever is going on?*
>
> *I think it will be easier for you if you sit in the back of the room, and we will keep the door open. Then when the phone rings, you can easily step out of the room to talk to your caller.*
>
> *Can you turn the ringer down on your phone?*

If the situation changes, and you need assistance, just catch my eye. I will launch a discussion group again and help you.
—LILLY WALTERS

Humorous

My audiences always try that one! You're not getting out of here that easy.
—DAVE CAREY

I think that's for me.
—BOB BURG

If that's Bill Clinton, tell him I'm busy.
Heck of a time for a civil defense drill.
—ROGER LANGLEY

I was waiting to see who would be first today.
—W MITCHELL

I sympathize, sir (madam). Never a free moment when you're a brain surgeon.
—LORIN PAULSEN

Whoops! Time to take a pill!
Tell 'em I want mine with mushrooms, onions, and extra cheese.
—JEFF SLUTSKY

That's your secretary reminding you to turn off your beeper.
I left strict word not to be disturbed unless it was absolutely impressive...er, necessary.
—From *Speaker's Idea File*, Original Humor
section by Gary Apple, June 1993

Another baby comes into the world!
—GEORGE GOLDTRAP

If that's for me, tell them I'm not here.
If that's my broker, tell him to buy all the stock he can in _____ (name of the company, group, or industry you are speaking for). I know sales are going to skyrocket.
If that's my mom, tell her she doesn't have to worry. I wore my scarf and mittens.
—TOM ANTION

Tell them I put the check in the mail!
                                   —LILLY WALTERS

Tell them I've already left, thanks.
                                   —MARIAN WOODALL

What *Not* to Say

I would really appreciate your turning that off.

...A Phone Rings

To Prevent It from Happening

Carefully check out your room. Look in the closets and cupboards to see if any phones are still set up from the previous meeting. Find out where they hook up and unplug them.

What to Do

First, make a joke. Then talk to whoever is on the line—this gets a bigger laugh. After you hang up, disconnect the phone from the wall, and carry on with your presentation.

What to Say

See the preceding section on pagers and personal phones. You can easily adapt the lines for an internal phone ringing in your room.

(Using the name of one of the attendees) Jane Smith, your baby-sitter wants to know the number of the fire department.
                                   —R. MICHAEL WALTERS

(Using the name of one of the attendees) Mark Jones, never mind about moving your car out of the way of the painters. Oh, and they said to tell you the color really matches pretty darn good.

Yes, dear, I'll pick up the milk and bread.

Mom! Geez! I did wear my jacket today!

I told you, the check is in the mail!

(Looking wide-eyed and horrified) What? Unzipped?

Answer that. It might be the phone.
                                   —LILLY WALTERS

(Call out in horror) What do you mean I've been served?!
                                   —TOM ANTION

...The Fire Alarms Go Off

Right after the infamous MGM fire in Las Vegas, new ordinances and rules were passed for hotels and meeting sites. It was almost impossible for meeting planners to keep up with them all. One planner told me she was having an elegant banquet in Vegas for 1500 members of a certain company. She noticed a fire chief and the hotel manager having an argument by one of the doors. She scurried over and questioned them. The fire chief was furious. "There are to be no open flames in these meeting rooms! Look at that! You've got 300 flaming candelabra in there! I want that room evacuated now!"

Seeing her major event about to go up in flames (sorry), she said, "Give me 2 minutes." She went over to the band, whispered something, and the music stopped. She grabbed the mic and said, "Ladies and gentlemen. We have a special treat today. There is a birthday boy here! We have placed the candles on your tables in his honor. Let's all sing him happy birthday, and when we're done, please *blow out the candles on your tables!* OK? Happy birthday to you! Happy..."

Smart lady.

What to Do

Most fire alarms in your meetings are going to be false alarms. Regardless, *act* as if the alarm is false, but *assume* it is real. Always act with blasé, calm self-assurance, as if you are positive it is a false alarm. Always assume it is a real danger and the lives of the people in that room are *your* responsibility. Most fires are going to burn faster than people can run. Many times the crowd panics and people are crushed at the doors—with escape so close—killing each other in their panic. Their lives are in your hands.

Before the audience ever enters your room, find out where all the closest fire exits are. Actually walk down them to the street. Twice when I was presenting in Africa, I tried to test an obvious fire exit in my meeting room only to find it padlocked. I asked the managers how we were supposed to get out in case of a fire. Both times the answer was "Oh, we don't have fires here. We are more worried about terrorists bringing bombs in, so we padlock these exits." (Not terribly reassuring.) I had them show me an alternate route out for us, just in case.

There is always the possibility that a fire will break out in your room. You need to:

- Know where the fire extinguisher is.
- Know where the fire alarm is.
- Know where the closest fire exit is and exactly where it leads.

Assign an assistant to be ready to go get the fire extinguisher. Don't give this role to the assistant you have already assigned to go the phone in a medical emergency. You want to have that one primed to go call for help while the other one gets the fire extinguisher. Make a decision as to which assistant will pass the fire alarm and can pull it on the way to his or her other task. Then calmly clear the room of the attendees.

> *The crowd of 400 is really cooking and I am in the middle of a funny story. Suddenly, the fire alarm clamors for their attention. I stop immediately. The tension must be alleviated. I assign someone to investigate and return to us with a report of what action the facility wants us to take. A few minutes later, we get an "all clear." False alarm. By now, of course, I've lost them and they chatter among themselves.*
>
> *I stride onto the stage, purposefully, seductively. Stand there for effect and attention. Put my hand on my hip as I swing it out. I look at them slowly. In my best Mae West voice, I murmur: "When I'm HOT...I'm HOT!"*
>
> *The explosive laughter suddenly brings us all together and once more, humor has saved the day.*
>
> —ROSITA PEREZ

What to Say

Serious

...When You Start Your Program

> *In the very unlikely event of a fire, the fire exits are _____ . When you walk down them, you will see _____. Please wait for me there, if it seems safe, and I will soon rejoin you to let you know where we will continue the meeting. If we do need to leave, note if people seated near you have a movement disability. Please help them out too.*
>
> —LILLY WALTERS

...For a Fire in Your Room

> *(Very calmly) All right. _____, call for help—you know where the phone is. _____, get the fire extinguisher. _____, activate the fire alarm. The rest of you please exit through the _____ door. Help anyone next to you with a movement impairment. We will meet at _____ (the place you have decided on) in 15 minutes to determine where we will resume this meeting.*
>
> —LILLY WALTERS

...For Fire Alarms Going Off

This is a special category because there is a real physical danger involved. Whether you like it or not, you are in charge of the calm evacuation of the room. You should already know where the exits are located, and have a plan in mind for an orderly exit. You must stay absolutely calm. The audience will take their cues from you. If you sprint off the stage screaming, you will be morally responsible for someone getting crushed in the ensuing stampede.

I calmly say, "Well it looks like it's time to take a break whether we need one or not. Please stay seated. It's probably a false alarm, but as a precaution we will go outside and see what is happening. Are there any handicapped persons who may have a difficult time moving toward the exit? One person on either side should assist them." Now direct the crowd, by rows if necessary, to calmly move toward the emergency exit. To recite the above directions calmly takes about 30 well-spent seconds.

—From *One Liners for Disaster*, by Tom Antion,
Anchor Publishing, 1993

Humorous

That's the signal for coffee.
—Doug Malouf

Someone tried to get over the wall!
—George Goldtrap

Now that's what I call enthusiasm!

Now that's what I call a clearly defined goal.

Looks like the soprano section is trying to tell us something.
—Deanna Jean Brown

Recess already?
—W Mitchell

(After evacuating the room or making sure there is no fire) See, _____ is such a hot topic it sets off fire alarms.
—Allen Klein

Who's wearing the super beeper?

When we get the OK from the fire department, remember the word of General MacArthur: "I shall return." And I hope you do too!
—Roger Langley

(Chances are you will get cut off in the middle of a sentence. Evacuate people calmly and as soon as you get everyone back into the room, pick up with the last few words you were saying—as if nothing ever happened. It will bring the house down.)
—Brad Plumb

...The Room Is Smoky and You Want to Discourage Smokers

In the USA, many meetings are designated as nonsmoking. This does not mean you won't have smokers. It does mean that if you don't have breaks frequently, you will have people who are at a need level where they can't listen to you. Usually, a problem arises only if you are teaching a session of longer than 90 minutes.

Oddly enough, many smokers tend to fall into the same personality category: the analytical self-contained type. If you allow smoking in your room, in a "smoking section," you create a whole group of people who are not as strong at sharing and open exuberance. Besides, nonsmokers profoundly hate to be in the same room as smokers who are smoking. Smokers are in the minority. So you may meet both groups' needs better by just not allowing smoking in your room.

Outside of the USA, there seem to be more smokers and fewer laws about where they can smoke.

To Prevent It from Happening

To discourage smokers, take the ashtrays out of your room. Announce at the beginning whether smoking is allowed and how often you will allow breaks (so the smokers won't panic). If you allow smoking, note which way the air-conditioning system is sucking the air. Place the ashtrays in the part of the room that is "down wind."

If your audience can't breathe, your seminar is worthless. To minimize the discomfort of the nonsmokers, set aside a smoking section. Look at the ceiling and note the vents. There will be two types: exhaust vents blow air out and return vents take air in. The return vent will have a slight buildup of dust on its grate from electrostatic bonding. The exhaust vent will usually have louvers or some other directional fins. Position your smokers under the return vents. That way the smoke will be sucked up and run through the environmental filters and then dispersed more evenly and finely throughout the room. The "smoky" odor will still be there, but your nonsmokers will breathe easier. Whatever you do, don't light a match to determine air flow, as the air density and carbon dioxide buildup of the audience will change the nondynamic air flow in the room.
—David R. Villanueva

We recently gave a talk in Frankfurt where we were in a closed in room. In Germany, everyone smokes. I don't, but I knew that if I told the audience that I didn't want them to smoke it would not win friends and influence people. So I asked for a vote. After explaining what I wanted them to vote on, I asked first for the nonsmoking voters to show their hands. There were only four of us, and I started to mentally prepare for an uncomfortable afternoon. Then I noticed that one of the four was our executive sponsor.

I asked for the votes of the prosmokers. Two hands went up. I went for broke and asked if the rest of the audience was just being polite, and got a strong yes. I thanked them sincerely.

Later I braved the walk into the gray cloud at a break and asked how they felt about the vote. To a person, they said that they were personally sorry that they couldn't smoke in the room, but glad to support the vote of the group.

Since then, we have done the same thing in the States, and the voting technique works very well. I have yet to suffer smoke at a talk.
—Peter Meyer

What to Do

Check the source of the smoke, and deal with any danger to your group. If the smoke is from cigarettes, not from fire, you will have to confront the smoking issue. If you politely ask people to stop *after* you have given them permission to smoke, you will have a problem. Smokers tend to get hostile, even offensive, if you ask them—after they have lit up—to stop. So, instead:

- Open the doors and/or windows.
- Try moving the group around to put the smokers by open windows.
- Try doing some exercises outside.

What to Say

See the preceding section on what to do if the fire alarms go off. Always check that there is no danger to your audience members. Get them out of danger first. If the cause of the smoke is harmless—say, cigarette smoke (OK, that's not *harmless*, but you get the idea)—then make some funnies.

(Make gestures as if pushing the smoke away) Ah, Bill Clinton smokers. None of you guys ever inhale.
—Lilly Walters

(Sing) On top of Old Smoky.

(Sing) When smoke gets in your eyes.

Fog lights will be distributed shortly.
—Tom Antion

I'm sorry, but we're going to take questions only from the smokers because they've got less time.
                                                    —ALAN PEASE

This is just like home—if you're Smoky the Bear.
                                                    —ROGER LANGLEY

May I remind you that smoking is permitted in designated areas only. Today's designated area is Bangor, Maine.
                                                    —TERRY PAULSON

As a smoker, I'm convinced that smoking is dangerous to one's health. When I light up in a restaurant, mobs of nonsmokers want to kill me.

Los Angeles wants to ban smoking in indoor, public places. So now if you want to cough and gag, you have to go outside and breathe the air like everyone else.
                                    —From *Speaker's Idea File,* Original Humor
                                    section by Gary Apple, August 1993

I understand they took a vote before the meeting—to smoke or not. The smokers won, so the eyes will get in their smoke tonight.
                                                    —BRAD PLUMB

...The Sprinklers Go Off

A film crew was taping my presentation. They put their hot lighting right under a fire sprinkler. Wouldn't you know? Just in the middle of the talk, the sprinklers went off! I quickly told everyone, "Well, the next portion of my talk will be held in the parking lot."
                                    —GENE MITCHENER, THE WHEELCHAIR COMIC

A meeting planner was setting up her upcoming event on the huge lawn of the venue. As she watched far-off sections of the lawn getting watered, she had no fears. The groundskeeper had assured her that their section would not be watered the day before or the day of the event. The automated systems kept turning on sections, closer and closer. "No," she thought. "It will be all right—the groundskeeper promised." Unfortunately, the guy who programs the sprinklers had made no such promise. It was not a pretty picture.

To Prevent It from Happening

Keep your eyes on where the production people put their lighting.
   If you are outdoors, always check with the groundskeeper and ask

for the name of the sprinkler programmer. It will at least remind the groundskeeper that someone else needs to be consulted.

What to Do

If the indoor sprinkler system goes off, people will immediately start to scream. You have about 2 seconds to get them out calmly. And they must go calmly or they might injure themselves or one another.

What to Say

> *(Yell loudly) Now we learn about teamwork! Grab your valuables and help the people next to you! There are eight exits; use all of them. Meet me in _____ (someplace close that gets people out of the room and away from the front doors of the venue, where fires trucks will be pulling up in seconds). Please see if anyone around you needs assistance.*
> —LILLY WALTERS

> *(Sing) Rainy days and Mondays always get me down.*
> *Man the lifeboats. Women and children first!*
> *Oh, no! I can't swim! Is there a lifeguard in the house?*
>
> *Would you like to see my Gene Kelly impression? (Sing) I'm singing in the rain, just singin'...*
> —TOM ANTION

> *Did anyone remember to bring an ark?*
> —ROGER LANGLEY

...Insects Are Flying or Crawling Around the Room

> *I never talk with insects flying into the light. At a County Fair on stage at an outdoor racetrack, I once inhaled a moth during a serious moment. I couldn't even pause to chew it up. I just swallowed it whole.*
> —ART LINKLETTER

To Prevent It from Happening

Insects are usually a problem at outdoor evening functions. Smear your face with insect repellent cream. Talk to your doctor or pharmacists about finding one that is good for your skin and doesn't cause you to have a reaction. Don't wait until the day of the presentation to find out if you are allergic. Also use a spray for your shoulders and hair.

Ask for the light projectors to be placed as far away from you as possible. Bugs are attracted more to the bulbs than to where the light is directed. Pulling the lights farther away from the stage will help a little.

For an indoor event, carry a small can or tub of insect repellent. Your audience can sit there swatting away, but unless it is part of a gag, it will be very distracting if you do it more than once or twice.

What to Do

In an outdoor event, with bugs around, all you can do is hope your insect repellent works. For indoor events, you have more options.

- Lead a group bug bashing.

- Launch into a discussion exercise (see Chapter 5) while you try to fix the problem. Close the offending windows and do whatever else you can.

- Ask management to spray the room while you take your group for break or a "field trip" sort of exercise.

> *Simulate watching a bee buzz around your head while making buzzing noises. Then smack yourself in the head as if you killed the insect.*
> —TOM ANTION

Taking Tom's idea of hitting yourself in the head (carefully please) in pretense of killing the bug, I think it would be fun to cross your eyes and roll your head. Then, *if* you have had training in falling and *if* you have practiced this recently and *if* you don't mind getting dirty, and *if* you are fully aware that you are taking a chance at hurting yourself and are doing so at your own risk, it would be funny to fall over onto the floor as *if* you knocked yourself out. A less dangerous— and cleaner—version would be drape yourself over the lectern as you fake the faint. Do not try the fall if you have no training in falling or have not practiced it recently!

What to Say

> *It's really amazing what we attract into our lives, isn't it?*
> —TERRY BRAVERMAN

> *(Looking at the insect) No, no, you're supposed to be at the meeting for _____ (a competitor).*

(Make a great show of smashing the bug.) That's the last speech you'll ever attend for free!

And they said I wouldn't even draw flies!

Is there an exterminator in the house?

Our next exercise involves the use of a volunteer. Ah, here he is now.
                                          —UNKNOWN

Wow! I'm so great they're crawling out of the woodwork to see me!

I'll pay five bucks for a fly swatter.

(After swatting at an insect unsuccessfully) Maybe I ought to call the SWAT team.

These bugs are bugging me.
                                          —TOM ANTION

You know what bugs me about this place? The bugs!

Where is the Orkin man when you need him?
                                          —ROGER LANGLEY

...You Need to Kill Time While Staff Takes Care of the Problem

To Prevent It from Happening

If you plan carefully, use the checklist in Chapter 7, and keep your fingers crossed, you won't have to worry about killing time while someone fixes the "problem." However, no plan is foolproof.

What to Do

Assuming they can still hear you, launch into a discussion exercise. (See Chapter 5 for examples.)

One way I always fill dead air time while people are trying to fix the slide projector, sound system, lights, etc., is that I say, "Well, everyone is always asking me for recipes, and since there seems to be a bit of time right now, get out your paper and pencil and I'll give you a dilly of a one." Everyone laughs and actually writes down the recipe! If the projector, or whatever is wrong, is fixed immediately, I address the audience and say, "Do you want me to finish the recipe or shall I go back to my speech?" The answer shouted from the audience is inevitably, "Finish the recipe!" Keep in mind these audiences are usually predominantly male executives, and that's why it's so funny. At the end of my entire program

I refer to the interruption by saying, "You've been a great audience, but your insistence on my finishing the recipe does not speak too well for my speech!"

—LETITIA BALDRIGE

What to Say

(Hum or whistle the Jeopardy timer jingle.)

I'd go over there and help them, but I'd make it worse!

Folks, we could just sit here and cry about this little problem, but I've got a better idea. When is the last time you took a patriotic break? (Lead singing of "Yankee Doodle," or "God Bless America.")

Who has a birthday this month? Please stand up (come up front). (Lead singing of "Happy Birthday.")

—TOM ANTION

Talk among yourselves.

—TOM OGDEN

No hurry—I'm flying TWA.

—GEORGE GOLDTRAP

How many of you went to camp as kids? Remember "You Are My Sunshine"? Well, let's all sing it!

—ROGER LANGLEY

...Any Type of Technical or Mechanical Problem Occurs

What to Say

We name all our machines in our home. We get attached. I remember when my first Mr. Coffee died. (Look at the faulty equipment) OK, Bertha! Let's talk this through!

I love the computer—it multiplies the number of mistakes I can make per unit of time.

With the luck I'm having with equipment lately, I'd better sit in that flight recorder black box on my flight home.

I have computer phobia. I'm afraid I'll hit the wrong key and _____ (the group's home city) will be gone.

—TERRY PAULSON

Some _____ (the faulty equipment) are better than others. This is one of the others.

—LEONARD RYZMAN

The tech guy promised me they tested this. It's not that he stretched the truth...but I was wondering why his friends called him Mr. Bungee Tongue.
—UNKNOWN

Was this machine provided by the low bidder?
—ED MCMANUS, THE JOKESMITH

Ah, the wonders of modern technology!

I see the techno-gremlins are operating again.

Oh, oh. I've offended someone.

Once again, a technical challenge!
—ROGER BURGRAFF

Well, that's one of my goof-ups for the day. I'm glad to have that behind me.
—PERRY BIDDLE, JR.

The man who can smile when things go wrong has thought of someone else he can blame it on.
—ARTHUR BLOCK, AMERICAN WRITER
(From *Great Book of Funny Quotes,* by Eileen Mason, Sterling Publishing, 1993)

Science is really going at a rapid pace. Now it's only 100 years behind the comic strips.
—JOEY ADAMS, AMERICAN COMEDIAN, BORN **1911**
(From *Great Book of Funny Quotes,* by Eileen Mason, Sterling Publishing, 1993)

We all know there is a right way and a wrong way. Now after I fix this, there will be two wrong ways.

This is why I had to give up sky diving. I could never remember which direction to go after I left the plane.

I can get a cut unwrapping a Band-Aid.

If I touched the Dead Sea Scrolls, they'd come back to life.
—Adapted from *Bigshots, Pipsqueaks, and Windbags,* by Gene and Linda Perret, Prentice-Hall, 1993

(Assuming you will never work for a competitor) This _____ (broken or malfunctioning item) must have been made by _____ (competing company).
—From *One Liners for Disaster,* by Tom Antion, Anchor Publishing, 1993

If it ain't broke, don't fix it. But in this case it is broke, so will someone please get this thing working?
> —From *Speaker's Idea File*, Original Humor
> section by Gary Apple, September 1993

We learn from our mistakes. For instance, I'm learning that I make a lot of mistakes.
> —From *Speaker's Idea File*, Original Humor
> section by Gary Apple, May 1993

I've heard that we use only use 25 percent of our brains. What I want to know is: What happened to the other 75 percent?
> —Unknown

The time when the machines take over is getting nearer.

What did we do for problems before we had technical problems?
> —Roger Langley

They always say about me that I really know how to get a program rolling. 'Course that's easy to do when you're going down hill.
> —George Goldtrap

Anyone know where the coin slot on this thing is?

These things always give me problems...hell, the microwave still confuses me!

Let's try to wring one last spectacular defeat from the jaws of victory.
> —Lilly Walters

4 Miscellaneous Maladies

WHAT TO SAY WHEN
...Your Introducer Is Awful

Quiet, please. Quiet, please. Let's come to order. It's time for the speaker.
You can enjoy yourselves some other time.
                                        —LARRY WILDE
                        (From *Library of Laughter*, Jester Press, 1988)

At a literary luncheon held shortly after the publication of her memoirs, Gypsy Rose Lee was preceded by author Walter Lord. At the conclusion of his talk, he remarked that just before the luncheon Gypsy had said to him: "Walter, your speech will be a hard act to follow, so to ensure close attention to my speech, I've decided to take all my clothes off!"

Gypsy rose from her seat, smiled demurely at the audience, and said, "Why, Mr. Lord, you know that isn't true. You know I'd never end a sentence with a preposition."

—ANONYMOUS

My brother Charlie* was speaking at a co-op annual business meeting in western Kansas. The manager who had hired him was—unfortunately—the same guy who forgot to schedule the freight car to pick up the co-op's grain in town. The elevator was still full of grain and the co-op members were broke and ticked off. One of the first points of business was to fire this guy, who was supposed to have introduced Charlie only a few minutes later. The manager got up and left in shame, and then the introducer said (or rather implied) that it was time for the "speaker this terrible mismanager has spent our money on" to speak. It took Charlie a good 10 minutes to set the mood again.

—BRAD PLUMB

To Prevent It from Happening

Control the introduction by bringing a short written intro, and a gift for the introducer. Rehearse the introducer.

—DOTTIE WALTERS

I do not provide them with an introduction. But I do ask that the one they prepare be short. When possible, I ask them to read it to me before we begin to make sure there is no misinformation.

—VINCENT BUGLIOSI

I give introducers a written introduction and ask them not to vary from it. Before my talks, I ask introducers to go over the introduction with me. (I want to see the introduction they have in their hands and make sure it's mine!) I always carry an extra copy with me if they don't have one. Even if they made up their own, I encourage them to use mine. This can be delicate. First, I praise the one they have written themselves, and tell them how much I appreciate the effort they have put into it. I explain that this introduction (giving them mine) has been tested over several hundred speeches and makes any talk more effective and impactful, since it doesn't give anything away that I'm going to say in my talk. It also gives introducers information that I won't be talking about. Although I would never

---

*Charlie Plumb, a POW in Vietnam, is a fabulous motivational speaker.

push it to the limit and insist—it's their show after all is said and done
and I'm their employee—they always use mine.
                                   —W Mitchell

My personal opinion is that you should always bring an introduction, and always have a private little rehearsal with the introducer. No doubt you will make the introducer think you are a bit of an egotist and a nit when you insist on a rehearsal. But would you rather have a rotten introduction or an introducer who is miffed at you? I actually make great effort to keep the introducer happy *and* have a good introduction.

In the long run, remember that less is better. The participants really do not care much about your credentials; they want to hear you speak. Most of them know something of your background, or they wouldn't be sitting in your audience. So make it quick. See Figure 4-1 for a sample introduction.

What to Do

If you have just had a horrid introduction, smile sweetly, say "Thank you," and jump into your presentation.

I can always plug up any bad introduction with my own, which is an electronic introduction with 130 slides and 70 seconds of music and a professional Nashville voice and music.

                                   —Michael Aun

I had gone over my introduction with the introducer. I was standing at the side with my mic on ready to go, near the AV person who would play my entrance music upon the last cue that the introducer gave.

When the introducer finished his introduction he stopped one line short of "Please welcome Mikki Williams," which is the cue for the music. I didn't know why, so I told the music guy to put the music on and I proceeded to walk to the podium.

At the same time, I saw another woman coming from the other side of the podium. The introducer on stage was kind of sandwiched between two women approaching the stage. He looked as confused as I was. I proceeded to go up there. The other woman reached the stage at the same point as I did and said, "Excuse me." She leaned over the microphone and announced, "Will the owner of the Chevy Cavalier, license plate..., please move your car." At that point the attendees fell silent. They didn't know what to do. It was probably the worst loss of momentum in an intro that I ever had.

The introducer walked off stage and shrugged his shoulders. He didn't know what to do. So, standing there at this point with no applause to even welcome me, I just looked at the audience and said, "That was by far the most unique introduction I've ever had. I wrote everything except the part about the car. I will now give you the last line. 'Please welcome Mikki

---

LILLY WALTERS' INTRODUCTION
(Please read this as it is written)

Today Lilly Walters, an international lecture agent,
  will share with us strategies, tips, and techniques of professional speakers
    to use in our presentations, speeches, and training sessions.

Lilly Walters is the Executive Director
  of Walters International Speakers Bureau,
a professional lecture agency with a database of 20,000
  speakers and seminar leaders.

She is author of
  ...the book *Secrets of Successful Speakers*, published by McGraw-Hill,
which was chosen as a major selection
  by the Fortune Book Club and several others. *Secrets of Successful Speakers* is a number-one best-seller for *Success* magazine in the USA
  and a number-one best-seller in Australia.

She is also the author of the best-seller from McGraw-Hill, *What to Say When...You're Dying on the Platform*, as well as several other books and video programs about the world of speaking and presentation skills.

Help me welcome Lilly Walters!

* * * * * *

After you introduce me, please...

- Turn to face the direction I am coming from and start applauding.
- Wait for me at the lectern.
- Leave the introduction on the lectern.
- Hold out your hand, get ready to greet me at the lectern by shaking my hand.
- After we shake, walk in front of me and leave the platform.

Figure 4-1. Sample introduction.

Williams.'" At that point they all clapped and laughed. My presentation was off to a great start and happened to be one of the best speeches to one of the best audiences I have ever given. Amen to that.
—Mikki Williams

If the introduction has set a truly horrendous mood, you must deal with it. If the audience is now grieving, or angered, you need to do something about it. (See also Chapter 2 on when the audience receives bad news.)

> I had a group of 50 salesmen I was speaking to. This fellow was going to introduce me and just talk to them for 5 minutes and tell them about a few changes that are going to happen next year—"and then you'll be on straight away." He got off for nearly 40 minutes and said to them, "Enjoy the company this year, because next year half of you won't be here! Your performance has been no good. You're going to be out, you're going to be finished. I'm not going to put up with these lousy standards. You have done this and you have done that. You are going to be demoted—pay reductions!" "Anyway," he concluded, "that's enough for me; here's our good speaker."
> Well, I stood up there. And these were all people who were faced with losing their jobs. They didn't want to hear from me. I stood up and said, "I can see you don't want to hear from anyone, and if I was you I wouldn't want to either. Let's have a 5-minute coffee break."
> So we go on a coffee break. Some of them went home.
> —ALAN PEASE

What to Say

> (If it was really dreadful) Let's take a 5-minute break. (It gives them time to start over.)
> —ALAN PEASE

> I'm so sorry my mother isn't here. Not only would she have loved the _____ (whatever was unusual on the menu); she would have believed every word of that introduction too!
> —LILLY WALTERS

> Sometimes I wish I was one of those men (women) who need no introduction.
> —ROGER LANGLEY

What *Not* to Say

> Well, it's the MC's job to make himself look bad and me look good. I'd like to thank our MC for doing just that.

> There's nothing like a good introduction—and that was nothing like a good introduction.

> Well, of all my introductions, that is the most recent.

...The "Other" Presenter Does Not Show Up

"Miss Walters, the presenter before you has not shown up. Can you go on now?"

"Certainly."

I start thinking that I don't really need to organize my thoughts on that little portion in the middle. "Do you still want me to speak for 30 minutes?" "Yes, just that."

Fifteen minutes into it, when the audience is doing a discussion, the planner taps me on the shoulder and says, "Everyone really is enjoying this!" (My ego is immediately deflated by the surprised look on his face.) "Why don't you just do this 30-minute segment, and the 30 minutes following?" Hmm. I came with only a total of 30 minutes prepared.

This is a common scenario for all presenters. You need to be flexible.

To Prevent It from Happening

You can't prevent someone else from not showing up. You can be ready to help carry the day off and turn the event's agony of defeat into a thrill of triumph.

What to Do

If the audience didn't realize that someone else was supposed to be on the program, ignore it. Carry on as if everyone always intended for you to do the amount of program you are doing.

If people realize that someone has not shown up, but you were the main attraction, make light of it. They won't care much anyway. Emphasize how delighted you are that you will now be able to give them a much more in-depth program than was originally planned for.

If the other presenter was the main attraction, show great concern and caring before you try any levity.

In all three case scenarios, never say anything derogatory about the other speaker's not showing up. Always try to make the announcement yourself. People may walk out if they hear the announcement from someone else. But if you make it yourself, and you are fairly dynamic and funny, they may stick it out to watch the new kid. Many a star was born when the understudy had to fill in.

Always work in modules. So if someone else does not show up, you are prepared to bring out more modules. Get the audience participating and continue.
—Dottie Walters

What to Say

The bad news is you don't get to hear _____ give her presentation. She got stuck and can't be here today. The good news is you are going to get to hear me give every speech I have ever memorized.

(Clearing throat loudly, take a "stance.") All right, I think that I shall never see a poem...*(By this time they should be groaning.)*
    No? *(Turning serious, but with a smile)* I am scheduled to talk to you in _____ minutes. Let's start now instead. I'm delighted to have the opportunity to turn my briefer program into a workshop to really find some solutions to the challenges facing you about _____ *(your topic that day).*
                                            —LILLY WALTERS

The bad news is the other presenter didn't show up. The good news is we will have more time to explore my topic together and, even better news, we may finish earlier than planned.
                                            —ROGER LANGLEY

That's OK, I'll handle it. I'll speak twice as slowly!
                                            —LORIN PAULSEN

...The Presenter or Jokester Before You Is Embarrassing

I had booked a "General George Patton" impersonator into a regional convention in California. As the introducer was reading the introduction, in through the door and up onto the platform walks a bimbo. (I'm struggling for a nicer word, but, well, *you know.*) She starts making erotic moves and petting the MC, with such tasteful comments as "Hi, honey. I loved our date last month in Mexico! But I've got bad news, I haven't had my period...." Hard to believe, but it got *worse* from there! She started to remove her clothing until she was down to her teddy.

Obviously it was a paid prank. Maybe in another setting it might have been a funny paid prank. But this business audience had no clue as to what was going on. It was all the more tragic because "Patton" must be set up just the right way for the presentation to work. He uses some light profanity, à la George C. Scott in the movie *Patton,* which works quite well—normally. Just for the record, it does *not* work at all when booked to follow a tasteless striptease at a business meeting! The audience's sensibilities were offended beyond repair. No one was amused—least of all me, who stood in the back of the room ripping my hair out and planning dire revenge on whoever set up the "prank."

So this section is in here because *I've* been burned. Knowing that the question is more important than the answer, I wanted answers available *to me* the next time it happens!

To Prevent It from Happening

You are doing a presentation. Someone plays a joke on someone else as you're speaking or right before you go on. Bingo! Now you want to know how to prevent it from happening? Sorry, I have no clue how to prevent it. The only things I can think of are ways to soften the blows after they hit.

What to Do

I was showing a bunch of 35mm slides to a group of executives, management, and staff. One of my staff people had "one too many" at lunch and thought it would be a tremendous joke to stick a picture of a nude model right in the middle of my slides. I'm flicking away, and up flashes this nude! There was stunned silence (including me). Then I said with a smile, "Apparently someone in this room is trying to set me up," and moved right on. It got a good laugh from the audience.
—Don Dewar

A well-known TV sex personality preceded me on the platform, and was giving advice with very graphic examples. People were so embarrassed they had their heads down. When I came on, I knew I had to bring them back onto the track in which they could learn. I said, "There are many different viewpoints in the world. What I would like to talk about is old-fashioned values and how these can help you with your career and your family. There are certain fundamentals..." and I went on with my talk. Now they were listening.
—Somers White

Don't lower yourself to the level of the crude, rude person sharing the program with you. Maintain your own dignity without frosting it with ice. Don't criticize him, but let your audience know you are not in agreement with his tactics.
—Letitia Baldrige

My motto is "Don't complain and don't explain." This is how I handle people who are rude, crude, or humiliating.
—Pat McCormick

What to Say

Serious

Mr. X and I obviously march to a different drummer, but we're alike in one way—we're both privileged to have an excellent audience like you with whom to communicate.
—Letitia Baldrige

There are many different viewpoints in the world. What I would like to talk about is old-fashioned values and how these can help you with your career and your family. There are certain fundamentals...
—Somers White

Humorous

Guess maybe Darwin was wrong.
                              —UNKNOWN

...The Presenter on the Platform with You Is Embarrassing

I've been asked to read this disclaimer: "The opinions expressed by this panel are not necessarily the opinions expressed by this panel."
                    —From *Speaker's Idea File*, Original Humor
                    section by Gary Apple, August 1993

Whether the presenter comes on stage before you (see preceding section) or with you, the same principles apply.

To Prevent It from Happening

This type of embarrassment is likely to happen only when you are asked to be part of a panel. Always ask who the others are and what they are like. Then you can prepare witty remarks and brilliant comments well in advance.

What to Do

Retain your dignity and your humor. It just makes other people look worse and you look better.

Be careful: "Let he who has not sinned, pick up the first stone."
    If you are not the moderator, you may want to ignore it.
    If you are the moderator, correct them with dignity. "In the interest of professionalism, may I suggest to our panel that we need to be very careful about how we use four-letter words like...love."
    If they do it again, quickly cut them off and say, "Thank you, we have heard from you, now onto..." and pick on someone else.
    What I like the best is giving the person a note with a suggestion that he may be hurting himself with the audience and making the whole panel look bad, and with a request to "play it in a softer key."
    If you are sharing the platform, rather than moderating a panel, don't correct the person in front of the audience. Don't try to be clever. Don't make a battle out of it. Avoid wars that you don't have to fight.
                    —SOMERS WHITE

...The Presenter Before You Attacks You

This section and the two that follow go together. Read all three.

To Prevent It from Happening

Personal attacks usually happen only in presentations that deal with political and social issues. If you are involved in sweeping changes, you are going to tick people off and they are going to attack you. It just goes with the territory.

It's a revolution damn it! We're going to have to offend somebody!
—John Adams, while discussing the massive changes being hacked into the Declaration of Independence in 1776

What to Do

Instead of an ad hominen attack on them, I substantively attack what they are saying, frequently by demonstrating that it is a distortion of the facts or of the official record. That way you maintain your credibility and you stay above the fray.
—Vincent Bugliosi

If people get nasty with me, they usually go for cutting comments about my shaved head. Tactical error on their part. If you know what they are bound to go after, you can prepare truckloads of funny comebacks that will get the audience laughing at the situation and back on your side.
—Jim McJunkin

What to Say

Serious

I think the prior speaker has a lot to defend. On the other hand, I think it's critical to maintain "humble disrespect for the status quo" and try to find better ways to do things we do well. Perhaps the prior speaker should look at a new way to think.
—Chris Hegarty

I'm sorry he had such nasty things to say about me. I always speak well of him, but of course I suppose we could both be wrong.
—Terry Paulson

Humorous

(In the same condescending tone as the preceding speaker's, say) Wasn't that a sweet little introduction (comment, speech).
—Gene Mitchener, The Wheelchair Comic

My opponent reminds me of Shakespeare: "much ado about nothing."
—Roger Langley

When you hear that someone has gossiped about you, kindly reply that he did not know the rest of your faults or he would not have mentioned only these.

—ANONYMOUS

(From *Great Book of Funny Quotes*, by Eileen Mason, Sterling Publishing, 1993)

What *Not* to Say

My opponent has made a good argument...for ignoring him.

Amazing the idiots they let in here!

...The Presenter on the Platform with You Attacks You

See the preceding and following sections.

To Prevent It from Happening

An on-stage attack is likely to happen only when you are asked to be part of a panel or debate and the presentation involves political or social issues. Always ask who the others are and what they are like. Then you can prepare witty remarks and brilliant comments well in advance for those areas where you know you are weak. Walk softly, and carry a big stick.

What to Do

If you are not a humorist and they are, you cannot win with the use of humor—but you can win.

Imagine my hand pushing against yours. We are both pushing with equal force, fighting each other. If I let go and step aside, you will fall forward from your own momentum. One of the best ways to win, when you are on the platform with people who are attacking and critical, is to let them fall over from their own force. You see, the more you fight, the worse it gets. If they are well known, or celebrities, you will come out on the bottom—if you fight.

During the American Civil War a man from the North went to Liverpool. Because of the cotton imported from the South for use in the textile industry, those in Liverpool wanted the South to win. The crowd booed and jeered him. He looked out at them and said, "I always heard the English had a sense of fair play; therefore I knew I would be given a chance to be heard tonight." The crowd immediately quieted.

You might try the same strategy, by saying, "I have always heard you had a sense of fair play, and as a result I have looked forward to sharing the platform with you. May I ask you a question?" (Say it softly and with dignity.) "Now are you in control?" If the person says no, he or she looks like a jerk. If the answer is yes, you are now able to bring the person back on track.

When people sling mud, a little always stays on their hand. Don't pick up any to throw back or it will be on your hands. Don't try to be clever or witty in your responses; it is too easy to leave you with some of that mud on your hands.

—SOMERS WHITE

What to Say

Uh, _____, you seem a bit off your normal jovial self. Let's take a quick break so you can take some Midol.

—LILLY WALTERS

What *Not* to Say

I had the choice to either appear on the program with you or work a leper colony. I think I made the wrong choice.

Why don't you go misrepresent someone else's thought?

...The Presenter After You Attacks You

Read this section along with the two preceding ones.

To Prevent It from Happening

There is not much you can do. But forewarned is forearmed. At least find out as much as you can about who will follow you on the platform.

What to Do and Say

Consider passing the chairperson a note. It might read, "I would appreciate the opportunity to make a final comment. When _____ is done, I suggest you say something to the audience like, 'We have heard from _____. I wonder if Mr. White has a short closing comment?'"

If you are given the opportunity, don't be defensive. The audience will remember what happens in the last few minutes of a program. Say something very positive and leave people with impressions of you in a good light. Perhaps something like, "In a couple of minutes you will be going home. You all have had an opportunity that is so important to Americans—to hear different points of views expressed in different ways. While your two speakers came from differing views, this is the essence to what makes America great; the ability to say what we think! Any one of us can make a joke about the President of the United States. Under fascism you could have lost your life for such a joke. Under communism you could have lost your life saying something about Stalin. Let's all say a word of thanks to the Almighty above for this wonderful land that we live in. And I think _____ will agree with me. God Bless America."

Where has this left you? The final impression about you is positive. You may even want to go over and shake hands with that other person. He'll never know what hit him!

—SOMERS WHITE

...The Presentation Before You Is So Outstanding, It's a Hard Act to Follow

I heard Dorothy DeBolt speak at a National Speakers Association annual convention. She and her husband founded the Association for Unadoptable Children. Her presentation was stunning and moving. There were very few dry eyes in the house when she finished with us. It was magic. When she sat down, the MC tried to move on, but it was obvious that the audience was still reliving the experience. The MC had the presence of mind to say, "Dorothy, come back for a moment." We all just gave her another standing ovation, she said thank you again, and we were able to move on.

To Prevent It from Happening

You don't want to prevent it from happening. People need all the magic moments in their lives they can possibly get.

What to Do

As you begin, let your body, voice, and mind show you were swept up in the love and emotion that the other presenter created. Do not allow your ego to get in the way and try to *bravado* your way over what you are feeling. The audience will love you more if you have just shared the same emotional experience they have. If you are moved to cry, then cry. Give praise back to the other presenter. Use the emotion that the other presenter has generated. Keep referring to his or her point or message as it relates to yours.

What to Say

Let's hear it for my opening act—wasn't he (she) great!
>—GENE MITCHENER, THE WHEELCHAIR COMIC

No one in his right mind would be on stage following _____. That's why they invited me.
>—TERRY PAULSON

Well, you won't believe this, but the guy (woman) before me said everything I was going to say.
>—From *A Funny Thing Happened on the Way to the Boardroom*, by Michael Iapoce, Wiley, 1988

I feel like the guy who had to replace Michael Jordan in the lineup.

I feel like a dish of vanilla ice cream after the world's greatest banquet.

Now I know how every speaker who had to follow Winston Churchill must have felt.

I feel like Elizabeth Taylor's fifth husband on their honeymoon. I know what to do, but how do I make it different?
>—ROGER LANGLEY

...The Presenter Before You Is So Boring, the Audience Is Dead

Roger Burgraff was asked to speak to a group of mainly female business executives in Orange County, California, near the U.S. Marine Corps base in El Toro. The two speakers before him were also men. The first one got up and said, "You know, I was a marine for 10 years. Seeing the base reminded me of a few things." He then spent the next 45 minutes on war stories. The women, of course, had no great connection with his stories and quickly got restless and bored. They were greatly relieved when the first speaker said thank you and stepped down.

The second gentleman stood up. "Hearing _____ speak reminded me of *my* days in the Marine Corps. Let me tell you about the time..." Roger was amazed! Another 45 minutes of leatherneck stories! Now the women were gritting their teeth.

As Roger stood up, there was not a friendly eye in the house. He said in a total deadpan, "You know, hearing _____ and _____ speak reminded me...I have *never* been a Marine." He almost got a standing ovation.

To Prevent It from Happening

Don't I just wish we could prevent it? Millions of audience members all over the world join us in our fervent prayer.

What to Do

Have the audience "change states" immediately. Ask people to stand up, or turn their chairs around—anything to show them that this will be a different program, a new topic, a new presenter. Note I said *show* them. Don't tell them. Never say anything about the presenter before you being a dud. Everyone knows, and people do not want to be reminded—especially the people who planned the event! So *show* them you will be a totally different experience by quickly strutting your best stuff.

...Someone Tells You Motivational Speakers Are Charlatans

I agree. Some speakers are charlatans. Some tell stories that are dated, and tired—which is almost an insult to the audience, because chances are that 80 percent of the audience has heard them before. Charlatans will make themselves the hero of every story, as opposed to the goat. They tell all the "I'm so wonderful and you can be just like me" stories. They never compile original research. Instead, they steal other people's material. Unfortunately, even the term "motivational speaker" has come to mean charlatan in some minds.

Fortunately, there are plenty of speakers out there who do it well. But occasionally even they will get a bad rap because of the nature of motivation itself. I like to draw an analogy between food and water and motivation. You can have a full meal, you can quench your thirst, but within a short period of time you are going to be hungry and thirsty again. Motivation is no different. It's nourishment for the mind and the soul. You can fill up with it, but a few days from now you'll need more. This is not the fault of any speaker. It's human nature.

—JIMMY CALANO

Unreasonable expectations are placed on you the moment you decide to take the platform. Small things you do will be judged in a very odd manner. If you say something a little off-color—just one time—years later you may find that someone from that audience still labels you as "crude." You may tell *one* humorous anecdote with a good result one time. From then on, some people obstinately refuse to think of you as anything but an absolute knee-slapping comic.

I had a young man in my office ask me, "What do you think of Anthony Robbins?"

"Well, I think he is an extremely successful motivational speaker."

"Yes, but I heard one of his original tapes, and in that tape he contradicts what he is saying today! How can anyone listen to someone like that? If people knew the truth about him, they wouldn't follow his advice any longer."

Sigh. I replied, "Have you learned anything in the last 5 years that has changed your prior opinions on anything?"

"Well, yes," he replied. "But I wouldn't go and *speak* about it!"

Isn't it strange that we judge presenters by standards and ideals that we don't use with others? Knowledge is a journey, often with no solid destination. What may be a beautiful truth to you today could be proved wrong tomorrow. All that teachers can do is present the knowledge they have today, the best way they know how—and hope they learn more tomorrow, so they can do it better the next time.

> *There are times I almost think I am not sure of what I absolutely know!*
> *Very often find confusion in conclusion, I concluded long ago!*
> —"A Puzzlement"
> (From *The King & I,* by Richard Rodgers and
> Oscar Hammerstein II, 1951)

To Prevent It from Happening

There is not much you can do about it except be aware that you are being judged harshly. Decide what image of yourself you are most happy with, then do your best to live up to it.

> *You will be respected more if you come off as a reporter, rather than an expert. For example, I say, "As we consider how people can improve their performance, we all owe a debt of gratitude to the most important psychologist who has ever lived in the area of human performance. I am referring to Dr. Robert Assagioli, the Italian psychologist. God, I wish he'd been Irish! (wait for laugh.) He developed...."*
> *This attitude is much better than conveying the feeling of "Here you go, boys and girls, listen to me. I'm the big expert." Give credit to others and you won't be viewed as a charlatan.*
> —Chris Hegarty

What to Do

> *If a person really feels that strongly, and uses a word like "charlatan," I don't think you get anywhere by trying to change that person's mind. You may be able to silence people, but I doubt you can change their minds. It's an uphill battle, because, unfortunately, there are some motivational*

speakers who are charlatans. The thing to identify is that there are some excellent, reputable, professional speakers. It may help to point out that it is unfair to make a flashy generalization about any group of people.
—BRAD PLUMB

I don't believe in "clever" responses or ones that in some subtle way put down the speakers, such as the way comedians deal with hecklers. Coming from my background in psychology, I am more interested in the source of the upset. Somewhere this person has probably been ripped off by someone who is or was a charlatan, so I would say, "What makes you say that?" or "Who, specifically, are you referring to?" or "Do you think I'm a charlatan?" If the person says yes, I would then ask, "In what way do I appear to be a charlatan?"

These kinds of questions can usually evoke the real concern. These concerns might include "You're only here to sell me your tapes." "You don't care about me; you're only in it for the money." "I got ripped off by someone once." "I wish I could do what you do." "I don't think anyone could really care as much as you say you do"—which usually leads to "I was hurt once and I am afraid to trust anyone again."
—JACK CANFIELD

What to Say

Serious

You must have had an unpleasant experience. Will you share it? (Often what people really want is a way to express their frustration.)
—LILLY WALTERS

I agree with you. In my mind I can't motivate you, I can only educate you.
—JIM McJUNKIN

I'm very proud that I care so much about what I do, that I made a profession of it.
What do you do that you are proud of?
—W MITCHELL

I know you already don't believe what I have to say. Would you be kind enough to listen closely? Then at the end, tell me what I've said that is wrong.
—TOM ANTION

...You Notice Misssspelllled Words in Your Materials

To Prevent It from Happening

■ Proof your materials again 24 hours *after* you create them.

- Use spell-check on everything.
- Always have an extra set of eyes check the materials after you have.

What to Do

You can just fess up and say, "Oops!" Or you can pretend you did it on purpose as an exercise for "creativity," or in the interest of "quality"—whatever you can do to tie it into your topic of the day. Make a game out of seeing who can discover the most typos.

What to Say

Serious

To make sure you are paying close attention today, we have hidden many typographical errors throughout the materials, both on the overheads and in the workbook. Each time you see one, don't tell your neighbor, just write it down, clearly stating exactly where you found it. Whoever finds the most gets a prize!
—TOM FARANDA

Humorous

Any misspelled words or punctuation errors have been added for comedic effect.
—GENE MITCHENER, THE WHEELCHAIR COMIC

I believe in accurate spelling...I don't practice it, but I believe in it.
—ROGER LANGLEY

I was in the half of the class that made the top half possible.
—MICHAEL AUN

There are those people who wait for the speaker to make an error. You know the ones, retired English teachers. They sit together and elbow each other—"Look at that—he dangled his participle." I like to bring a thrill to retired teachers 'cause they don't get many thrills.

I am such a bad speller my spell-checker laughs at me.

I am not a lousy speller, I'm just creative.

I've always been known as a poor speller—backed up by lots of data.

We added that little mistake so you would have some joy in this presentation.
—TERRY PAULSON

Oh! I apologize. My word processor had a virus.

That is the Swahili/Pig Latin spelling.

That was put in there to test you.

I knew I shouldn't have had my dog proofread this.

—From *One Liners for Disaster*, by Tom Antion,
Anchor Publishing, 1993

Quote Mark Twain: "Never trust anyone who can't spell a word more than one way!"

—**ALLEN KLEIN**

I believe your education is not complete if you cannot spell a word three different ways!

—**UNKNOWN**

I feel it is my duty to keep the proofreaders of America employed.

—**LILLY WALTERS**

...Your Luggage Has Been Lost

To Prevent It from Happening

My father has always said, "There are two kinds of luggage: carry-on and lost." Whatever you must have to do the performance, you must carry on with you. I always carry a business suit, my notes, and my overheads (if I'm using them). That way, when I land and my luggage doesn't, I will at least be able to perform.

What to Do

If your notes get lost, just do the presentation without them. You know what you know. Make it work without the things you don't have. If your business clothes didn't arrive, do it in what you have. Consider not making reference to your attire at all. People will most likely think you are a trend setter, or trying to teach them some deep message with your unusual clothing. Speakers are an eccentric lot. It is almost expected that you will show up wearing something unusual. Go with it.

What to Say

I'm delighted to be back in _____ (city you are in). This is my third visit to _____. My luggage has only visited once.

—**JEFF DEWAR**

I am delighted to have been brought to _____ (town of presentation)

to speak. I am delighted to be here and I understand my luggage is delighted to be in Tibet, so I hope you will forgive my unusual attire.
—LILLY WALTERS

I must explain my inappropriate attire at this formal banquet. I knew what to pack but I had a moment of temporary insanity and checked my bag at the airline counter. It may arrive one day—possibly at the Cairo airport.

—ART LINKLETTER

You'd be surprised how much it costs to dress this cheap.
—DOLLY PARTON, AMERICAN ENTERTAINER
(From *Great Book of Funny Quotes,* by Eileen Mason, Sterling Publishing, 1993)

The scientific theory I like best is that the rings of Saturn are composed entirely of lost airline luggage.
—MARK RUSSELL, AMERICAN COMEDIAN, BORN 1932
(From *Great Book of Funny Quotes,* by Eileen Mason, Sterling Publishing, 1993)

They say clothes don't make a man or woman, but let me tell you, they sure help you avoid a lot of embarrassment.

Let me assure you that my message will be more appropriate than my clothes.
—ROGER LANGLEY

As you can tell, I'm taking a fashion risk.
—PHIL CASS

For me, dress for success means tucking in my shirt.
—TERRY PAULSON

Clothes make the man. Naked people have little or no influence on society.
—MARK TWAIN
(Submitted by Terry Paulson)

...Your Clothes Tear While You Are Speaking

To Prevent It from Happening

Always wear your clothes in an active situation *before* you present in them. Presenters have a very bad habit of buying a lovely new outfit just for the talk, and wearing it into action for the first time that day. Bad plan.

Carry safety pins and a needle and thread in your travel kit. If the damage isn't too bad, you may be able to make a mad dash to your room to fix it.

What to Do

Of course, it depends on what tears and where, but you have a few options:

- Carry on.
- Launch into a discussion exercise (see Chapter 5) and make a mad dash to your room.
- Make a joke about it.

What to Say

I knew I shouldn't have eaten that extra chocolate fudge sundae.
—DIANNA BOOHER

Looks like everything is having a ripping good time here today.
Funny? So funny I thought my pants would split—and they did.
Is there a tailor in the house?
—ROGER LANGLEY

Uh oh! It sounds like Calvin just split with Klein.
—TOM OGDEN

...Part of You Is Showing That Shouldn't Be

Campaigning Senator John F. Kennedy had made powerful speeches all over America. One night a man came backstage to meet the handsome senator. Hoping to gain the secret of Kennedy's tremendous power over his audience, the man asked, "What is the last thing you do before you go out to deliver one of your lectures? Do you read a favorite passage in Shakespeare or recall an inspiring bit of Shelley's poetry?"

"None of those," replied Mr. Kennedy. "I just feel to see if my pants are zipped up!"
—LARRY WILDE
(From *Library of Laughter*, Jester Press, 1988)

Once I was asked to participate in another speaker's presentation. She called me up and asked me what I would do if, in a hypothetical circum-

stance, I was speaking to a large audience and I looked down and noticed my fly was open. I said, "Well, like all good speakers, I would resort to a poem." She then asked what that poem would be. I said, "If there's anyone here who likes what they see, there's a lot more showing in Room 323." It was slightly naughty, but it got giant laughs.
—Gene Perret

To Prevent It from Happening

While you are in the restroom for that last relief break, always, always check yourself in the mirror carefully from the front and back. You may find all kinds of interesting things—even a few exciting items trailing along behind you.

What to Do

Make a joke and fix it—whether it's a wayward brassiere strap or an open fly. Give a quick prayer of thanks that you finally did see "it" before you went through the whole talk that way. Remember, no one really cares as much as you do about it. They are all only immensely relieved that you fixed it, because every person out there had been wishing there was some way to tell you.

What to Say

Excuse me, my clothes need a little more zip.
—Roger Langley

(At one point I noticed—right in midsentence—that my fly was open. I panicked! I reached down and looked right at the first person and said)
Mary, why didn't you tell me my fly was unzipped? This was a test to see how observant we are in here. You've got to do better than this next time!
(It wasn't that great of a line—but, hey, I was in a severe panic.)
—Dave Carey

Pardon me. I didn't intend to expose any of my shortcomings.
—Terry Braverman

(Stare at the offending garment and give the audience a mock devil-may-care look.) "It's the latest fashion from Paris...honest!"
—Lilly Walters

...You Spill Something on Yourself During the Meal

What to Do

...They had an electrical storm. The power was out, and the meeting was lit by candlelight, and of course the mic didn't work. During the dinner by candlelight, I managed to drop the baked potato in my lap. I thought, "Well, it's great the lights are out so no one will ever see the enormous spot in the middle of my silk skirt." So, I was conjuring all the one-liners about "darkness into light," etc., etc., when—right before I was scheduled to speak—the power came on, and I was introduced to an enthusiastic group who applauded not only me but the light going on. I was faced with a 4-inch in diameter grease stain, and no shawl to casually wrap around my lower half.

I decided to incorporate it into my speech. I opened with, "A Negaholic (my book and presentation topic) beats himself up because he or she does something stupid like dropping the potato in her lap during a power outage. I, however, am a recovering Negaholic, and therefore am not beating myself up for the spot on my skirt!" They applauded, I forgot about it, and so did they.

—Chérie Carter-Scott

What to Say

Humorous

And my children wonder why we've never been invited to the White House.

—Gene Perret

Never eat more than you can lift.

—Miss Piggy, Muppet character
(From *Great Book of Funny Quotes*, by Eileen
Mason, Sterling Publishing, 1993)

I wish this suit had come with gutters.

—George Goldtrap

On the long drive home tonight I'll still be able to sample the cuisine!

—Lorin Paulsen

It's times like these I wish I were wearing a sponge suit.

What I like best about this suit is that is goes well with everything—the gravy, the dressing...

—Roger Langley

This would happen on the day I forgot to bring my designer bib.

—Art Gliner

...The Meal Is Served
Very Late
To Prevent It from Happening

You can help the novice event planner estimate how long those dinners will *really* take. Novices always think dinner will be served faster than it really will be.

What to Do

If you are the one planning the event, you can comment on the meal being late, make jokes, and so on. If you are the guest speaker, make *very* light jokes. Believe me, the event planners and host *know* dinner is late and are feeling terrible that you—and the group—are being held late. You are treading on very dangerous ground to "snicker" about it.

What to Say

> If good things come to those that wait, that was one hell of a good meal we had.
> —ROGER LANGLEY

...The Food Is Very Strange
or Odd
To Prevent It from Happening

Prevention is possible only if you are on the planning end. Never serve the untested!

What to Do

Weird food is a great opportunity for humor. But make sure you cloak the humor in lots of praise about other things that were done well. The event planner really doesn't want to be reminded that the meal was a bomb.

What to Say

> I really appreciated the Venusian meal!
> —LORIN PAULSEN

That was some dinner. Are you sure McDonald's started out like this?

I have had a great many meals in many great restaurants, but this meal tonight—and I mean this sincerely—was the most recent.
—Roger Langley

I'll try not to repeat myself, and I hope the dinner does the same.
—From *Speaker's Idea File,* Original Humor
section by Gary Apple, premiere edition

What a great meal. I've never had leg of oat bran before.
—Terry Paulson

What *Not* to Say

What was that we had for dinner? Looked kinda like veal cordon Jeffrey Dahmer.

What exactly was that we all just ate for dinner? Just think we should find out now. The paramedics might need to know.

It's not that dinner was bad, but three terrorist groups have called in to claim responsibility.

The bad news—tonight's dinner. The good news—there wasn't much of it.

...The Weather Is Bad

What to Do

For cold or rainy weather. While you are holding your workbook or textbook, say, "Don't you love this kind of weather? Makes you want to curl up by a fire with a good book." Then you open the book and flames burst out! You can purchase one of these magic-trick books and just paste the cover of your own book over the top. Fun.

What to Say

Oh, the weather outside is frightful, but the crowd inside's delightful!
—Roger Langley

My great, great granddaddy used to say, "Everyone bellyaches 'bout the weather but nobody does nothin' 'bout it." Well, the weather is bad, but the company is good.
—Tom Antion

I have an announcement before we begin. Will the owner of an ark, license number "2BY2," please see the parking attendant? Your giraffes are eating the foliage.

—From *Current Comedy Newsletter,*
October 21, 1991

Because of the rain, it took me forever to get here. Traffic on the highway was slowed to 15 knots.

—From *Current Comedy Newsletter,*
December 9, 1991

...You Rush into the Wrong Meeting

John Wayne Lee's plane was late. He rushed to the event, ran into the room he was scheduled to be in, and there was the crowd, waiting. He immediately began his presentation. About 8 minutes into it, he realized something was very wrong. So he asked. You guessed it. John Wayne Lee was not the speaker they were waiting to hear! The planners had changed the room he was to present in. Oops.

To Prevent It from Happening

Always arrive early! Try to be the first person at the event. Your clients should find you waiting when they arrive.

Consistently check with the event planner on the evening before your presentation (or as soon as possible) to confirm that the meeting will still be in the same room you thought it was to be in. Actually go into the room so you know where it is.

What to Do

If you are getting an odd response from your audience, stop and find out what is going on. If you are in the wrong room, first, apologize; then, assign someone from their audience to find out what happened to their program. Go find your poor audience, who is by this time tapping their feet in impatience.

What to Say

I guess you are all wondering why I called you here.
Surprise!

I hope you like my presentation, but you'll have to come to another room to hear it.

Let's have a big hand for your speaker (directed toward the speaker in the room as an apology for interrupting).

I think everyone here except me is in the wrong room.

I hope I didn't keep you waiting long.

Is this where I sign up for squash lessons?

I just stopped in to let you know, if you need me I'll be in the _____ (conference room, Jefferson Room, etc.).

I just thought I'd drop in to say Hi!

Did someone here order a pizza?
>   —From *One Liners for Disaster*, by Tom Antion,
>   Anchor Publishing, 1993

I'm either the wrong speaker in the wrong meeting, or the wrong speaker in the right meeting, or the right speaker in the wrong meeting, but I'm definitely not the right speaker in the right meeting.
>   —ROGER LANGLEY

...Terrorists or Gang Members Crash Your Presentation

If you can keep your head while all about you are losing theirs, it's just possible you haven't grasped the situation.
>   —JEAN KERR, AMERICAN WRITER
>   (From *Great Book of Funny Quotes*, by Eileen
>   Mason, Sterling Publishing, 1993)

In February 1994, as a roundtable discussion session was in progress at the Holiday Inn in Torrance, California, a gunman ran into a meeting in progress and waved his gun, screamed something to the effect of "This is a robbery!" and fired a shot into the air. Not a pretty picture for any presenter to be faced with or to be prepared for. But this robber had made a particularly bad call, since this meeting was a team-building workshop for the Palos Verdes Estates Police Department. Several officers immediately tackled him to the ground—unfortunately, not before two of the officers were killed.

>   *...I looked up and saw one of the attendees in my seminar (to law enforcement personnel) cleaning his gun at his desk (weapons are not allowed in*

class unless for instruction). My first reaction was to make light of the situation, so I said with a grin, "Hey,_____, I really don't think you'll be needing that gun for the next segment on dealing with 'problem subordinates!'" Everyone else in the class laughed, but the guy with the gun looked up and said, "Oh, I never go anywhere without Veronica."

At that point I had a couple of decisions to make. The first one was to continue the class until the normal break time. I figured that the gun was dismantled and wouldn't fire so the danger right then was minimal. I set the class to working on a group exercise and asked one of the members of the local host agency to slip out and let some folks know what was going on.

When I brought them back from the exercise, the guy with the gun was starting to put it back together and the cavalry had not yet arrived. I picked the guy's magazine off his desk and told him one of the other guys in class was real interested in the kind of ammunition he carried. Then I passed the magazine to another class member, who made a big show of examining it carefully. By the time he had strung that out for a bit, I saw the administrator and my "messenger" in the back of the room.

We went to break and had a chat with our friend. The outcome was that he was subdued and transported to a local hospital, where he was admitted to the psychiatric unit.

—WALLY BOCK

To Prevent It from Happening

I don't know how you can prevent terrorism from happening. God willing, no one reading this book will ever need to deal with this issue.

What to Do

I wish there was a smarter thing for me to suggest to you. I feel like a doctor explaining a number of horrible choices you can try to combat a terminal illness. But consider this: You have the lives of others in your hands when you are on the platform. A privileged position. The best way to keep people alive is to set your pride aside, calmly find out what the threatening person wants, and hand it over. This is not the time for you to launch into your Sylvester Stallone impression.

What to Say

(With no sarcasm or hostility, in a low calm voice) What do you want? (Give it to the person.)

—LILLY WALTERS

...Other People Want
Permission to Quote You

As you start to get better at the craft of presenting, you will also be asked to make audiotapes and videos, and to write articles and books. People will ask if they can quote you.

The harsh reality is that people are going to use "adaptations" of the things you have said and written—*whether they ask your permission or not.* Most people feel they can "adapt" what others say and do, but they just shouldn't "adopt" it.

What to Do

If you are lucky enough to have people *ask* you if they can quote you, for heaven's sake, say yes! If you say no, they are going to use something very similar and not give you credit. Being quoted by others gives you greater prestige, credibility, and exposure.

What to Say

Thank you! I'd love you to quote me. By the way, how were you planning on crediting me? Can we just doublecheck that you have the references right?
　　　　　　　　　　　　　　　　　　　　—LILLY WALTERS

Spell my name right.
　　　　　　　　　　　—ROGER LANGLEY

...Your Cyberspace Lecture
Goes into Meltdown

Cyberlectures. The computer has brought a whole new realm of experience to the world of speaking. You sit in front of your computer (maybe even snuggled up with your laptop as you are propped up in bed in your jammies) and type your thoughts to hundreds of people who sit watching their screens (maybe in their jammies). There are many on-line computer companies now. I have given several lectures on America OnLine (affectionately called AOL to its devotees) and Genie. Mainly you follow a Q&A format in a cyberspace talk.

When I got done with that first on-line seminar, I was—literally—sweating. It was amazing—no, flat-out frightening! My first experience was with AOL, which advertised my program daily to its 500,000 membership—very good for my ego! The big day arrived. AOL had it set up so that every user who logged on would see an icon that said, "Come see Lilly Walters! Learn the 'Secrets of Successful Speakers' in the Small Business Center Conference Room." The user just clicks on the icon and gets popped into the "room." Uh-huh, sure. I guess everyone in the universe was in the mood for "Secrets" that day. Users began *flooding* into the room! All of a sudden, we went into a major meltdown. Some high-tech gremlin just threw me out of my lecture room! I'm sitting at my screen, frozen out of participating, but able to see all the questions my audience was trying to ask me. Then I watched in horror as they got angry with me for being "rude" and ignoring them! They began leaving in a justified huff. To my amazement, it all took on a fantasy air—like being on the bridge of a starship in a major catastrophe. In the back of my mind, I could hear Scotty yelling, "Captain! I can't hold her together any longer!"

Finally AOL got it sorted out, and on we went.

The terrible frustration for me was seeing the questions come up. I wanted to answer each one with a paragraph, at least—but knowing it just takes too long to type that much, I had to get each answer pruned down to a short sentence.

After those first 2 hours, I felt five times more exhausted than I have after any full day I have ever done. But I have learned a few things since, which I now pass on to you.

BEING A GUEST AT AN ON-LINE CONFERENCE
by Janet Attard

Being a guest at an on-line conference is a little like being the guest on a radio call-in show. The two main difference are that (1) people type their questions instead of speaking them into a telephone and (2) people pay by the minute while they wait for you and others asking questions to type.

Usually a lot of people attending the conference will want to ask a question. To get to as many as possible in the course of the hour or two that most conferences last, about all you can do is toss out the equivalent of brief sound bites—nuggets of wisdom that pertain to the question. In addition, be ready with a phone number that people can call for additional information or an address they can write to for information from you. Be sure it gets mentioned several times in the course of the seminar.

Be prepared for "guests" who aren't going to stay in their virtual seats, either. Some leave as soon as their question has been answered; others leave if you don't get to their question fast enough. Others drift in and out for the duration.

(Continued)

In fact, be prepared for almost anything to happen. The entire virtual conference room may stall, or even electronically capsize—dumping you out of the conference room or even off line.

One of the things you have to remember as a "lecturer" is that if you have to answer with a whole paragraph of information (as opposed to one brief sentence) you should type the information in spurts, hitting the return key frequently so that information gets sent to the screen and people know you aren't ignoring them. Ellipses at the end of each line let people know you aren't finished typing yet.

It's a good idea to send a list of potential interview questions to whoever is hosting the conference, so that if no one has questions (or worse, not many show up) or if the conference gets off topic, the host can prime the pump or steer the conference back onto the topics you want to cover.

Find out in advance how "crowd control" will be handled. Will there be a way of choosing who can ask a question and when the next question will be heard? Is there some way to block off all unwanted messages to the screen?

Check the calendar and think about what news-related off-line events might be going on at the same time as your conference. Super Bowl Sunday, the World Series or Olympics, presidential speeches, and similar events will keep people from logging on to "hear" you.

Besides all that—the best thing to remember is to enjoy the experience!

To Prevent It from Happening

Since surviving my first—terrifying—experience, I have a few tips to add to Janet's (see above). Meeting and event planners have differing experiences and knowledge. There is nothing wrong with your helping them along with ideas of how your particular presentation might run a bit more effectively. There are many types of "conference rooms" in on-line systems. You need to find out how yours will work and suggest that the host find a way of keeping the throng in control. Some rooms allow "guests" to see only the input of "lecturer" and "host." The guests type their questions and send them, but the questions don't appear on screen. Only the host can see them. When the lecturer finishes a thought, the host comes back with a comment like, "Interesting. Now Susie has a query related to that."

Other rooms are more like a free-for-all. Anyone can throw out any question at any time. So people who are just passing through will pop in and throw out questions or comments that are very bizarre, off your topic, or otherwise disruptive. If this is the sort of "conference room" you are presenting in, you should consult with your host.

If the system allows private messages to be sent, encourage the host to have assistants who will send a private message to each guest as he or she arrives in the room—something along these lines:

"Welcome to the _____ Conference. Today our presenter is Lilly Walters on *Secrets of Successful Speakers: How You Can Motivate, Captivate, and Persuade.* If you would like to ask a question, please type a '?' We call on you in order. Thank you."

If you are not a speed typist (I do about 60 words per minute), consider hiring a typist who can do 130 words per minute and who knows you very well. Then you can just dictate your lecture.

There are many software programs called "macros" that will allow you to preset your text. These need to be prepared in small sound bites (type bites?) of no more than three sentences. Many people's screens will allow them to see only that much at a time. You must rehearse using your macros in the room in which you will present! It is devastating to get there and find that all the preparatory work isn't usable in that particular environment.

What to Do

The main problem for traditional speakers is that this media form is so new. It is so much slower, and unusual to us, that we panic the first few times. If you are giving a conference on line and you begin to have problems, relax. Just let the audience wait. Keep typing away, at the speed you are able, and relax. People will usually assume you are slow because of an overload in the system.

What to Say

In this case, it is what to "type." You must keep your response very brief. There is a whole new language of codes and acronyms for online users. Some of these may help you get your feelings across when you just don't have time to type it all. They are called emoticons.

As you examine the list below, look at the codes sideways—:) is a smily face sideways.

:) = smile

;) = wink

:D = smile/laughing/big grin

:(= frown

:'(= crying

:X = my lips are sealed

:P = sticking out tongue

:* = kiss

O:) = angel

}:> = devil

LOL = laughing out loud

BRB = be right back

<g> = grin

{{{{{{{person's name}}}}}}} = a hug

Other nonverbal emotions are often displayed this way:

:::::scratching head:::::

:::::wondering what the heck he is thinking!!!!:::::

::::::looking at door, hoping to sneak out before she notices:::::

...You Want to Keep Roasts from Going Up in Flames

First, let's define some terms:

Roastmaster—the master of ceremonies

Roaster—the individual participant doing the roasting

Roastee—the guest of honor

To Prevent It from Happening

1. *Make sure the "roastee" wants to have a roast. Don't surprise the guest of honor or the result may be unpleasant.*
2. *Help the guest of honor prepare a counterroast. The counterroast is a reversal of roles in which the "guest of honor" turns the tables and roasts his or her "roasters" and the "roastmaster." It's an important part of the show, toward the end of the program.*
3. *As roastmaster, take a few shots at each roaster just before he or she gets up to speak.*

4. As roaster, take a few shots at the other people participating in the roast; it helps to create balance.

5. The roaster's job is not to fill time, but to be good. Better to do 2 minutes of funny stuff than fill a requested 5-minute slot.

6. Don't hit sensitive issues. A good way to avoid them and be funny is to exaggerate so much that, even though what you've said is pointed, people know that you made it up. For example, for a single woman: "She has 5 inches of dust under her bed—because she read in the Bible that man was created from dust!" No one will believe she really has all that dust under her bed.

7. As roastmaster, preface the roast with the fact that you give roasts only to people you like—that it's an honor to be roasted. It helps to set the scene.

—John Kinde

What to Do

- Joke about things that are obviously untrue. Then exaggerate them to make them more obvious:

To an AT&T executive: "If the Martians called Ed's office to contact earth, he'd try to sell them on the benefits of our new 800 service."

- Keep remarks focused on unimportant things that can't be damaging:

"Folks we are here tonight to roast _____. I'm particularly happy to be here because I can now say in public all the things I've been saying behind his back. He is man of the world—and you know what bad shape the world is in."

- Direct your insults to areas of recognized strength and superiority:

To a great family man or community leader: Joe's _____ (neighbors/ business/associates/preacher) all say what a wonderful team he and his wife make—if it weren't for Joe."

To a well-known philanthropist: "He is a man of rare gifts—he rarely gives them."

- When choosing the butt of a story, pick big targets. Never make fun of a small target (clerk or secretary).

- Make fun of the boss. He or she is still the boss.

- Members of the "in group" can joke about their peers. Bob Hope makes fun of Ronald Reagan. Everyone knows they are buddies.

- If you spread an insult or collection of insults widely, the group can laugh together. No one is individually embarrassed. The same remarks aimed at an individual removed from the cohesive influence of the group might cause someone to get upset.

- Always make fun of yourself first. If you kid yourself first, the members of the audience will be more receptive when you kid them.

At a program with a long head table with lots of speakers an MC might say: "The MC's job is not to be wise or witty. In fact, it is his job to appear *dull so that the speakers on the program will shine in comparison. Tonight it looks like I'm going to have to rise to the new heights of boredom."*

Another good MC line: "I'm glad to be here tonight to look into your faces—and God knows there are some faces here that need looking into."
—TOM ANTION

What to Say

As I look back over her checkered career, _____ has been a modest person—with so much to be modest about.

I don't know what you could say about _____ that he hasn't said about himself.

He's got the kind of face that belongs on radio.

_____ said he was kept up all night by two women banging on his door. He finally had to get up to let them out.
—UNKNOWN

Weighty Wisdom

You will do better to use the following on people who are slender, or on yourself. Be careful about using "fat" jokes on people who are overweight—they may *seem* to be laughing, but often they are not. In your research and interview with the roastee, you can ask permission about what is acceptable and what is not.

_____ is a light eater. As soon as it's light, she starts to eat.
—HENNY YOUNGMAN, AMERICAN COMEDIAN, BORN
1906
(From *Great Book of Funny Quotes*, by Eileen
Mason, Sterling Publishing, 1993)

You go in and get your shoes shined and you have to take the guy's word for it.

I beat anorexia.

The reason I don't play golf is that when I put the ball where I can see it, I can't hit it. When I put the ball where I can hit it, I can't see it.
—MICHAEL AUN

Bald Lies

Always clear baldness jokes with the roastee.

It's a solar panel for a sex machine.

_____ would give anything to have a "bad hair day."

Grass doesn't grow on a busy street.
—MICHAEL AUN

Miscellaneous Material

In all or most of the following, try substituting the roastee's name for the pronouns "he/she" or "I" or for the notable person mentioned.

Dear Randolph, utterly unspoiled by failure.

> —NOEL COWARD ABOUT RANDOLPH CHURCHILL
> (From *Great Book of Funny Quotes*)

Frank Harris is invited to all the great houses in England—once.

> —OSCAR WILDE, IRISH POET, PLAYWRIGHT, AND
> NOVELIST, BORN 1856
> (From *Great Book of Funny Quotes*)

Sometimes when you look in his eyes you get the feeling that someone else is driving.

> —DAVID LETTERMAN, AMERICAN TELEVISION HOST,
> BORN 1947
> (From *Great Book of Funny Quotes*)

A mind so fine, no ideas could violate it.

> —T. S. ELIOT ABOUT HENRY JAMES
> (From *Great Book of Funny Quotes*)

Some men are born mediocre, some men achieve mediocrity, and some men have mediocrity thrust upon them.

He was a self-made man who owed his lack of success to nobody.

> —JOSEPH HELLER, AMERICAN NOVELIST,
> BORN 1923
> (From *Great Book of Funny Quotes*)

Harold could be the best conversationalist in the world—if he ever found anyone he thought worth talking to.

> —HERBERT ALEXANDER ABOUT HAROLD ROBBINS
> (From *Great Book of Funny Quotes*)

His enemies might have said before that he talked rather too much; but now he has occasional flashes of silence that make his conversation perfectly delightful.

> —SYDNEY SMITH, ENGLISH CLERGYMAN, BORN 1771
> (From *Great Book of Funny Quotes*)

I often quote myself; it ads such spice to my conversations.

> —GEORGE BERNARD SHAW, IRISH PLAYWRIGHT,
> BORN 1856
> (From *Great Book of Funny Quotes*)

Since we have to speak well of the dead, let's knock them while they're alive.
> —JOHN SLOAN, AMERICAN PAINTER, BORN 1871
> (From *Great Book of Funny Quotes*)

He's so generous he'd give you the sleeves out of his vest.
> —ANONYMOUS
> (From *Great Book of Funny Quotes*)

His descriptive powers were remarkable, but his ideas cannot too soon be forgotten.
> —BERTRAND RUSSELL ABOUT D. H. LAWRENCE
> (From *Great Book of Funny Quotes*)

I never forget a face, but in your case I'd be glad to make an exception.
> —GROUCHO MARX, AMERICAN ACTOR AND COMEDI-
> AN, BORN 1890
> (From *Great Book of Funny Quotes*)

The affair between Margot Asquith and Margot Asquith will live as one of the prettiest love stories in all literature.
> —DOROTHY PARKER, AMERICAN WRITER, BORN 1893
> (From *Great Book of Funny Quotes*)

There is absolutely nothing wrong with Oscar Levant that a miracle can't fix.
> —ALEXANDER WOOLLCOTT, AMERICAN JOURNALIST
> AND CRITIC, BORN 1887
> (From *Great Book of Funny Quotes*)

Our guest is familiar to many of you. And if it's any consolation, he owes me money, too.

Our guest is a little depressed today. His shrink canceled his appointment because he wanted to concentrate on a patient he could help.

Our guest is the greatest guy in the world. And that's not my opinion—it's his.
> —From *Speaker's Idea File*, Original Humor
> section by Gary Apple, premiere edition

_____'s popularity is up slightly in the polls. He's now somewhere between IRS agents and Jehovah's witnesses.
> —From *Speaker's Idea File*, Original Humor
> section by Gary Apple, September 1993

_____ is living proof that there is life after death.

Yup, _____ has the highest reputation for integrity that money can buy.

I'd like to introduce _____, who has been called rude, fat-headed, self-centered, and egotistical—but that's just opinion, the opinion of his friends.

You always leave people with such a good feeling—like, oh, the feeling you get when you stop banging your head against a wall.

You're just like a daughter (son) to me! Uncivilized, offensive, insulting.

You just don't seem yourself lately. We've all noticed the improvement.
                                                                    —UNKNOWN

...The Speech Bombs—Your Ego Is Shattered

My favorite Art Linkletter story is one he tells of a lady who thought she recognized him but could not remember his name. She tried several times...Walter Cronkite? Hugh Downs? Arthur Godfrey? Attempting to assist her memory, the acclaimed star of radio and TV said, "Art Linkletter." "No," she said, "that's not right either."
                                                                    —GEORGE GOLDTRAP

Failure is an event, not a person.
                                                                    —UNKNOWN

To Prevent It from Happening

Practice, rehearse, and drill yourself on your presentation. (See the section in Chapter 6 on polishing your delivery.) Research your audiences; know their needs so you can better meet them. As Mary Martin said, "Care more about them than you care about yourself." Most audiences will forgive you anything if you are the kind of presenter who forgets about "you" and honestly cares for them.

What to Do and Say

Even a brilliant presenter has a bad day. The better you get, the more critical you will become of yourself. That simple little mistake you made may not even be noticed by others. But even the very best presenters may bomb. You may bomb for many reasons—you aren't feeling well; you have had bad news—all the things discussed in this book.

But if you *are* bombing, cut your losses—cut to your best close and cut a swathe off the stage. Then go and evaluate why the presentation bombed. If you can, fix it for your next one. Life is a learning process. Use the lesson you learned to elevate yourself to the next level. It can be one of the most significant emotional experiences in your life.

Success is seldom final; failure is seldom fatal.
                        —Jeff Dewar

...Your Ego Is Overdone

Egotist: a person...more interested in himself than in me.
                        —Ambrose Bierce, American journalist, born
                        1842
                        (From *Great Book of Funny Quotes*, by Eileen
                        Mason, Sterling Publishing, 1993)

Egotism is the anesthetic that dulls the pain of stupidity.
                        —Samuel Goldwyn, American producer, born
                        1882
                        (From *Great Book of Funny Quotes*)

To Prevent It from Happening

A speaker is a person who, if you are not talking about him (her), is not listening.
                        —Anonymous

How many speakers does it take to turn a light bulb? Only one. He holds the light bulb and the world revolves around him.
                        —Mike Walters

Tired of jokes like the two above? Me too. But we all hear them all the time when we begin speaking and training—because, unfortunately, there is a grain of truth in the kidding.

What to Do

We are in an industry whose practitioners are often called motivational, fabulous, awe-inspiring, egotistical, arrogant, and difficult to get along with.

All of the above...sometimes. If you decide to tackle the challenge and take the platform, you have a right to feel pride. I think we are called arrogant and difficult because the pressure of the challenge makes us a little crazy.

It is easy to get caught up in the glitter and glamour of the platform and forget the caring and sharing. For the most part, when speakers put on the facade of arrogance, it's because we get scared. We realize we didn't lift and inspire, teach and change, the way we wanted to that day. So we put up a false bravado. Inside, we know the truth.

When I am honest with myself and to others about the pain I feel when I don't do a good job, I am much more attractive. Charles "Tremendous"

Jones, a wonderful motivational speaker, tells a story of a young city minister who goes out into the country to give a sermon. The man is excited. These country folk are in for a treat; they will never have heard the like of his message! He swaggers up the steps into the pulpit and lets loose! After a while he realizes he is in trouble—they aren't responding in the right places! They don't laugh at his great lines! He tries harder—nothing works. When he is finally done, he hangs his head and quietly walks off the dais. An old man puts his hand out and whispers in the young man's ear, "Son, if you'd gone up there the way you'd come down, you could have come down the way you'd gone up."

> —From *Secrets of Successful Speakers: How You Can Motivate, Captivate, and Persuade,* by Lilly Walters (McGraw-Hill, 1993)

What to Say

Praise is like perfume—it's all right to smell it as long as you don't swallow it."

> —ATTRIBUTED TO ADLAI STEVENSON

Miscellaneous Funnies You Can't Wait to Use

Actually, I couldn't find a good place to use the following, but they were fun, so here they are!

The difference between the right word and the almost right word is the difference between lightning and the lightning bug.

> —MARK TWAIN

(Announcing good news) I have bad news for all you pessimists in the audience.

> —From *Current Comedy Newsletter,* November 25, 1991

(Announcing bad news) Let's face it. Communism had a better quarter than we had.

> —From *Current Comedy Newsletter,* September 23, 1991

I go to my radio voice and make the announcement utilizing my "Walter Cronkite" imitation.

> —MICHAEL AUN

We have now reached the highlight of today's meeting—a 15-minute break.

It's time for a brief break. You may prefer to view it as a 15-minute parole.

Now that we've stretched your patience, feel free to stretch your legs.

We will now take a brief break. Don't even think of leaving. We have samples of your clothing and bloodhounds to track you down.
—From *Current Comedy Newsletter*,
June 10, 1991

We will now take a 10-minute break. Those of you who are asleep can wake up. And those of you who remained awake can take a nap.
—From *Current Comedy Newsletter*,
June 24, 1991

I'm parked outside at a meter—so we'll be taking a break every 30 minutes.
—From *Current Comedy Newsletter*,
November 25, 1991

Now that everyone has had a nice long nap, why don't we have a 15-minute break?
—From *Current Comedy Newsletter*,
December 9, 1991

Either they brought in some empty chairs or some of you have left.
—From *Current Comedy Newsletter*,
July 15, 1991

Welcome back. You'll be pleased to know that while you were out, I managed to think of something more to say.
—From *Current Comedy Newsletter*,
December 23, 1991

I'm not one of those speakers who will bore you with a long speech....I can do it just as dandy with a short speech.

I bet some people tell you I have wit, interest, and humor. Some tell the truth.
—Unknown

(Appearing before a sales meeting of realtors in Southern California during a slump) I knew this was going to be a glum audience, but I misjudged you a trifle. Therefore I will begin by saying, "Dearly beloved..."
—Art Linkletter

(When you can't find the opening in the curtain) What did they do—sew it up? (After you break through) It healed!
—Tom Ogden

(Since I collect bumper stickers, I keep dozens of them on hand to relate to a particular situation. Here are just a few.)

Children, tired of being harassed by your stupid parents? Act now! Move out! Get a job! While you still know everything!

Ask some teenagers. They know everything.

*"My child is in the top half of the class at Lakeview Elementary School."
My response: "Who cares? My child made it possible!"*

(On the back of a Mercedes with a beautiful blonde inside) Was his!

I didn't claw my way to the top of the food chain to eat vegetables.

(On the back of a heavy-set man's car) I beat anorexia.

Money isn't everything but it does tend to keep the children in touch.

If the Yankees were so smart, why'd they keep the North?

Best oxymoron: "Greater Cleveland."

Never eat the yellow snow.

(On a car in Florida) When I get old I'm going to move up north and drive slow.

Lawyers eat their young.

So many pedestrians...so little time.

Happiness is seeing your mother-in-law's picture on a milk carton.

The more you complain, the longer God lets you live.

Do you know where you'll be when your laxative starts working?
—Michael Aun

(I am a professor. Some people consider that title as stuffy.) Well, like Henry Kissinger, I'll settle for your highness or his excellency.
—Gerald C. Meyers

(An audience member is waving an arm to get your attention) Excuse me, are you trying to land a jet?
—Terry Braverman

Lectern? Wasn't he the bad guy in Superman?
—Jeff Slutsky

Rostrum? You mean the place you excuse yourself to when the speaker is boring?
—Mike Walters

It's great to be among friends—pity none of them are here.
—Max Hitchins

I must be a very entertaining speaker. Every year the IRS invites me back to explain my tax return.
—From *Speaker's Idea File*, Original Humor
section by Gary Apple, premiere edition

They say you should never overstate your argument. And here are 147 reasons why this is true.
> —From *Speaker's Idea File*, Original Humor
> section by Gary Apple, May 1993

Stop me if you've heard this joke before. Actually, you may want me to stop me if you've heard me tell any joke before.
> —From *Speaker's Idea File*, Original Humor
> section by Gary Apple, June 1993

I believe there is one thing that all successful people have in common— and I'd sure like to know what it is.

I went to a stress workshop and had terrific results. Now I worry much more effectively.
> —From *Speaker's Idea File*, Original Humor
> section by Gary Apple, September 1993

What time is it?...Oh, no! I've been asking people for the time all day, and each one tells me something different.
> —Leonard Ryzman

One of my attendees came up to me after a speech. "Jeff, I bet a lot of people tell you funny jokes and stories."
"Why, yes, they do."
"Well then, why don't you use them?"
> —Jeff Dewar

I'd like to say I'm happy to be here...so I will. I'm happy to be here.

I'd like to say a few words. Sponge, toothpick, shoe, and bottle cap. Later, I'll say a few more.
> —Roger Langley

In preparing this speech, I used the great ideas of Churchill, Gandhi, Confucius, and Jesus. In case you disagree with anything I've said, go talk to them.
> —Lilly Walters

My brother Marc and I were giving a presentation together when one of the audience members said, "Are you married?" Without missing a beat, we both said at exactly the same time, "No, we're brothers."

Sometimes people ask my brother and me if we're twins. I say, "Yea, and we were born 16 months apart. It was a very difficult birth."

Oftentimes before a big program the audio people need me to do a sound check on the mic. Instead of "testing one, two, three" like most people do, I recite "you got trouble in River City" from Music Man. Really impresses the hell out of the support staff and once in a while the client hears it too.
> —Jeff Slutsky

Storyteller Harry Hershfield was the MC at a big New York banquet. He began his remarks to the audience: "My job is to talk to you and your job is to listen. If you finish first, please let me know it."
> —LARRY WILDE
> (From *Library of Laughter*, Jester Press, 1988)

I was going to read a speech titled "Our Overdependency on Technology," but my laser printer broke down.
> —From *Speaker's Idea File*, Original Humor
> section by Gary Apple, May 1993

Do you know the difference between education and experience? Education is when you read the fine print; experience is what you get when you don't.
> —PETE SEEGER

Do you know the difference between training and education? How many of you have teenage daughters? (Wait for the raised hands) Would you rather they had sex education or sex training?
> —STEVE GOTTLIEB

Thrusting my nose firmly between his teeth, I threw him heavily to the ground on top of me.
> —MARK TWAIN

I've already told you more than I know.
> —DIANNA BOOHER

I didn't mind the ones glancing at their watches, it was the ones shaking them that bothered me.
> —UNKNOWN

Harvey Korman used to speak to the audience between acts when I was working on the Carol Burnett show. He used to get laughs with this line: "How many think I look taller in person than I do on TV? How many think I look shorter? How many don't give a damn?"
> —GENE PERRET

The House of Lords is like a glass of fine champagne that has stood for 5 days.
> —WINSTON CHURCHILL ABOUT CLEMENT ATTLEE
> (From *Great Book of Funny Quotes*, by Eileen
> Mason, Sterling Publishing, 1993)

He can compress the most words into the smallest idea of any man I ever met.
> —ABRAHAM LINCOLN, SIXTEENTH U.S. PRESIDENT,
> BORN 1809
> (From *Great Book of Funny Quotes*)

If they try to rush me, I always say, "I've only got one other speed, and it's slower."
—GLENN FORD, AMERICAN ACTOR, BORN 1916
(From *Great Book of Funny Quotes*)

Ninety percent of the politicians give the other ten percent a bad name.
—HENRY KISSINGER, AMERICAN POLITICAL SCIENTIST, BORN 1923
(From *Great Book of Funny Quotes*)

It is best in theater to act with confidence, no matter how little right you have to it.
—LILLIAN HELLMAN, AMERICAN PLAYWRIGHT, BORN 1905
(From *Great Book of Funny Quotes*)

I'm going to speak my mind because I have nothing to lose.
—S. I. HAYAKAWA, AMERICAN POLITICIAN AND EDUCATOR, BORN 1906
(From *Great Book of Funny Quotes*)

Diplomacy is the art of saying "nice doggie" until you can find a rock.
—WILL ROGERS, AMERICAN HUMORIST AND ENTERTAINER
(From *Great Book of Funny Quotes*)

An expert is a person who can take something you already know and make it sound confusing.
—ANONYMOUS
(From *Great Book of Funny Quotes*)

The most important thing in acting is honesty; once you learn to fake that, you're in!
—SAMUEL GOLDWYN, AMERICAN PRODUCER, BORN 1882
(From *Great Book of Funny Quotes*)

(On being asked what he thought of Western civilization) I think it would be a good idea.
—MAHATMA GANDHI, INDIAN POLITICAL AND SPIRITUAL LEADER, BORN 1869
(From *Great Book of Funny Quotes*)

There is only one thing in the world worse than being talked about, and that is not being talked about.
—OSCAR WILDE, IRISH POET, PLAYWRIGHT, AND NOVELIST, BORN 1859
(From *Great Book of Funny Quotes*)

Getting a dog is like getting married. It teaches you to be less self-centered, to accept sudden, surprising outbursts of affection, and not to be upset by a few scratches on your car.
—WILL STANTON, AMERICAN WRITER, BORN 1918
(From *Great Book of Funny Quotes*)

Computers come in two varieties: the prototype and the obsolete.
—ANONYMOUS
(From *Great Book of Funny Quotes*)

A promotional piece for a private club's gala event installing its new president read: "The evening will conclude with a toast to the incoming president in champagne, kindly supplied by the outgoing president, drunk as usual at midnight."
—ANONYMOUS
(From *Great Book of Funny Quotes*)

I know a man who gave up smoking, drinking, sex, and rich food. He was healthy right up to the time he killed himself.
—JOHNNY CARSON, AMERICAN TELEVISION HOST
AND COMEDIAN, BORN 1925
(From *Great Book of Funny Quotes*)

Somebody's boring me...I think it's me.
—DYLAN THOMAS, WELSH POET AND PLAYWRIGHT,
BORN 1914
(From *Great Book of Funny Quotes*)

Success didn't spoil me; I've always been insufferable.
—FRAN LEBOWITZ, AMERICAN JOURNALIST, BORN 1950
(From *Great Book of Funny Quotes*)

Only the mediocre are always at their best.
—JEAN GIRAUDOUX, FRENCH DIPLOMAT, NOVELIST,
AND PLAYWRIGHT, BORN 1882
(From *Great Book of Funny Quotes*)

The advantage of the incomprehensible is that it never loses its freshness.
—PAUL VALÉRY, FRENCH POET, ESSAYIST AND CRITIC,
BORN 1871
(From *Great Book of Funny Quotes*)

You can always spot an educated man. His opinions are the same as yours.
—ANONYMOUS
(From *Great Book of Funny Quotes*)

If only I had a little humility I would be perfect.
—TED TURNER, AMERICAN ENTREPRENEUR, BORN 1938
(From *Great Book of Funny Quotes*)

Get your facts straight; then you can distort them as you please.

Suppose you were an idiot; and suppose you were a member of Congress; but I repeat myself.
                    —MARK TWAIN, AMERICAN JOURNALIST, LECTURER,
                        AND AUTHOR, BORN 1835
                        (From *Great Book of Funny Quotes*)

Life is the art of drawing sufficient conclusions from insufficient premises.
                    —SAMUEL BUTLER, ENGLISH SATIRIST AND NOVELIST,
                        BORN 1835
                        (From *Great Book of Funny Quotes*)

It is part of prudence to thank an author for his book before reading it, so as to avoid the necessity of lying about it afterwards.
                    —GEORGE SANTAYANA, AMERICAN PHILOSOPHER,
                        POET, AND NOVELIST, BORN 1863
                        (From *Great Book of Funny Quotes*)

An expert is a man who has made all the mistakes which can be made in a very narrow field.
                    —NEILS BOHR, DANISH PHYSICIST, BORN 1885
                        (From *Great Book of Funny Quotes*)

"Gee, wouldn't it have been easier to let us do a little work today?"

5 Group Therapy: Simple Audience Participation Exercises

As you have seen in almost every panic situation, a good audience participation exercise can be an excellent learning device that allows you time to fix a crisis. But more than that, it is an exceptional way to teach.

A man who carries a cat by the tail learns something he can learn in no other way.

—Mark Twain

Language is the most imperfect and expensive means yet discovered for communicating thought.

—William James

People do not stop playing because they grow old; they grow old because they stop playing.
                                   —UNKNOWN
                                   (Quoted in *Eat Desert First* by Steve Wilson,
                                   DPT Enterprise, Inc., 1990)

I pay the schoolmaster, but 'tis the schoolboys that educate my son.
                                   —RALPH WALDO EMERSON

WHAT TO SAY WHEN
...You Need to Reach the
Audience in the Way They
Listen

Some of your listeners are *visual processors*—they need to "see" things to understand them. Some are *auditory*—they need to "hear" to learn. Some are *tactile*—they need to "do" things. All people need *some of each*, but the magic is in the mix. A brilliant presentation uses some of each learning mode. Most presenters have auditory teaching skills down but find it harder to use the tactile. Hence, this chapter of ideas.

Edgar Dale, a researcher, developed what is now known as "Dale's cone of experience." He says people will remember:

20 percent of what they hear

30 percent of what they see

50 percent of what they see and hear

80 percent of what they hear, see, and do

I hear, I forget,
I see, I remember,
I do, I understand!

                                   —CONFUCIUS

...You Need to Explain How
to Do a Participation
Exercise

Smart people get downright dumb when they do a group exercise. You need to make your instructions very simple and very clear, as if you were teaching a 12-year-old. No, I'm not kidding. People get so preoccupied that they don't concentrate on what you are saying. I like to follow these five steps:

1. Have the instructions written out—in workbooks or on slides or overhead transparencies.

2. Read the instructions to the participants, as they read along with you.

3. Reexplain the instructions simply, "So, in other words..."

4. Ask one member of the group to tell you his or her interpretation of what you said. (Handle this step with care. You want the group to feel you are asking one of them to explain, not because that one person is so smart and the rest are dense, but because you have difficulty conveying just what you want when you explain this exercise, and you need their help. They will love you for your humanness.)

5. Walk an "example group" through the exercise while the rest watch.

Don't be surprised when they still don't get it!

...You Have to Leave the Room in a Hurry! Try These, Simple and Quick

All the exercises below are great for those moments when you are in trouble and need to leave the room *now*.

Discussion Exercises

There are endless variations on group exercises. Almost any topic—or "pretext"—will do. Here are some examples.

(Hold up a pencil or a piece of paper—anything that at least most of the audience members will have with them.) Tell the audience: "Gather into groups of three or four. Find 25 uses for this object. Go."

Take the next 5 minutes and turn to your neighbor (or your group of _____) and discuss the two best ideas you have learned today, and how you will apply them to your own situation at work/home. You have 5 minutes. Go ahead.

(Use the exercise above, but conclude with...) When we resume, be prepared to tell the rest of the group one of your neighbor's applications of today's idea. You have 5 minutes. Go ahead.

Take the next 5 minutes and turn to your neighbor (or your group of _____). Please develop two questions you wished I had answered more fully. Please elect a group leader (if the group you have assigned is bigger than three people). You have 5 minutes. Go ahead.

Take the next 5 minutes and turn to your neighbor (or your group of _____). If you were going to teach _____ (your topic), what three things would you want your listeners to take home? Please elect a group leader (if the group you have assigned is bigger than three people). You have 5 minutes. Go ahead.

Think of the three best ideas you have gained so far today. Write them down in your diary or calendar on the day you intend to take action upon them—specify exactly what you intend to do. You have 5 minutes. Go ahead.

Take the next 5 minutes and turn to your neighbor (or your group of _____). Finish these sentences:

1. *I am worried about attempting to do _____ (whatever the topic is you are covering) because...*
2. *I am excited about attempting to do _____ because...*

Please say what you feel, visualize these things in your mind, and on a piece of paper verbalize the way you hear the answers in your mind.
Finish those two sentences: "I'm excited because..." and "I'm worried because..."
Please elect a group leader (if the group you have assigned is bigger than three people). You have 5 minutes. Go ahead.
　　　　　　　　　　　　　　　　　　—LILLY WALTERS

Team up into groups of three. I'd like you to identify three companies that you perceive to be successful. For each of those companies, identify three reasons for their success. You have 5 minutes. Let's go to work.

What I'd like you to do is get out a piece of paper. I want you to answer these three questions.

1. *How do your customers perceive you?*
2. *How do you want them to perceive you?*
3. *What can you do to change?*

(You can quickly write on a flipchart or board the three key words "perceive," "want," and "change.")

What I'd like you to do is team up into groups of 3. Imagine an organization that has everything working right. (Alternate wording: imagine your department without any problems—working perfectly.) Sit down for a minute, by yourself. Imagine what that organization looks like. Then team up into groups of three and draw that picture as a team. There is flipchart paper up here.
　　　　　　　　　　　　　　　　　　—JEFF DEWAR

(Great way to open) Turn to your neighbor and describe an event that had the most positive effect on your life. Be prepared to tell the rest of us about your partner's experience.
　　　　　　　　　　　　　　　　　　—JIM McJUNKIN

When you get back to the audience, you need to have closure on any of the above exercises. Allow a few minutes for individuals or groups to share with the rest of the audience or with a smaller subgroup or to do something with what they have just discussed. Perhaps have them write down any great ideas they have just learned in their calendars or on an action item list.

TIPS ON HOW TO FACILITATE DISCUSSIONS

The University of Georgia recently surveyed 50 facilitators to find out what they consider the top skills required of a good facilitator. Here is what to try for.

1. **Planning.** The facilitator involves the meeting leader or initiator in planning; develops clear meeting outcomes (goals); designs an agenda and selects group processes on the basis of those outcomes; clarifies ground rules; learns about the group members ahead of time; and uses appropriate tools, such as visual aids or meeting software.

2. **Listening.** The facilitator really listens to what the group is saying and makes an effort to make sense out of it; clarifies goals, terms, and definitions; reiterates participant responses; remembers previous comments to reconnect information; and helps organize information into themes.

3. **Flexibility.** The facilitator adapts the agenda or meeting activities on the spot, as needed; handles multiple tasks smoothly; adapts personal style to the group; and tries new things.

4. **Focus.** The facilitator has a definite direction and knows where to go next in the agenda; clearly communicates the task to the group; and keeps the group's comments relevant to the desired outcome.

5. **Encouraging participation.** The facilitator draws out individuals by asking questions; gets people involved early on; controls dominant people to ensure equal participation; provides anonymity and confidentiality when needed; acknowledges and is open to the group's contributions; and uses humor, games, music, and play to enhance an open, positive environment.

(Continued)

6. **Managing.** The facilitator leads the group through the meeting process; uses the agenda to guide the group; sets time limits, enforces ground rules, and limits choices; provides models, frameworks, and processes to guide the group; uses breaks effectively; and checks progress and reactions with the meeting leader and group.

7. **Questioning.** The facilitator considers how to word questions that encourage thought and participation, and develops thoughtful questions on the spot, when necessary.

8. **Promoting ownership.** The facilitator helps the group take responsibility for the meeting and its outcomes; helps the group create follow-up plans; turns the floor over to others; permits the group to call its own breaks; and encourages the group to evaluate the process.

9. **Building rapport.** The facilitator demonstrates responsiveness and respect for people; is sensitive to emotions; watches and responds to nonverbal signals; empathizes with individuals who have special needs; helps develop constructive relationships with and among members; greets and mingles with the group; and uses the group's own words and symbols.

10. **Self-awareness.** The facilitator recognizes and deals with his or her own behavior or feelings; behaves confidently; behaves honestly—openly admits mistakes and lack of knowledge; shows enthusiasm; and keeps his or her ego out of the discussion.

11. **Managing conflict.** The facilitator encourages the group to handle conflict constructively; provides techniques to help the group deal with conflict; helps the group gain agreement and consensus on issues; and allows the group to vent negative emotions constructively.

12. **Broadening discussion.** The facilitator encourages looking at issues from different points of view, and uses techniques, metaphors, stories, and examples to get the group to consider different frames of reference.

13. **Understanding the technology.** The facilitator is familiar with any technology used; clearly understands tools and their functions and capabilities; and solves common technical difficulties.

---

14. **Presenting information.** The facilitator gives explicit instructions; uses clear and concise language in presenting ideas; gives the group written information such as handouts and printouts; provides research and background information; presents models and framework clearly; and makes important information visible on flipcharts or overhead transparencies.

The University of Georgia Study was conducted by Dr. Victoria Clawson and Dr. Bob Bostrom.

To facilitate discussions, don't stand. You stand only to give directions or to regain control. Sit with them if you want them to speak. People always expect the one standing to "take the lead." If you really want them to discuss, "Get out of the way of their education!"

—MICHAEL PODOLINSKY

Self-Quizzes

Self-quizzes can often be even more effective than writing quizzes yourself. Break the audience into groups; each group writes a quiz they will give to the others. To ensure simplicity, the questions must be in true-false or multiple-choice form. Then have each group elect a group leader. The group leader reads the questions to the rest of the audience, who try to answer. This exercise is lots of fun, with great sharing and repetition of information.

Do the math in your head quickly on this. If you have 50 people and you break them into 5 groups, that's 10 people per group. If each group comes up with a quiz of 5 questions each, that's 50 questions. In this case scenario, that might be a bit long. I find a total of 40 questions is fun and a great review. Consider breaking the audience into bigger groups with fewer questions. This will take less "quiz" time. You will need to make a quick decisions when the time arises.

Don't have each group read all of its questions at once. Have the first group read one, then move to the next group, and so on. Otherwise, the chances are good that by the time you get to the end, all the questions will have been read (repeat questions are common), and the last groups will feel a bit cheated.

(To get the audience into it) Break into groups of _____. You are going to write a quiz for the rest of the group, just five questions

about_____. The answers to these questions must be true-false or multiple-choice.

Please elect a group leader (if the group you have assigned is bigger than three people).

Now, you don't want the answer to be easy, but you must be able to answer it yourself. Also, the other group will be able to challenge your answer.

You have 5 minutes. Go ahead.

(To launch into the quiz giving)

All right, let's start with this group. Read us just your first question. Then we'll go on to the next group until we have gone all the way around the room. Then we'll start over with this group. We'll go on this way until we have asked all the questions from all the groups. There will, of course, be some duplicate questions, so if you have a question that has already been asked, please just skip it.

—LILLY WALTERS

T-Diagrams

A T-diagram (see Figure 5-1) encourages members to look at both sides of any issue. It can be effective in helping to change your listeners' mindset. T-diagrams are a good warm-up to move into a new topic area. They are very versatile and applicable to any topic.

T-Diagram	
People will say that participating on a team is…	
Constructive, rewarding, fulfilling when…	Destructive, frustrating, lonely when…

Figure 5-1. Sample T-diagram for team participation. (*Reproduced with permission from* Building Enthusiastic Teams *workbook by Jeff Dewar*)

In the following example, the topic was the advantages of team participation, part of a "Building Enthusiastic Teams" seminar by Jeff Dewar. Jeff breaks the group into subgroups of three to eight people. They elect a group leader. The leader conducts the discussion first on the constructive, then on the destructive aspects of working on a team. Of course, you could use this to generate discussion on any topic which you are presenting.

> *Elect a group leader. Group leader, have one of your group take a piece of paper or use the back of your handout (or whatever else you know they have) and make a big "T" on it. (It helps if you have a flipchart or blackboard of some type.) On the left side above the "T," write "Constructive, rewarding, fulfilling when...." On the right side above the "T," write "Destructive, frustrating, lonely when...." As a group of* _____ *(however many is convenient), brainstorm as many experiences as you have had, or that you imagine you might have had, about our topic today: _____. On the left you will write all things that make _____ (the topic at hand) constructive, rewarding, and fulfilling. On the right side you will write all the reasons it is destructive, frustrating, and lonely. You have 10 minutes. Go.*
> —Jeff Dewar

Goal Letters

You can have participants write a letter to themselves saying what they hope to accomplish *in a month* using the information they learned during your program (see Figure 5-2). Have them address the letter to themselves. Keep all the letters and mail them a month later.

Props and Preparation: Exercises for Getting Everyone Involved

Follow the Bouncing Ball

At the end of the day, I like to go back over the objectives which in the morning the participants said they wanted to cover. I take a big beach ball and throw it into the group. Whoever catches it first tells how her objectives were met and throws the ball in the air. Whoever catches it next tells what he learned. You can adapt this exercise to large groups by having them report table by table.

Judge and Jury

Design a positive statement and a negative statement about the topic of your presentation. The whole group acts as jury while the con and

(Today's date)

(Your address)

_____

_____

_____

_____

Dear:

I attended a great seminar today about enhancing my presentation skills. These three things were the most important to me personally:

1. _____

   _____

2. _____

   _____

3. _____

   _____

You have such great potential as a presenter! I hope you might find something of value in these ideas too!
I believe in you!

Love,

(Your signature)

Figure 5-2. Sample goal letter. (*Courtesy of Lilly Walters*)

the pro argue the point, with questions being thrown from the jury. Put the audience in a semicircle, with the prosecutor and the defendant in front.

This game must be prearranged with the key players—the prosecutor and the defendant. Otherwise you're not going to get any participation whatsoever! It's a very good opener for total group involvement.

Quizzes and Question Sheets

If you hear something six times, chances are good that after 30 days you're going to remember about 90 percent of it. It won't surprise anyone that just repeating something six times verbally is not incredibly effective. The trick is to find alternative ways to present the same information.

In longer sessions, I have the audience do brief quizzes at the end of each section, and a final exam at the end of the day, that bring those important points back into their minds. It's amazing how giving them a quiz multiplies the times that the audience will hear your information!

1. They heard it when you said it the first time.
2. The group leader reads them the questions you have set up at the end of each section in the quizzes.
3. They have workbooks in front of them, from which they are reading as well.
4. They discuss among themselves what the answers might be. Since this creates discussion, you may get up to six repetitions right here, but just in case...
5. They write the answer on blanks in the workbooks.
6. At the end of the workshop they take the final review during which you might have them incorporate their own objectives for attending that day.

Sample Quiz: Total Quality Discussion Questions

Figure 5-3 is a good example of how QCI, International, developed an audience participation device to warm the audience up to a topic. (Only sample questions are given; the original QCI quizzes are 12 questions long.) A quiz like this can be given to individuals, or to small groups to come up with group answers. I prefer the group method. If someone in a group is new to the topic, or just a slow learner, he or she won't feel embarrassed when it comes time to share the answers.

TOTAL QUALITY DISCUSSION QUESTIONS

Quality has become a leading topic of conversation in boardrooms and among employees at all levels of the organization. However, not everyone is in agreement as to what it really means.

A. Respond to the following statements for organizations in general.

   A = Agree   D = Disagree   I = It Depends

1. Everyone in the organization has a customer.   A   D   I
   Your immediate supervisor is one of your
   customers. In fact, your supervisor is your
   most important customer.

2. Awareness of the requirements of your   A   D   I
   customers is not necessary. If they are
   buying, you obviously are filling their needs.

3. An employee's boss is not necessarily in the   A   D   I
   best position to evaluate the quality of his or
   her work.

4. Quality will improve most when line   A   D   I
   managers take the time to identify problems at
   the operating level and to recommend
   improvements.

B. Your answers to the following questions indicate what quality means to you.

   T = True   F = False   ? = Maybe

1. From a quality standpoint, a choice cut of steak   T   F   ?
   is better than a fast-food hamburger.

2. Quality means meeting the requirements of   T   F   ?
   the customers—nothing more, nothing less.

3. Quality issues are more important than   T   F   ?
   schedules and financial matters.

4. The cost of quality for our organization can   T   F   ?
   be determined as accurately as the cost of
   owning a home.

Figure 5-3. A quiz can be used as an audience participation device. (*Reproduced with permission from* Fundamentals of Total Quality, *by QCI, International*)

Sample Question Sheet

In Figure 5-4, the presenter's topic is employee involvement. The presenter would say to the group, "Let's talk about group dynamics." The audience would discuss the answers in groups of three to eight. Then each group would pick a group leader. The group leader would share the answers with the whole group.

Debates

Debates are easy and fun. Break the group into two to five groups, each defending a different position of what you are trying to teach. One of the best ways to teach something to is find ways to have people support a position on it, even though they may be forced to defend a side they are opposed to. Making them present on the positive aspects of it will force them to think through their position. It may reinforce their old ideas or it may help them better understand the ideas you are trying to teach, but it will force them to think.

Leave a few people out to act as the judges. (Two or three judges are plenty.) Let these people know that they must decide who has won, and explain why they feel that way.

QUESTION SHEET

What Would You Do as a Team Leader in Each of the Following Situations?

1. Your team has one member who is very quiet. During a brainstorming session, she rarely does more than to say "pass." Her attendance is regular and she seems to like the other members of the team. *How can you get her involved?*

2. Your team has one man who is constantly talking. His ideas are generally good, but the other team members are being turned off because they don't get an opportunity to express themselves. *What should you do?*

3. One of your team members disagrees with nearly every suggestion made. The other members are fed up with this excessive negativism and are threatening to drop out unless something is done. *What can you do?*

Figure 5-4. Question sheet on employee involvement. *(Reproduced with permission from* The Employee Facilitator Handbook *by QCI, International)*

(To run the debate)
In your group, I want you to take the next 10 minutes and develop a 60-second presentation on why _____ is a better position (idea, concept) than the others. Elect a spokesperson from your group to deliver this presentation to the rest of the participants. You have only 60 seconds. Judges, you must decide who has won, and tell the rest of us why you feel that particular group had the best answer. To recap: You have 10 minutes to write your 60-second argument, which your spokesperson will deliver to the rest of us. Go.
—Lilly Walters

Hidden Messages

Tape a piece of paper on everyone's back with something written on it. For instance, when I do my seminar, I generally use it as an icebreaker when people come in. I have five tables set up for five people at each. One of the things I want people to start thinking about is "using participative methods to teach." So, I write down five different audience participation devices (five times each) and tape one to the back of each attendee as he or she arrives. As they are drinking coffee and waiting for the other attendees to arrive, they try to guess what is on one another's back. This technique is applicable to almost any topic. As an added benefit, I use it to break up the cliques as they come in, because when the attendees finally sit down I say, "All right, the people who had 'video' on their backs sit at this table, those with 'skits' sit at this one...."

Use topics that are specific to the objectives of your presentation. For example, if you are speaking on effective communication, you might say, "On your back I have taped the name of a communication device of some type."

I find hidden messages good as a method of:

- Breaking up attendees from the groups they came in with
- Getting everyone to loosen up
- Encouraging people to talk to one another
- Getting people started thinking about the day's topic

Instructor's Notes for Hidden Messages

1. Make yourself a list ahead of time of all possible topics, related to your presentation, that would make good items for people to try to guess. For example: when Jeff Dewar and I do "Games Presenters Play," we tell them we have taped the name of an audience participation device of some type on their back. We came up

with a list of 30 such devices: humor, overheads, field trips, music, movies, and so on.

2. Get an estimate of how many people will be in the audience. Then divide the number of attendees by the number of tables. If you have 60 attendees and your tables will hold 6 each, you will need 10 tables. Make up 10 topics, with 6 copies of each.

3. Well before the attendees start to arrive (preferably even the night before), write out the messages on sheets of paper. I get about four messages from each $8\frac{1}{2}$" × 11" sheet.

4. Collate the topics in order—one each of all 10 topics, then starting over at number one again—until you have one big pile.

5. Put the instructions of how this game works on the first page of your workbook (if you have one) *and* reproduce the instructions as an overhead slide that welcomes people as they come in (see Figure 5-5).

6. Hand the registrar your pile of topics face down so the attendees can't read them.

7. As each attendee comes in, the registrar takes the top piece of paper, asks the attendee to turn around, and tapes the item on the attendee's back with clear tape.

8. The registrar explains to each attendee how the exercise works and points out where the instructions are (in the front of the workbook and/or on an overhead).

HELLO!

Welcome to "Games Presenters Play" by Lilly Walters and Jeff Dewar

1. On your back is an audience participation device of some type.

2. Try to figure out what is written on your back.

3. People may reply to your questions only with "yes," "no," or "maybe."

4. Help others figure out what is on their backs.

5. As long as they get pretty close, give it to them!

6. Go sit at a table that has five other people with the same message on their backs as you have on yours.

Figure 5-5. Sample instruction sheet for hidden messages.

9. The registrar tells the attendee to find all the other people who have the same topic on their backs.

10. The hitch is: They can find out who the other people are (with the same topics) only by first finding out what is on their own back. They go up to people and ask. Everyone is allowed to answer questions only with a "yes," "no," or "maybe."

Preferred Results Sheet

Jeff Dewar passes out a "preferred results sheet" (see Figure 5-6) at the beginning of a seminar. The attendees fill it out and pass it back immediately. Jeff displays the results of this survey on a flipchart or overhead for the group. It gives the attendees a sense of involvement and ownership of the contents of the presentation they are about to hear. It also enables the presenter to quickly customize the presentation to the needs of the audience. Often attendees have special issues they need discussion on before they will be able to focus on the mission of the original agenda. Jeff says this technique is most effective for in-house presentations.

Flowcharts

Figure 5-7 is an example of how an experiential exercise can be used to teach the audience how to make a flowchart. First, the instructor gave a lecture followed by a demonstration. Then he had the group do the exercise shown.

The Uniqueness and Commonalities Exercise

Here is a great discussion exercise I first saw used by Bob Pike of Creative Training Techniques Seminars. It can serve as an icebreaker or as a way to get the audience thinking about a subject, to gather information, or to initiate discussion.

I divide the audience into small groups. Each group takes a piece of paper (flipchart or regular paper) and draws a circle in the middle. Group members put their names around the outside (see Figure 5-8). Then they decide what "things" they have in common. Those go in the center of the circle. Those things that are unique to just one person go under his or her name. Things that some have and some don't, don't go anywhere.

I often use the uniqueness and commonalities exercise as part of my "Secrets of Successful Speakers" workshop, in the section where I talk

---

PREFERRED RESULTS SHEET

Date _____

Name _____ Position _____

Following are some of the major benefits of enthusiastic teams. Please circle the *three* that would be of greatest value to your organization right now.

1. **More teamwork and cooperation among departments**—eliminating finger pointing; everyone being made aware of the responsibilities of others.

2. **Greater employee pride in the organization**—knowing that it provides some of the best products or services.

3. **More satisfied customers**—resulting in greater loyalty.

4. **Better managers**—by understanding that people really want to do their best, and creating the environment to make it so.

5. **Development of new skills**—using problem solving as a vehicle to increase employee knowledge and skill level.

6. **Improved morale**—owing to less rework and frustration, and the opportunity to help improve the organization.

7. **Reduced mistakes**—lower reject level, less scrap and waste, lower warranty costs.

8. **Competitive edge**—earning a reputation for quality in the marketplace.

9. **Increased profits**—through higher productivity.

The **one** benefit which is most important to my organization at this time is number _____.

Figure 5-6. Sample preferred results sheet. *(Reproduced with permission from* Building Enthusiastic Teams *workbook by Jeff Dewar)*

about audience participation. First, I have them select a group leader. Next they discuss the games they have used in the past, trying to figure out which ones are unique to just one person—the uniqueness—and ones they have all used—the commonalities. It gets them thinking about audience participation exercises and different ways to use them. As a follow-up to this exercise, I often have them go back and decide what points each game best makes.

DEVELOP A FLOWCHART

A catalog order company requires that payment be made with orders. After an order is received, filled, and shipped, the order is filed away. However, occasionally an order is received with no enclosed payment. When that occurs, the clerk examines credit information on that customer. If the credit rating is good, the customer is invoiced and the order is filled and shipped. Following that, the order is filed. If the credit rating is bad, the customer is notified to pay before the order is filled.

Assignment:
Use flowchart to graphically describe the above situation.

Figure 5-7. Flowcharts can aid in understanding concepts. *(Reproduced with permission from* Fundamentals of Total Quality, *by QCI, International)*

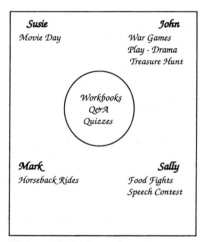

Figure 5-8. Sample uniqueness and commonalities diagram.

Matrixes

A matrix can be designed to match any speech topic. If you were speaking on goal setting, you might make a matrix that looked like Figure 5-9.

Jeff Dewar developed the customer service matrix in Figure 5-10 for his presentations.

	Tomorrow	Next Week	Next Month	Next Year	3 Years
Money					
Love					
Business					
Education					

If all your dreams could come true, where would you like your life to be in each of the following categories, by each of the corresponding dates?

Figure 5-9. Goal-setting matrix.

Potato Rewards

Bob Pike showed me another wonderful experiential exercise. When attendees participated by asking or answering a question, he threw them a big raw potato. No explanation, other than "With risk comes reward," and he tossed it to them! People were dying to figure out what in the heck he was up to. At the end of the seminar, he had all the "potato people" come up front and showed them how to put a thin plastic straw through the potato in one thrust! The message Bob used for this exercise was to *follow through,* which is the secret of making the straw go through the potato.

Instructor's Notes for Potato Rewards

1. Buy nice big and long potatoes.
2. Have the participant hold the small end.
3. Make sure the participant's fingers are not underneath the place where the straw will go.
4. The straw should be held at arm's length, like a dagger, with the thumb over the end of the straw.
5. Both arms are held at arm's length, with locked elbows, at chest height.
6. Have the participant take three long, slow, deep breaths.
7. The arm with the straw makes several "fake" passes next to the potato. Have the participant visualize the straw going all the way through.
8. Say: "OK, on three. One...two...three!"

	Expected Level				Actual Level			
	Low	Medium	High	Exceptional	Low	Medium	High	Exceptional
Situation 1								
Situation 2								
Situation 3								
Situation 4								
Situation 5								

In your group, think of customer service situations. Then place checks for each situation in the matrix below. One under the level of "expected" customer service and one under the "actual" level of service you offer. After we are done, we will compare what you are delivering to your customers as compared with your customers' expectations. — JEFF DEWAR

Figure 5-10. Customer service matrix.

At least one participant from the group won't make it the first time. Usually the participant doesn't keep the elbows tight and isn't thinking hard enough. It is an excellent lesson for the rest of the audience to watch why this person can't—and a great feeling when the person finally succeeds.

Reporting Assignments and Reviews

Reporting assignments need at least a 3-hour program to work well. Early in the day, I break the participants into groups of four to six and have each group come up with a list of reasons they are attending my seminar. Then as a room we come up with a master list—typically between 13 and 18 reasons. (I have never had a group come up with more than 32 reasons!) I write each one down on a sheet of flipchart paper and stick the papers up around the room. I then divide up the room by the number of objectives, and have people sign their name on one of the flipchart pages.

It is important to have an equal number of people on each chart—this takes some watchdogging. Make sure participants understand that they cannot put their name on a chart with more than _____ names already on it, and that they can't put their name on two separate charts.

Announce at the beginning of the day that each group will be giving a report back to the others on what it learned about that topic. Every hour or so, stop and break the room into discussion groups to brainstorm on the various objectives. This is where the real learning occurs, so it is important to make up new groups at each break so people will learn new ideas each time. At the end of the day, allow time to complete the exercise. Have people gather into groups according to who is on each objective sheet. In other words, you say, "All those on sheet 1 (you stand there holding that paper) go sit at that table (you point to a table). All those on sheet 2, go sit at that table." Tell them to prepare a 60-second presentation on just the three best ideas they gained about their topic.

A variation of this is to have people prepare quizzes. Break them into groups of up to 15 people each, hopefully with no more than 6 groups total. Each group writes a quiz to give to the others in the room.

One of the best ways for people to learn anything is to present it themselves. So finding ways for attendees to present to others in your audience is an excellent learning tool. However, it can be terrifying for some people, so use it with care. You may want to try a group report. You assign a small group to prepare the report and to come back in a specified time—anywhere from 5 to 60 minutes later, depending on the topic. You may ask them to elect a group leader to present, or you could give them the option of each person doing a small part, with some holding the visual aids, and so on. It is "safer" and less threatening if you have people present to small groups, seated. This is also a fast way to close out the exercise: you can have 20 presentations going on at 20 tables at the same time.

Role Playing

My objection to using the term "role-play" with the audience is the negative learning experiences many have. They think, "I'm not good at acting!" Call it an opportunity to practice the skill.
                                                    —BEVERLY SMALLWOOD

When you use role-play, it is often good to assign three parts: one player for each opposing role, and one "coach" to keep them in line. Make sure you switch parts so everyone does all three jobs. For example, when I did some customer service training, I had one person be the "angry" customer, a second, the employee trying to handle the situation, and a third, the "coach" who was checking the strategies we had just discussed for the past 20 minutes.

Pantomimes

Pantomime can be great fun. Have people pair off. Each partner tells the other the most valuable thing that he or she has learned in the presentation so far—without saying a word! This exercise gets people up and moving, but it continues the learning process by having them mentally repeat the most valuable things they have learned thus far.

Competitions

Pick a panel of three or four judges. Bring them to the front behind a table. Divide the remaining attendees into subgroups of two to eight people. (From four to six people in each subgroup is ideal.) Give all the groups a problem or question to resolve in 5 minutes. A spokesperson gives each group's answer, and the judges decide which one is the best. Create a fun, competitive atmosphere, with lots of cheering and shouting.

Team Drawing

Break people into subgroups and say, "Draw a picture of your image of _____ (whatever point you are trying to get across)." Have each group elect a group leader to explain what its drawing means. This exercise helps open people's minds by allowing them to view a concept through a window other than the verbal or written.

Setup and Practice: Exercises for Building Experiential Learning

Field Trips

Take people out to a site and let them see the concept, product, or service you are talking about in action. Make sure you design a discussion time before and after to help them process their conclusions.

Case Studies

A case study is another method of allowing your audience to experience learning.*

Types of Case Studies

Real-Life versus Fictitious Cases. Case histories are actual stories of situations or events. They allow the audience to see the good or bad results of some company, service, or product they (hopefully) all know. These are great to make your point. Good sources for case histories include *Inc., Business Week, Forbes, Fortune, The Wall Street Journal,* and *Harvard Business Review.*

Fictitious case studies are those that are "made up" by the presenter. Actual case histories are more credible, but the fictitious ones can be tailored to the exact learning point. They can also be used as an experiential device. Once you present the fictitious study, you say, "Now, go and decide in your group what your strategies would be to accomplish _____ (your objectives for this particular experience)."

Activity-Oriented versus Narrative Cases. In activity-oriented cases, the participants are given a set of rules and a task and are asked to attempt to achieve something, usually by doing something physically. An example is tossing ping-pong balls into a box and then brainstorming *why* all the balls didn't go into the box.

Narrative case studies are simply read by the group and then discussed, with the group attempting to answer some preestablished questions.

---

*Adapted with permission from *Games Presenters Play* workbook by Jeff Dewar and Lilly Walters.

Designing Case Studies

- *Give complete information and instructions.* Include facts, figures, and histories. Keep in mind the types of learners in your audience. Some require more "stats" than others, some more pictures, and so on. In giving instructions for group exercises, it is better to err on the side of over-explanation than worry about being verbose. You are so familiar with the material, you will easily *assume* that people understand the exercise. Remember you are 100 times more acquainted with this case study than they are. They will always need much more explanation of the study to understand what is expected of them than you think they will.

- *Make your objectives crystal clear.* Always think through the "where" and "why." (See the section on setting objectives in Chapter 6.)

- *Test beforehand.* What seems great on the drawing table always comes off a little different in a presentation. If possible, test your case study on your staff, friends, or family.

- *Allow adequate time.* It is very easy to underestimate the amount of time needed. The bigger the group, the longer it takes.

CABLE SHOP CASE STUDY

You are a member of a team in a cable shop. Your work area is a large room in which about 50 other people are doing the same type of work. The work consists of assembling cables and wire harnesses to a wide variety of connectors. The workload on each cable is sporadic and requires that everyone in the shop be able to do nearly all tasks required on the various cables. The work requires the use of several types of unique and expensive hand tools. There are only two sets of tools available, consisting of five tools each. Much of the work is done by hand, and each tool is used for only a short time.

All the tools are stored in a centrally located cabinet. Usually the person needing the tool finds that it is not where it belongs. It is being used, has not been returned, is mixed in with other hand tools, has been misplaced, or is missing for some other reason. The person needing the tool must then search through all the other tools in the cabinet, walk along all the workbenches looking for the needed tool, or simply wait until it shows up.

Management has been asked to authorize the purchase of additional tools. It has refused because of the expense. Team members are frustrated by this situation and decide to attempt to correct it.

Figure 5-11. Sample case study. (*Reproduced with permission from* The Employee Involvement Handbook *by QCI, International*)

- *The more universal the better.* Design a case study situation that the majority of your participants will have knowledge about. Very few people understand electronics, but most understand driving a car. Unless the group (and especially you!) has specific knowledge on a certain subject, lean toward a more universal case study.

A sample case study is presented in Figure 5-11.

Magic Tricks

Magic tricks do more than entertain, as the best magic consultants know. They also serve to break the ice, reinforce ideas, and convey subtle visual messages. Here are some of the best.

THE JUMPING RUBBER BAND
by Tom Ogden, Master Magician and Corporate Magic Consultant

Effect: The magician places a rubber band around the first and second fingers of the right hand and closes the hand into a fist. When the hand is opened, the rubber band jumps to the third and fourth finger.

The trick was invented by Stanley Collins and first written up in *The Magician Monthly* in December 1911.

Possible icebreaker lines: Elasticity (Ability to stretch)
Mobility ("Let's move it!")
Stress ("I'm about to snap!")

Setup: None; one or more rubber bands required.

Method: Place a rubber band around the first and second fingers of the right hand, moving it all the way to the base of the fingers. Show both sides of the hand to the audience.

Close the right hand into a fist. At the same time, the left thumb and first finger secretly stretch the band (on the palm side) around all four fingertips of the right hand.

This action can be covered in the following manner: Hold the right hand palm down with the tips pointing toward the spectator. Using the left fingers, stretch the band along the back of the right hand to show that it is an "ordinary" rubber band. Hold up the right hand with the palm toward yourself. The left hand stretches the band on the palm side as the right hand is closed into a fist. The back of the right hand covers the secret "move."

(Continued)

The back and knuckles of the right fist are shown to reinforce that the rubber band is still in place. When the hand is opened and the fingers are extended, the rubber band appears to "jump" to encircle the third and fourth fingers. (Alternatively, under cover of a broad up-and-down swing of the arm, the fist can be quickly opened enough to make the band jump and then re-closed. This was the inventor Collins' favorite presentation.)

If a second band is twisted around the tips of the right fingers before the hand is closed into a fist, it seems to make it impossible for the lower band to move or escape. The second rubber band does not in any way impede the jumping band. (This idea was first published by Harlan Tarbell in Volume 1 of his *Tarbell Course in Magic*.)

The same handling can be used, of course, to "magically" return a single band from the third and fourth fingers back to the first and second fingers. A few people are dexterous enough to use the thumb to stretch the rubber band around the fingertips. (This was perhaps first noted by Stanley Collins in *A Conjuring Melange* in 1947.)

Frederick Furman suggested a routine (first published in *Thayer's Magical Bulletin* in January 1921) in which two different-colored rubber bands are used. One is wrapped around the first and second fingers; the other is placed around the third and fourth fingers. If both bands are stretched and placed around all four fingertips as the hand is closed into a fist, the bands will appear to change places when the fist is opened.

From the video training program *Teaching and Training with Magic*, © 1993 by Tom Ogden, Hollywood, CA. Reprinted with permission.

THE VANISHING PEN AND BUSINESS CARD
by Tom Ogden, Master Magician and Corporate Magic Consultant

Effect: The magician holds out a business card and offers to make it vanish by tapping it with a magic wand (a pen). On the third tap, the pen suddenly disappears instead. The magician explains the joke: The pen was stuck behind the ear. Looking back to the magician's hand, the spectator sees that the business card has now disappeared.

Possible icebreaker lines: Making the competition disappear
Making problems vanish into thin air

Setup: None; a pen and business card required, also a coat (or pants) with side pocket or an open shoulder bag.

Method: This routine is best performed with your spectator standing or sitting to your left side. Hold the business card in your left hand. Hold the pen in your right hand over the business card.

Explain that you will make the card vanish on the count of three. In a broad swing, raise the pen up beside the right side of your head. Bring the arm down and tap the pen on the card as you count, "One."

Again, swing up the arm, then bring it down to tap the card as you say "Two."

Raise the arm up beside the head again, but this time shove the pen behind your right ear. (If this is difficult to do, or the pen repeatedly fails to balance and falls, try shoving it under the coat or shirt/blouse collar.)

Without pausing, bring the right hand down as if it were still holding the pen. Say "Three" as you pretend to tap the business card. Look at the right hand and say, "Wait! The pen vanished instead!"

Turn your right side to the spectator. Point with the right hand to the pen and pick it up, saying, "See it was only a joke. I put it behind my ear."

As all eyes are looking at where you are pointing, the left hand simply drops the business card into the left side coat pocket, pants pocket, or open handbag.

After you retrieve the pen, face the spectator. Hold out your empty left hand as if you were still holding the card. Say "Three" and tap the pen against your open left palm. The card has now disappeared!

If you do not wish to make the card disappear, or do not have an open pocket, you can perform the same trick as a way to magically *print* business cards. Hold the card, printed side down, in the left hand. Perform the routine as described; but as you show the pen has "vanished" behind the ear, simply flip the business card over in the left hand. The final tap of the pen will appear to "print" the business card.

From the video training program *Teaching and Training with Magic,* © 1993 by Tom Ogden, Hollywood, CA. Reprinted with permission.

SAWING A PERSON IN HALF
by Tom Ogden, Master Magician and Corporate Magic Consultant

Effect: The magician offers to visibly saw a person in half. For the faint-hearted in the group, the magician will use two lengths of rope rather than a buzzsaw. The magician wraps two long ropes around a spectator, and two more spectators hold the ends of the ropes. Suddenly, the ropes come free as the spectator walks through the ropes.

Possible messages: Getting out of impossible situations
Seeing our way through hard times
Teamwork and cooperation

Setup: Two ropes, each approximately 72 inches (183 cm) long are required. Before the performance, the ropes are set side by side, then tied together near the middle of the lengths of rope with a single piece of white thread. Each rope is then folded back on itself, so that you have, in effect, two folded lengths of rope, tied at the curve by a thread. This junction, held in the palm of the hand, will give the illusion of two long single pieces of rope.

Method: Ask for three assistants and place them in a row. Let's call the volunteers, from left to right, A, B, and C.

Place the ropes behind B so that the secret junction is at the center of the back, away from the audience. Hand one set of ends of the ropes to A and the other set to C. The illusion to the audience is that A and C are holding two long ropes that pass behind the back of B.

Take either one of the two ends that A is holding and either one of the two ends that C is holding and tie them in a single knot around and in front of B. Give the ends back to A and to C. (Note that tying the knot will switch the ends: A will receive the end formerly held by C and vice versa.)

A and C are asked to hold their ends *tightly* with both hands. Caution them not to drop the ropes. (If they drop them, the effect is ruined!)

On the count of three, A and C are to gently pull their ends of the rope taut. B is to take one step backward. If the ropes pass through B's body, you will have been successful at sawing a person in half.

One, two, three: *MAGIC!*

From the video training program *Teaching and Training with Magic,* © 1993 by Tom Ogden, Hollywood, CA. Reprinted with permission.

"You're on next, Mrs. Mooney."

6 "An Ounce of Prevention!"— Speech Design and Preparation Strategies

I think it's almost impossible to make any presentation "bomb" proof, but we can at least reinforce it a bit. Rather than worry about what to do only *after* disaster has struck, in this chapter we will explore how to design the presentation to be a bit more substantial under pressure!

HOW TO DESIGN YOUR SPEECH
Choosing the Topic

You might have thought that naming this book *What to Say When* meant I was going to help you pick an overall general topic. Well, it seems to me nobody is going to read this book unless a topic or an audience has already been selected. (Either that or you thought this was a book of famous pick-up lines, in which case I suggest you get a refund.)

The best way to find a subject that audiences are excited to hear is to start from the marketplace. In other words, "find a need and fill it." Attend meetings relating to your field of expertise and listen. When you hear people say "I need...," "I have a problem...," or "I wish I could find...," you have heard the seed of a seminar or speech topic for which people are waiting.

If you don't have a "field of expertise," study the topic until you become an expert. Look into your own life and think about what you are passionate about. Can you tie that passion into your topic? If you are passionate on anything, you will naturally become an expert in short order. Besides, as you study and contemplate a given subject, you will gain a perspective that is unique. It's rather like adding all the ingredients for a good soup and simmering it. When you taste the finished product, you'll find it has a quality all its own.

> *If you give one hour extra per day of study to your chosen field, within 5 years you will be a national expert!*
>
> —JIM CATARACT

If you need some more help on picking a topic, I strongly suggest you read Chapter 5 of my last book, *Secrets of Successful Speakers* (McGraw-Hill, 1993).

Setting Clear Objectives

You are preparing an "address." When you address a letter, you direct it to a certain party or place. When you address an audience, you direct your words toward your listeners, with the intent of having them take direction from the message. An early meaning of the word *address* was to "prepare." So what exactly are you trying to prepare people to do?

Preparing a presentation without clear-cut objectives gets you nowhere. It's like constructing a building without a blueprint. When you're thinking through the objectives, you must define the "what" and "why." Some group of people—your audience and/or an employer—will be investing a great deal money in you, even if it's just the value of time (our most valuable resource).

To help you define your objectives, ask yourself:

- What do you hope the return on their and your investment will be?
- When attendees leave the event, what do you want them to *do* differently?
- When attendees leave the event, how do you want them to *feel* differently?
- When attendees leave the event, how do you want them to *think* differently?

Establishing Time Limits

Less is always better. People rarely complain that a speech is too short.

Check with whoever is planning the event for the time limit you are expected to stay within.

Prepare twice as much information as you will need. This ensures that you will be viewed as an expert and feel like one yourself. Then practice the presentation so that it takes only about 80 percent of the time allotted. The reason? A presentation always takes longer than you think it will. If you practice your whole speech, word for word, on a tape recorder, you will get a much better idea of how long it will take.

Don't go over the time limit! It's the sign of a rank amateur and really ticks people off.

Short? No one was ever booed off a stage for talking too short. Only go as long in a speech as is minimally needed to get the point across. They don't need to know the sum total of your life's experience...even as important as it may seem to you to be. Don't be a speaker who is "a legend-in-his-own-mind"!
　　　　　　　　　　　　　　　　—MICHAEL PODOLINSKY

It is very complex to make something simple, but very simple to make things complex.
　　　　　　　　　　　　　　　　—JEFF DEWAR

I find, as a humorist, that 45 minutes is the longest presentation that can remain effective, even when you are "killing." I should say, "Especially when you are killing." Leave them wanting more.
　　　　　　　　　　　　　　　　—ANITA CHEEK MILNER

Finding Appropriate Material

Constantly look for information. There are countless formal and informal sources available to you.

- *Libraries.* All the great minds of the world are there waiting to give you their information. Always check with the reference librarian.

- *Bookstores.* There is something new every day.

- *Used bookstores.* I found some great things by getting an old 1958 *Reader's Digest Treasury of Wit and Humor.* It is old enough that the material should seem new to most people.

- *Resource books.* Quote books, dictionaries, joke books, and concordances are all great places to start. I found the most wonderful things by spending time with my dictionary.

- *Phone books.* Who and where are the people who are in business in your topic area? Call them and ask to interview them by phone. Most people are flattered to be asked.

- *Schools and colleges.* Note where the topic you need is taught. Ask the teachers and professors for interviews.

- *Computer search systems.* Many systems are available for your personal computer. Libraries and colleges all have computer search services you can subscribe to. You give them the topic; they obtain all the articles that have been written about it in the time frame you request.

- *Trade associations and publications.* Most of the real learning and exchange of business information in the world take place at those industry associations. Members sit and discuss the real problems current in their work, and come up with the modern-day solutions. Join these groups. Subscribe to the magazines, newsletters, and other publications in your area of expertise. Lists of these materials are available from the library.

- *Other speakers on your subject.* You can find them speaking at conferences and seminars in your area.

- *Other sources.* Educational videos, comedy shops, friends and colleagues, and churches are only some of the wide range of sources available. Always keep your eyes open. When you are in an airplane, don't just sit there. Read all the magazines and newspapers! Keep your scissors out and be ready to snip any goodies that have been printed on your topic.

Be a voracious note taker.

—W Mitchell

I find bits to spice up talks by using quotes from unusual places—like movies. I quote from The Godfather—Part II when Michael Corleone is reminiscing: "My father always told me, `You keep your friends close, but your enemies closer!'" I thought that was a profound observation about knowing your competition.

Biblical quotes can be good, slightly changed or embellished. There is one that I use to explain that once you have made the sale, get out—otherwise you will talk the buyer out of the sale. To make this point I say, "It is said that Samson killed a thousand Philistines with the jawbone of an ass. Every year the same number of sales are lost with the same weapon."

—Jeff Slutsky

Material is everywhere. Ask the people selling products and services to your audience what they need to know and you will get an earful.

—Michael Podolinsky

Gathering Your Thoughts and Ideas

When I help people write a speech, I like to use the worksheet shown in Figure 6-1 to help them gather their thoughts and consider the possibilities.

Building Audience Retention

A month after hearing you, people will remember only about 10 percent of what you tell them. So why tell so much? Think of that 10 percent they must remember, and design the presentation around it. Give them the rest in a handout.

Retention is aided when you repeat the information. Studies show that people who hear information only once retain less than 10 percent of it, whereas those who hear the same information six times retain more than 90 percent of it. Here are some tips to help with the retention of information.

- *The simple approach.* As the adage goes, "Tell 'em what you're gonna tell 'em. Tell 'em. Tell 'em what you told 'em." Then get off the platform.

- *Visual aids.* Charts, graphs, videos, and slides

Figure 6-1.

INFORMATION-GATHERING WORKSHEET

Introduction

Simply state your mission and the three key strategies they will need to know to accomplish the mission. Keep this to no more than three sentences.

1. _____

2. _____

3. _____

Body

"Now let's talk about those three points one at a time."

A. Explain key strategy 1 in a fuller sentence.

Why is it important?

_____

Who else says so? Any studies to back this up?

_____

What will it mean to the audience members if they don't apply strategy 1?

_____

Is there a humorous story or joke that makes this point?

_____

Is there a heart story that makes this point?

_____

Is there an audience participation experience that makes this point?

_____

Is there a visual that makes this point?

_____

Restate the point again in one clear sentence.

_____

B. Explain key strategy 2 in a fuller sentence.

Why is it important?

_____

Who else says so? Any studies to back this up?

_____

What will it mean to the audience members if they don't apply strategy 2?

_____

Is there a humorous story or joke that makes this point?

_____

Is there a heart story that makes this point?

_____

Is there an audience participation experience that makes this point?

_____

Is there a visual that makes this point?

_____

Restate the point again in one clear sentence.

_____

C. Explain key strategy 3 in a fuller sentence.

Why is it important?

_____

Who else says so? Any studies to back this up?

_____

What will it mean to the audience members if they don't apply strategy 3?

_____

Is there a humorous story or joke that makes this point?

_____

(Continued)

Figure 6-1. (*Continued*)

Is there a heart story that makes this point?

_____

Is there an audience participation experience that makes this point?

_____

Is there a visual that makes this point?

_____

Restate the point again in one clear sentence.

_____

Conclusion

"So, in order to _____."

You need to restate your three main points just as you did above.

_____

_____

_____

- *Workbooks.* Workbooks reinforce what people have learned and greatly help them retain information.

- *Silence.* People need to absorb what you say. It's very powerful to make the point and then just be silent and let your listeners think about it. Let them reach the conclusion by themselves.

- *Audience participation exercises.* Audiences need to participate in learning. I have a whole slew of ideas (Chapter 5) on how you can design ways for them to experience the concepts.

- *Humor and heart stories.* You may not remember the exact information, but chances are you'll remember the joke or the story. These are largely graphic images, and images are more easily remembered than abstract information.

- *Acronyms.* I'm really talking about a special type of acronym here, an acrostic. An acrostic spells out a word—for example, FEAR (false evidence appearing real). An acronym does not necessarily spell a word: IBM, CBS, CNN. Acrostics are easier to remember. When done right, they are fabulous memory aids to organize material. A good acronym—in order of importance—does the following:

1. Is designed to fit your presentation. Don't try to design the presentation to fit an acronym!
2. Is easily remembered.
3. Has each letter represent the key thought in the concept you want people to remember.
4. Substantiates your mission.

Back up your points with visual aids (oversized props...charts...blown-up letters, etc.). People watch television...they only listen to a radio. [Using props, etc.] lets you become a video...ALIVE...and you will be refreshing and unique.
>   —IRA HAYES
>   (Quoted in *Secrets of Successful Speakers,* by
>   Lilly Walters, McGraw-Hill, 1993)

A story full of sparkling wit will keep its audience grinning.
Especially if the end of it is close to the beginning.
>   —ANONYMOUS
>   (From *Great Book of Funny Quotes,* by Eileen
>   Mason, Sterling Publishing, 1993)

Polishing Your Delivery

Practice, Practice, Practice

Winston Churchill estimated that it took him 6 to 8 hours to prepare a 45-minute speech. Roger Burgraff, one of the speakers I often engage on the topic of advanced communication strategies, says that it takes 1 hour of preparation for each minute of speech.

But, as the saying goes, "It's not practice that makes perfect. It's *perfect* practice makes perfect." Practice effectively. For example, don't just practice silently to yourself; do it out loud. Then try your material out at parties, at home, or even with friends on the phone.

Doug Malouf of Dougmal Training Systems in Wollongona, Australia, is a fantastic presenter. He suggests that you practice your speech, especially your opening, to a spot on the wall. He feels that those first few minutes in front of an audience are the most neurotic moments for a speaker. So he says to memorize a dynamite opening word for word. Practice it while you are staring at a spot on the wall. Doug says you develop such fantastic confidence that it carries you through the rest of the speech.

Local Toastmasters groups are another great way to try out new material.

How to Rehearse a Presentation

1. Write it.
2. Read the speech over several times silently.
3. Read the speech several times aloud.
4. Practice your delivery, including the entire address, standing in front of a mirror.
5. Read the speech into a tape recorder and listen to the results.
6. Listen to the results again.
7. If you have cooperative family members or friends, deliver the speech to them and ask for their honest comments; tape this.
8. Write the final draft, word for word.
9. Read it into a tape recorder.
10. Listen to this final taped version over and over (while you shower, in the car, as you fall asleep).
11. Make an outline to use on the day of the presentation.

If this speech is really important, also add these steps:

12. Give the presentation, from the outline, to a few friends or family members. (Tell them they need to act as polite and businesslike as any real audience. I find my closest friends and family members are the worst at this!) Tape the presentation.
13. Listen to the tape. Did you say things you didn't mean to? Did you go overtime? Did you add some things you really like? Then what are you going cut to make room for these new things?
14. Make a final audiotape. Duplicate the tape from step 12 onto a clean tape. When you get to the spots you want to fix, stop the step 12 tape and edit the new tape. Depending on what you are trying to fix, you will either continue the new tape—taping your new, correct words—or you will fast-forward over the bad part of the old tape until you come to the part where you want to start back up again. Then you continue dubbing.

(If there are many corrections to be made, you will go insane trying to do this. Instead, have a transcript made of the tape in step 12. Read it. With a highlighter, just cut out all the phrases you didn't want to say. Carefully write in exactly what you did hope to say. Now read this final transcript into a tape recorder.)

Whichever way you get your final tape, live with it for a few days. Play it while you shower, sunbathe, and drive. It will help you learn the phrases just the way you want to say them, and when you want to say them.

Now that I've taken you through all these steps, you may be surprised to learn that I do not suggest you memorize the presentation word for word. I suggest all of the above steps for those presentations that are very important to you. Going over the words again and again will bring you to a place where you can use those brilliant, pithy phrases to best advantage. You will also have the confidence in your material to ad-lib and be natural in your delivery.

> *Polish your delivery by practicing in your car, to and from work. The other drivers around you may think you are nuts, but that quiet time is great for honing skills in schedules that are usually too busy for practice.*
> **—MICHAEL PODOLINSKY**

> *I continue to give speeches aloud in the shower, or car, or virtually any place else when I'm alone, long after I'm fully familiar with the material. The way a speech is delivered is at least as important as the content itself. I'm constantly fine-tuning my inflections, attitude, and delivery.*
> **—DICK FLAVIN**

> *I simply speak with true-to-life animation and logical emphases on words. A drama teacher once told me that when you're on a stage you should emphasize only the important words in a sentence—in other words, the audience should not be confused as to what point you're trying to make. An example of doing this improperly is standard flight attendant talk: "Please remain seated with your seat belt fastened until we have come to a complete stop at the terminal building." The important words in this sentence are really just "complete stop," but you'd never know it.*
> **—HOPE MIHALAP**

> *It takes me at least 3 weeks to prepare an impromptu speech.*
> **—MARK TWAIN**

SIMPLE SPEECH OUTLINES AND MODELS
Half-Sticky Method for Developing a Presentation Quickly

One simple model designed to organize material (available in complete form in my books Speaking to a Group *and* 14 Reasons Corporate Speeches Don't Get the Job Done) *revolves around these two key principles:*

1. *Create a one-sentence take-away message—what it is you want the audience to learn or know as a result of your time together. It not only provides focus, it also enables you to respond wonderfully when the decision maker stops you at the door with this comment, "I can't stay today. What are you going to tell us?"*

2. *Use the analogy of the presentation-as-a-journey to keep focused on who the speech is for: the journey is for the audience.*

—MARIAN WOODALL

Marian Woodall has also developed a shortcut, template method that uses only a single sheet of paper with stickies (Post-its or their clones) (see Figure 6-2) all over it. Each sticky has just the key word that represents the main thought she wants people to remember. Since most presentations should only focus on three key thoughts, the presenter needs to hone in on key issues. The main conclusion is followed by a quick sum-up, which Marian says is that last "half sticky."

The Jigsaw Management Model

Most speakers put too much talk into their talk. There is only so much you can cover in an hour and expect learning to occur. We have started to follow a specific model to make sure that we do not break this rule. I call it Jigsaw Management.

As you lay out your ideas, imagine that you are going to ask your audience to assemble a large jigsaw puzzle from scratch. Your ideas are the pieces. Actually, if you think about it, this is pretty much what each of us is doing whenever we talk. The difference is that we force the audience to put all of the ideas together in an hour instead of taking their own time.

When you are doing a puzzle, the first thing that you do is to look at the boxtop. Your talk should have one of those. It tells you which pieces you want to present.

Now, how many ideas to you have in your puzzle? Remember how much harder it is to assemble a 1000-piece puzzle than a 100-piece one if you only have an hour to do it? If you have more than a few main ideas, you have too many. I keep my talks to three ideas max, and that can still be too much for an hour.

Ask yourself another question before you start organizing your talk. If you were playing with a puzzle and you had only an hour to finish, would you want the person with the puzzle to hide the boxtop from you? Would you want the person to add extra pieces to the pile? Don't be guilty of the same when you do your talks.

In other words, no matter how wonderful the idea is to you, don't include it unless it fits exactly into the picture on your boxtop.

Second, as you start the talk, be sure to tell your audience what the boxtop looks like. Tell them what you will show them, so they know where the ideas fit.

—PETER MEYER

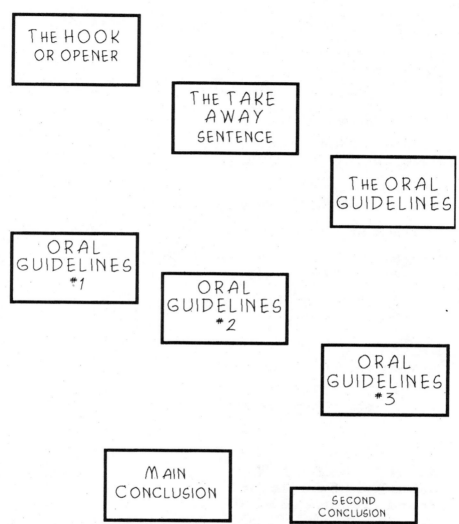

Figure 6-2. Shortcut method for organizing a presentation.

The Adendorff Speech Model

Peter Adendorff, a South African trainer, has developed the following speech model:

Opening

- State the purpose of the presentation.
- Explain why it is important.
- Provide the structure for the presentation.

Generate interest and clarify understanding

- Describe the current situation.
- Describe the problems experienced.
- Explore the consequences.
- Elicit the benefits of a solution for the audience.

Introduce proposals and recap

- Present your solutions to overcome the problems.
- Elicit reaction from your audience.
- Elicit implementation suggestions.
- Develop the most appropriate course of action.

Closing

- Recap the main points of agreement.
- Ask for an appropriate commitment.

WHAT TO SAY WHEN
...You Need Funnies for
Your Introducer to Read

What to Do

I find it valuable to prepare a short introduction, with simple words, to give to the MC with the hope that it will be delivered intact. No more than one page, double spaced.
—PHILIP CROSBY

The following lines are ones you will write into your introduction for the introducer to read. It is rare that you'll get an introducer who can handle humor well—so beware of what funny "bits" you use. Make sure you have time to rehearse in private with the introducer.

Also, ask the event planner for an introducer who will have the *time* for a rehearsal. This ensures that the event planner will ask the introducer for a rehearsal and gives everyone a way to "save face" if the introducer feels insulted that you want rehearsal time.

Some presenters effectively avoid the issue of horrid intros by introducing themselves. You might try this yourself. Make the introduction a joke by putting on silly glasses or a hat and reading it yourself.

What to Say

You never know what this guy will talk about. And when he's finished, you may still not know.

Every now and then a gifted speaker hits the circuit who's unique, insightful, and entertaining. Unfortunately we couldn't afford her, so let me introduce...

I'd like to bring out a wonderful, sensitive, and gifted man who taught me everything I know...including this introduction.
—From *Speaker's Idea File*, Original Humor
section by Gary Apple, August 1993

Our speaker tonight needs no introduction. So I'm going home.
—From *Speaker's Idea File*, Original Humor
section by Gary Apple, September 1993

We wanted to make sure our speaker was rewarded handsomely for tonight's presentation—so we have given him a picture of Paul Newman.
—From *Speaker's Idea File*, Original Humor
section by Gary Apple, May 1993

(Sometimes I have the introducer say) Our speaker today needs no introduction. (Then I jump up, push him aside, and say) Good, I need all the time I can get!
—GEORGE GOLDTRAP

Never will I forget the first time I met _____, but I'm giving it a darn good try.
—UNKNOWN

Some of you may have heard Jeff Dewar before. Those of you who haven't may be looking forward to it.
—JEFF DEWAR

(After all the credits, have the introducer say)...obviously he can't hold a job.

...he has just returned from a tour of Tijuana and Stanton.
—JOHN PATRICK DOLAN

...You Open the Speech

What to Do

People will remember the first 30 seconds. So state the mission of your presentation and the main points you want them to remember. In my talk on presentation skills I often open with, "Passion and compassion, with a purpose. (Pause) The secret of successful speakers? Passion and compassion, with a purpose. When you leave today you will have several 'whys' and 'hows' to create...passion...and compassion...with a purpose." (I bet you can guess what my mission is for this talk by now...huh?) Now I can go on and make a joke or announce some housekeeping items.

> *Psychologists have shown that the first 30 seconds have the most impact. So don't waste time. Don't say, "Ladies and gentlemen, it's a pleasure to be here." Come out punching.*
> —PATRICIA FRIPP

Tips for Delivering a Good Opening

1. Make the audience think about your mission.
2. Let the audience subtly (almost subliminally) know you are an expert and an "important" person.
3. Quickly get to the point.
4. Speak on a subject that is important *to the audience.*
5. Grab the audience's attention.

It's always clear why a topic is important to you. Really think this through and find the benefit to your audience. To capture people's attention, *be enthusiastic.* A Stanford University study showed that only 15 percent of success in sales was due to knowledge; the other 85 percent was from *enthusiasm.*

> *To ensure audience attention in the beginning I relate a personal experience that occurred in their field. Usually this is as a participant, but it can be as a customer, or a victim.*
> —PHILIP CROSBY

For Starts

A good opening line is priceless, and can come from any source.

- *Question.* "Were you there when..."
- *Historical reference.* "Fourscore and seven years ago..."

- *Dictionary definitions.* Unusual or little-known definitions are often insightful, and a great way to open.

- *Famous or unusual quote.* If you are lucky, you will find a great quote that tells the mission of your talk—one you can repeat over and over.

> *I like to open with comments that are designed to slightly startle the audience. This wakes 'em up after their rubber chicken dinner, and gets their attention. Example: "The earth is shrinking."*
> —TONY KING

> *I open with "Have you ever been in prison? I have." Then I go on to explain how situations in your life can create a prison and how I've escaped.*
> —W MITCHELL

- *Song lyric.* There are many famous lyrics that you can use. For time management you might try, "If I could save time in a bottle..." Michael Aun rewrote the start of "I've Been Working on the Railroad" to open his presentation.

- *Poem or rhyme.* In her sales talk to salespeople, my mother (Dottie Walters) often stresses the importance of caring about your customers. She uses:

> "Why does the Lamb love Mary so?"
>   The eager children cry.
> "Because Mary loves the lamb you know,"
>   The teacher doth reply.

- *An unusual sound.* Try learning a rare bird call.

- *Anything unexpected.* The "startle" effect is always an attention grabber.

> *Many times I find the audience has been sitting through several other speakers. I'll often have them stand and give one another a back rub.* As they're doing this, most are laughing and having a good time. I'll say the following, "I couldn't help but notice that a few of you were taking advantage of the situation. You may be seated. I do that little exercise for two reasons. First, it gives you all an opportunity to stretch and get your seats turned around. Second, I don't know about you, but my underwear rides a little high and it gives you a chance to readjust it."*
> —MICHAEL AUN

---

*Always be careful using any exercises that require members of the audience to touch one another—especially before the audience has had an opportunity to learn to trust you. Michael Aun, who suggests the back rub technique, has had years of experience in when to use it and when not to. Before you try it, calmly ask yourself if you are comfortable with it. If you are, chances are your audience will be too.

- *Promise.* "When you leave today, you will have the solution to..."
- *Humor.* Use it only if it helps to get your main message across.

> *(All my talks have a common message of laughing at yourself. I am totally bald. I find out who the bald guys are in the group that have a good sense of humor. I talk to them myself to make sure they have a sense of humor. Then I open with)*
> You know, we just don't give enough recognition. I want to take a moment to praise one of your members who is kind, cheerful, brave, reverent...and handsome beyond all imagination, always shining in a crowd. Let's give a hand to _____.
> *(I have the bald guy stand up.)*
> —JIM MCJUNKIN

> *If the audience is not fully aware of your credentials, tell a story that embellishes your image and ends in a joke on yourself. I open by telling of an incident in Italy where I gave out my autograph as a "famous" author. Then the person realized I wasn't the famous person he wanted at all! This gives me the chance to tell of my six published books and 30 years of international experience, yet end with a "simpatico" joke on me.*
> —PAUL DINSMORE

> *Brevity is the soul of many things, including opening statements of speeches—if the situation permits it. These executives get to the point quickly:*
>
> *Rawleigh Warner, Jr. of Mobil Oil Corporation: "I plan to talk with you today about negative factors affecting private sector research and development in our country, particularly as these factors bear on small companies."*
>
> *Irving S. Shapiro of DuPont: "There has been lots of talk about America losing its lead in technology."*
>
> *John R. Beckett of Transamerica Corporation: "This morning I will be talking about five subjects: customers, employees, education, executives, and the importance of the `concept of commitment.'"*
>
> *Richard J. Ferris of United Airlines: "Today I'm going to tell you what United has done to get ready to do business in the future. I am talking about the short-term future—a period that'll be dominated by high fuel costs and the recession. And I'm talking about the long-term future, after the economy pulls out of the recession."*
>
> *Establish a clear and simple two-part outline in the mind of the listeners, as in "I'm going to talk about _____ (subject) and*
>
> *...how it...*
> *...why it...*
> *...what it...*
> —From *Openings,* by Robert O. Skovgard,
> Executive Speaker Company, 1984

After your initial opening, somewhere in the first 10 minutes you really should make a point of mentioning

- Where the fire exits are
- When you will take breaks
- What time lunch is
- An overview of how they will travel through the day
- A request that they turn off their pagers and cellular phones

What to Say

Also, in the unlikely event of a fire, the emergency exits are... (Then to lighten the mood)

You don't have to leave; survival is not compulsory. You all just follow me out. I'll be the one frantically running to the door.

(In a serious tone again)

If we do need to leave, please very calmly leave by those exits and assist any of those around you with movement disabilities.
—JEFF DEWAR

(After a flowery introduction)

That was powerful. Will you stay after and work on my résumé?

I just hope I grow up to be the person my dog thinks I am.

Amazing, they can get you to clap for almost anything.

I loved it when _____ first called me. _____ said, "I need something light with no message, and you came highly recommended."
—TERRY PAULSON

(After a flowery introduction) May God forgive this man (woman) for his (her) excesses—and me for enjoying them so much!
—UNKNOWN

(After a warm welcome) Please, I don't want you to make a fuss over me. Just treat me as you would any other great man.
—From *Current Comedy Newsletter,*
June 10, 1991

(After a warm welcome) Mother Teresa, eat your heart out!
—From *Current Comedy Newsletter,*
December 9, 1991

I guess you're all wondering why I sent for you.
—UNKNOWN
(Supplied by Tom Ogden)

My talk has only three points. This does two things. First, it keeps the talk organized; second, it gives you hope.
—UNKNOWN
(Supplied by Jeff Dewar)

I was a little puzzled by what _____ (chairperson) said to me before I came up here. She said, "Shall we let them enjoy their dessert and coffee a little longer, or shall we have your speech now?"
                                                              —JEFF DEWAR

Hello, my name is Gene and I'm an alcoholic! Oops, wrong meeting.
                                          —GENE MITCHENER, THE WHEELCHAIR COMIC

I am not going to bore you with a lot of statistics. I'm going to bore you without them.

I had planned to open with a few witty ad-libs (pat pockets), but I seem to have left them at home.
                                          —From *Current Comedy Newsletter,*
                                          June 10, 1991

In the interest of being politically correct, I've deleted all controversial material from my speech. (Pause) Thank you, and good night.
                                          —From *Current Comedy Newsletter,*
                                          July 15, 1991

That was the strangest introduction I have had since 5 years ago at a convention when the introducer said, "Many of you may have heard Mr. Linkletter before; others will have something to look forward to."
                                          —ART LINKLETTER

How does one begin a speech? A very important decision. Some speakers jump right in with a relevant statement. Others stall with generic questions like "How does one begin a speech?"
                                          —From *Current Comedy Newsletter,*
                                          July 29, 1991

I'd like to thank all of you for coming today, especially those who knew I'd be speaking and came anyway.

I'm going to throw away my prepared statements—just as soon as I finish reading them to you.
                                          —From *Current Comedy Newsletter,*
                                          September 23, 1991

A good speaker should always know his audience. And if I'm not mistaken, that's you folks, right?
                                          —From *Current Comedy Newsletter,*
                                          December 9, 1991

I have always been short, but today I'll be brief.
                                          —From *Current Comedy Newsletter,*
                                          December 23, 1991

If everything goes as planned this evening, we shouldn't run more than an hour late.

I wasn't their first choice as a speaker. But fortunately for me, Socks the White House cat couldn't make it.

—From *Speaker's Idea File*, Original Humor
section by Gary Apple, premiere edition

We wanted to give you a multimedia presentation, but none of us could program the VCR.

After that introduction, I'm beside myself—and it didn't describe either one of me accurately.

(When you're the final speaker in a long program) I'll keep my comments brief...I disagree with everything everybody else has said. Goodnight!

—From *Speaker's Idea File*, Original Humor
section by Gary Apple, August 1993

I must warn you. When all is said and done, I have a tendency to keep right on talking.

Some of you in the rear may not be able to hear me. Those of you in the front may wish to go back and join them.

I see a lot of smiling faces in the audience—I guess you have kids going back to school too.

—From *Speaker's Idea File*, Original Humor
section by Gary Apple, September 1993

(I have the person introducing me say)

Terry Braverman is a comic/impressionist who has opened for Ben Vereen. As a professional speaker, he has worked for Northrop Corporation....

Unfortunately, Mr. Braverman couldn't make it at the last minute, but we did find an obscure comedian to take his place. So let's give a big welcome to Mr. George Burns!

(I come out with the cigar and glasses on, and start my talk as George Burns.)

—Terry Braverman

I haven't decided what I am going to do. That's neither a plus nor a minus. It's just a fact. I'm just going to take the time to kind of size you up. And you, sir (point to someone in the front row), look like about a 44 long.

—Steve Allen

(I open with brief questions relating to the topic)

How many of you spend more than 50 percent of your workday on the telephone?

How many of you receive calls from people who don't know what they want?

(Then often the third question is humorous)

How many of you feel like cutting the cord and throwing the phone out the window?

—ROGER BURGRAFF

(I especially enjoy using this opening when I'm giving a speech relatively close to home—at the school, the women's club, or something in the neighborhood.) This is a real luxury for me to give a speech so close to my home. I can leave this auditorium, hop in my car, and be in the safety of my own home within 5 or 10 minutes. Now that may not mean much to you, but with the talk I give, to me it can be a lifesaver.

(Comedian Slappy White used to use this opener effectively.)

You know, I hear speakers and comedians saying "A funny thing happened to me on the way to the theater...." I've been working in show business for 25 years and nothing funny ever happened to me on the way to the theater...until tonight. (Then he'd tell his opening story. It worked well.)

—GENE PERRET

When _____ (the challenge the audience is currently facing) began about _____ years/months ago, we at _____ (their company/ association) had some choices. We could have supported the status quo and worked to defeat _____ (the challenge). We could have supported small and cosmetic changes to _____ (their company/association or situation). Or we could have supported—and did (or will) support— sweeping change!

—LILLY WALTERS

What *Not* to Say

Thank you, _____, for that great introduction I wrote.

Thank you for reading that introduction just the way I wrote it.

It's nice to see so many smiling faces. And it's good to see the rest of you too.

I really get annoyed when I hear any version of the three "not to says" above. They are so clichéd, chestnutted, overdone, and outdated. When I hear them, it's like nails on a chalkboard! Just in case I'm not making myself clear here: My opinion on using them is almost unprintable.

...You Can't Figure Out Who Really Said It

Some things have been said so often, you're just not sure who said it the first time. Or the source you pulled it out of didn't write down where it came from originally, so how can you know?

In my last book I wanted to quote the saying "Humor is tragedy plus time." I had first heard it said by the famous comedy writer Gene Perret. So I asked him who said it.

"I have no idea."

OK. I asked the research librarian to work on it. Two weeks later she came back to me with a report of over 63 sources her people had checked. They had thought, as I did, that it must be an ancient Greek saying. But the only place they found it in print attributed it to Carol Burnett! Well, well, well. Guess who one of Carol's main writers is? You got it, Gene Perret! As I was doing the research for this book, I found it again, this time attributed to Mark Twain. Oh, well.

I had someone stop me in the middle of a presentation when I said, "I've always said, 'People support what they help to create.'"

"Excuse me! Isn't that Jeff Dewar's line?!?!"

Well, yes it is. I wrote that particular line with Jeff Dewar when I was helping him develop his talk. In his written works he attributes it to me. When he speaks, he doesn't. After all, I came up with it *for* him. I often attribute it to him.

OK, your turn to figure out the ethics on that one.

What to Do

Just because you can't attribute it, doesn't mean you can acquire it. But even though you can't source it, you can still say it. Make a reasonable effort to find the source—check your quote books and ask your library—if that doesn't work, admit you don't know who said it.
—MARK SANBORN
(Quoted in *Secrets of Successful Speakers,* by
Lilly Walters, McGraw-Hill, 1993)

What to Say

Serious

Does anyone know who said this?

I don't know who said this, but it sounds pretty good and makes good sense to me.
—TOM ANTION

As a wit once said…

You've heard it before, but it's still true….
—STEVE ALLEN
(Quoted in *Secrets of Successful Speakers,* by
Lilly Walters, McGraw-Hill, 1993)

Humorous

(Ham it up) My old Aunt Maude used to say...
I think _____ said this, but he (she) is dead, so I can't ask....
                                —TOM ANTION

A wise person, whose name escapes me, once said...
                                —ROGER LANGLEY

...You Want to Touch Their Heartstrings

The appeal to emotion is particularly effective when the speaker seeks nothing for himself but asks us to care about others.
                                —STEVE ALLEN

What to Do

What stories from the newspaper make your emotional motors start to roar?

What in your own life has taught you a lesson?

What's the most painful experience you've had in your life, or have perhaps heard about?

What makes you cry?

What did this experience help you do better than you did before?

Is that a lesson you can use to support your mission?

Answer these questions and you have the basis for finding those wonderful "heart" stories that can change lives.

That which cometh from the heart will go to the heart.
                                —JEREMIAH BURROUGHES
                                (From *Hosea,* 1652)

If you would have me weep, you must first of all feel grief yourself.
                                —HORACE

Personal stories about how you failed at what you are now good at, how you turned life around for yourself, really turn the group on. They create a "yes I can" or a "so can I, me too" type of tone in the audience. People leave full of hope. What more could you ask for?
                                —DANIELLE KENNEDY

Heart stories in business are always where a group of "little people" proved to be smarter than the big bosses.
—Philip Crosby

You find the best humor and heart stories by simply watching the human dilemma. I used to tell jokes, but there are too many funny and heart-touching things I find by just walking around businesses and airports.
—Ken Blanchard

I like stories that tug at the heartstrings, but as a humorist, I also like to turn it lighthearted again at the end. I've had some fun with this device of reading a heart-tugging letter and then ending by saying: "That's what makes the work that you do so worthwhile, when you get letters like that. And if you don't get letters like that, just do what I do—write your own."
—Gene Perret

Heart stories come best from life experiences. If you have none that touch your heart, either you are made of stone or you need to get involved in your community. Suggestions: Go to a home for handicapped or retarded children or adults. Share experiences. Go to a Salvation Army soup kitchen and listen to the stories. Visit a crime victim center and experience their trauma firsthand. Personally, anyone offended by any of these ideas maybe doesn't deserve to be on the platform.
—Michael Podolinsky

While I'm basically a humorist, I have discovered over the years that some of my humorously told stories have moving messages behind them. Almost ALL of these stories are about members of my family. For me, there is no substitute for real life—that is true and has happened to me— in the search for heart-tugging stories. Much of this material is about children, a fact that has made female speakers hesitant to use it to business audiences because of feminist concerns. I say, if Robert Fulghum can do it, why can't I?
—Hope Mihalap

Information promotes thinking. Emotion promotes action.
—Alan J. Parisse

What to Say

David, my next door neighbor, has two young kids—5 and 7. One day he was teaching his 7-year-old son, Kelly, to push the gas-powered lawn mower around the yard. As he was teaching him how to turn the mower around at the end of the lawn, his wife, Jan, called to him to ask a question. As David turned around to answer the question, Kelly pushed the lawn mower right through the flower bed at the edge of the lawn—leaving a 2-foot wide path level to the ground!

When David turned around and saw what had happened, he began to lose control. David had put a lot of time and effort into making those flower beds the envy of the neighborhood. As he began to raise his voice to his son, Jan walked quickly over to him, put her hand on his shoulder, and said, "David, please remember...we're raising children, not flowers!"
—JACK CANFIELD

Motivational "heart" stories are all in the telling, as Mark Victor Hansen's signature story of Terry Fox reveals. Sentences in his narrative may seem awkward at times, since it is transcribed from an actual live presentation. Mark uses the story to make the point of goal setting.

THE STORY OF TERRY FOX
by Mark Victor Hansen

Terry Fox, as you may remember, was an outstanding athlete, ready to go in pro sports. Started having problems with his right leg. Went to the medical doctor; they checked it out and found out he had cancer ravaging itself through his leg. Doctor came back into the consulting room, said, "Boy I'm sorry to tell you this, you've got cancer shooting through your leg; we're going to have to amputate today, about here. And you're over 21, you've got to sign off on your own leg."

Terry signed off his own leg, bit the bullet, sucked it in, and toughed it out. The next couple of days he's convalescing in the hospital bed and he flashed on one little thoughtful affirmation his high school coach gave him, and that was, "Terry, you can do anything if you want to do it with your whole heart."

He decided what he wanted to do was to run from one end of Canada to the other, raise $100,000, give it to the youth research, so no other young person would suffer the pain, anguish, torment, and travail that he'd gone through.

And he got out of the wheelchair, he got fitted for a prosthesis, false leg. Stated hobbling around. He got his strength and courage up.

Terry wanted to call it *Terry Fox's Marathon of Hope.* Announced it to his parents and his parents said, "Look boy, it's a noble idea, but just now, we've got enough money and we want for you to go back to college and make a real contribution, and drop all this silliness and nonsense."

On the way to school he stopped at the cancer society and he announced his intent. They said, "We think you're right, it's a noble idea, but just now we've got to procrastinate. Come back and see us some *other* time."

Talked his college roommate into dropping out of school; they fly out to Newfoundland, Canada. Drops his crutch in the great Atlantic. Starts trucking through French-speaking Canada.

Essentially gets no media attention.

Breaks into English-speaking Canada and is instantly front-page media sensation. You saw the blood was trickling down his prosthesis. He had a grimace across his face.

Kept on trucking.

Got to meet the Prime Minister, who wasn't reading his vita that day, and said, "Forgive me, but who are you?" and Terry said, "My name is Terry Fox and I'm doing the Marathon of Hope. My goal is to raise a hundred grand—as of yesterday, we got that. I thought with your help, Mr. Prime Minister, we'd go a million dollars."

That's the first time you started seeing him in the U.S. on TV. "Real People" came up and filmed him. And as they skated him across hockey rinks, they collected buckets of money in the grandstands.

He kept on trucking valiantly and vigorously at 31 miles a day. More than a Boston marathon daily. Got to Thunder Bay, Canada. By this time he had deep respiratory problems.

Next town the medical doctor said, "Terry, you've got to cease and desist." He said, "Doc, you don't know who you're talking to. In the beginning my parents told me to buzz off. Provincial government has told me I'm cluttering the highways, I've got to cease and desist. Cancer society would not assist me. I decided to raise a hundred grand. I did that. I extended it to a million, 3 days ago we got a million. When I leave your office, I'm collecting one dollar from every living Canadian, 24-point-one million dollars."

Doc said, "Look, kid, I wish you could do it, but the truth is, you've got cancer ravaging itself up through your chest. Top end, you're probably only going to live another 6 or 8 hours. You've got an Air Force jet, 'cause the whole country's behind you. You've gotten us to drop language barriers and provincial nonsense. You've become the nation's hero. You should be put on a pedestal. We're going to fly you back to BC and we've taken the liberty to call your parents. They'll be there when we get there."

Many of you remember watching the evening news as they rolled him in the emergency room. A 19-year-old journalist, hot for a story, comes lobbing on top of Terry in bed with a microphone and TV cameras going into the ER, and said, "Terry, what are you going to do next?"

(Continued)

Looking into the eye of media, he was a pro until the end. He said, "Are you going to finish my run? Are you going to finish my run? Are you going to finish my run?"

As you know, he died a short time after that. By Dec. 24th that year, millions of individuals had gone out, and they had raised $24.1 million dollars (or $1 for every living Canadian). That was his vision.

You see, some of you will come to this meeting and say, "Well, what can I do. I'm so weak and helpless. There's nothing I can do."

But God, in all His wisdom, said just build a better you. The good news is, as good as you are, you can be even better, if you really want to with your whole head and heart.

Ladies and gentlemen, it has been my honor to be with you this afternoon. Thank you for having me.

CHICKEN SOUP FOR THE SOUL
by Jack Canfield and Mark Victor Hansen

The 26-year-old mother stared down at her son, who was dying of terminal leukemia. Although her heart was filled with sadness, she also had a strong feeling of determination. Like any parent, she wanted her son to grow up and fulfill all his dreams. Now that was no longer possible. The leukemia would see to that. But she still wanted her son's dreams to come true.

She took her son's hand and asked, "Bopsy, did you ever think about what you wanted to be when you grew up? Did you ever dream and wish about what you would do with your life?"

"Mommy, I always wanted to be a fireman when I grew up."

Mom smiled back and said, "Let's see if we can make your wish come true." Later that day she went to her local fire department in Phoenix, Arizona, where she met Fireman Bob, who had a heart as big as Phoenix. She explained her son's final wish and asked if it might be possible to give her 6-year-old son a ride around the block on a fire engine.

Fireman Bob said, "Look, we can do better than that. If you'll have your son ready at 7 o'clock Wednesday morning, we'll make him an honorary fireman for the whole day. He can come down to the fire station, eat with us, go out on all the fire calls, the whole 9 yards! And, if you'll give us his sizes, we'll get a real fire uniform made for him, with a real fire hat—not a toy one—with the emblem of the Phoenix Fire Department on it, a yellow slicker like we wear, and rubber boots. They're all manufactured right here in Phoenix, so we can get them fast."

Three days later Fireman Bob picked up Bopsy, dressed him in his fire uniform, and escorted him from his hospital bed to the waiting hook and ladder truck. Bopsy got to sit up on the back of the truck and help steer it back to the fire station. He was in heaven.

There were three fire calls in Phoenix that day and Bopsy got to go out on all three calls. He rode in the different fire engines, the paramedics' van, and even the fire chief's car. He was also videotaped for the local news program.

Having his dream come true, with all the love and attention that was lavished upon him, so deeply touched Bopsy that he lived 3 months longer than any doctor thought possible.

One night all of his vital signs began to drop dramatically and the head nurse, who believed in the Hospice concept that no one should die alone, began to call the family members to the hospital. Then she remembered the day Bopsy had spent as a fireman, so she called the fire chief and asked if it would be possible to send a fireman in uniform to the hospital to be with Bopsy as he made his transition. The chief replied, "We can do better than that. We'll be there in 5 minutes. Will you please do me a favor? When you hear the sirens screaming and see the lights flashing, will you announce over the PA system that there is not a fire? It's just the fire department coming to see one of its finest members one more time. And will you open the window to his room? Thanks."

About 5 minutes later a hook and ladder truck arrived at the hospital, extended its ladder up to Bopsy's third-floor open window, and 14 firemen and 2 firewomen climbed up the ladder into Bopsy's room. With his mother's permission, they hugged him and held him and told him how much they loved him.

With his dying breath, Bopsy looked up at the fire chief and said, "Chief, am I really a fireman now?"

"Bopsy, you are," the chief said. With those words, Bopsy smiled and closed his eyes for the last time.

From *Chicken Soup for the Soul,* by Jack Canfield and Mark Victor Hansen, Health Communications, 1993, pp. 61–63.

After you have finished your story, you will need to come to some type of closure. You can sum up to the audience, or make a comment directed at yourself.

Maybe you are sitting in the seat of someone like that.

I'm not crying; my eyes are sweating.

—TERRY PAULSON

...You Want to Joke About Location

What to Do

First, what *not* to do: Don't make jokes about *their* country, *their* culture, or *their* company! When I was speaking in Sydney, Australia, my hosts were trying to help me come up with some good humor. "You know, there is a big rivalry between Sydney and Melbourne," they told me. "Poke fun at them!"

All right. So at the appropriate moment in one of my talks I said, "Oh, that reminds me of what the people at *that* table were just explaining to me. You know? Now I don't believe it myself, but they were telling me the difference between Melbourne and yogurt is that yogurt has an active living culture."

Very mild titter. Uh oh.

I *should* have said, "The difference between Los Angeles (where I live) and yogurt...." That would have gotten a laugh. But I should *not* have said it about anything Australian. It is perfectly acceptable for me to pick on my sister, but I'll start snarling at *you* if you try to pick on her. Nobody wants to have an outsider poke fun at his or her ways. You will be the loser if you try.

What to Say

(I have the announcer say, "Please help me welcome, from Azusa, California, Jim McJunkin!" Then I come on and say)
Who was laughing?! I'll have you know that Azusa is a very famous city. I'll have you know the inventor of liquid manure lives there. Our city bird is the med-fly. But the thing I am most proud of is that Azusa is the only city in the world that ever had a McDonald's close its doors.
—JIM MCJUNKIN

The trouble with Oakland is that when you get there, it's there.
—UNKNOWN

I have just returned from Boston. It's the only thing to do if you find yourself there.
—FRED ALLEN, AMERICAN HUMORIST, BORN **1894**
(From *Great Book of Funny Quotes*, by Eileen Mason, Sterling Publishing, 1993)

The difference between Los Angeles and yogurt is that yogurt has a living, active culture.

—Anonymous
(From *Great Book of Funny Quotes*, by Eileen
Mason, Sterling Publishing, 1993)

...You Close the Speech

What to Do

At the end of your presentation, call people to the action dictated by the objectives you set for the presentation. Restate the theme you established in your opening.

Since I speak on humor as a stress relief tool, I like to end by asking the audience to make a commitment to get more laughter in their life. I ask them to take a "Humor Oath."

I say, "Raise your right hand. Take your right index finger and put it on your nose. Take your left hand and hold someone else's earlobe. Now repeat after me: `Starting right now (audience repeat), I will (audience repeat) get more laughter (audience repeat) and play (audience repeat). In my life (audience repeat) I will take what I do seriously (audience repeat). But I will refuse to take myself seriously (audience repeat). So help me Groucho Marx (audience repeat).'"

—Allen Klein

I close with what is now the moniker of my message and career: "It's not what happens to you, it's what you do about it."

—W Mitchell

Open with a laugh—close with a tear.

—Dottie Walters

I always sum up the points I made. And I give them a really funny story. Or I give them some funny lines. I start off humorous and end off humorous. All the stuff I teach is really serious. I teach heavy-duty psychology. But I teach it in a really funny way.

—Alan Pease

I was struggling one day over how to close an upcoming presentation. I kept thinking and reflecting on my theme. I finally got inspired and wrote a poem that sums up my thoughts and presentation skills—which are my main topic.

CURTAIN CALL
by Lilly Walters

We've shown you the challenge
　Many skills to enhance.
It's all set before you.
　Will you join in the dance?

Your words can bring hope
　And joy and new powers
For somebody crying,
　In desperate hours.

You stride to the footlights
　The crowd is so still.
Will they clap and applaud
　And stand with the thrill?

Or...Will glitter and glamour
　Cause you to forget
The caring and sharing,
　And your mission neglect?

The speech is now over
　And gone is the crowd.
Did anyone hear you?
　Did you come on too proud?

Reliving it later
　Sadly parked in your car.
So much farther to go,
　Yet already *so far.*

Then, a kid at your door,
　Says, "'fore you're off to bed,
Would you tell me more?
　I *loved* what you said."

Was unsure of my part.
　I was crying today
Then your words touch'd my heart.
　Do you mean what you say?

Were you to talking to me?
　I've a race to be run.
Is there power in me?
　Did ya mean...*I'm* the one?"

Well...
We've shown you the challenge
　Will lives you enhance?
It's all set before you.
　Will you join in the dance?

What to Say

...and remember, make everyday above ground a great day.
—Jim McJunkin

Please remember, if you enjoyed hearing me today, my name is John Nisbet. And if you didn't enjoy it, that's _____ (the CEO of their company, a famous person, or even something neutral like John Smith).
—John Nisbet

Please drive carefully. The IRS needs you.
—Anonymous
(From *Great Book of Funny Quotes,* by Eileen Mason, Sterling Publishing, 1993)

As you slide down the banister of life, may the splinters never face the wrong way!
—UNKNOWN
(Submitted by Mikki Williams)

The race is not always to the swift, nor the battle to the strong, but that's the way to bet.
—DAMON RUNYON

I need to go now...they don't even know I left the hospital yet.
—GENE MITCHENER, THE WHEELCHAIR COMIC

I could go on and on, but I see a lot of you are dozing off and off.
—From *Speaker's Idea File,* Original Humor
section by Gary Apple, premiere edition

The longest journey begins with one step...and ends with one, too. Goodnight.
—From *Speaker's Idea File,* Original Humor
section by Gary Apple, August 1993

I'm not afraid of tomorrow. I've seen yesterday and I'm in love with today.
—GEORGE GOLDTRAP

Follow your heart, but do it with your head.
—STEVE JOBS
(Quoted by Jimmy Calano)

(After dinner) I hate to bring this up, but which one of you is leaving the tip?
—From *Current Comedy Newsletter,*
September 9, 1991

As Lady Godiva said when she stepped off her horse, "I've come to my clothes."
—GENE MITCHENER, THE WHEELCHAIR COMIC

...You Are Asked to Speak to the Same Group Again

Ira Hayes had a speech he perfected to brilliance. For many years he said, "I have only one speech. It's much easier to find a new audience than it is a new speech!" That is just what he did!

To Prevent It from Happening

If your market is very small (your topic is only appropriate to the same association, company, or geographic area), you will find yourself forced to present to the same group over and over. Here are some ideas for remaining fresh:

- Keep track of what you do, and whom you do it for.

- Constantly develop new material. Keep yourself in a high research mode. Always carry a note pad or small recorder with you to jot down ideas when they come to mind.

- Find ways to creatively embellish the old stuff.

> *I have a sheet that's got about 400 key words on it. Each key word represents my different openings, closings, stories, physical humor—my humorous stuff. Then I have two columns for the speech. Before I start, I write the name of the company at the top, and then I'll take whatever bit of humor I think I could use to open and close. When I've used it, I'll put a line through it so at the end of the speech I know what I've used. That way, if I speak to the same company next year, I won't use the same stories. With this system, I have marked exactly—for the last 10 or 15 years—every line, every quip that I've used.*
>
> *In America you just have to change cities and you've got a whole new audience. But here in Australia, and New Zealand—where there aren't that many cities—you get the same people over and over in your audience. You must make sure you do not duplicate material. At the start of the meeting, I always do a survey and say, "How many of you people have seen me before?"*
>
> *There are only one or two options as a speaker when you're in a small market—either you get new material or you get new audiences. As a result of being a speaker in this market, I've been forced to expand my repertoire. So, now I can speak competently on at least 10 different areas all within the same general umbrella, say, of "selling"...whereas in America I'd only have to have one.*
>
> —ALAN PEASE

> *I keep outlines and notes on every presentation I make so that I know what I've already said. This is critical.*
>
> —MARK SANBORN

> *I always plant a "teaser" about past programs—to say just enough about those past topics to make them go to the meeting planner and ask for the old tape or book. If I create enough interest this way, the whole cycle starts over. The meeting planner calls me back the next time to repeat the first program.*
>
> —DIANNA BOOHER

What to Do

I was speaking to an association in Southern California. I had presented to the group every year for the preceding 3 years; this was my fourth talk. I have three subjects on which I give keynotes and workshops: "Secrets of Successful Speakers," "Games Presenters Plays," and "How to Organize Meetings, Seminars, and Workshops with Pizzazz!" Well, I had done all of these already, but the event planner felt that, since the presentations had such a tremendous turnout in the past 3 years, and the association had a great deal of turnover, I could start over with "How to Organize Meetings, Seminars, and Workshops with Pizzazz!" So, after I said "Hello," I asked: "How many of you heard me 4 years ago on this topic?" Ninety-five percent of the room raised their hands!

Uh oh. I laid down my notes, and said, "Super. We are going to take up from where we left off. This time you are going tell me exactly what we most need to work on, and strategies to work on those issues!" I then launched into a group discussion activity. I hardly said a word for the 45 minutes I was with them. They talked, came up with ideas, which being their own they thought were just terrific (and frankly they were), and I mainly sat there and nodded. My ego was a bit bruised at all the folks who afterward said, "This was the *best* you've done for us in 4 years!"

There are many way to facilitate a problem-solving session. (See the section in Chapter 5 on discussion groups.) One simple way is to break people into groups of three to six, and have them come up with the three worst problems facing their company, industry, or association. Assemble a master list of these problems. Then reassign the problems to new teams within the same audience. Let them come up with all the answers they can think of. You just comment on the results.

First I make sure how much of the audience has actually heard me before. Many times, even though I've spoken to this group three plus times, there are always some who are hearing me for the first time. I do this right at the beginning with a show of hands. It can also be done by my introducer. If half or less than half have not heard me before, I can use many of the same stories. Even so, I need some new materials or the other half will feel cheated.

I always get people who come up afterward and says something like, "You know, I've heard you five times now and I learn something new each time."

I look back at my notes from the previous speech to that group and see what stories I've used, and make sure I use as many different stories and examples as possible that also are pertinent to the points I'm making. Even so, I have several stories that I always use and that are expected of me. (Like my friend Henny Youngman saying, "Take my wife ...please." You've heard it a million times, but every time you see him, you want to hear it again.)

I might interview a number of participants who heard my previous speech to this same group, and who will be there again, and see what they've done to implement the ideas I've shared with them. The client usually knows who these people are. Then I can tell the same idea to the audience, tailor it more to their industry, and give them a success story from their own ranks. Very powerful, even though it's essentially the same material.

— JEFF SLUTSKY

What to Say

Serious

It's nice to be back with old friends and have an opportunity to go deeper and to cover advanced ground with you. So much of consulting and speaking is "Blow in, blow off, and blow out," without ever really knowing what happened and with no accountability for results. I enjoy the opportunity to have this ongoing relationship with you and your organization (company, school, association, etc.). It allows us to work in depth over time and really create some spectacular results together. So let's get started.

— JACK CANFIELD

When I was here _____ years ago, I looked out at an audience that was battling with _____ (the challenges they faced, over which they have achieved success). I thought about the magnitude of that challenge, and as I was speaking then I wondered, "Can they do it?" Today I look out at an audience, and I'm thinking, "What have I done in my life to deserve the honor of addressing people who can meet, defeat, and exceed that kind of challenge?"

Thank you.

Today we look at the battlefield and see _____ (the new challenge). This time I am not thinking, "Can they do it?" This time I wonder, "How fast will they advance right through this skirmish to seek out the next?"

— LILLY WALTERS

Humorous

Some of you may have heard a few of my stories before. If you have, please don't yell out the punch lines!

— MARK SANBORN

You people are getting to be family.

This is the third year in a row they've asked me back—they're hoping I'll get it right this time.

This is my third session. I've just about told you more than I know.

— DIANNA BOOHER

They say the third time's the charm. I don't know who they are, but I hope that's what you'll say when I'm done!

Don't worry! My third talk is always the best.

I have a personal rule—"Never speak to the same group three times"—but I broke it for you because I couldn't stand to see _____ (insert name of meeting planner, someone well known to the group) crying and begging.

There's only one thing more difficult than speaking to a group for the third time and that is listening to the same speaker for the third time.
        —TOM ANTION

...You Are Asked to Give the Same Speech to the Same Group Again

To Prevent It from Happening

You can just say no. Many entertainers refuse to present to the same group 2 years in a row. They insist on a lapse time of *at least* 2 years or more. During that time, most group's rank-and-file will have changed at least a little. Often they have changed a great deal. If you wait at least 2 years, the audience members who still remember you as a presenter will be eager to "replay" the great experience. Besides, by this time you will have at least *some* new stuff.

When they keep inviting you back it not only means they love you, it means they love what you are saying. Speakers often think they need to have all new material when they are invited back to a group. But the truth of the matter is that often one of the reasons they have been invited back is because the people want to relive the wonderful experience they had the previous times. They want to hear what they heard the other times—and if you don't tell the favorites stories they remember from the previous visits, they may well be disappointed.

Have you ever had a favorite movie that you have gone back to see more than once? Sure you have. You may even have taken a friend along to share your experience. It is often that way with speakers. People in the audience may be there because a friend has wanted to share your message with them.
        —RALPH ARCHBOLD

Can you imagine someone inviting Neil Diamond or Luciano Pavarotti to sing at an annual meeting and saying "Here are the words to our company song, our company motto, and our sales brochures—please be sure to sing only these words and phrases, not those popular, meaningful songs you perform so well that have made you famous and inspired millions of people"?

> —ED FOREMAN
> (Quoted in *Secrets of Successful Speakers*, by
> Lilly Walters, McGraw-Hill, 1993)

What to Do

Audiences remember only about 10 percent of what you say. Usually that 10 percent is those terrific stories that you would like to use a second time. So think of different points you can make using those same stories again, but apply them to their new challenges and needs.

> *Whenever I am speaking to a group that has invited me back, I am sincere in expressing my appreciation for the exceptional honor, and work very, very hard to make sure they are as pleased with my third performance as they were with my first.*
>
> *Obviously, my objective is to develop a presentation with primarily new material. However, I find that most stories, if they are really good, are enjoyed as much and more in the retelling—as long as the audience knows you know they've heard them before.*
>
> *A helpful twist or two:*
>
> *I use a "rest of the story" approach. If the group has already heard my Fred the Postman story, I offer an update: "Fred left my route, but sent a letter and here's what he said...."*
>
> *Also, you can tell the same story—or a synopsis of it—and make a different point. "You may remember...(story). Today I'd like you to consider a different conclusion." Most excellent illustrations are multifaceted and lend themselves well to this.*
>
> —MARK SANBORN

What to Say

> *I am delighted to be with you again. I know many of you have heard me talk before, which puts me in a rather bad spot of having to keep my stories straight. I also know you will hear several new, thought-provoking, and different ideas tonight, which gives me courage to press on! This evening I'd like to talk about...*

> *I am delighted to be with you again. I know some of you have heard me talk before, so I'll try to keep my stories straight. By the way, if you hear me once more, you will be qualified to give this presentation yourself! If you have heard me before, I know that tonight you will hear something unique in a number of my comments. This evening I'd like to talk with you about...*
>
> —DAVE CAREY

> *If you have heard me say any of this before, the redundancy is for emphasis!*
>
> —MARK SANBORN

For those of you who haven't heard this before, there's an important point to make. For those of you who have, consider it a review.
                                    —JEFF SLUTSKY

SUREFIRE SAVERS FOR ANY SITUATION

I am wary of typical saver lines that comedians use—such as "I'm going to fire that writer" or "Anybody awake out there?" or other things that aren't funny. I think it's sometimes a danger to try to use saver lines—the possibility exists that the audience might not have even noticed that you're dying.
                                    —HOPE MIHALAP

Point is: If you're going to use saver lines, make them fresh. And don't complain about others, or grovel! Here are some winners.

David Letterman, on his TV show one night, gave me a great opportunity at self-promotion when, upon my entrance while introducing me, he accidentally knocked my book The Executive Memory Guide *off his desk and onto the floor. I scooped it up before I sat down, placed it back on his desk, and announced gingerly, "See, Dave, my book is already on the rise."*
                                    —HERMINE HILTON

We'll pause for a moment...while I try to think of what the heck to do next.

Well, nobody's perfect...except grandchildren.
                                    —ROGER LANGLEY

Now what's wrong with this picture?

(Look pained at the situation) Goes to show ya, not all the suffering is over in third world countries and at _____ (the group's major competitor).

I've had a wonderful day—but this wasn't it.
                                    —LEONARD RYZMAN

Everything is funny as long as it is happening to somebody else.
                                    —WILL ROGERS

That was done on purpose. It's part of my presentation...It wasn't yesterday, but it is today.
                                    —RON DENTINGER

Seriously, most of you know where I was going anyway. While I fix this, go ahead without me.

These are not tears you see—my eyes are sweating.

Is this Candid Camera?

Did you ever have a day when you felt like a fire hydrant and all your friends were dogs?

Some days you're the pigeon; some days the statue.

Some days you're the bug; some days the windshield.

This is probably as bad as it gets, but don't count on it.

I love the bumper sticker: "If at first you don't succeed, do what your wife told you."

Someday I'll laugh at this—so why wait?

Some days I speak on optimal performance; other days I can't even say it.

After this program, please keep the razor blades away from me for an hour.

(Pull out a small retake clapboard from behind the podium and clap it together, saying) Cut! Take two!

(Reach into your wallet and pull out a card; pretend to read.) Get out of jail free.

This feels like that day when I had to sell my house and move into one of those pandemoniums.
—TERRY PAULSON

If you want a place in the sun, you have to expect a few blisters.
—LORETTA YOUNG, AMERICAN ACTRESS, BORN **1912**
(From *Great Book of Funny Quotes,* by Eileen
Mason, Sterling Publishing, 1993)

If at first you don't succeed, try, try again. Then give up. No use being a damn fool about it.
—W. C. FIELDS, AMERICAN ACTOR AND COMEDIAN,
BORN **1880**
(From *Great Book of Funny Quotes*)

If at first you don't succeed, failure may be your style.
—QUENTIN CRISP, ENGLISH ACTOR, POET, WRITER,
AND CRITIC, BORN **1908**
(From *Great Book of Funny Quotes*)

There are three rules for writing a novel.* Unfortunately, no one knows what they are.
—W. SOMERSET MAUGHAM, ENGLISH NOVELIST,
BORN **1874**
(From *Great Book of Funny Quotes*)

---

*Substitute "telling a joke," "giving a speech," or "fixing an overhead projector."

A man of genius makes no mistakes. His errors are volitional and are portals of discovery.

> —JAMES JOYCE, IRISH NOVELIST AND POET, BORN **1882**
> (From *Great Book of Funny Quotes*)

If I ever wanted a brain transplant, I'd use a sportswriter* because I'd want one that had never been used.

> —NORM VAN BROCKLIN, AMERICAN FOOTBALL PLAYER, BORN **1926**
> (From *Great Book of Funny Quotes*)

The world is so overflowing with absurdity that it is difficult for the humorist to compete.

> —MALCOLM MUGGERIDGE, ENGLISH EDITOR AND JOURNALIST, BORN **1903**
> (From *Great Book of Funny Quotes*)

Education is when you read the fine print. Experience is what you get when you don't.

> —PETE SEEGER, AMERICAN SINGER AND COMPOSER, BORN **1919**
> (From *Great Book of Funny Quotes*)

My philosophy of life is to live one day at a time...and skip ones like today!

> —From *Current Comedy Newsletter*, June 24, 1991

Sometimes you just need to look reality in the eye—and deny it.

> —GARRISON KEILLOR
> (Submitted by Terry Paulson)

Life is a test—it is only a test. If it had been a real life, I would have received further instruction on where to go and what to do.

> —UNKNOWN
> (Submitted by Terry Paulson)

Please, no individual laughing or clapping. Stay with the group.

> —PHIL CASS

I'm not out of control. My life just gives a whole new dimension to the definition.

> —LOU BROWN

---

*Substitute appropriate person or industry for the group you are presenting to.

Now for an encore, ladies and gentlemen, I will...
—From *One Liners for Disaster,* by Tom Antion,
Anchor Publishing, 1993

I should say something funny now, but my mind just took a sabbatical (vacation, leave of absence, went AWOL, etc.).
—TOM ANTION

(When it's time to get back on track, affect the voice of a radio announcer.) We now return to our previously scheduled program, in progress.
—DICK FLAVIN

"He's so sure, he wrote an acceptance speech."

7 Master Checklist So You Don't Need to Worry About Dying on the Platform

Long Before You Arrive

Get it in writing! All arrangements, agreements, fees, and other terms should be written down, including how, when, and to whom to make payment. Carry copies of your correspondence and the contract with you in your briefcase or purse. If your meeting planner has been fired, you may have been replaced without notice. Be ready with proof.

Who pays for workbooks and handouts? Will pencils, pads, and other items be paid for by the hotel, the planner, or the presenter? Find out who will set the materials out and pay for the labor costs.

Get a deposit in advance. For overseas programs, get full payment in advance.

Who will pick you up at the airport? Have that person's home and work phone numbers and another emergency number. Be sure to take this information with you in your briefcase, not in your suitcase.

Pack what you absolutely must have with you as a carry-on. There are only two kinds of luggage: carry-on and lost!

Dress appropriately for the group. Check with the planner. The theme of the whole convention may be "Western," but you may be speaking at a formal banquet. The presenter should always look businesslike and professional. Plan to dress slightly better than the audience, without being out of place. Never dress down. Look successful and elegant, not "loud" or ostentatious. Also check on the colors of the meeting room. Will your clothes clash with the site?

Carry a kit of emergency supplies. Essentials include tape, scissors, extension cords, chalk, whistle, flashlight, aspirin, small can or tube of insect repellent, anti-itch cream, needle, thread, and safety pins. I always carry a daytime hot tea flu remedy—one of those sneezing, coughing, stuffy head, sore throat, fever concoctions. (Ladies should also remember feminine supplies.)

The mind can accept only what the seat will endure. Find out what is on the program in the 3 hours before and after your presentation. Will the crowd need a stretch or a bathroom break before you can begin? Will people slip out before you are finished because they have another event in a different location? Work with the meeting planner in advance on the flow of the meeting. A receptive audience will take in the best you have to offer. Make suggestions on breaks to the planner to help make the meeting a success.

Tell catering to stop all activities when your program starts. Let the planner know it's not effective to have catering serve or clear while the presentation is in progress. Often the planner will forget to inform catering of this ahead of the event. Ask the planner's permission to speak with the catering people directly. They will need to plan to stop clearing even if they are not finished yet.

Doublecheck all details before you leave home. Call your client *no more than* 4 days before the event to confirm *everything*. You will be amazed that even the state and date can change without anyone letting you know. One presenter arrived at the right place and time, but the wrong year. Another arrived at the hotel only to be told the meeting (out of country) had been canceled. Always confirm.

Get a map. Doublecheck the event location, addresses, and phone numbers at the site. Find out about alternative transportation in case the person who is to pick you up does not show up.

Bring props with you. The meeting planner has 1000 details to attend to. Don't ask for difficult or hard-to-get props. If they *must* be there, design your presentation in such a way that you can carry them on the plane with you.

Who is the contact person when you arrive on site? Where will he or she be located? Often the main planner assigns someone else the task of "presenter sitting" you once you arrive.

Send a copy of your introduction in advance. The planner or the introducer usually wants to practice before the event.

Plan how many assistants you need. Let the planner know. Contact the assistants if needed before you arrive to set up a rehearsal time.

Prepare a seating setup chart. Submit it to the planner several weeks before the event for approval. Also give a copy to catering a few days before the event (ask permission of your planner first). Always pack an extra copy or two.

Request that the location and title of your presentation be printed on the program.

Request that signs be posted outside the presentation room door. Bring signs if your client does not have them. Get easels from the hotel. Attendees choose which breakout session to attend, and the presenter is judged by the number who do. Be sure they can find you!

Ship your materials to the bell captain. Call several days ahead of the meeting to check that anything you sent is there. Use a second-day type carrier. It's not as expensive as next day, yet still gets there quickly. If things get there earlier, they are often lost by the hotel.

Arrange to have your presentation taped. Use a top-quality reproduction company if possible and affordable. These tapes can be used as demo tapes and products for resale. Only one in 10 will be good enough to use, so try to tape all your presentations. If the planner is not taping you, ask the hotel if it has an audiovisual department that can do so. Often local colleges and universities will send out students to tape you at a low cost. (Murphy's Law for presenters is: "You never manage to tape your best presentations.")

Request two mics: one on you and one on the audience. You want the tape to pick up the audience's laughter.

Is the client taping? You are within your *legal* rights to refuse to allow planners to tape your presentation. You can require royalties, or a reproduction fee. If you forget to check with the client about taping before you arrive, you can still refuse to perform. Your *ethical* rights are in question for not being responsible enough to check before the event.

Write articles or press releases for the client's house publication and for industry magazines. This sets you up before the event as an industry authority and helps promote your image as a celebrity to the group.

Brainstorm with the client's publicity or public relations team.

Negotiate for a publicity day with the client. The client may arrange interviews with TV, radio, and publications. You are paid an extra fee for the day.

Mention the host organization in all media coverage that the client helps you with. Also mention the event you are speaking at, your name, the location and time of the event, and your presentation title in any PR you do for that client or for publications that are distributed to those industries.

What are the client's special objectives and needs? What level of person are you addressing? Has the audience heard someone on your topic before? What were the good and bad aspects of that presenter?

Poll part or all of your audience ahead of the event. Learn people's specific needs, problems, and sensitive topic areas. Tailor your material to them. For example, if the audience is 90 percent female, do not use football stories. Speak in terms of their interests.

Research current news about the industry. Check the papers, magazines, and TV. There are services available, through libraries and universities, that will give you copies of all articles written on a specific topic.

Emergencies and Delayed Travel

Book safe travel. It is your obligation when you accept a fee for your speaking services to arrive ready and refreshed at the site. Do not book yourself so tight that you must take "red eye" flights each night. Plan to arrive at least 4 hours before the event—preferably the day before. If your plane is delayed, you need the leeway to find alternative travel in case of cancellations and weather problems.

Find out whom to contact if an emergency or delay occurs. If everyone is already at the event and your transportation is delayed, you need at least one other contact with the host organization to help get the message through to the right people. Call ahead to both the hotel and the planner.

Compile a list of several other presenters who speak on your subject. Professional presenters say the only reasons for "no shows" are death (preferably yours) and natural disasters that would stop even Superman from reaching the meeting site. If either of these situations occurs, you (or your next of kin) should be prepared to have someone fill in. Some organizations require this "standby" on the contract.

After You Arrive (Well Before the Presentation)

Let your contact know at once that you have arrived. Never let your client worry and wonder. You are there to help the meeting planner.

Make yourself known to the hotel's switchboard and message center people. Establish contact as soon as you arrive. Say something nice. Tell them you just wanted to say hello. Let them know you are expecting important calls and you wanted to thank them in advance.

Go to a hall phone and ask to be transferred to yourself. Even after you have been there 30 minutes, they still may not know you are registered there! Your meeting planner may call and become panicked, assuming you had plane trouble and are not going to make the meeting!

Check up on your presentation room. If it has not been set up yet, give the catering people the extra copy of the room setup chart you brought with you; they will no doubt have lost the original. If the room is set up, picture yourself as an audience member. Go sit in the audience. Can the entire audience get the full benefit of your visuals with this seating arrangement? Will people be looking into the open windows behind you? If the room is not set up correctly, check with the planner. Sometimes it is just impossible to adjust the room to your needs because the next group needs it set up another way. Try for a compromise, and *offer to fix it yourself.*

Doublecheck with the event planner to make sure of exactly which room you are to present in.

Ask the hotel people what the emergency procedures are. Each venue has different procedures for fire, earthquake, medical emergencies, and so on. Where are the exits and house phones located? Actually walk the fire exit paths to the street.

Find out where the closest fire extinguisher and fire alarm are.

Assign one of your assistants as the person to call for help in emergencies. Show your assistant where the phones are yourself so you are both clear as to medical, fire, and other emergency procedures.

Assign one of your assistants to get the fire extinguisher in case of a fire in your room. Actually walk this person to where the fire extinguisher is housed and discuss how it is pulled out of the wall and how it is used. I suggest a large, burly person—fire equipment can be heavy. Assign this person, or the one who is to go call for help, to activate the fire alarm.

Assign people to help you distribute your handouts in the quickest manner possible. Discuss exactly how and when this will be done. At meal functions materials must be passed out after the dessert. In workshops they can be waiting for attendees on their seats. Include the evaluation forms.

Check camera angles if videotaping. While you look through the camera lens, have someone stand where you will be speaking from and walk around as you do when you are speaking. Is anything distracting to the viewer's eye in the background? Will the lectern be in the way of the screen? Are unneeded chairs in the way? When you write on a flipchart or blackboard, is your back to the camera? Where are the dark spots? Stay in the light.

Practice any prop moves, lighting changes, and other signals. Practice all moves alone or with your assistants, the light-switch people, the introducer, or the projectionist, as needed. Appoint someone to each light switch. Practice your signals. Test your visuals in various dimmed lighting conditions.

Practice adjusting the mic stand up to your height.

Get all the electrical equipment up and running. Will you pull too much power when it all goes on and blow a fuse?

Bring *extra* bulbs and batteries. Pack them in your purse or briefcase. Do not leave them in your hotel room.

Safely tape down extension cords.

Write down the names and addresses of your assistants. Send thank-you notes and/or bring small gifts to present to them at the meeting. They will never forget you.

Be sure *you* are spotlighted. Never work on stage in the dark. Some presenters carry their own spotlights and extension cords. You are the star, not the slides. Bring the lights up full as soon as possible. The audience needs only a few moments to review each slide. Then people *need* to see your face again, not a dark shadow. Doublecheck that your slides are in the right order and right side up *before* your presentation.

Check the staging. What will the audience see directly behind you on the stage? A blank wall or drapes are ideal. (Mooseheads should be removed—unless they are owned by your client.) Open windows must be free of sun glare—and the view of bikinis at the pool should be blocked.

Unscrew the lights behind you. If there are wall lights directly behind where you will be standing, unscrew them. You don't want the audience trying to stare into a light bulb.

Fix the seating if the house is light. Take the seats away in the back.

Make sure your mic is working. Check the mic before the audience enters. Find out where static and squelch sounds occur. Avoid that part of the room. Cordless mics are great. Many presenters bring their own. These mics allow the presenter the freedom to move all over the auditorium in an arc as big as a football field. Some are handheld; others fasten on the presenter's clothing. But be sure to turn the equipment off when you are finished.

Practice with your introducer. Bring an extra copy of your custom introduction (the one you sent usually will be lost). Give the introducer a gift—just a small remembrance to say thank you for doing a good job of getting the presentation off to a good start.

Ask someone to time your presentation. Wear a watch with a very large face, or bring a clock to put just out of sight on the lectern. Don't go over your time limit. If you are forced to start late, check with the meeting planner. Are you to cut your presentation time down, or give them the full time? Adjust to what your client wants.

Get pronunciations of names, titles, and current company status correct. Pronunciation is critical if you use stories that involve members or employees of the organization you are addressing. Print names on a card in bold black pen and tape the card to the lectern where you can glance at it easily.

Post signs to divide the room into smoking (with ashtrays) and nonsmoking. Test air flow. Put the smokers *down wind.*

Know where the facilities person will be at all times. You don't want to hunt if you're in trouble. One presenter discovered an error as she began her presentation. Her mic would not work, and the program from the adjoining room was piped into her room full blast.

Where are the air-conditioning controls? Remember, it gets a lot hotter when the room fills up with people. You should feel cool when you are in there alone.

Ask the head of catering not to allow serving or clearing while you speak. Even if you have asked before, reconfirm about an hour before you go on.

Do not drink alcohol. Many people may be offended. Even if you are drinking a soda, people will often assume it is mixed with alcohol. Consider carrying the bottle or can of your nonalcoholic beverage around with you when you mingle and set it on the table with you at meals.

As the Audience Begins to Come In

Speak with the audience members. Get a feeling for whom you can "play" with.

Ask permission of your participants. If you plan on going over the edge with a member, take him or her aside privately and ask.

Ten Minutes Before You Go On

Use the restroom.

Check that your water glass is in place.

Visually check that your props are in place.

Check with the event planners on what time they *really* want you to end your talk.

When You Step Up to the Lectern

Smile.

Take a deep breath.

Look into several people's eyes and make *contact*.

Start your talk.

During the Presentation

Mention emergency procedures. If the MC or the announcer has not done so, casually mention to the group that "in the unlikely event of a fire, the fire exits are there and there. Please notice if anyone next to you needs assistance in leaving the room."

Ask your attendees to please turn off their pagers and phones. Or have your assistant collect them and handle calls.

Distribute your handouts in the quickest manner possible. At meal functions, handouts must be passed out after the dessert. In workshops they can be waiting for attendees on their seats. Include the evaluation forms.

Let the audience stand up to stretch at least every 2 hours. Every hour is better. In long sessions (over 1½ hours) include a participative section in which each member of the audience speaks to another, stands and shakes hands with a neighbor, and so on.

Do not allow the catering staff to clear while you are speaking. Don't try to talk over a meal service. Make a joke and calmly, with a smile, ask the servers to leave. (Before you ask catering to leave the room, make sure the planner knew and agreed to there being no clearing going on during your presentation.)

Remind the attendees several times to fill out the evaluation forms. Allow a few moments at the end of your presentation for people to fill out the forms before they leave for the next event.

If you are taping, repeat the questions from the audience. Audience comments will not pick up well on the tape, even if the floor is mic'd—unless someone is walking a mic right up to the question askers.

Right After the Presentation

Gather your materials. Don't forget to look under the lectern.

Ask for a copy of the tape. If the client made a tape, make sure you receive a personal copy.

After You Go Home

Send a thank you. Send thank-you notes and/or bring small gifts to present to them at the meeting to the assistants who helped you. They will never forget you.

Never let your clients forget you. Send them news of new products and subjects that relate to their interests. Let them know you remember them.

When it's all over and everyone says, "I guess this sort of thing comes easily for you," **just smile!**

Resources

Publications

Executive Speeches, published bimonthly, includes the full text of 10 to 20 current contemporary speeches as well as bibliographic listings of other speeches on the same topic.

Executive Speaker Company
P.O. Box 292437
Dayton, OH 45429
Editor/publisher: Bob Skovgard
Phone: 513-294-8493; fax: 513-294-6044

The Executive Speaker, a monthly newsletter, features a variety of the best openings and closings from current speeches by executives, as well as examples from the body of the text. Also publishes the *Quote...Unquote* ® newsletter.

Executive Speaker Company
P.O. Box 292437
Dayton, OH 45429
Editor/publisher: Bob Skovgard
Phone: 513-294-8493; fax: 513-294-6044

Speechwriters Newsletter is a publication for speechwriters.

Lawrence Ragan Communications, Inc.
212 West Superior Street, Suite 200
Chicago, IL 60610
Phone: 312-335-0037; fax: 312-335-9583

Speaker's Idea File is a monthly compendium for speakers and speech-writers.

Lawrence Ragan Communications, Inc.
212 West Superior Street, Suite 200
Chicago, IL 60610
Phone: 312-335-0037; fax: 312-335-9583

The Jokesmith is a monthly newsletter of current comedy and humor.

Ed McManus, Consultant
44 Queen's View Road
Marlborough, MA 01752
Phone: 508-481-0979

Current Comedy Newsletter is a selection of bimonthly updates to *American Speaker*, a guide published by Georgetown Publishing House.

Georgetown Publishing House
1101 30th Street, NW
Washington, DC 20007
Phone: 800-368-0115

Sharing Ideas Among Professional Speakers, a newsmagazine, discusses issues, news, tips, and trends for professional speakers.

Royal Publishing
P.O. Box 1120
Glendora, CA 91740
Phone: 818-335-8069

The Toastmaster publishes monthly how-to articles about public speaking and other communication-related topics. The official publication of Toastmasters International.

Toastmasters International
P.O. Box 9052
Mission Viejo, CA 92690-7052
Phone: 714-858-8255

Speech Consultants

Tom Ogden, executive magic consultant; $1529\frac{1}{2}$ North Bronson Avenue, Hollywood, CA 90028; phone: 213-461-7038, fax: 213-461-5067

Lilly Walters, presentation skills, professionalism, and content design; P.O. Box 1120, Glendora, CA 91740; phone: 818-335-8069, fax: 818-335-6127

Tom Antion, humor consultant; P.O. Box 2630, Landover Hills, MD 20784; phone: 301-459-0738, fax: 301-552-0225

Roger Langley, humor consultant; Comedy College, 625 Smallwood Road, Rockville, MD 20850; phone: 301-217-6560

Ed McManus, The Jokesmith; 44 Queens View Road, Marlborough, MA 01752; phone 508-481-0979

Educational Materials for Speakers

Speak and Grow Rich, by Dottie and Lilly Walters. How to increase your income in the world of professional speaking.

For an autographed copy contact the authors at

P.O. Box 1120
Glendora, CA 91740
818-335-8069

Secrets of Successful Speakers: How You Can Motivate, Captivate, and Persuade, by Lilly Walters. Design your presentation using the secrets of the master speakers.

For an autographed copy contact the author at

P.O. Box 1120
Glendora, CA 91740
818-335-8069

Persuasive Platform Presentations—Secrets of Successful Speakers, by Lilly Walters. A $4\frac{1}{2}$-hour audio album with 70-page workbook.

Royal Publishing
P.O. Box 1120
Glendora, CA 91740
818-335-8069

How to Prepare, Stage, and Deliver Winning Presentations, by Thomas Leech.

AMACOM
135 West 50 Street
New York, NY 10020
212-586-8100

Games Presenters Play, by Lilly Walters and Jeff Dewar. A 2-hour training video on designing audience participation exercises.

Royal Publishing
P.O. Box 1120
Glendora, CA 91740
818-335-8069

Games Trainers Play, More Games Trainers Play, and *Still More Games Trainers Play,* by Ed Scannell and John Newstrom. Books on training exercises.

McGraw-Hill, Inc.
Order Services
P.O. Box 545
Blacklick, OH 43004-0545
800-722-4726

Speaking with Magic, by Michael Jefferies. How to use magic in speeches.

Royal Publishing
P.O. Box 1120
Glendora, CA 91740
818-335-8069

Teaching and Training with Magic, by Tom Ogden. Video seminar on using magic.

Tom Ogden, Consultant
1529 ½ North Bronson Avenue
Hollywood, CA 90028
213-461-7038

or

Royal Publishing
P.O. Box 1120
Glendora, CA 91740
818-335-8069

Associations

Toastmasters International
P.O. Box 9052
Mission Viejo, CA 92690-7052
714-858-8255

International Platform Association (IPA)
2564 Berkshire Road
Cleveland Heights, OH 44016

National Speakers Association (NSA)
1500 Priest Drive
Tempe, AZ 85281

Glossary of Speaking Terms

Please, enjoy. I had a great deal of fun digging into the history of these words. But I am truly embarrassed that it was so easy! Since my school days, I have never thought to spend time with such a simple tool as a dictionary! What a treasure—so easy and so valuable. I highly recommend it to you.

This glossary serves two purposes. The first is to give you an idea of the definitions of some slang terms in the speaking and meeting industry. (Some of these are not yet in any dictionary.) Many English words have a wealth of secondary meanings. I have included the meaning of the word or phrase as it applies to those who take the platform.

The second purpose is to give you a history of some of the words we use so freely from the platform: lectern, podium, rostrum, enthusiasm. Often I added the history of the word because its derivation gave the word new meaning and life for me. The definition or history of a word can be used effectively to open a presentation or to make a point.

I am not a linguist or an expert in the field of word histories. However, I checked *most* of the words and phrases in this glossary against the following three sources (all of them against a minimum of two out of three):

1. *Random House Unabridged Dictionary*, 2nd ed., CD-ROM version, © 1993 Random House

2. *Funk & Wagnalls Dictionary*, Microlibrary 1.1, © 1990–1992 Inductell

3. *Webster's Third New International Dictionary*, unabridged, © 1976 G. & C. Merriam, Co.

Enjoy!

Accolade: Any award, honor, or praise. From the Latin *ac-* at + *collum* neck. In the sixteenth century it became a ceremony which included an embrace to confer knighthood, sometimes done symbolically by tapping the sword on each shoulder. When a speaker receives acco-lades from audiences, it shows they are "embracing" his or her work.

Acronym: A word formed from the first letter or syllables of other words, as in IBM (from International Business Machines). From the Latin *acr-* topmost, extreme + *onym* to combine. Compare **acrostic.**

Acrostic: A series of words, lines, verses, or other compositions in which the first, last, or other particular letters when taken in order spell out a word or phrase. In the example below, FEAR is the acronym. "False Evidence Appearing Real" is the acrostic. From the Latin *acr-* top-most, extreme + the Greek *stichis* line (akin to "go to" and "stair").

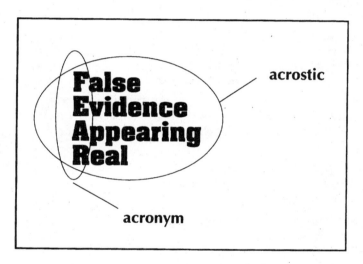

Address: (1) To speak to a group. (2) The speech or written state-ment itself. From the Latin *dresser* arrange, set in order. The archaic meaning was to give direction to or aim. When you address a letter, you direct it to a certain party or place. When you address an audi-ence, you direct your words toward the listeners, with the intent of their taking direction from the message.

Ad hominem: (1) Directing an argument to people's personal feel-ings, emotions, or prejudices rather than their intellect or reason. (2) Attacking an opponent's character rather than answering his argu-ment. The literal meaning is "to the man."

Adjunct: Something joined or added to another thing, but not essentially a part of it. For speakers, this refers to a thought added on. The word originated in 1580–90, from the Latin *adjunctus* joined to, yoked.

Ad-lib: To improvise words or gestures that were not in a speech or script. From the Latin *ad-* at + *libitum* pleasure—as opposed to *obligatus* bound, obliged. In music an *obbligato* (Italian) is something you are "obliged" to perform. When you ad-lib, you are not bound or obliged; you deliver at your pleasure—hopefully giving a good measure of pleasure in return.

Agenda: A list of things to be done or acted upon, especially a program of business at a meeting. Plural of the Latin gerund *agendum*. Today "agenda" is regarded as a singular noun; its plural is usually "agendas." The singular "agendum," meaning an item on an agenda, is uncommon.

Amateur: One who speaks or practices his or her craft for the love of the craft rather than for pay. In Europe a gentleman often engages in sports as an amateur: Prince Phillip is an *amateur* equestrian. In the USA, where skills are thought of in more monetary terms, an amateur is often perceived to be—incorrectly—a person with less skill.

Ambiance: The special atmosphere, mood, character, quality, or tone created by a particular environment, especially one of a social or cultural nature. From the French equivalent to *ambi-* surrounding.

Amplify: To make larger, greater, or stronger; to enlarge or extend. This can apply, for instance, to a speaker's comments, such as when more information is given, or to the method of increasing volume by use of a sound system.

Amuse: To occupy the audience in an agreeable, pleasing, or entertaining way. To cause people to laugh or smile by giving them pleasure. If you amuse your audience, you are usually playful or humorous and please their fancy. Now, the history of this word has me baffled. It comes from the Old French *muser* to stare. Hmm. Does this mean that in order to divert people, you need to concentrate so intently on them and their needs that you have to stare?

Maybe the French got it from **Muse,** as in the nine daughters of Zeus and Mnemosyne, who presided over various arts. I have often heard it said that when you are inspired to create, the "muse" has grabbed you. So it made good sense to me that "a-muse" meant one of those Muses had grabbed you. This was what I was hoping to prove, but alas, it remains my own little unsubstantiated theory.

Analogy: A comparison of the similarities between two things that are otherwise unlike in kind, form, or appearance. Examples include "the brain is like a computer," or "the heart resembles a pump." These are analogies and refer to similarities. From the Latin *ana-* according to + *logos* proportion.

Anecdote: A short narrative, story, yarn, or reminiscence of an interesting, amusing, or curious incident, often biographical and generally involving human interest. From the Greek *an-* not + *ek-* out + *dotos* given. Originally anecdotes were items not to be published or given out. We all know the best stories are those we are not supposed to tell!

Announcer: A person who makes announcements. The term came into being in radio in 1920–25, and today it is used often in public speaking. See also **Introducer, MC, Toastmaster.**

Aphorism: A tersely phrased comment or opinion stating a general truth, an astute observation, or a principle. Also a proverb, an adage, or a maxim. For instance, "Power tends to corrupt, and absolute power corrupts absolutely" (Lord Acton). From the Greek *apo* from + *horizein* to divide. So you should obviously use an aphorism when you want to make a point which divides the fluff from the facts and important stuff.

Apron: The part of a theater stage in front of the curtain.

Argument: (1) A quarrel or disagreement. (2) Discourse intended to persuade or to convince. (3) A short summary of a piece of subject matter. A speaker's "argument," like a lawyer's, gives the reason or reasons offered for or against something.

Articulate: (1) Presented clearly and with good logic. (2) To enunciate words well and distinctly. From the Latin *articulare* to divide into joints, to utter distinctly. Originally, "articulate" referred to something that had a clear definition, as in clear segments or joints. In speech, it came to mean clear enunciation, with each part of a word clearly segmented.

Attendee: A person who is present at a meeting or event.

Attention: The act or faculty of attending, usually by directing the mind to an object or concept. From the Latin *attendere* (*tendere* = stretch) to apply the mind to. When you capture people's attention as a speaker, you get them to stretch their minds and thoughts toward you.

Audience: Those who hear your message, whether it is an assembly of listeners or those who are reached by a book, audiotape, television show, or radio program. From the Latin *audire* to hear.

Audience participation: Involvement beyond that of listening to a lecture or speech. Examples include discussions, games, quizzes, and competitions. Some would argue that when audience members are actively listening, they are participating as well.

Auditorium: A room occupied by the audience to hear the speaker. From the Latin *audire* to hear + *orius* a place for.

Autograph: A signature written in one's own hand. From the Greek *aut-* self + *graphos* written.

Autograph table: The table, usually at the back of the meeting room, on which speakers sell their products.

A/V: Abbreviation for "audiovisual." Refers to all the audio and visual requirements of an event: overhead projectors, tape recorders, video players, microphones, and so on. This term came into usage in 1935–40.

A/V booth: Area of the **venue** where the A/V technology is controlled. See also **Sound booth, Tech booth.**

Back-of-room (BOR) sales: The selling of a speaker's books and other products at the back of the room, usually immediately after the speech.

Bandy words: To exchange words back and forth—a give-and-take—often in a glib or argumentative manner. Bandy was a game played with a ball and racket.

Bio: Shortened form of **biography.** See also **Biographical sheet.**

Biographical sheet: Usually referred to as the bio, curriculum vita, CV, or vita. A list of the speaker's credits and a brief history of his or her career. For speakers and presenters, this is not a job résumé. It typically ranges from one paragraph to one double-spaced page.

Biography: A written history of a person's life. A speaker's biography is usually tailored to his or her experience in the topic area in which the speaker is presenting. From the Greek *bios* life + *grapho* write.

Black and white: See **Glossy.**

Black humor: According to the *Random House Dictionary,* "a form of humor that regards human suffering as absurd rather than pitiable, or that considers human existence as ironic and pointless but somehow comic."

Blocking: (1) The way you position yourself on stage, including your props, lighting, and equipment. (2) The path of action you take to move from one spot on stage to another. If done well, blocking gives the greatest clarity of movement to the communication.

Blue humor: Risqué and naughty humor. Near as I can tell, back in the 1300s the meaning of "blue" was to be sick. But in the USA in the early 1800s, "blue" also became a slang adjective for being drunk, possibly because those who overindulge get a bit "blue around the edges." Hence "blue laws" forbid you to drink during certain days and times. Later in that century "blue" came also to mean risqué and naughty. So *my* theory is: folks tend to get crude when they get drunk, their humor representative of their state of inebriation; *maybe* this is where we get the term "off-color." Perhaps too much black humor and too much blue humor will bruise the audience—leave people black and blue. (OK, OK, it's weak.)

Bomb: In the USA, starting in the 1960s, a slang word for an absolute failure, a fiasco. The British use it to mean an overwhelming success. (Go figure!)

Bombastic: All the definitions of this word in my dictionaries were very negative, and referred to the inappropriate use of elaborate or theatrical language: "a verbose grandiosity or pretentious inflation of language and style disproportionate to thought." (This seems rather *bombastic* if ya ask me!) Bombast or bombase was the cotton used to stuff or pad garments. It then came to mean a pretentious inflated style (kinda "stuffy") of speech or writing—in other words, a "stuffed shirt."

Book: To reserve a date for a speaking engagement. The term originally meant to reserve something by entering it in a book of record.

Booking: The condition of being engaged to speak.

Bore: To weary yourself or others by dullness, as by being long-winded. One source says it comes from the Old English *bor auger*—which, more or less, meant a spear, a tool to go through something. Perhaps we use it as we do today because boring your listeners is like wounding them.

Breakout (session):   The splitting up of the main group into smaller groups. A session at a convention or meeting where attendees are divided into several concurrent sessions to hear material on differing special-interest topics.

Brochure: For a presenter, a listing of speech titles, past speaking clients of importance, and quotes from clients and/or other famous people about the speaker. From the French *brocher* to stitch—a brochure often being a few pages stitched together.

Bromide: (1) No longer a common term in the USA, but still used loosely to mean a photo-quality original, mainly one to be used for reproduction. (With the development of laser printers, terms like "bromide," "velox" and "slicks"—all referring to a photo-quality original—will soon be only historical notations.) See **Camera-ready.** (2) A person or expression which is flat, dull, trite, and/or boring.

A bromide is a chemical, a compound of bromine, which is used in film for black-and-white photography. Today old photographs are still often referred to as "bromides." Bromide as a slang term for a bore comes from the fact that bromides were also used as sedatives.

Buyer: The person or group who signs the **contract** and pays for the speaker.

Byline: The line at the head of a news story or article in a newspaper, magazine, or other publication giving the name of the writer. The term originated in U.S. journalism in the 1920s: "Well! Where is the line saying who the darn thing is by?" "The byline is right here, chief!"

Camera-ready: A piece of material that is of a quality ready to be photographed for reproduction by a printing press, copy machine, or camera. Presenters often develop handouts or workbooks to supplement their talks, and are asked to supply an "original" (the master image from which identical copies are produced) for event coordinators. Most coordinators request this master original to be "camera-ready" so they will not need to have the piece "typeset."

Over the years many processes and systems were used for the preproduction composition of a camera-ready master—from an inscription engraved in stone to an illustration cut into a wood block or a text stored as digital information in a computer. With the development of the laser printer, the middle step of creating a clean, clear copy for reproduction was taken care of automatically by the computer. Yet the old terms still hang on. When you are asked to submit an original, don't be surprised if you hear old-fashioned process words like "bromide," "velox," "PMT," and "slick." Today these words are *usually* a request for a camera-ready master.

Canned: For speakers, a standard speech or presentation. The term originally referred to music that was recorded and stored in a cylinder, rather than live. The myth is that if a speech is "canned," the audience is left feeling that it has been listening to the same old thing, like a recording. This happens only when the speaker loses enthusiasm for a speech—and shows his or her lack of interest to the audience.

Caricature: A representation ludicrously exaggerating and/or distorting the peculiarities or defects of persons or things, to produce an absurd effect. From the Italian *caricare* to load, exaggerate, distort. See also **Characterization.**

Characterization: An array of physical mannerisms, tones of voice, rhythms, and other features that create a convincing and/or humorous portrayal of a fictitious character or persona. See also **Caricature.**

Charlatan: A person who pretends to be more knowledgeable or skilled at something than he or she is; an impostor; quack. From the

Old French *ciarla* chat, idle talk. Interesting that a charlatan is especially associated with those who offer "idle chat." The French word stems from the Old Italian *cerretano,* meaning an inhabitant of Cerreto, a village near Spoleto. Its archaic meaning was "a baker of dubious remedies." Which just makes you wonder about the guys from Cerreto.

Chautauqua circuit: According to the *Random House Dictionary:* "1. An annual educational meeting, originating in the village of Chautauqua (New York) in 1874, providing public lectures, concerts, and dramatic performances during the summer months, usually in an outdoor setting. 2. Any similar assembly, especially one consisting of a number of meetings in a circuit of communities. 3. Of or pertaining to a system of education flourishing in the late nineteenth and early twentieth centuries, originating at Lake Chautauqua, New York." The Chautauqua circuit followed the railroad lines and boasted such celebrities as Charles Dickens, Ralph Waldo Emerson, Mark Twain, and P. T. Barnum. See also **Circuit.**

Cheap laugh: (1) A laugh that anyone can get, because it stems from an obvious or easy joke, like a sight gag. (2) An unkind, tasteless, or unsportsmanlike laugh derived from preying on sexual or other stereotypes. An example is saying to a woman, "Now clear your mind!...Oh? So quickly!" In other words, a "cheap shot."

Chestnuts: Stories, jokes, or songs that have been overused and are stale. From the 1880s. Nobody could tell me exactly why a nut became a synonym for an old, tired joke. One source said that a plausible explanation "is that it comes from an old melodrama, *The Broken Sword,* by William Dillion. In the play Captain Zavier is retelling, for the umpteenth time, a story having to do with a cork tree. His listener Pablo breaks in suddenly, correcting cork tree to chestnut tree, saying, `I should know as well as you, having heard you tell the tale these twenty-seven times.' Popularization of the term is attributed to the comedian William Warren, who had played the role of Pablo many times."* My guess is that chestnuts were so plentiful then that a common story got called a chestnut.

Circuit: (1) A periodic journey from place to place, usually including one or more presentations at each location. (2) A group of associated theaters presenting plays, films, or other performances. A single sponsor may set up a series of engagements.

The term is used by judges to hold court, by ministers to preach, and by salespeople to cover a route. ("She is on the circuit this month.")

Picturesque Expressions: A Thematic Dictionary, 2nd ed., edited by Laurence Urdang, Gale Research Co., 1985.

For presenters, it is most often a reference to the old **Chautauqua circuit** days, when speakers were sent around the country on a speaking circuit or speaking tour.

Classroom-style seating: Seating for the audience that is set up with tables in front of the seats. Compare **theater-style seating.**

Cliché: A trite, stereotyped sentence or phrase. Originally a printing press used wooden blocks (later metal, to cope with the stress of bigger runs) called clichés or stereotypes. Since a cliché was used over and over, some clever person adopted the word to mean an expression that is used over and over.

Client: Whoever is paying for the service. A company or association is the client when it hires the speaker. Speakers may be the clients of an agent who is paid, or receives a commission on earnings, to "manage" them.

Clique: Any small, exclusive, clannish group of people. In an audience, attendees tend to form in, or associate in, cliques. In training and seminar settings, learning levels are considered to increase if attendees are broken out of the cliques they arrived in. From the 1700s, possibly a likening of the Middle French *clique* latch.

Close to the edge: See Edge.

Community service speakers bureau: A **speakers bureau** that sends presenters into a community or industry, usually at little or no cost, to speak on topics that promote the sponsoring company or on public awareness issues.

Compassion: Deep sympathy for the needs of another with the desire to help or spare. From the Latin *com-* together + *pati* to feel. As a speaker, you attempt to bring your own feelings for others "together" with their feelings and needs.

Conclude: To bring to an end; finish; terminate. From the Latin *com-* thoroughly + *claudere* to close, shut off.

Concluder: In a speech the final remarks said to finish the presentation. A concluder is the speaker's way of closing a presentation. It also refers to the remarks the MC or announcer makes to conclude that particular session.

Concurrent (session): A simultaneous **breakout** session.

Connection: The bonding, association, or relationship of the presenter with the audience's emotions.

Consult: To seek advice, guidance, or information from someone; to give such advice. From the Latin *consulere* to seek advice.

Consultant: A person who gives professional or technical advice. Speakers often consult with clients to prepare customized material for programs or workbooks for an added fee. An example is an expert who sits in on telephone complaint calls in order to prepare material for workshops to train employees in handling problem customers. The term came into use in the late 1600s.

Content: That which a thing contains. In presenter's terms, the subject matter—as in "We want a speaker with content!" Audiences want speakers who have usable data and ideas—as opposed to "fluff"—that they can apply to their own situations.

Contract: A formal legal instrument used to delineate an agreement between speaker and client, and/or bureau. It details the exact terms of payment and performance.

Convey: To communicate; transmit; make known. From the Latin *com-* together + *via* road, way. When we teach, we use the roadway of words to bring together the mind of the speaker and that of the listener.

Cordless: Slang for cordless microphone; wireless mic. A cordless may be a handheld device or a lavaliere. It works by radio waves sent through the **PA** system.

Curriculum vita (vitae):   Also called just plain vita, vitae, or CV. A brief biographical résumé of the presenter's career and training. This term is most commonly used by the academic community. See also **Biographical sketch.**

CV: See **Biographical sketch, Curriculum vita.**

Dais: A raised platform, usually at the front of a room, where the speaker presents from. Also called platform, podium, riser, or stage. From the Latin *discus* table.

Deadpan: A completely expressionless face; a comedic technique that uses a completely expressionless face. U.S. slang from the 1920s: "*Pan* has been used since at least the early 19th century to mean 'the face,' possibly because the face is 'broad, shallow and often open,' as *Webster's* suggests, but just as likely because pan meant 'the skull or head' as far back as the early 14th century and was used by Chaucer."*

Demo: An audio or visual demonstration tape used to promote speakers' services or speeches to buyers.

Desultory: Jumping from one thing to another; unmethodical, random. Roman acrobats who jumped from one fast-moving horse to

---

*Encyclopedia of Word and Phrase Origins, by Robert Hendrickson, Facts on File, 1987.

another were called *desultores*—leapers. If you deliver a speech in a desultory fashion, you leap from one thought to another.

Diad, dyad: A group of two; couple; pair.

Digress: To step away from the main subject; to ramble or wander. From the Latin *di-* away, apart + *gradi* to go, step.

Discourse: (1) To send forth one's ideas concerning a subject; to communicate thought by words. (2) Talk; conversation. From the Latin *dis-* apart + *cursus* running.

Discuss: To have as the subject of conversation or writing; especially, to explore solutions. From the Latin *discutere* to discuss: *dis-* apart + *guatere* to shake. Interesting. As a speaker, when you allow people to discuss, are *they* shaken apart? Or is it the topic? I rather think both.

Downstage: At or toward the front of the stage. In olden days, theaters were often set up across a small ravine. The audience was on one hillside, the stage on the other. Downstage was the point farthest down the hill. Upstage was the point farthest up the stage, up the hill. This made it easier for the audience to see and hear. Even today a speaker will say, "Come on down here with me!"—meaning come downstage to where I am. Compare **upstage.**

Dynamic: Powerful, active. A dynamic presentation is filled with energy and/or effective action and forcefulness. From the Greek *dynamis* power.

Easel: A folding frame or tripod used to support flipcharts or other visuals. In Dutch, a donkey is called an *ezel*. A donkey is a wonderfully patient assistant that bears its burden without complaint for hours— hence, the artist's *ezel* would hold his or her burden. Today a speaker has this same faithful (inanimate) friend in meetings. See also **Flipchart.**

Edge: The limit or extreme of what is expected and/or acceptable. The term originated in the early 1900s. Hence the expressions "over the edge," "close to the edge," "on the edge." A humorist may have the audience rolling on the floor with mildly racy humor (close to the edge), but may then go too far (over the edge). That is when the audience starts to think, "That's not funny, it's just plain gross." The challenge to you as a presenter is to discover and ride this edge for yourself and your audience.

Elocution: The art, study, and practice of public speaking or reading aloud in public, including vocal delivery and gestures; also one's manner of speaking.

Elocutionist: Someone adept at public speaking and at voice production. An older term, no longer widely used. From the Latin *e-* out + *loqui* to speak.

Eloquence: The quality of speaking in a moving, forceful, or persuasive way. An eloquent speaker uses fluent, polished, and expressive language. From the Latin *e-* out+*loqui* to speak.

Emcee: An informal term for master of ceremonies, often abbreviated MC. See **Announcer, Introducer, Master of ceremonies, MC, Toastmaster.**

Emotion: According to *Funk & Wagnalls:* "A strong surge of feeling marked by an impulse to outward expression and often accompanied by complex bodily reactions; any strong feeling, as love, hate, or joy." From the Latin *e-* out + *movere* to move. The expression "to move an audience"—when we have "touched their emotions"—undoubtedly comes from this Latin root.

Energetic: To have or exhibit energy; powerful or vigorous in action. From the Greek *en-* in + *ergon* work. Interesting. Speakers know that being energetic on the platform can be achieved only by hard work.

Enjoy: To experience with joy; to take pleasure in. From the 1350s Middle English *enjoyen* to make joyful; in turn, from the Old French *enjoier* to give joy to. Rather a lovely moral message to realize that both roots involve the giving of joy. How wise of our ancestors to know that to get it, you must give it first.

Enthusiasm: A keen, animated interest; an absorbing or controlling possession of the mind by any subject, interest, or pursuit. From the Greek *entheos, enthous* inspired, possessed. Originally the term was applied to people who seemed so inspired as to be possessed by god— *theos.* The expression has almost lost its religious meaning—a passionate elevation of the soul. As speakers, we have all felt the wonderful filling up with spirit that happens when we are speaking well, and the joy that follows as that spirit pours from us into our listeners and they become filled with enthusiasm—as if filled with God's spirit.

Enunciate: To pronounce words distinctly; to use articulate sounds. From the Latin *e-* out + *nuntiare* to announce.

Eulogize: To extol or laud; to speak or write in high praise. Often associated with the address (eulogy) given at a funeral. From the Greek *eu-* well + *legein* to speak.

Expatiate: To elaborate at length with copious descriptions or discussion. From the Latin *ex-* out + *spatiari* to wander about. The archaic meaning was to move around intellectually and imaginatively.

Experiential exercise: An **Audience participation** exercise in which the lessons learned are derived from direct experience. If you touch a hot stove when you are young, you have learned a lesson by the experiential method.

Expostulate: To reason earnestly with a person against something he or she is inclined to do. The term came into use in the 1520s, from the Latin *expostulātus* demanded urgently, required.

Extemporaneous: (1) Impromptu, spontaneous. (2) Prepared with regard to content but not read or memorized word for word. From the Latin *ex-* out + *tempus, temporis* time.

Flesh out: The process of adding more material to a written speech for length and substance.

Flipchart: A chart with bound or loose pieces of paper, usually set on an **Easel.** Used by speakers to clarify their points.

Flippant: Given without forethought; often characterized by levity or lack of seriousness, as in a flippant remark.

Flop: (1) To be completely unsuccessful. (2) A failure. A speaker's entire talk may be a flop, or just a portion—one joke or anecdote—could "flop." From the late 1890s.

Flop sweat: (1) Fear and trauma about performing. (2) Actual perspiration when fearful of performing.

Fluent: Capable of speaking or writing with effortless ease. From the Latin *fluens, fluere-* to flow. Fluent speech flows easily, like a stream of water.

Flush out: The process of cleansing a written speech of the least important pieces.

Flyer: A one-sheet printed advertisement, usually letter or legal size. Often produced to promote the presenter's program, products, or services.

Focus: The concept or idea on which the mind is centered. From the 1630s, an extension of the Latin *focus* hearth. The Roman fireplace was the center of family life. The root of this same word came to mean the central point of interest; it has a similar meaning in optics, physics, and geometry. More than one writer has noted the close tie between fire and focus: "Walt Whitman said of himself, 'I was simmering, really simmering; Emerson brought me to a boil.' What an apt description of a personality, gifted but lacking in power until the fire of enthusiasm brought it to the boiling point."

Foil: (1) A person or thing that makes another seem better by contrast; this person could be, but is not necessarily, a **Plant.** When the foil stops being a "good" contrast for the presenter, he or she might be categorized as a **Heckler.** (2) An overhead slide transparency—a term commonly used in aerospace and high-tech companies, and in Europe. It is derived from a 1950s method of producing overheads on foillike material. (3) Any metal in the form of very thin sheets. From the Latin *folium* leaf. Later, in Old French, it came to mean a leaflike decorative design, often in thin metals.

Forte: A person's strong point, something at which he or she excels: "Tom is a humorist, but magic is his forte." A two-syllable pronunciation (fÔr'tā) is often heard, perhaps confusing this word with the musical term *forte,* pronounced in English as (fÔr'tā) and in Italian as (fÔr'te), which means loudly and forcefully. The historical pronunciation is one-syllable: (fÔrt) or (fõrt). Both pronunciations are acceptable. The word is derived from the French word *fort* strong.

Fulminate: To explode suddenly and violently, like a chemical. Speakers fulminate when they make loud or violent denunciations or scathing verbal attacks or when they give a scathing rebuke or condemnation. From the Latin *fulmen, fulminis* lightning.

Gab: To talk, chatter, yak, rap, schmooze, or chat idly. *Funk & Wagnalls* traces the word to the Old Norse *gabba* to mock. But *Random House* feels it comes from the Scottish Gaelic *gob* mouth (1540–50). Even the Old French *gobe* means "mouthful." When you have the "gift of gab," you are gifted with the use of your mouth.

Gag: As used in the theater, a joke or any built-in piece of wordplay or horseplay. Historians seem to be puzzled by its origin. Some speculate that jokesters would finally annoy the audience so badly that people would want to "gag" them!

Garble: To mix up, jumble, or confuse facts, ideas, or words, usually unintentionally or ignorantly. From the Arabic *gharbala* to sift or purify. "But by the seventeenth century it had come to mean 'sifting' information maliciously—putting together selected bits to distort the meaning. Nowadays, the malice has dropped out, and the information is merely muddled."*

Loose Cannons and Red Herrings, by Robert Claiborne, Ballantine Books, 1980.

General assembly (session):   A convocation of all attendees at a meeting or convention, usually implying a session other than a meal function. A general assembly often, but certainly not always, follows a meal session, in the same room because everyone is already sitting in that location.

Genre: A class or category of artistic endeavor having a particular form, content, or technique: "the genre of Western cowboy comedy," "the genre of fire-and-brimstone oratory." The term came into use in the mid-1750s and can be traced to the Latin *genus* race, kind—the same root that "gender" is derived from.

Gesticulate: To use emphatic or expressive gestures, especially in an animated or excited manner. From the Latin *gesticulus,* diminutive of *gestus* mode of action, which is where we get the word "gesture."

Gig: Slang term for engagement or **booking.**

Glib: Marked by ease and fluency, with little forethought or preparation. A glib talker is more superficial than sincere. From the Middle Low German *glibberich* slippery.

Glossary: A list of terms in a special subject area, explaining the technical, obscure, difficult, or unusual expressions used; a list of the same at the back of a book, explaining or defining special terms. From the Greek *glôss*- tongue. It is easy to see how a glossary came to mean a collection of words with which the tongue might have trouble.

Glossy: Slang for a glossy photograph; usually a black-and-white promotional photograph of the presenter. Also called a black and white, or B&W.

Greenroom: A "backstage" room in a theater, broadcasting studio, or the like, where speakers can relax when they are not on stage or on camera. *Random House* dates its usage from the late 1600s. The real reason it is called a greenroom is lost to antiquity. One drama friend of mine recalls a story associated with the Globe Theatre in England. The actors performing in Shakespeare's open-air theater had to face the summer sun all afternoon. So legend has it that the actors' resting space backstage was painted green as a restorative to the eyes. Another would-be historian says the terrible glare from the "limelights" was so harsh that actors needed a dark place to rest after a show—hence a room painted dark green.

   More official sources tend to downplay the significance of the color green: "[It] probably takes its name from such a room in London's Drury Lane Theatre, which just happened to be painted green sometime in the late 17th century. Most authorities reject the old story that the room was painted green to soothe the actors' eyes."* Hmm. Note that this is 100 years later than *Random House* cites; but it first appears in print in 1678, so maybe *Random House* is right. Another: "It was also known as the Scene Room, a term later applied to a room where scenery was stored, and it has been suggested that 'green' is a corruption of 'scene.'"** So only the ghosts of actors past know the truth about greenroom.

Gross fee: The total fee that the buyer is charged for a booking, including agents' fees, but excluding expenses.

Hack writer: One who hires out writing services, especially for routine work. The result is often writing that is stale or trite because of constant use. In England, a hack (short for hackney) is a horse let out for common use, often old or worn-out as a result. In the USA, perhaps by extension, a hack refers to a taxicab or driver.

Ham: A presenter or an actor who overacts or exaggerates. The history of this term is varied. It has been said to derive from "lower order" actors who removed their makeup with inexpensive ham. However, according to *Random House:* "1880–85; short for hamfatter, after 'The Hamfat Man,' a black minstrel song." Finally, my nephew Michael thinks it is because presenters tend to "hog" the limelight, so they are hams. Sometimes simple is best.

Handheld: Slang for a handheld microphone. A handheld comes in a cord or cordless version.

Handout: Any informative or educational material "handed out" to the audience at the speaker's presentation.

Hands-free mic: A microphone that attaches to the speaker's clothing. See **Lavaliere.**

Harangue: A lengthy, loud, and vehement speech; a tirade. From the Old High German *hari* army, host + *hringa* ring.

Head table: The table at the front of the room, reserved for key people at a meeting.

Heart story: A story that touches the heart, spirit, or soul of the listener. Heart stories are usually thought of as vignettes that bring a tear to the eye.

---

*Encyclopedia of Word and Phrase Origins, by Robert Hendrickson, Facts on File, 1987.
**The Oxford Companion to the Theater, 4th ed., by Phyllis Hartnall, Oxford University Press, 1983.

Heckle: To annoy with taunts, questions, or verbal abuse. "The original verb meant to straighten and disentangle the fibers of flax or hemp, by drawing them through a heavy, sharp-toothed iron comb; later it took on the additional meaning of 'scratch.'"* Speakers who face severe heckling may well feel like they are being scratched with an iron comb.

Heightening: Intensifying awareness, sensitivity, or understanding of a subject. Presenters are heightened when, through their presentation, they create a greater enthusiasm and/or a greater "connection" with the audience. The audience is heightened if the connection is made and understanding and enlightenment dawn in people's minds.

Hem and haw: To equivocate, hesitate, or avoid committing yourself, particularly when you are at a loss for words. Typically you say things that really are not saying much of anything: "Well, ah, you see, um, I was just...well, I had thought that...uh." From the sixteenth century. A "hem" (or "hmm") is the vocalized sound of clearing the throat; a "haw" is an imitative sound of hesitation.

Hoarse: Describes a voice that has a husky, gruff, or croaking quality, which can be harsh and grating in sound.

Honorarium: A payment for a service (such as speaking or consulting) in situations where custom forbids a price to be set.

House: Slang expression for the building in which you are speaking, or for the number of attendees in the building. "How's the house?" means how many audience members are sitting in the **venue.** "The house is dim" means the room is lighted poorly.

House lights: The lights that illuminate the audience rather than the stage.

Humor: The quality of anything that is funny or appeals to the comic sense. From the Latin *umere* to be moist. In ancient physiology, the four principal bodily fluids were called the cardinal humors: blood, phlegm, choler (yellow bile), and melancholy (black bile). They were believed to influence health and temperament according to their proportions in the body.

Idiom: (1) An expression peculiar to a language and not readily understandable from the meaning of its parts; an expression whose meaning is not predictable from the usual or literal meanings of its constituent elements—for example, "to put up with," "kick the bucket," "hang one's head." (2) A language, dialect, or style of speaking

---

Loose Cannons and Red Herrings, by Robert Claiborne, Ballantine Books, 1980.

peculiar to a people or region. (3) The special terminology of an industry, class, or occupational group. From the Greek *idios* one's own.

Impresario: A producer or sponsor of public entertainment programs—operas, concerts, sports events, and the like. Speaking programs organized by impresarios are usually held in large sports arenas or auditoriums.

Improve: To become or to make better; to raise to a higher or more desirable quality, value, or condition. From the Old French *en-* into + *prou* profit.

Improvise: To compose and perform or deliver a speech (or music, verse, drama) without previous thought or preparation. From the Latin *in-* not + *provire* to foresee.

Influence: The power the presenter has to have an effect on the actions or thoughts of others. From the Latin *in-* in + *fluere* to flow.

In-house: When a presenter's audience is composed only of employees of the client company.

Inspire: To have an invigorating influence on someone; to move someone to a particular feeling, idea, or action. To breathe life into an idea in other people's minds. From the Latin *in-* into + *spirare* to breathe.

Instruct: To impart knowledge or skill. To build a new knowledge base in the minds of others. From the Latin *in-* in + *struere* to build.

Interact: To act on each other. In public speaking, members of the audience may communicate with one another and/or with the presenter in a verbal or nonverbal manner.

Interpretation: The presenter's or the audience's explanation and/or understanding of the ideas under discussion.

Intro: Slang term for **introduction.**

Introducer: The person who introduces the speaker and usually gives the audience a brief look at the speaker's history. From the Latin *intro-* within + *ducere* to lead. See also **Announcer, Emcee, Master of ceremonies, MC, Toastmaster.**

Introduction: A carefully written opener about the speaker, used by the **Introducer** at the beginning of a speech. It usually includes a halo—listing the speaker's credits, achievements, and honors—and a statement of "why this speaker, for this crowd, on this date, for this audience."

IPA: The International Platform Association, a USA-based organization for public speakers.

Irony: A sarcastic or humorous way of speaking in which you say the opposite of what you mean: "Isn't that sweet?" (read, "That's hideous"). See also **Sarcasm.**

Juice: Electricity or electric power.

Keynote: The main speech at a meeting; originally, the fundamental point of a speech. The keynote is one of the featured spots of an event, usually connected with a prime time—such as the opening, the sit-down meal, or the closing—and is given to the entire convention in the main room. Often delivered by the celebrity speaker, the keynote speech sets the tone of the convention and carries out the theme.

Laugh: (1) An expression of mirth, merriment, scorn, or derision. (2) Something that causes laughter, such as a joke, gag, or anecdote: "I get the laugh by doing a pratfall as I enter."

Lavaliere: A "hands free" microphone worn around the neck or attached to an article of clothing, as opposed to a stationary or hand-held mic. Can be on a cord or cordless. Derived from the French *lavallière*, a round or oval ornament worn on a chain around the neck. Named after Louise de La Vallière, 1644–1710, mistress of Louis XIV.

Lectern: A small desk or stand with sloping top from which the speaker delivers a **lecture.** It may include a stationary or handheld mic, a shelf underneath, and a light. Sometimes called (many will argue incorrectly) the **podium.**

Lecture: A discourse given before an audience. The archaic meaning is "the act of reading aloud." From the Latin *agere* to read.

Lighting: The providing of light or the state of being lighted; the way a stage or presentation area is illuminated.

Limelight: According to *Funk & Wagnalls:* "1. Public attention or notice. 2. A bright light used to illuminate a performer, stage area, etc., originally produced by heating lime to incandescence."

Lingo: The specialized vocabulary and **idiom** of a profession or class, as in medical lingo. From the 1600s, an apparent alteration of the Latin *lingua* tongue.

Malapropism: The absurd misuse of words. From Mrs. Malaprop, a character in R. B. Sheridan's play *The Rivals* (1775), who made endless verbal blunders. Today, comedian Norm Crosby is a master of the malapropism.

Master: (1) A person eminently skilled in something, as an occupation, art, or science; in presentations, a master of the spoken word. (2) Of or pertaining to a master from which copies are made: in photography, a master film (also called a "copy negative"); in recording, an audio or video tape or disk from which duplicates may be made; in printing, the **camera-ready** piece used to make other copies for handouts, workbooks, or overheads.

Master of ceremonies: The person who acts as a moderator and connects the separate sessions of an event together. See also **Announcer, Emcee, Introducer, MC, Toastmaster.**

Materials: Handouts, products, giveaways, workbooks, and all other items used in a presentation.

MC: Pronounced MC, as it is written; an abbreviation of master of ceremonies. Sometimes spelled emcee and used as noun or verb: "Mary is the MC tonight" or "John is going to MC the event." See also **Announcer, Emcee, Introducer, Master of ceremonies, Toastmaster.**

Media: (1) All the ways of communicating with the public—radio and television, newspapers, magazines, and so on. (2) An area or form of artistic expression, or the materials used by the artist or presenter. A speaker's media are the "tools" that he or she uses, such as overheads and videos. Dianna Booher, business communications expert, extends this definition to include "pantomime, magic, drama, or any other means of conveying a message or feeling other than words." The term "medium" (the singular form of "media") was first used in reference to newspapers two centuries ago and meant "an intervening agency, means, or instrument."

Meeting planner: The person in charge of planning the meeting—including logistics, meals, hotel arrangements, room sets, travel, and often the hiring of speakers. Often called the organizer, the coordinator, or just the planner.

Mellifluous: Flowing sweetly, like honey. From the Latin *mel*-honey + *fluere* to flow. A mellifluous voice can be a speaker's greatest asset.

Mesmerize: To hypnotize. A presenter can so captivate an audience that people seem to be hypnotized. From the 1820s, referring to the infamous Austrian physician and rather dubious pioneer of hypnosis, Franz (Friedrich) Anton Mesmer, 1733–1815. "Often accused of being a magician and charlatan, Mesmer treated neurotic patients using iron magnets and hypnosis, which he originated. Hypnosis, or 'mesmerism,' later became an accepted psychotherapeutic technique."*

---

*New Grolier Multimedia Encyclopedia, Release 6, Grolier, 1993.

Metaphor: A figure of speech in which one object is likened to another by speaking of it as if it were that other object. Typically a term or phrase is applied to something to which it is not literally applicable in order to suggest a resemblance, as in "A mighty fortress is our God" and "He was a lion in battle." From the Greek *meta-* beyond, over + *pherein* to carry. Compare **simile**.

Mic: Print slang for **microphone**. Pronounced "mike." Mic was considered an incorrect abbreviation of microphone for many years. But the newer dictionaries have given in to the influence of the notation on the back of all those tape players. You know, back there where you plug in the microphone—that hole that says "mic."

Microphone: An instrument which causes sound waves to be generated or modulated through an electric current, usually for the purpose of transmitting or recording speech or music. There are many types. The most common for presenters are **handheld**—with or without a cord; **stationary**—usually attached to a lectern or a mic stand; and **lavaliere,** or hands-free.

Mike: Slang for **microphone**.

Mixed Metaphor: The use in the same expression of two or more images that are incongruous or illogical when combined: "The president will put the ship of state on its feet." "She kept a tight rein on her boiling passions." See also **Metaphor**.

Module: A self-contained section of a presentation.

Multimedia: The combined use of several **media,** such as sound and full-motion video in computer applications. A speaker may use overheads, videos, and live music in a multimedia presentation.

Muse: (1) Any one of the sister goddesses of Greek mythology—originally given as Aoede (song), Melete (meditation), and Mneme (memory), but later and more commonly as the nine daughters of Zeus and Mnemosyne—who presided over the various arts: Calliope (epic poetry), Clio (history), Erato (lyric poetry), Euterpe (music), Melpomene (tragedy), Polyhymnia (religious music), Terpsichore (dance), Thalia (comedy), and Urania (astronomy). (2) More generally, any power regarded as inspiring; the genius or inspirational power characteristic of presenters, poets, thinkers, and the like. Since ancient times, these artsy sorts have invoked the appropriate Muse for aid when performing and creating.

Nonverbal: Relying on unspoken methods—gestures, games, sight, sound, feeling, touch, smell—to communicate.

NSA: National Speakers Association (of the United States). There is also a National Speakers Association of Australia.

Off-color: Material that is naughty, indelicate, indecent, or risqué. See also **Blue humor.**

Off the cuff: Without preparation. Apparently afterdinner speakers would make notes on the cuffs of their shirtsleeves at the last minute, as opposed to preparing a speech well in advance. The expression originated in America in the 1930s.* My mother remembers her grandfather speaking of this practice. He said they used to have celluloid cuffs—the print would wash right off after the talk.

On-site: Where an event is held. Also, meeting planners may hold an "on-site" to preview a hotel or **venue** as a prospective meeting location.

Orator: A person who delivers an elaborate discourse (oration), with great eloquence and formality. From the 1300s, derived from the Latin *oratio* speech.

Overhead projector: A projector of images from transparent pieces of film onto a screen.

Overhead slide transparency: See Slide.

Over the edge: See Edge.

Oxymoron: A figure of speech in which incongruous, seemingly self-contradictory terms are brought together, as in "cruel kindness," "make haste slowly," and "O heavy lightness, serious vanity!" From the Greek *oxys* sharp + *moros* foolish.

PA: Public address system—the loudspeaker equipment which amplifies sound to the audience.

Panel: A small group of presenters selected to hold a discussion on a particular subject. Audiences are usually encouraged to participate in a question-and-answer period.

Pantomime: (1) The art or technique of conveying emotions, actions, and feelings through gestures, without speech. (2) A play or acting style characterized by such a performance. From the Greek *panto(s)* of all + *mimos* imitator.

Passion: Any intense, extreme, or overpowering emotion or feeling. From the Latin *pati* to suffer.

Patter: (1) Specialized technical phrases and terminology exclusive to an industry. (2) The usually glib and rapid speech or talk used by a

---

*Have a Nice Day—No Problem, by Christine Ammer, Dutton, 1992. A concise dictionary of slang and unconventional English.

humorist magician while performing, (3) Standard material used by presenters to accompany their **shtick.** Any rapid-fire staccato speech can be called patter. Radio disk jockeys are well known for their patter between songs.

The term is derived from the Middle Ages, when Catholic priests prayed daily in Latin. The priests would say their *Paternoster* in a very fast, mechanical manner; the practice came to be known as "patter." Truly.

Philosophy: (1) The study of the principles of reality in general. (2) The love of wisdom, and the search for it. (3) The general laws that furnish the rational explanation of anything: the philosophy of banking. (4) Practical wisdom; fortitude. From the Greek *philosophos* lover of wisdom.

Photo-quality: See **Camera-ready.**

Pit: (1) The area of the theater where the musicians are located. (2) The main floor of the auditorium of a theater, especially the rear part. (3) The audience sitting in this section. (4) A position of great distress or trouble, as when the presenter feels he or she is doing a poor job: "I'm dyin' up here! I'm in the pit."

Pithy: Forceful, effective; brief and meaningful in expression; full of vigor, substance, or meaning; succinct, pointed, meaty, concise. A Middle English term from the 1300s. Pith is the important or essential, the core or heart of a matter. The archaic meaning was the spinal cord or bone marrow.

Plagiarism: An act of artistic or literary theft. The word goes back to the Latin *plagiarus* kidnapping—especially in relation to stealing and keeping the child, not holding it for ransom. So when you use someone else's words or thoughts as your own, you kidnap them.

Planner: See **Meeting planner.**

Plant: A person set up in the audience to help the speaker by asking a prearranged question or participating in a predesigned act. The plant's rehearsed (prepared) reactions and comments are meant to appear spontaneous to the rest of the audience. See also **Shill.**

Platform: (1) The raised area where speakers stand when they address an audience. Also called dais, podium, riser, or stage. (2) A public statement of principles, objectives, and policy, particularly of a political party. My theory is that since politicians traditionally stated their policy from the platform, the statement itself eventually became known as the platform.

Plug: An informal advertisement, usually a verbal mention from the platform or a casual reference in a publication, to help promote a product or service.

PMT: Photomechanical transfer. See **Camera-ready.**

Podium: Often a riser or risers; a small stage; also called dais, platform, or riser. This word comes from the same root as pedal and podiatrist (the Greek *podion*—diminutive of *pous, podos*—foot). So the *podium* is the place you step on, although common usage is wearing away at the precise meaning of this word. Some (not all) new dictionaries have given in to those who insist on calling the lectern a podium (or vice versa). Both the unabridged *Funk & Wagnalls* and *Random House* say a podium *can* be called a lectern, but they list it as the third and last definition. However, the abridged *Funk & Wagnalls* does not list a lectern as a correct choice for a podium. So you can call the lectern a podium if you like, but those of the old school will raise a condescending eyebrow.

Polish: To add those final touches of refinement to your presentation to make it complete and perfect. From the Latin *polire* to smooth.

Pontificate: (1) To act or speak pompously or dogmatically, with an attitude of "I don't care to be questioned or challenged. I am the expert!" (2) To perform the office of a pontiff. This older meaning, going back to the early Roman Catholic church, helps explain the word's history. In ancient Rome, a pontifex was a priest belonging to the Pontifical College, the highest priestly council, which had supreme jurisdiction in religious matters. From the Latin *pons, pontis* bridge + *facere* to make. One source suggests that *pontis* is related to *puntis,* meaning a conciliatory offering.* I prefer my own interpretation: a pontifex helped religious understanding by making a bridge for the mind.

PR: Public relations. Promotion, publicity, advertising, and all the other tools used to keep a speaker in the public eye.

Pratfall: (1) A humiliating fall, often on the buttocks. (2) In the theater, a fake fall. Thought of as U.S. slang from the 1930s, but some trace it back to the sixteenth century and earlier. There is an Old English word *praett*, chiefly Scottish, meaning a low-down trick. However, by the 1500s *prat* was an established word meaning buttock. This seems its most likely origin.

*Oxford English Dictionary, compact ed., Oxford University Press, 1973.

Preoccupation: The state of being fully engaged and engrossed mentally, with one's energy and attention fully directed at some objective. From the Latin *praeoccupare* to seize beforehand.

Press kit: A promotional package which includes the speaker's letters of recommendation, audio and/or visual tapes, bio, articles written by and about the speaker, and other promotional materials. The name originates from promotional packages that were originally sent to the "press"—newspapers, broadcast media, and so on—to help promote a presenter or performer.

Problem solving: A system of teaching through audience involvement exercises that present a problem to the group or subgroups for which they attempt to find solutions.

Process: The logical series of steps that the listener or presenter must take to complete an exercise or deliver a concept.

Processing: The contemplation of ideas presented; the logical series of thoughts that listeners must send through their minds to arrive at a conclusion.

Product: Any item that the speaker has available for sale. Books, audio cassettes, videos, workbooks, and posters are the most common.

Production company: A vendor that helps "produce" a meeting or event. A production company might handle the taping, lighting, and sound and on occasion even bring in the speakers and entertainers.

Professional speaker: A public speaker who is paid a fee for performances.

Project: (1) To use words or force of character to send forth a visualized idea or concept into the minds of the listener. (2) To use the voice so it can be heard clearly and at a distance. From the Latin *pro-* before + *jacere* to throw.

Projector: An apparatus for sending a picture onto a screen: overhead projector, slide projector, film projector.

Promotional package: See Press kit.

Prompter: (1) Someone who follows the lines of a script and prompts the performer. (2) An electronic display of magnified written text that is visible on a clear screen to the presenter but is unseen by the audience. The trade name TelePrompTer has come to stand for the device itself, just as we often call any copy machine a Xerox, or any personal computer an IBM—regardless of whether it was manufactured by another company.

Prop: In general, any portable object—projector, overheads, notes, flipcharts, marker pens, notepad, calendar, slides, multimedia shows, whiteboard, chalkboard—used in a presentation. Although "prop" is thought to mean anything that "props up" (supports) the presentation, that is a "folk derivation"; the term actually comes from the theatrical slang for "stage property."

I did a survey of 75 presenters on this one word, trying to get a consensus of what current common usage dictates. It appears that there is a second, but not universal, school of thought that draws a clear distinction between "traditional" visual aids or learning aids (overheads, flipcharts) and less traditional paraphernalia (puppets, musical instruments). This group feels that only "less traditional paraphernalia" qualify as "props," and that true props are three-dimensional. Jack Mingo (famous for his *Couch Potato* book) says, "If I were feeling literal, technical, grouchy, and argumentative, I would refer to chalkboards as part of the 'set'; flipboards, slides, chalk, and pointers as part of the 'visual aids' (the tools that make the presentation possible); and the stuffed animals, puppets, birds' nests, and other cool stuff as 'props.'"

Psychobabble: The use of words from psychiatry or psychotherapy in a ponderous and often not entirely accurate way. Popularized in a book of the same title (1977) by U.S. journalist Richard D. Rosen. Compare **technobabble.**

Public domain: Intellectual property for which the copyright or patent has expired or which never had any such protection. This is material that anyone can use, without credit.

Public seminar: A seminar that is open to the public. Tickets are sold to individuals, as opposed to organizations.

Public service bureau: See **Community service speakers bureau.**

Public speaker: Someone who speaks in public.

Pulpit: An elevated stand or desk for a presenter. Most often used in reference to a preacher in a church. From the Latin *pulpitum* scaffold, stage.

Punch line: The line or word that delivers the impact, the fun—the hit—of the message. From the 1920s.

Q&A: The question-and-answer session of a presentation.

Rapport: Harmony or sympathy of relation; agreement; accord, fellowship, camaraderie, understanding. From the French *rapporter* to bring back or report.

Rehearse: To prepare for a public performance by going over all the rough spots until they are smoothed out. From the Latin *herce* to harrow. A farmer harrows the ground over and over to break up the hardened soil.

Repartee: A quick and witty reply, or a succession of clever retorts to give quick thrust, as in verbal fencing, that will slice (divide) the listener in two. This rather grim analogy is in order: the word comes from the Latin *re-* again + *partir* to part or divide.

Repeat engagement (booking):   A second **booking** for the same client.

Repertoire: The complete list or supply of dramas or pieces that a person is prepared to perform. For speakers, the speeches and/or **Modules** that are ready and available. From the Latin *repertorium* catalog, inventory. Compare **Repertory.**

Repertory: (1) A place where something may be found. (2) A company that presents several different productions, usually alternately in the course of a season. (3) **Repertoire.**

Resistance: Unwillingness of the audience or the presenter to understand a concept, idea, or experience.

Retort: To cast back a similar reply, or hurl back a comment. From the Latin *re-* back + *torquere* to bend, twist. From the same root word as "torture." (Interesting!)

Risers: Short, portable platforms used to raise an area in the front of the room so that the presentation may be more easily seen by the audience. A portable dais, platform, podium, or stage.

Roast: An event in which the guest of honor is criticized and/or ridiculed severely in the name of fun. Participants include:

> *Roastee:*   the guest of "honor"
> *Roaster:*   individual participants doing the roasting
> *Roastmaster:*   the master of ceremonies

Role-play: An audience participation exercise in which a member of the audience and/or the presenter pretends to have the attitudes, actions, and dialogue of another, usually in a make-believe situation. Role-play is used to heighten understanding of social interaction or differing points of view.

Rostrum: The dais or stage area used by a speaker. The platform for speakers in the ancient Roman Forum was decorated with the bows of ships captured in war. Guess what these bows were called? You got it: *rostra.* The singular, *rostrum,* came to mean any platform for speakers.

Running gag: A series of jokes, phrases, or fun bits of business that make reference to others told before.

Sarcasm: A sharply satirical remark describing a person's weaknesses, vanities, or absurdities in subtly disparaging terms. **Irony** is a more limited form of sarcasm. From the Greek *sarkazein* to tear flesh (*sarx*), gnash teeth.

Saver: Anything used to salvage a part of the presentation that seems to need rescuing. A saver may be a witty ad lib or a pratfall.

Seasoning: (1) Anything that increases the enjoyment, zest, and/or impact of a presentation. (2) The act or aging process by which the presenter, much like lumber, is rendered fit for use; all the experiences that makes the presenter a better communicator and performer.

Segue: The act of making a smooth transition from one topic to another in a conversation or speech. From the Latin *segui* to follow, go after. Originally a direction in music, meaning to proceed without pause from one musical number, sound effect, or theme to another.

Ideally, a segue (pronounced "seg-way") is logical or seamless. Let's say you open your talk on leadership with, "My, the weather is terrible today. And speaking of weather, great leaders need to use their skills in all weather—good and bad. So turn with me to page one of your handout." The transition from "weather" to "leaders" is a segue. The second transition, from "weather" to "handouts," is merely a change of thought.

Seminar: A classroom-type lecture, usually an educational session, lasting anywhere from an hour to several days. At a convention, the **breakout** (concurrent) sessions are often referred to as seminars. A seminar is usually thought of as having more of a lecture format than a **workshop.**

Sharing: (1) Inclusion of the audience in the magic and **ambiance** that the presenter tries to create. (2) The moment when a presenter or an audience member publicly acknowledges a personal thought or feeling, possibly with some self-disclosure.

Shill: A **plant** in the audience, with the additional, negative connotation of being connected with a hustle. An example is someone who poses as a bystander and decoy to encourage an audience to bet, buy, or bid. The word seems to date from the 1920s.

Shtick: From the Yiddish *shtik* prank, and the German *stück* bit, part, or piece. In the USA about 1960, it came to mean a performer's special piece of business, an attention-getting device. "That joke is always part of his shtick."

Sight gag: A comic effect produced by visual means rather than spoken lines, such as a pie in the face or a **pratfall.** The term came into use in the mid-1940s.

Sight line: A line extending from the viewer's eye to the stage or presentation area. When presenters are "off stage," they are out of the sight line, in a place where the audience can't see them.

Signature story: A story that is credited to a specific person—one as unique as the person's own "signature." It is considered very bad form to use someone else's signature story, especially without crediting the owner. Compare **public domain.**

Simile: A figure of speech in which two unlike things are *explicitly* compared, as in "she is like a rose." Similes use the words "like," "as," and "so" as distinguished from **metaphor.** According to *Funk & Wagnalls:* "Simile is a literary device to conjure up a vivid picture; 'an Alpine peak like a frosted cake' is a simile. A metaphor omits 'like' or 'as,' the words of comparison; 'the silver pepper of the stars,' is a metaphor. A comparison brings together things of the same kind or class."

Site: The location of the meeting. See **Venue.**

Slander: An oral utterance of false charges or misrepresentations that damage another's reputation or means of livelihood. (The written or pictorial defamation of character is known as "libel.") From the Latin *scandalum* stumbling block.

Slapstick: Means broad comedy with a great deal of boisterous action, as in throwing pies in the presenter's face, mugging, and obvious farcical situations and jokes. This term comes to us from the late 1890s when a stick or lath was used by harlequins, clowns, etc., for striking other performers. This stick was often made in such a manner that a loud, clapping noise occurred, without hurting the person struck.

Slick: See **Camera-ready.**

Slide: In the United States, a 35mm photographic plate. In other English-speaking countries, usually an overhead slide transparency.

Sound booth: The area housing the controls for the **sound system**—referred to as a "booth" regardless of how it is set up. It may be set up on a dais in a corner of the room, combined with the **tech booth.** Also called the **A/V booth** or A/V area.

Sound system: The audio amplification system for speakers. "How's the sound in the house?"

Speakers bureau: A booking or sales company which provides speakers and humorists for meeting planners. Speakers are usually represented on a nonexclusive basis.

Special-events company: A company that brings all kinds of special effects and theatrical acts (and occasionally presenters) to an event.

Spokesperson: A person who speaks for, or in the name of and/or on behalf of, an individual, a company, or an association.

Stage: (1) Any place where a speech, play, or production is delivered. Also called dais, platform, podium, or riser. (2) To plan and organize the presentation for its best dramatic effect.

Stage fright: Fear and nervousness at appearing before an audience.

Stage left: The side of the stage that is left of center as the presenter faces the audience. Also called left stage.

Stage lights: The lights that illuminate the stage area.

Stage right: The side of the stage that is right of center as the presenter faces the audience. Also called right stage.

Stammer: To speak or utter haltingly, with involuntary repetitions or prolonged sounds, or with irregular repetitions of syllables or sounds. Often a temporary condition, caused by stage fright or some other strong emotion; sometimes a psychological condition that can be aided by professional treatment. From the German *stammern* to stammer.

Stationary: A microphone attached to a stand or lectern.

Stock-in-trade: For presenters, the stock used in the craft of speaking—stories, statistics, music, videos, and the like. Also, the standard business of a presenter: "Magic is his stock-in-trade."

   The term came into use in the 1600s to mean the goods kept on sale by a dealer, shopkeeper, or peddler—sometimes referred to as "stock-of-trade"—or the equipment in the conduct of a trade or business. By the 1770s it also came to mean what you kept on hand in your mental facility.*

Swan song: A farewell appearance; an artist's last work. From the ancient Greek myth that swans are mute but burst into song just before they die.

*Oxford English Dictionary, 2nd ed., Vol. 16, Clarendon Press, Oxford, 1989.

Symposium: (1) A meeting to discuss a particular subject. (2) A collection of comments or opinions brought together, as in a series of essays or magazine articles on the same subject. From the Greek *symposion* drinking party. Yes, drinking party.

Tailoring: The speaker's adjustment of the material to the particular needs of the audience.

Talent: (1) A special natural ability or aptitude. (2) The speaker or performer, as in "The talent hasn't arrived yet." (3) An ancient unit of weight or money. From the Greek *talanton,* pan of a scale, weight.

The New Testament parable Matthew 25:14–30 tells the story of the master who gave away talents to three of his servants. When the master returned, two of the servants had invested the talents and doubled their wealth. The third had just buried his talent in the ground. The first two servants were praised and given more to work with. The third servant not only did not receive more; his master was so angry that he took the talent away from him and sent the servant out into sorrow.

Today, by extension, talent has come to mean special ability. The moral is clear: "Use it or lose it"!

Tantalize: To tease or torment by repeated frustration of hopes or desires. Derived from the myth of Tantalus (a son of Zeus), who was sent to Hades. His punishment was to sit in a big pool, ever thirsty. The water would draw back every time he tried to drink; the fruit trees at the edge would pull their fruit away whenever he tried to reach them—"tantalizing" poor Tantalus. Speakers often use more benign forms of torment (such as suspense) to tantalize their audience.

Tech booth: The area of the meeting room from which the sound, lights, and technical equipment are controlled—referred to as a "booth" regardless of how it is set up. Often it is set up on a dais in a corner of the room, combined with the **sound booth.**

Tech crew: The people who operate the sound, lights, and technical equipment.

Technobabble: Using words from technology that are ponderous and often not entirely accurate. Compare **psychobabble.**)

TelePrompTer: See **Prompter.**

Testimonial: A statement of benefits received (usually a written letter of recommendation) from a former client who is familiar with a speaker's work.

Theater-style seating: Audience seating that is set up in rows, much as in a theater, with no tables. Compare **classroom-style seating.**

Theme: The moving thread that weaves throughout a presentation.

Toast: The act of drinking to someone's health or to some sentiment and the person named in the sentiment. How the custom began is unknown. But raising a glass in a toast is steeped in "antiquity." Ulysses drank to Achilles' health in the *Odyssey*; Atilla drank to the health of everyone in the *Rise and Fall of the Roman Empire*. In the Shakespearean era, along came the custom of placing a spiced piece of toast in a drink to flavor it. Perhaps "toasting" to someone's health comes from the notion that the person being honored added flavor by his or her very existence. From the Latin *torrere*, to parch.

Toastmaster: A person who presides at public dinners, announcing each **Toast**, calling upon the various speakers, and so on. See also **Announcer, Emcee, Introducer, Master of ceremonies.**

Toastmasters International: One of the largest personal development associations in the world to assist in building confidence in public communication skills.

Tongue in cheek: Spoken with irony or humor. "It first appeared in print in a book published in 1845 called *The Ingolds by Legends*, in which the author, Richard Barham, reports a Frenchman as saying, 'Superbe! Magnifique!' (with his tongue in his cheek)."*

Track: The type of communication or vehicle used at any given time to teach—video, audio, lecture, audience participation, and so on. The expression comes from the recording industry, where it refers to a discrete, separate recording that is combined with other parts to produce the final aural version.

Trainer: A person who conducts workshops and training sessions. Participants receive assignments, break into small groups, and then come back together to discuss the results.

Transcribe: To copy or recopy in handwriting or typewriting, or electrical recording, a presentation or program of any type. From the Latin *trans-* over + *scribere* write.

Transparency: See **Slide.**

Trany: British slang for overhead slide transparency. See also **Slide.**

Triad: A discussion group of three people.

Two-step seminar: A free seminar in which attendees are encouraged to buy a second seminar or purchase a set of products.

Morris Dictionary of Word and Phrase Origins, 2nd ed., by William Morris, Harper & Row, 1988.

Understand: To come to know the meaning or import of; to have comprehension or mastery of. From the Anglo-Saxon *understandan,* to stand under or among (hence, to comprehend). I wonder if this is where we get the expression "over their heads"? Just a bit of artistic speculation on my part.

Up one's sleeve: Possessing a backup strategy, idea, or solution that will somehow serve in time of need. From the audience perception that a magician, who makes things happen suddenly and mysteriously, can achieve that result only by having something "up his sleeve."

Upstage: (1) The part of the stage farthest away from the audience. Compare **downstage.** (2) To overshadow another presenter or performer by moving upstage and forcing the performer to turn away from the audience. (3) To steal the "focus" of the audience in any way. (4) To outdo another professionally or socially.

In the olden days, when theaters were set on a hillside, with the audience viewing across a small ravine from another hillside, "upstage" and "downstage" had very literal meanings.

Velox: A brand name for film paper. See **Camera-ready.**

Venue: (1) Site of the meeting or event—often a hotel, conference or convention center, college, or restaurant. (2) The position, side, or ground taken by the presenter in a presentation, argument, or debate. Originally used to mean the place where the "action" was. In Middle English *venyw* meant the action of coming, or an attack—probably from the Latin *venir* to come. No doubt the cry of "They're coming! They're coming!" could easily come to signal an attack.

View-graph: The original term (no longer in use) for an overhead transparency.

Vignette: A short, descriptive literary sketch, subtly and delicately told. In the mid-1700s the title page of a book or the beginning or end of a chapter would often have decorative designs or small illustrations, typically with lovely, delicate vines running through them. Hence, the French word *vignette, vigne* vine + *ette* (diminutive).

Vita: See **Biographical sketch, Curriculum vita.**

Wings: The sides of the stage in an auditorium, out of sight of the audience.

Wireless: A wireless mic. See **Cordless.**

Workshop: An educational, classroom-type session, usually with handouts or workbooks, ranging from a minimum of an hour to as long as long as many days. Usually considered to include more **audience participation** and **experiential exercise** and assignments than a **seminar.**

Index

About the Author

Lilly Walters is executive director of Walters International Speakers Bureau, which accesses 20,000 speakers, conducts seminars, and publishes *Sharing Ideas,* the world's largest circulation magazine for the professional speaking industry. She is the author of *Secrets of Successful Speakers—How You Can Motivate, Captivate, and Persuade* and coauthor with her mother, famed speaker Dottie Walters, of the 50,000-copy best-seller *Speak and Grow Rich.*